Strengthening the Rule of Law through the UN Security Council

The UN Security Council formally acknowledged an obligation to promote justice and the rule of law in 2003. This volume examines the extent to which the Council has honoured this commitment when exercising its powers under the UN Charter to maintain international peace and security. It discusses both how the concept of the rule of law regulates, or influences, Security Council activity and how the Council has in turn shaped the notion of the rule of law. It explores in particular how this relationship has affected the Security Council's three most prominent tools for the maintenance of international peace and security: peacekeeping, sanctions and force. In doing so, this volume identifies strategies for better promotion of the rule of law by the Security Council.

This book will be of interest to scholars and students of international law, international relations, international development and peacekeeping.

Jeremy Farrall is Fellow at the Asia-Pacific College of Diplomacy in the Coral Bell School of Asia Pacific Affairs at the Australian National University, and Australian Research Council Linkage Industry Fellow at the Centre for International Governance and Justice in the Regulatory Institutions Network, also at the Australian National University.

Hilary Charlesworth is Distinguished Professor, Australian Research Council Laureate Fellow and Director of the Centre for International Governance and Justice in the Regulatory Institutions Network at the Australian National University.

Challenges of globalisation

Edited by Charles Sampford and Carmel Connors

Griffith University, Australia

This series seeks to make systematic contributions to international debates over two intimately related issues:

- The values that should inform the governance of modern states and the globalising world in which they are increasingly enmeshed, in particular whether the liberal democratic values that sought to civilise the sovereign state need to be reconceived as global values.
- The institutions that are needed to realise those values, be they local, national, regional, international, transnational or global.

1 **Globalisation and Equality**
Edited by Keith Horton and Haig Patapan

2 **Globalisation and the Rule of Law**
Edited by Spencer Zifcak

3 **Environmental Values in a Globalising World**
Nature, justice and governance
Edited by Jouni Paavola and Ian Lowe

4 **Globalisation and Citizenship**
The transnational challenge
Edited by Wayne Hudson and Steven Slaughter

5 **Global Democracy and its Difficulties**
Edited by Anthony J. Langlois and Karol Edward Soltan

6 **New Visions for Market Governance**
Crisis and renewal
Edited by Kate MacDonald, Shelley Marshall and Sanjay Pinto

7 **Shifting Global Powers and International Law**
Challenges and opportunities
Edited by Rowena Maguire, Bridget Lewis and Charles Sampford

8 **Institutional Supports for the International Rule of Law**
Edited by Charles Sampford and Ramesh Thakur

9 **Access to International Justice**
Edited by Patrick Keyzer, Vesselin Popovski and Charles Sampford

10 **Strengthening the Rule of Law through the UN Security Council**
Edited by Jeremy Farrall and Hilary Charlesworth

Strengthening the Rule of Law through the UN Security Council

Edited by Jeremy Farrall and
Hilary Charlesworth

Routledge
Taylor & Francis Group
LONDON AND NEW YORK

First published 2016
by Routledge
2 Park Square, Milton Park, Abingdon, Oxon OX14 4RN

and by Routledge
711 Third Avenue, New York, NY 10017

First issued in paperback 2017

Routledge is an imprint of the Taylor & Francis Group, an informa business

British Library Cataloguing in Publication Data
A catalogue record for this book is available from the British Library

Library of Congress Cataloging-in-Publication Data
Names: Farrall, Jeremy Matam, editor. | Charlesworth, Hilary, editor.
Title: Strengthening the rule of law through the UN Security Council / edited by Jeremy Farrall and Hilary Charlesworth.
Description: Milton Park, Abingdon, Oxon : Routledge, 2016. |
Series: Routledge/challenges of globalisation | Includes bibliographical references and index.
Identifiers: LCCN 2015039248 | ISBN 9781138959033 (hardback) |
ISBN 9781315660868 (ebook)
Subjects: LCSH: Rule of law. | United Nations. Security Council.
Classification: LCC KZ4992 .S77 2016 | DDC 340/.11–dc23
LC record available at http://lccn.loc.gov/2015039248

ISBN 13: 978-1-138-48819-9 (pbk)
ISBN 13: 978-1-138-95903-3 (hbk)

Typeset in Times New Roman
by Wearset Ltd, Boldon, Tyne and Wear

Contents

Illustrations

Figures

Tables

Contributors

Karine Bannelier holds a PhD in International Law from the University of Paris Panthéon-Sorbonne. She is Associate Professor of International Law at the Faculty of Law of the University of Grenoble-Alpes (France) and Director of the Master's Degree on International Security and Defence Studies. She has published seven books, including as co-editor of *Use of Force under UN Security Council Mandates: Issues of Law and Responsibility* (Pedone, 2014) and *The Protection of the Environment in Time of Armed Conflicts* (Pedone, 2001). She is also author of more than 25 articles and book chapters on international law.

Alex J. Bellamy is Professor of International Security at the Griffith Asia Institute, Griffith University, Australia, and Non-Resident Senior Adviser at the International Peace Institute, New York. He is also Honorary Professor of International Relations at the University of Queensland, where he serves as Director (International) of the Asia Pacific Centre for the Responsibility to Protect. His recent books include *Massacres and Morality: Mass Killing in an Age of Civilian Immunity* (Oxford University Press, 2012), which won the 2012 International Studies Association Ethics Section prize for best book, and *Understanding Peacekeeping* (2nd edition, Polity, 2010), with Paul D. Williams.

Théodore Christakis is Professor of International Law at the Faculty of Law of the University of Grenoble-Alpes, France, since 2002, and also teaches International Law at the Paris School of International Affairs, Sciences Po, since 2006. In 2015 he was appointed as a Senior Member at the Institut Universitaire de France. He is Director of the Centre for International Security and European Studies, CESICE, Grenoble, and Director of the Master's degree in International and European Law offered by the Grenoble Faculty of Law. He has published or edited eight books and more than 55 articles and book chapters on international law.

Annemarie Devereux is an international and constitutional lawyer whose major practice has been with the United Nations and the Australian Government. She undertook Law and Arts honours degrees at the Australian National

University, an LLM at Columbia University, and a PhD at the Australian National University. Her engagements with the United Nations (2000–2009, and since 2011) have included working in human rights components of three peacekeeping missions, heading up the Legal Unit for OHCHR–Nepal, and working as a legal adviser for the International Commissions of Inquiry for Libya and Timor-Leste.

Laura Grenfell is an Associate Professor at the University of Adelaide Law School where she teaches and researches in public law. She is also Director of the Law School's Human Rights Internship Programme. Before joining academia in 2002, she practised constitutional law with the Crown Solicitor's Office of South Australia and was an associate in the Supreme Court of South Australia. In December 2009 she was awarded a Doctor of Philosophy from the Australian National University. Her book, *Promoting the Rule of Law in Post-conflict States*, was published by Cambridge University Press in 2013.

Joanna Harrington is a Professor in the University of Alberta Faculty of Law. Co-author of the Canadian text *International Law: Doctrine, Practice and Theory* (2nd edition), she has combined an academic career with experience as a legal adviser and university administrator, serving from 2006 to 2008 as Scholar-in-Residence with the Legal Affairs Bureau of Canada's Department of Foreign Affairs and International Trade, and from 2010 to 2015 as Associate Dean with the University of Alberta's Faculty of Graduate Studies and Research. She holds a BA from the University of British Columbia, a JD from the University of Victoria, and a PhD in Law from the University of Cambridge, where she was a Tapp Scholar.

Gina Heathcote is a Senior Lecturer in International Law and Gender Studies at SOAS University of London. She has published in the areas of collective security, feminist perspectives, the prohibition on the use of force, the war on terror and human rights. She is the author of *The Law on the Use of Force: A Feminist Analysis* (Routledge, 2012), and co-editor with Dianne Otto of *Peacekeeping, Gender Equality and Collective Security* (Palgrave, 2014). She is currently writing her second book on the role of feminist perspectives in twenty-first-century international law, entitled *Feminist Dialogues on International Law: Successes, Tensions, Futures.*

Martin Krygier is Professor of Law and Co-Director of the European Law Centre, University of New South Wales. His work overlaps legal, social and political theory. He is interested in exploring variations in the characters, consequences and worth of large institutions, and the interrelations between such variations and morally justifiable social practices. His latest book is *Philip Selznick: Ideals in the World* (Stanford University Press, 2012). He has also written extensively on the prospect of rule of law, especially in post-communist Europe. He holds a BA and LLB with honours from the University of Sydney, and a PhD from the Australian National University.

Marie-Eve Loiselle is a doctoral scholar in the Centre for International Governance and Justice, RegNet, at the Australian National University. She holds a Bachelor of Laws from the University of Montreal, a certificate in Transnational Law from the University of Geneva, and a Master in Strategic Studies from the Australian National University. She worked as an external collaborator at the International Training Centre of the International Labor Organisation, and interned with the Office of the Legal Adviser to the NATO Communication and Information Systems Services Agency, and has two years' corporate law experience with a firm in Montreal.

Usha Natarajan is Assistant Professor of International Law at the American University in Cairo. Her research engages postcolonial approaches to international law, the laws of the use of force, law and development, and sustainable development. Her recent publications examine different facets of the ongoing Arab revolutions. Her PhD dissertation examined the role of international law in the 2003 Iraq invasion. She has worked with UNDP, UNESCO and the World Bank on law reform initiatives in Asia and the Arab world, including Indonesia during its democratic transition, post-independence Timor-Leste and constitutional reform during the Arab uprisings.

Mary Ellen O'Connell holds the Robert and Marion Short Chair in Law and is Research Professor of International Dispute Resolution, Kroc Institute, University of Notre Dame. She is author or editor of numerous books and articles on international law on the use of force and international legal theory. She was a Vice President of the American Society of International Law (2010–2012), chaired the Use of Force Committee of the International Law Association (2005–2010) and has been a faculty member at the Ohio State University, Johns Hopkins University and Indiana University. She holds a JD from Columbia Law School.

Bruce 'Ossie' Oswald is Associate Professor in the Melbourne Law School at the University of Melbourne. In 2012–2013 he was a Jennings Randolph Senior Fellow at the United States Institute of Peace. His interests in law and practice are in the areas of international humanitarian law, peace operations, state building, accountability and responsibility, and the application of human rights law to military operations. Ossie has served in the Regular Australian Army as a legal officer. He has seen operational service in Rwanda, the Former Yugoslavia, Timor Leste, Iraq and Afghanistan.

Kimberly Prost is the Ombudsperson for the Security Council Al-Qaida Sanctions Committee. Before that she served as an *ad litem* judge of the International Criminal Tribunal for the former Yugoslavia (2006–2010). She has also served as Chief of the Legal Advisory Section of the UN Office on Drugs and Crime, as Head of the Criminal Law Section of the Commonwealth Secretariat, and as a Federal Prosecutor with the Canadian Department of Justice. She was also a member of the Canadian delegation for the negotiation of the

Convention against Transnational Organized Crime, the Convention against Corruption and the Rome Statute of the International Criminal Court.

Charles Sampford is the Director of the Institute for Ethics, Governance and Law. He is also President of the International Institute for Public Ethics, and Foundation Dean and Professor of Law and Research Professor in Ethics at Griffith, as well as Adjunct Professor at QUT and York. He holds a DPhil from Oxford University. In 1999 he became Foundation Director of the Key Centre for Ethics, Law, Justice and Governance. He has published numerous articles and essays and completed 28 books and edited collections. He won a Senior Research Fellowship at St John's College Oxford and a Fulbright Senior Award to Harvard.

Richard Zajac Sannerholm heads the Rule of Law Programme at the Folke Bernadotte Academy, and conducts research on measuring rule of law in public administration, monitoring administrative justice, rule of law and security sector reform, and an empirical project on mapping UN rule-of-law reform in post-conflict settings. His previous assignments include research and programming on legal education, public administration reform, rule of law training, customary law and issues of harmonisation and human rights. His most recent publication is *Rule of Law after War and Crisis: Ideologies, Norms and Methods* (Intersentia, 2012).

Gerry Simpson holds the Kenneth Bailey Chair of International Law at Melbourne Law School. He is also a Visiting Professor of International Law at the London School of Economics, where he held a chair until 2009, and a Soros Fellow, based in Tbilisi, Georgia. He has been a Senior Lecturer at the Australian National University (1996–1998) and a Visiting Scholar at Harvard Law School (1999). His most recent book is a collection of essays entitled *The Margins of International Law* (CMP, 2014). He is currently working on a book about the literary life of international law.

Veronica L. Taylor joined RegNet at the Australian National University in 2010 as Professor and was Director until 2014. She now serves as Dean of ANU College of Asia and the Pacific. She was also Director of the Asian Law Center, University of Washington (2001–2010), and remains an Affiliate Professor of Law and Senior Adviser there. In 2010 she was inaugural Hague Visiting Professor in Rule of Law, hosted by the Hague Institute for the Internationalization of Law and Leiden University's Van Vollenhoven Institute. She also has over 25 years' experience designing and leading rule of law and governance projects.

Peter Thomson is a Principal Legal Officer at the Australian Government's Attorney-General's Department. Previously he was seconded as Governance and Rule of Law Adviser at the Australian Civil-Military Centre. During this time, Peter was the designer and co-facilitator of the Centre's Rule of Law Roundtable in post-conflict situations, held in October 2010. He also was project-lead for two training documentaries developed by the Centre in partnership with the UN, and event-lead and Co-Chair of the 'Protection of Civilians: AU Drafting Workshop' held in Queanbeyan in 2009 on drafting Guidelines for the Protection of Civilians in African Union Peace Support Operations.

Frida Wall works as Desk Officer, Rule of Law Programme, Folke Bernadotte Academy. She holds a Degree of Science with Law as her main field of study. Together with Richard Zajac Sannerholm, she has operational lead on the Academy's research project on UN Peace Operations and Rule of Law Assistance. She also works on a project on Local Self-Government and Rule of Law in Ukraine, where she is responsible for issues in relation to rule of law, public administration and gender. She also has a strong interest in the Swedish feminist foreign policy and gender in post-conflict justice and security.

Erika de Wet is Co-Director of the Institute for International and Comparative Law in Africa and Professor of International Law at the University of Pretoria. She also holds a part-time position as Professor of International Constitutional Law at the Amsterdam Center for International Law, University of Amsterdam, and lectures at the University of Zurich and the University of Bonn. Her *Habilitationsschrift*, completed at the University of Zurich in 2002, was published as *The Chapter VII Powers of the UN Security Council* (Hart, 2004). Her most recent book (with Jure Vidmar) is *Hierarchy in International Law: The Place of Human Rights* (Oxford University Press, 2012).

Jeni Whalan is Lecturer in International Security and Development at the University of New South Wales, and a Research Associate of the Global Economic Governance Programme at the University of Oxford. Her research focuses on peacekeeping, the United Nations, fragile states, post-conflict economies, and international security governance. Her book *How Peace Operations Work* (Oxford University Press, 2013) investigates what helps and hinders peacekeepers in achieving the change they want in post-conflict societies. Jeni holds a DPhil and MPhil in International Relations from the University of Oxford, where she studied as a Rhodes Scholar.

Foreword

Alan Ryan

This is an important book, but not perhaps, dear reader, as you might imagine. It arises from a collaboration between an arm of the Australian Government, the Australian Civil-Military Centre, and a diverse and brilliant group of scholars. The excellent scholarship, I should emphasise, is all down to the contributors. Professor Hilary Charlesworth and Dr Jeremy Farrall have done a brilliant job of shepherding this work through a process of collective engagement with some of the most noted and emerging international scholars in the field. They are to be congratulated on this, the product of their labours.

This genesis is not perhaps unique – what is truly interesting is the engagement that this book represents between the academic world and that of the practitioner of international relations. More to the point, it deals with the issues faced by participants in the highly charged political processes that provide the context in which United Nations Security Council (UNSC) members work.

Which, reader, brings us back to you. It is more than likely that you are reading this text as part of your academic studies. You may be an academic seeking for proofs to advance a thesis. It is highly unlikely that you will be a government official seeking enlightenment as you seek to develop a brief or determine a course of action. Unfortunately, that is a fact little appreciated outside government. John Lewis Gaddis diagnosed the problem when he wrote that:

> Part of the problem is that policymakers almost never build into the schedules time to think about fresh approaches to what they do. Leaders rarely 'gain in profundity while they gain in experience', Henry Kissinger has reminded us; the convictions that high officials form before reaching their positions tend to be 'the intellectual capital they will consume as long as they are in office'.[1]

He did not close out the quote though. Kissinger famously concluded: 'There is little time for leaders to reflect. They are locked in an endless battle in which the urgent constantly gains on the important.'[2] It is entirely possible that you will pursue a career in which you will consume the intellectual capital contained in these pages. You may have to live with the frustration of never knowing enough and the responsibility of having to provide advice without adequate reflection.

So the value of this collection lies in the sense that you will take away from it, of a dynamic and evolving notion of the role of the UNSC in upholding concepts of a rule of law (ROL) for which there is no authoritative definition, much less consensual support.

Too often, scholars, particularly legal scholars, focus on admiring the fragile beauty of the law. At the same time, practitioners seem doomed to constant disappointment as international organisations, states and individuals conspire to frustrate common application of laws that meet even the most basic notions of human rights norms and standards.

It would be easy to become cynical – and too many have fallen into that trap.

This collection reminds us that the realisation of humanity's aspirations is a matter of hard work, intellectual rigour, and international commitment. It requires states, particularly great powers, to hold to the standards they profess.

The UNSC might exist to serve the higher aspirations of the UN Charter, but it was founded to attempt to do what its high-minded predecessors in the League of Nations could not – to take action 'to maintain or restore international peace and security'.

The UNSC is ultimately a political institution that serves a vital function, operating on political rather than purely legal norms. It is not wholly representative, transparent, accountable or subject to judicial review.[3] It can confer legitimacy on the use of force or the application of sanctions in support of international legal norms, but it is not obliged to. The UNSC is more than the sum of its parts, but it is grounded in political reality.

Successive UNSC statements have reiterated its commitment to 'an international order based on the ROL and international law, which is essential for peaceful coexistence and cooperation among States in addressing common challenges'.[4] The UNSC has called upon member states to comply with their obligations to end impunity for those responsible for serious breaches of international law and to settle their disputes by peaceful means.

At the same time, the UNSC has accepted its own responsibility to construct mandates for operations that will promote peacebuilding through observance of domestic and international law. But the tenor of these statements from the UNSC over the past decade leaves us with a strong sense that the UNSC cannot do it alone, that it requires a level of assurance, currently lacking, that states and international organisations will be able to coordinate their efforts at least to the point where they are not acting at cross-purposes to each other.

A recent UNSC presidential statement on the ROL captured this problem, expressing 'its commitment to ensure that all UN efforts to restore peace and security themselves respect and promote the rule of law'.[5] This was followed two years later by another presidential statement emphasising that the success of the UNSC's efforts was ultimately reliant on achieving greater international civil–military–police coordination than is currently possible:

> sustainable peace requires an integrated approach based on coherence between political, security, development, human rights, including gender

> equality, and rule of law.... In this regard the Council emphasizes the importance of the rule of law as one of the key elements of conflict prevention, peacekeeping, conflict resolution and peace building.[6]

The UNSC might agree to take action to support the ROL between or within states by taking action under the UN Charter to keep or enforce the peace. It takes steps to protect civilians, to highlight gender and children's issues. Ultimately, however, the international community must rely on the commitment of communities and national authorities to achieve these objectives. The UNSC does not, by itself, have the tools or the span of control to react to all breaches of the ROL at the national or sub-state level – and it is unreasonable to judge it on that basis.

If the UNSC cannot, by itself, ensure respect for the ROL within states, then in the international domain it seems unrealistic that we should hold it responsible for enforcing the notion of an indefeasible concept of international law. It is a body that was never designed, nor constructed, to do so. What we can expect, or at least investigate, is the possibility of how participating states and international organisations can coordinate their efforts to achieve a more consistent and coherent recognition of the value of an international legal order.

To assist the UNSC to support the international ROL, we must first have a clear appreciation of how states behave in their relations to the UNSC and to each other. The composition and operation of the UNSC, with permanent and non-permanent members, a challenging agenda and a dynamic international situation, does not lend itself to the disinterested contemplation of black letter law. Rather, UNSC member states are challenged to formulate considered positions on the vast body of work that confronts them on a daily basis. National interests are clearly in play – as they must be – because solutions need to be based on the practical consideration of possibilities and values as well as those understandings that have been absorbed into international law through agreement and observance. Common interests are also relevant as states work, through political negotiation, to form reasonable and reasoned positions that can be agreed by 15 varied member states – five of whom hold the veto power.

We also need to understand the complex web of relationships between the over 40 UN agencies involved in rule-of-law issues. Responsibility for the coordination of ROL work within the UN does not lie with the UNSC, but is essentially a function of non-political delivery agencies. The UN Rule of Law Coordination and Resource Group (ROLCREG) is chaired by the Deputy Secretary-General and includes representatives from 19 agencies.[7] It does not include representatives of the UNSC, though the UNSC has recorded its support for the establishment of ROLCREG and has urged 'greater efforts by the Group to ensure a coordinated and coherent response by the UN system to issues on the Council's agenda related to the rule of law'.[8]

Most of the work that is done by these agencies focuses on capacity building for the ROL at the national level and is most often involved in crisis-affected states. These agencies, and the UNSC, have to deal with what 'is' rather than what 'ought' to be. The UN as a whole is still a long way from realising an objectively agreed and understood legal regime to apply to the full range of crises and contingencies that evolve faster than the international community can possibly expect to coordinate a response.

The problem is perhaps not that the UNSC, as an imperfectly representative body, cannot ensure the international ROL, but that it finds it difficult to agree to act in ways that are always consistent with a contested international legal regime. If it is to do so, it must build capacity from the very basis of international understanding.

We need to imagine what a UNSC that always supports the ROL might look like on the ground in New York. The well-constructed theories of legal scholars need to be robust enough to survive contact with that reality. To do that we need to start with a practical conception of what is possible.

To go forward, then, we need to consider the extent to which all members of the UNSC understand and agree on their common objectives, the tools at their disposal and the way that those tools will be used. To achieve that, the UNSC needs the active assistance of all UN member states to build common understanding of peacebuilding efforts, of lexicons, and of the lessons of our recent past. This collection represents a valuable contribution to that understanding.

The UNSC cannot be the author of its own transformation. It needs first- and second-track collaborative efforts to work through potential responses to contingencies; to build agreement on what can be achieved and what cannot; and to establish pragmatic links between those national and international organisations that support the UNSC's ability to observe and apply the ROL.

In a 2013 report on the effectiveness of the UN's support of the promotion of the ROL, the UN Secretary-General made clear that the '[r]ule of law is central to the challenges facing the global community'; not only do '[s]tates need support in strengthening national institutions and the rule of law', but '[e]qually, given the transnational nature of many challenges, normative and operational tools at regional and global levels are a crucial complement to nation-state responses'.[9]

This collection provides practical considerations and tools to promote that more robust international conception of the ROL. I implore readers not to see it as merely an intellectual exercise. Hopefully in the years ahead, the aspirations contained in these pages will be realised, at least in part. If they are, it will be in no small part due to the efforts of those who made this work possible.

Notes

1 John Lewis Gaddis, 'Expanding the Data Base: Historians, Political Scientists, and the Enrichment of Security Studies' (1987) 12(12) *International Security* 3–21.

2 Henry A. Kissinger, *The White House Years* (Boston, Little, Brown and Company, 1979), p. 54.

3 Erik Voeten, 'The Political Origins of the UN Security Council's Ability to Legitimize the Use of Force' (2005) 59(3) *International Organisation* 527–57.

4 UN Doc. S/PRST/2010/11 (29 June 2010), para. 1. See also UN Doc. S/PRST/2003/15 (24 September 2003); UN Doc. S/PRST/2004/2 (26 January 2004); UN Doc. S/PRST/2005/30 (12 July 2005); UN Doc. S/PRST/2006/28 (22 June 2006).
5 UN Doc. S/PRST/2010/11 (29 June 2010), para. 9.
6 UN Doc. S/PRST/2012/1 (19 January 2012), para. 6. See also references in note 4.
7 UN Rule of Law, 'Rule of Law Coordination and Resource Group': www.unrol.org/article.aspx?article_id=6.
8 UN Doc. S/PRST/2010/11, para. 11.
9 UN Doc. S/2013/341 (11 June 2013), *Report of the Secretary-General on Measuring the Effectiveness of the United Nations System's Support to the Promotion of the Rule of Law*.

Preface

This book brings together contributions from well-established academics and newer scholars. Through the lenses of their own discipline, the authors approach the relationship between the Security Council (UNSC) and the rule of law from a range of perspectives, and advance new ways of thinking about how the UNSC might better promote and respect the rule of law. The papers that make up this collection were originally presented in a series of workshops held from 2011 to 2013 at the Australian National University (Canberra) and the Australian Permanent Mission to the United Nations (New York). Each Canberra workshop, and its mirror workshop in New York, concentrated on one of three themes: peacekeeping, sanctions and the use of force. We found that these subjects best reflect the areas where the relationship between the UNSC and rule of law is manifest. For this reason, we structured this collection according to the same three themes. The chapters that follow convey hope, and sometimes doubt, about the potential for the UNSC to strengthen the rule of law through its activities for the maintenance of peace and security. Overall they carry the message that achieving a greater respect for the rule of law at the international level is achievable.

We express our gratitude to all participants to the workshops and contributors to this volume. Not all papers presented at the workshops are reproduced in the following pages; notwithstanding, these contributions were valuable to our analysis of the UNSC functions and working methods. They also proved useful in understanding the practical implications of peacekeeping, sanctions, and use of force activities for the rule of law at the national and international level.

The financial support of both the Australian Research Council (ARC) and our partner organisation, the Australian Civil-Military Centre (ACMC), supported the research project and workshops that led to the publication of this book (ARC Linkage Project LP110100708). We are particularly grateful for the dedicated support of the ACMC. A special thanks goes to Dr Alan Ryan, Executive Director of the ACMC, as well as his predecessor, General (retired) Michael G. Smith, and all their ACMC colleagues, including in particular Dr Jeni Whalan, Kelisiana Thynne and Olivia Cribb.

We would like to underline the outstanding research assistance and administrative support that Marie-Eve Loiselle and Shane Chalmers provided at different times throughout the life of the project. Their support in the conduct of workshops and the preparation of the manuscript for publication was invaluable. Jane McCosker meticulously proofread and offered insightful feedback on the contributions contained in this volume. We also thank Charlotte Endersby, Andrew Taylor and their colleagues at Routledge for their work towards the publication of this book.

Finally we would like to thank our colleagues at the ANU Centre for International Governance and Justice, the Regulatory Institutions Network, the Asia-Pacific College of Diplomacy and the Coral Bell School of Asia Pacific Affairs, as well as our families. Jeremy thanks Lyn, Jemma and Maya, and Hilary thanks Charles, Stephanie and Will.

Abbreviations

ACT	Accountability, Coherence and Transparency
ANP	Afghan National Police
AU	African Union
BRICS	Brazil, Russia, India, China, South Africa
CAR	Central African Republic
CFI	Court of First Instance
CIDA	Canadian International Development Agency
CJEU	Court of Justice of the European Union
CNDP	Congress for the Defence of the People
CPI	Corruption Perceptions Index
DDR	disarmament, demobilisation and reintegration
DDRRR	disarmament, demobilisation, reintegration, resettlement and repatriation
DPA	UN Department of Political Affairs
DPKO	UN Department of Peacekeeping Operations
DRC	Democratic Republic of the Congo
ECHR	European Convention of Human Rights
ECJ	European Court of Justice
ECtHR	European Court of Human Rights
EU	European Union
FARDC	Forces Armées de la République du Congo
FBA	Folke Bernadotte Academy
FIB	UN Force Intervention Brigade
GC	General Court of Europe
GFP	UN Global Focal Point
HAP	Humanitarian Accountability Partnership
HRDDP	UN Human Rights Due Diligence Policy
ICC	International Criminal Court
ICCPR	International Covenant on Civil and Political Rights
ICGLR	International Conference on the Great Lakes Region
ICISS	International Commission on Intervention and State Sovereignty
ICJ	International Court of Justice
ICRC	International Committee of the Red Cross

ICTY	International Criminal Tribunal for the former Yugoslavia
IDP	internally displaced person
IEMF	Interim Emergency Multinational Force
IHL	international humanitarian law
IHRL	international human rights law
ISAF	International Security Assistance Force
LOAC	law of armed conflict
M23	March 23 Movement (DRC)
MINUSCA	UN Multidimensional Integrated Stabilization Mission in CAR
MINUSMA	UN Multidimensional Integrated Stabilization Mission in Mali
MINUSTAH	UN Stabilization Mission in Haiti
MONUC	UN Mission in the DRC
MONUSCO	UN Stabilization Mission in the DRC
NATO	North Atlantic Treaty Organization
NDS	National Directorate of Security
NGO	non-governmental organisation
NIF	Neutral International Force
OCHA	UN Office for the Coordination of Humanitarian Affairs
OHCHR	UN Office of the High Commissioner for Human Rights
ONUC	Opération des Nations Unies au Congo
POC	protection of civilians in armed conflict
R2P	responsibility to protect
RAMSI	Regional Assistance Mission to the Solomon Islands
ROE	rules of engagement
ROL	rule of law
ROLCREG	UN Rule of Law Coordination and Resource Group
RWP	responsibility while protecting
SADC	Southern African Development Community
SML	Senior Mission Leadership
SRSG	Special Representative of the UN Secretary-General
SSR	security sector reform
TCC	troop-contributing country
TRC	Truth and Reconciliation Commission
UDHR	Universal Declaration of Human Rights
UN	United Nations
UNAMA	UN Assistance Mission in Afghanistan
UNAMIR	UN Assistance Mission for Rwanda
UNAMSIL	UN Mission in Sierra Leone
UNDP	UN Development Programme
UNEF	UN Emergency Force
UNGA	UN General Assembly
UNHCR	UN High Commissioner for Refugees
UNIOSIL	UN Integrated Office in Sierra Leone
UNIPSIL	UN Integrated Peacebuilding Office in Sierra Leone
UNMIK	UN Mission in Kosovo

UNMIS	UN Mission in Sudan
UNMISS	UN Mission in the Republic of South Sudan
UNMIT	UN Integrated Mission in Timor-Leste
UNODC	UN Office on Drugs and Crime
UNPROFOR	UN Protection Force (former Yugoslavia)
UNSC	UN Security Council
UNSG	UN Secretary-General
UNSMIS	UN Supervision Mission in Syria
UNTAC	UN Transitional Authority in Cambodia
UNTAET	UN Transitional Administration in East Timor
USAID	United States Agency for International Development
WJP	World Justice Project
WPS	women, peace and security

1 Regulating the rule of law through the Security Council

Hilary Charlesworth and Jeremy Farrall

Introduction

On 24 September 2003 the United Nations (UN) Security Council (UNSC) inaugurated a new agenda item entitled 'Justice and the Rule of Law', acknowledging the UNSC's 'heavy responsibility to promote justice and the rule of law in its efforts to maintain international peace and security'.[1] This book examines how the UNSC has responded to this mandate, particularly in the areas of peacekeeping, sanctions and the use of force. The contributors to this volume discuss both how the concept of the rule of law (ROL) regulates, or influences, UNSC activity and how the UNSC has in turn shaped the notion of the ROL.

The UNSC's designation of the ROL as an important theme offers principled law as the solution to the problem of unprincipled politics, and stable peace as the alternative to destabilising war. The idea is that threats to peace and security should be managed in accordance with the norms and values enshrined in the UN Charter. However, as many contributors to this collection note, the concept of the ROL is famously opaque and contested. Some commentators question the ability of the ROL to guide actions to maintain international peace and security on the basis that it is insufficiently coherent.[2] Others criticise attempts to transplant a notion with western origins and an associated suite of western rule-of-law institutions into other contexts.[3] The veto power accorded to the UNSC's five permanent members by the UN Charter is also regarded as undermining the capacity of the ROL to temper the exercise of raw power in and through the UNSC.[4]

The relationship between the UNSC and the ROL provides a fascinating case study of how powerful actors both shape and are shaped by powerful ideas. Terence Halliday has pointed to the tension between two different modes of UNSC interaction with the ROL – the external and the internal. Halliday describes the UNSC's external invocations of the concept as ROL 'on the offense' and claims of internal disregard of the ROL placing the UNSC 'on the defence'.[5] It is difficult for the UNSC to claim to act in the name of the ROL externally, without at the same time accepting the concept's applicability to the internal workings of the UNSC. Given these tensions and weaknesses in the ROL, how does it regulate behaviour in the international arena?

While much of the literature on UNSC activity focuses on either its legal or political dimensions, theories of regulation can also contribute to understanding the way the UNSC operates. The work of regulatory theorists has shown the limited power of legal systems alone to influence behaviour.[6] In the international realm in particular, the idea of any type of 'top-down' or coercive enforcement of legal principles is compromised by the nature of political interests.[7] Regulatory scholars have emphasised the multiplicity and complexity of both actors and motives in the international sphere, identifying the existence of regulatory webs of influences.[8] They have observed that, at the global level, each separate regulatory control tends to be weak, and that strength comes through weaving frail strands together to form a web that can be strategically activated by networks of regulatory actors. The idea of regulation and governance through networks explains why it is sometimes possible for those in a weak position to prevail over the strong. These perspectives suggest that a concept such as the ROL can influence the UNSC when it is deployed by a network of actors and when the regulation is responsive. Responsive regulation means encouraging self-regulation, initially through building strengths by persuasion and support, and only escalating to tougher enforcement measures when self-regulation has manifestly failed.[9]

The contributors to this collection approach the regulatory dimensions of the UNSC's relationship with the ROL from a range of perspectives. Part I examines various pressing theoretical questions prompted by promoting the ROL through and in the UNSC. Parts II, III and IV then address issues that arise when the UNSC engages with the ROL as part of its efforts to maintain international peace and security through the use of peacekeeping, sanctions and force, respectively.

1 Theorising the rule of law

Many efforts to define the ROL distinguish between 'thin' or formal interpretations and 'thick' or substantive understandings.[10] According to a 'thin' conception, the ROL depends on procedural safeguards that aim to guarantee the equal application of the law.[11] On this view, the ROL should increase the chances of a just outcome, but the ROL itself does not contain value judgements about what is just or right.[12] Justice is the result of the ROL rather than an inherent ingredient. Thick or substantive approaches to the ROL, by contrast, proceed from the assumption that the ROL depends on commitment to substantive values such as justice or human rights.[13]

In August 2004 UN Secretary-General Kofi Annan proposed a definition of the ROL with both 'thin' and 'thick' elements to guide UN activities in post-conflict environments. He defined the ROL as:

> a principle of governance in which all persons, institutions and entities, public and private, including the State itself, are accountable to laws that are publicly promulgated, equally enforced and independently adjudicated, and which are consistent with international human rights norms and standards.[14]

Part I of the book offers a range of lenses to scrutinise this definition. In Chapter 2, Martin Krygier urges greater attention to the purpose of the ROL, an element absent from the Annan definition, but essential for a responsive regulatory approach. While the Annan formulation sets out various features of the ROL, Krygier draws us back to the idea of the ROL as a counterpoint to the arbitrary exercise of power. This approach encourages a more flexible approach to the institutions that may be necessary in particular contexts to constrain arbitrary power.

Veronica L. Taylor (Chapter 3) examines the international rule-of-law industry, based on the Annan definition, which she labels 'Big Rule of Law'. Her focus is the regulation of this industry through soft law instruments and technical assistance programmes. Taylor is critical of the packaging of the ROL as a consumer product that can be identified through 'objective' indicators. In line with Krygier's analysis, Taylor concludes that rule-of-law promotion has lost sight of the goal of restricting arbitrary use of power and has become a technique of transnational policy intervention.

Usha Natarajan's contribution (Chapter 4) argues that a strong rule-of-law culture can only emerge from a particular mix of historical, cultural and economic factors, which are absent from the UNSC system. The partiality of the UNSC's decision-making processes and the unequal representation of states within it undermine prospects for observance of the ROL. Charles Sampford (Chapter 5) shares similar concerns but investigates in particular how the ROL might be applied to the UNSC's work and the countries taking part in UNSC peacekeeping missions, for example through the drafting of peacekeeping mandates.

The relationship between the ROL, hegemony and humanitarianism is Gerry Simpson's focus (Chapter 6). He examines how the ROL might be developed to constrain institutionally organised interventions, suggesting that the notion of 'humanity' seems to be increasingly regulating UNSC action with respect to force. Simpson points to the irony that, although the UN Charter system aims to deter the use of force, the concept of humanity in effect allows 'improvisational' use of force.

2 The Security Council, peacekeeping and the rule of law

The UNSC's interest in the ROL is most visible in the field of peacekeeping. The task of strengthening the ROL, broadly interpreted by the UN Department of Peacekeeping Operations (DPKO) to mean the (re)construction of institutions connected with the legal system, including courts, police, prisons and human rights bodies, is now routinely included in the mandates of contemporary multidimensional peacekeeping operations.[15] The chapters in Part II examine how the commitment to the ROL is translated in practice and all cast doubt on the success of this enterprise.

Richard Zajac Sannerholm and Frida Wall (Chapter 7) draw on data on UN rule-of-law assistance covering two decades of peacekeeping and peacebuilding in Africa (1989–2010). They examine the relationship between policy and practice in UN rule-of-law assistance, identifying a divergence between the broad approach set out in UN policy and the narrow 'securitised' focus taken by DPKO in its peace operations.[16] Sannerholm and Wall's chapter questions the relevance of the UN's rule-of-law commitment in war-torn societies, the capacity and preparedness of the UN, the mechanisms and tools for cooperation and joint initiatives between different UN entities, and the quality and coherence of policy and practical guidance. The implication is that UN rule-of-law assistance is not regulating the problem of arbitrary use of power in post-conflict situations in a responsive manner.

The role human rights play in contemporary UN rule-of-law discourse and practice is taken up by Annemarie Devereux (Chapter 8). The Annan definition gave priority to human rights norms as a basis for the ROL. Devereux shows, however, the difficulties both in conceptualising what a human rights-based approach means and in translating this to the field. While human rights can be seen as the 'unruly cousin' of the ROL, Devereux shows how human rights can be promoted in transitional justice programmes, constitution-making processes and in technical assistance programmes. Laura Grenfell (Chapter 9) focuses on UN translation problems in providing assistance to post-conflict states to draft new constitutions. The UN's main strategy is to encourage states to incorporate international human rights standards, reducing their capacity to articulate a national identity and norms. This can undermine the local legitimacy of new constitutions. Using the example of Timor-Leste, Grenfell argues that to achieve a 'rule-of-law constitution', the constitution-making process should be conceived as a long-term process of reconciling international and national norms.

If the function of the ROL is to reduce arbitrary exercise of power, the notion of accountability is central. Jeni Whalan (Chapter 10) offers a positive example of a mechanism used to hold a multidimensional peacekeeping operation accountable to the populations of the states in which they deploy. Whalan describes a pioneering experiment conducted by the UN Transitional Authority in Cambodia (UNTAC) in the early 1990s to address community concerns about peacekeeper misconduct with the creation of a Community Relations Office. She suggests that this local accountability forum for peace operations, albeit flawed in its UNTAC form, provides a valuable model of accountability. She identifies five features that would help refine the model for future operations: answerability, independence, accessibility, responsiveness and legitimacy.

Gina Heathcote's analysis of the UNSC's response to sexual violence within UN missions also takes up the theme of accountability (Chapter 11). She argues that the UNSC's women, peace and security (WPS) agenda is used to justify the use of force in humanitarian crises and post-conflict situations by identifying a category of vulnerable civilians, usually peopled by women and children. On this analysis, regarding young people and women as active participants within their community would unravel the legitimacy of the authorisation to use force, including robust peacekeeping mandates. Heathcote highlights the tensions between the UNSC's promotion of the ROL and its WPS agenda, particularly the UNSC's implication that widespread and systematic sexual violence may function as a trigger for the authorisation to use force.

The linkages between the ROL and protection of civilian agendas in peacekeeping missions are investigated by Peter Thomson (Chapter 12). He contends that rule-of-law programmes are essential to the protection of civilians in the context of peacekeeping in order to support the building of a sustainable peace. Thomson suggests, however, the inadequacy of the UN protection of civilian strategy, which prioritises certain short-term objectives over longer-term rule-of-law activities, such as institutional strengthening and transitional justice.

3 The Security Council, sanctions and the rule of law

Sanctions are a prominent UNSC Chapter VII measure for maintaining international peace and security. When paving the way for a June 2010 meeting on the ROL, the President of the UNSC described sanctions as 'highly efficient tools for promoting compliance with international law and are indispensable in the international fight against terrorism'.[17] When the UNSC applied sanctions against Libya in February 2011, Brazil (then President) emphasised that the sanctions sought 'to ensure the protection of civilians and promote respect for international law'.[18]

Yet sanctions can also undermine the ROL, as illustrated by the disproportionate humanitarian and economic impact of the comprehensive UN sanctions against Iraq and Haiti in the 1990s upon both civilians and third states.[19] The UNSC now uses the language of 'smart sanctions', such as travel bans and assets freezes, aiming to minimise humanitarian impact,[20] but these also have implications for the ROL.[21] Not long ago the notion that international courts might engage in effective judicial review of the UNSC's use of sanctions was considered far-fetched. While international courts have traditionally hesitated to scrutinise the UNSC's discretion to take Chapter VII action to maintain international peace and security,[22] the various stages of the *Kadi* case demonstrate that challenges to the UNSC's Chapter VII discretion are no longer simply academic.[23] Although the European Court of Justice Grand Chamber's decision addressed the European Commission rather than the UNSC, the message is clear: the UNSC does not accord individuals on assets-freeze lists sufficient due process guarantees to enable their assets to be frozen in European jurisdictions.[24]

The chapters in Part III examine these developments and how they affect the UNSC's relationship with the ROL. In Chapter 13 Kimberly Prost, the former UN Ombudsperson for the Al-Qaida sanctions regime, discusses whether the Ombudsperson procedure meets the requirements for a fair process. She identifies components of fair process in the context of targeted sanctions by the UNSC and discusses how the various phases of the Ombudsperson process are designed to address these requirements. Prost also considers the effect of the overall process in terms of the independence of its review. She concludes that the Ombudsperson process represents an important step towards supporting the ROL in the UNSC.

Erika de Wet turns to the role that courts, particularly in Europe, have played in the enforcement of UNSC resolutions affecting states' international human rights obligations. Drawing closely on the *Kadi* case, de Wet discusses benchmarks for judicial protection of European Union (EU) due process rights for individuals and other entities subject to the UNSC's targeted sanctions. She identifies challenges, particularly the problems facing states that are members of both the EU and the UN and which may be unable to honour treaty obligations under one system without violating similar obligations under the other. De Wet examines how the European Court of Human Rights has attempted to overcome such issues by applying a presumption of human rights friendliness. In a similar vein to Prost, de Wet regards the expansion and refinement of the office of Ombudsperson within the UN sanctions system as a constructive way to increase procedural fairness.

4 The Security Council, force and the rule of law

The relationship between force and the ROL is complex, whether in the national or international context. On the one hand, the resort to force represents a breakdown in peaceful relations, challenging the ROL. On the other hand, legal theorists have long argued that law gains its imperative, binding character when it is backed up by the legitimate monopolisation of the use of force. Article 42 of the UN Charter empowers the UNSC to 'take such action by air, sea, or land forces as may be necessary to maintain or restore international peace and security'. Yet the Charter vision of a UNSC that would itself take such action has lain largely dormant.

When the UNSC authorises force it generally delegates to designated states or groups of states the power to use 'all necessary means' or 'all necessary measures' to pursue particular goals.[25] The UNSC has also granted limited authorisations to peace operations to use force. At their most robust, these authorisations have mandated peace enforcement, such as in Somalia.[26] More commonly, however, the UNSC has provided peace operations with Chapter VII authorisations to use all necessary measures to protect civilians and to implement their mandates.

Concern that the UNSC might employ or delegate force in an unprincipled manner led the UN Secretary-General's 2004 High-level Panel to recommend a series of guidelines designed to regulate the UNSC's use of force, reasoning that UNSC decisions to authorise the use of force should be both legal and legitimate.[27] It emphasised that, in order to secure maximum legitimacy for decisions to use force, the UNSC should adopt guidelines designed to ensure not simply that force *could* be used, but that it *should* be used in a given situation.[28] The Panel proposed that these guidelines should include five basic criteria: seriousness of threat; proper purpose; last resort; proportional means; and balance of consequences.[29]

In his 2005 report to the World Summit, *In Larger Freedom*, UN Secretary-General Annan recommended that the UNSC should come to 'a common view' on how to embed these criteria of legitimacy in its decision-making on the use of force.[30] However, while the World Summit endorsed the Panel's proposed new norm of the responsibility to protect (R2P), which itself might result in a decision to use force through the UNSC, it remained silent on the applicability of the criteria of legitimacy.

Unease about the UNSC's discretion to authorise the use of force is not limited to the legitimacy of the UNSC's initial decision concerning whether to authorise the use of force. Concerns are also raised about the subsequent legitimacy of the exercise of force by member states acting under the authority of a UNSC mandate. Indeed, disquiet surrounding the implementation by the North Atlantic Treaty Organization of UNSC Resolution 1973 (2011) in Libya has led to calls for greater accountability in the authorisation and use of force in the name of R2P. These concerns have been framed as 'responsibility while protecting' (RWP).[31] The primary focus of RWP is on the UNSC's duty to ensure that its authorisations of force are implemented in good faith and are not exceeded or abused. While the UNSC generally requests states using force in accordance with a UNSC mandate to report to it on such action, such reporting has not always been regular or fulsome.

Part IV of the collection explores the twists and turns in how the ROL affects the UNSC's use of force. Karine Bannelier and Théodore Christakis (Chapter 15) investigate UNSC authorisations of states or coalitions of states to use force for the maintenance of international peace and security, decentralising UNSC functions. This system of 'delegation' of the power to use force to individual states raises the concern that some states might use these UNSC authorisations as a cover to achieve their own agenda and justify otherwise unlawful intervention and interference. It also increases the risk of non-compliance and abuse of UNSC mandates. Bannelier and Christakis assess nine proposals to strengthen the oversight and control of use-of-force mandates. They frame their assessment as a balance between the need for transparency and accountability, on the one hand, and flexibility, on the other.

Joanna Harrington (Chapter 16) addresses the controversy over the R2P doctrine which emerged from *In Larger Freedom*, exacerbated by the UN-approved military intervention in Libya in 2011. She reviews the proposal made by Brazil the same year to combine a doctrine of RWP with the concept of R2P. Harrington concludes that too often efforts to achieve respect for the rule-of-law focus on the substance of a legal framework, while discounting possible benefits to be gained from undertaking procedural reforms, such as enhancing the perceived legitimacy of the decision-making process.

In Chapter 17 Bruce Oswald analyses the implications of the establishment by the UNSC in March 2013 of its 'first-ever "offensive" combat force', entitled the Intervention Brigade. This Brigade was mandated to undertake military operations against armed groups in the Democratic Republic of the Congo. Oswald focuses on legal issues that arise with the creation of the Brigade, including whether the authorisation of offensive military operations renders the Brigade and by extension the broader peace operation of which it forms part, parties to the conflict? If so, does that in turn mean that the parties subject to the Brigade's offensive military action are entitled as a matter of international humanitarian law to target members of the Brigade in particular and of the broader operation more generally? He cautions that these legal issues should be resolved before the UNSC establishes another peace operation under UN command and control with a mandate to undertake offensive operations.

Mary Ellen O'Connell (Chapter 18) argues that the UN has fallen short of fulfilling its purpose of saving 'succeeding generations from the scourge of war'.[32] O'Connell proposes a new strategy for the UNSC to strengthen the ROL, which would support the UN's mission of preserving the peace. The strategy involves the UNSC, both as a body and in the individual capacity of members, modelling 'law compliance' with respect to the use of force. This approach echoes the work of regulatory theorists who argue that positive modelling is an effective regulatory strategy to promote self-regulation.[33] According to O'Connell, the principles of necessity and proportionality must govern not just the way force is used, but also the initial decision to authorise force in the first place. Similarly, the UNSC must respect important structural rules of the international legal system, in particular the principle of non-intervention.

Alex J. Bellamy (Chapter 19) examines current debates about the UNSC's management of the use of force for protection purposes in tracing the UNSC's response to the crisis in Syria and arguments about 'voluntary veto restraint'. He suggests that deepening the UNSC's consensus on the use of force for protection requires recognition of two main concerns of member states: that protection rhetoric is sometimes used to support other agendas; and that states acting on UNSC mandates are not held accountable to the UNSC itself. Like Joanna Harrington, he explores Brazil's RWP proposal, focusing on three elements: agreement on decision-making criteria to guide decision-making, 'judicious analysis' in advance of decision-making and the establishment of an accountability mechanism. Bellamy concludes that, while decision-making criteria have limited utility when it comes to the concerns mentioned above, judicious analysis and accountability measures might make a useful contribution to deepening consensus within the UNSC, especially if those measures are grounded in the Charter and the UNSC's own practice.

5 Conclusion

The book concludes with Jeremy Farrall and Marie-Eve Loiselle returning to Terence Halliday's characterisation of the UNSC's two modes of engagement with the ROL – as an external phenomenon to be promoted on the offence, and as an internal phenomenon to be respected on the defence. Farrall and Loiselle thus examine the key insights to emerge from the chapters of this collection in terms of the UNSC's actions as rule-of-law *regulator*, on the one hand, and as rule-of-law *subject* or *regulatee*, on the other. They then turn their analysis to the future, presenting provisional policy recommendations for strengthening the ROL through the UNSC that have emerged both from contributions to this volume and from the broader research project of which the volume forms part.

These policy recommendations for strengthening the ROL through the UNSC proceed from the premise that the best prospects of improving the UNSC's rule-of-law practice lie in convincing the UNSC to self-regulate its relationship with the ROL. By taking steps to ensure that its practice across the areas of peace-keeping, sanctions and force both *promotes* and *respects* the ROL, thus reconciling Halliday's external and internal modes of rule-of-law invocation, the UNSC can retain the trust and confidence of UN member states and bolster its legitimacy, credibility and effectiveness. This would be a constructive way to harness the tensions both in the concept of the ROL and in the UNSC's engagement with that concept.

Notes

1 UN Doc. S/PV.4833 (24 September 2003), p. 2.
2 Joel M. Ngugi, 'Policing Neo-Liberal Reforms: The Rule of Law as an Enabling and Restrictive Discourse' (2005) 26 *University of Pennsylvania Journal of International Economic Law* 513–99, 516.
3 Outi Korhonen, 'The "State-building Enterprise": Legal Doctrine, Progress Narratives and Managerial Governance', in Brett Bowden, Hilary Charlesworth and Jeremy Farrall (eds), *The Role of International Law in Rebuilding Societies after Conflict* (Cambridge, Cambridge University Press, 2009), pp. 15–37, 28; Amy Chua, *World on Fire: How Exporting Free Market Democracy Breeds Ethnic Hatred and Global Instability* (New York, Doubleday, 2003).
4 Hans Köchler, *The Voting Procedure in the United Nations Security Council: Examining a Normative Contradiction and its Consequences on International Relations* (Vienna, International Progress Organization, 1991), p. 28.
5 Terence Halliday, 'Rule of Law on the Offence and Defense in UN Governance', paper presented at a workshop on Strengthening the Rule of Law through the UN Security Council, New York, 14 June 2013.
6 See, e.g.: Ian Ayres and John Braithwaite, *Responsive Regulation: Transcending the Deregulation Debate* (Oxford, Oxford University Press, 1992); Neil Gunningham and Peter Grabosky, *Smart Regulation: Designing Environmental Policy* (Oxford, Oxford University Press, 1998); John Braithwaite and Peter Drahos, *Global Business Regulation* (Cambridge, Cambridge University Press, 2000); Christine Parker, Colin Scott, Nicola Lacey and John Braithwaite, *Regulating Law* (Oxford, Oxford University Press, 2005); Robert Baldwin, Martin Cave and Martin Lodge, *Understanding Regulation: Theory, Strategy and Practice* (New York, Oxford University Press, 2011); David Levi-Faur, *Handbook on the Politics of Regulation* (Cheltenham, Edward Elgar, 2011).
7 See, e.g. Hilary Charlesworth, 'Not Waving but Drowning: Gender Mainstreaming and Human Rights in the United Nations' (2005) 18 *Harvard Human Rights Journal* 1–18.
8 Braithwaite and Drahos, *Global Business Regulation*, pp. 550–63.
9 John Braithwaite, 'Fasken Lecture: The Essence of Responsive Regulation' (2011) 44(3) *University of British Columbia* 475–520.
10 Paul Craig, 'Formal and Substantive Conceptions of the Rule of Law: An Analytical Framework' (1997) *Public Law* 467–87; Brian Z. Tamanaha, *On the Rule of Law: History, Politics, Theory* (Cambridge, Cambridge University Press, 2005), pp. 91–113.
11 John Rawls, 'The Law of Peoples', in Samuel Freeman (ed.), *Collected Papers* (Cambridge, MA, Harvard University Press, 1999), p. 118.

12 Hans Kelsen, *General Theory of Law and State* (New York, Russell, 1961), p. 113; H.L.A. Hart, 'Positivism and the Separation of Law and Morals' (1958) 71 *Harvard Law Review* 593–629; Joseph Raz, 'The Rule of Law and its Virtue' (1977) 93 *Law Quarterly Review* 195–211, 207.
13 Lon L. Fuller, *The Morality of Law*, 2nd edition (New Haven, CT, Yale University Press, 1969); Craig, 'Formal and Substantive Conceptions', 467, 477–84.
14 UN Doc. S/2004/616 (23 August 2004), *The Rule of Law and Transitional Justice in Conflict and Post-conflict Societies: Report of the Secretary-General*, para. 6.
15 Jeremy Farrall, 'Impossible Expectations? The UN Security Council's Promotion of the Rule of Law after Conflict', in Brett Bowden, Hilary Charlesworth and Jeremy Farrall (eds), *The Role of International Law in Rebuilding Societies after Conflict* (Cambridge, Cambridge University Press, 2009), pp. 134–156, 153.
16 See also Shane Chalmers and Jeremy Farrall, 'Securing the Rule of Law through UN Peace Operations in Liberia' (2014) 18 *Max Planck Yearbook of United Nations Law* (in press).
17 Office for the Coordination of Humanitarian Affairs, *Aide Memoire for the Consideration of Issues Pertaining to the Protection of Civilians in Armed Conflict*, 4th edition (New York, United Nations, 2011).
18 UN Doc. S/PV.6491 (26 February 2011), p. 7.
19 Elizabeth D. Gibbons, *Sanctions in Haiti: Human Rights and Democracy Under Assault* (Westport, CT, Praeger, 1999); Sarah Graham-Brown, *Sanctioning Saddam: The Politics of Intervention* (London, I.B. Tauris, 1999).
20 David Cortright and George Lopez (eds), *Smart Sanctions: Targeting Economic Statecraft* (Lanham, MD, Rowman and Littlefield, 2002).
21 Vera Gowlland-Debbas, 'Security Council Change: The Pressure of International Public Policy' (2009–2010) 106 *International Journal* 105–25; Antonios Tzanakopoulos, *Disobeying the Security Council: Countermeasures against Wrongful Sanctions* (Oxford, Oxford University Press, 2011); Erika de Wet, *The Chapter VII Powers of the Security Council* (Portland, OR, Hart Publishing, 2004); Alexander Orakhelashvili, 'The Impact of Peremptory Norms on the Interpretation and Application of United Nations Security Council Resolutions' (2005) 16 *European Journal of International Law* 59–88; Alexander Orakhelashvili, *Peremptory Norms in International Law* (Oxford, Oxford University Press, 2006), chapters 12–14.
22 *Yassin Abdullah Kadi* v. *Council and Commission*, Court of First Instance, Case T-315/01, 21 September 2005, (2006) 45 *ILM* 81, para. 289.
23 *European Commission, Council of the European Union, United Kingdom of Great Britain and Northern Ireland* v. *Yassin Abdullah Kadi, French Republic*, Grand Chamber, Cases C-584/10 P, C-593/10 P and C-595/10 P, 18 July 2013, OJ 2013/C 260/02.
24 Ibid.
25 For discussion, see the chapter by Bannelier and Christakis in this collection.
26 See SC Res. 794 (3 December 1992).
27 See UN Doc. A/59/565 (2 December 2004), *A More Secure World: Our Shared Responsibility – Report of the Secretary-General's High-level Panel on Threats, Challenges and Change*, para. 207.
28 Ibid., paras 184, 204–9.
29 Ibid., para. 207.
30 UN Doc. A/59/2005 (21 March 2005), *In Larger Freedom: Towards Development, Human Rights and Security for All*, para. 126.
31 UN Doc. S/2011/701 (11 November 2011), Annex: *Responsibility While Protecting: Elements for the Development and Promotion of a Concept*.
32 UN Charter, Preamble.
33 See, e.g. Braithwaite, 'Fasken Lecture'.

Part I

Theorising the rule of law

2 The Security Council and the rule of law

Some conceptual reflections

Martin Krygier

Introduction

In recent years, the rule of law (ROL) has become a central part of the rhetorical armoury of the United Nations (UN) generally and the UN Security Council (UNSC) more particularly. Of course, it is not merely the UN that has fallen for the ROL; the concept has enjoyed a stellar rise to international celebrity, since and in large part because of the end of the Cold War.[1] The shift from sidelines to centre stage has been vividly evident in the UN, however, since the major protagonists are assembled there, and the change was public and swift.

Though lip service was occasionally paid to it earlier, the ROL only became an agenda item in the UN General Assembly (UNGA) in 1992.[2] By 2012, a High-level Meeting of the UNGA was devoted to it. And as Farrall has pointed out, while the ROL was rarely mentioned by the UNSC for the whole of the Cold War, it figures in 69 UNSC resolutions between 1998 and 2006.[3]

As the UN Secretary-General (UNSG) reported to the UNGA in 2008:

> the integration of rule of law activities into our major country-level operations is relatively recent. Since the 1990s, there has been a prominent shift towards more engagement at the country level. United Nations development, peace and security, and human rights actors increasingly provide rule of law assistance in countries at the request of Governments. The demand for United Nations rule of law assistance at the national level continues to grow.[4]

Indeed, supply seems to have matched demand, perhaps stimulated much of it, even taken on a life of its own.[5] Of course, the ROL is notably absent from many of the places and predicaments the UN deals with, so demand may well have been high in any event, but then that absence was already evident for decades before the UN began to talk about the ROL. There are likely to be other reasons for its invocation than the need for it, now that the ROL has become such an omnipresent hurrah phrase. Some of these are conceptual.

I begin in this chapter by noting the 'unclarity' inherent in many standard uses of the term 'rule of law'. I suggest this has both contributed to its omni-popularity and also might have allowed its proponents to pursue endeavours that could cause controversy if otherwise named. I then turn to the conventional debate over whether the ROL should be theorised as a 'thick' or 'thin' concept, to show how neither alternative helps get us closer to a conception of the ROL that might usefully guide UNSC-mandated interventions. In light of this, I set out in Section 3 an approach that begins at the other end, that is, not by specifying the content of the concept (whether thick or thin) but with the political ideal, the achievement associated, by many, over long stretches of time, with the ROL. Following this approach, I set out what I see as one central, if not the most important, end of the ROL: to temper and channel the exercise of power, and more specifically to protect against its *arbitrary* exercise. I then discuss how, having started with an attempt to identify the point of the ROL, one might begin to think about how to achieve that end. Finally, I return to the UNSC to draw out the implications of this approach for what it does, how it should do it and how it and we might think about these questions.

1 The uses of emptiness

Farrall has observed that:

> [t]he Security Council tends to refer to the rule of law as if the concept is both clearly understood and inherently desirable.... The Council does not see the need to clarify the meaning of the rule of law, nor to explain why it is a positive phenomenon. It simply presents the rule of law as something that is essential to peaceful society.[6]

As he also notes, this combination of conceptual unclarity with professed enthusiasm is not confined to the UN.

The combination is not accidental. Chesterman speculates that '[s]uch a high degree of consensus on the virtues of the rule of law is possible, in part, because of relative vagueness as to its meaning'.[7] And the fuzziness of the concept is not without other uses. The combination of vagueness with universal acclaim also allows the ROL to act as camouflage for more controversial activities, which can be pursued without being named. As the Security Council Report has observed, 'the rule of law has been used as an umbrella or gateway for the Council to involve itself in human rights-related activities in conflict situations without framing them as such'.[8]

Other qualities can mix helpfully with vagueness as well. Thus, some suggest, actors may use the language of the ROL as a cover, allowing them to appear committed to justice and good governance without having to confront more obviously controversial issues of human rights violations.[9] If this is so, it will not be the first time that 'rule of law' is a convenient way of re-labelling activities that might otherwise draw controversy, even censure.[10]

For believers in consensus, the ROL and human rights, there might seem nothing wrong with drawing on the tactical uses of this newly fashionable, though not newly minted, slogan. However, for those who have thought the ROL might add *specific* value, over and above its usefulness in clothing or promoting other purposes, something might appear to have been lost in the translation. What might that be?

2 Thick and thin

Writers on the ROL often distinguish between 'thin' or 'formal', on the one hand, and 'thick', 'substantive' or 'material' conceptions of it, on the other. The former locate the ROL in formal properties of laws and legal institutions and approved ways of operating them. The latter require substantive elements from a larger vision of a good society and polity – democratic, free-market, human rights-respecting or some such – to be present.

'Thin' and 'thick', 'formal' and 'substantive', conceptions compete in countless discussions of the ROL, among legal philosophers, comparative lawyers and rule-of-law promoters.[11] Positivist legal philosophers, and legal comparativists, tend to favour 'thin' conceptions of the concept, what might be called rule-of-law-lite for its lack of normative ballast: easier to identify and able to travel further, because it carries less baggage. Many governments, too, particularly authoritarian ones, prefer to be assessed against thin formal criteria, easier to satisfy than thick morally demanding ones. Today international businesspeople, unwilling to buy into controversial questions about democracy, human rights and other large values in, say, Singapore and China (with both of which they might want to do business), often prefer a formal, thin conception too.[12]

Partisans of 'thick' think differently. For them, thin accounts miss what is at stake in the ROL; that stake or those stakes are what fatten up their conception. As Kavanagh and Jones point out in the UN context, the thick conception:

> denies that mere procedural formality can protect individuals or groups from oppression and insists that effective rule of law requires a deeper set of constitutional and legal norms, ranging from guarantees of full citizen equality, recognition of alternative dispute resolution mechanisms, and political participation, to the panoply of contemporary international human rights and broader range of political institutions that can facilitate the provision of human security and development.[13]

According to Kavanagh and Jones, in the UN the competition between thick and thin occurs in an interestingly complementary and intertwined way. On the one hand, UN policy statements, they argue, are increasingly expressed in 'thick' language. On this account:

> the rule of law guarantees the protection of the full range of human rights, brings citizens and non-citizens alike legitimate avenues of recourse in cases of abuses of power and allows for the peaceful and fair resolution of disputes.... Strengthening the rule of law fosters an environment that

> facilitates sustainable human development and the protection and empowerment of women, children and vulnerable groups, such as internally displaced persons, stateless persons, refugees and migrants.[14]

On the other hand, they claim that:

> UN rule-of-law support on the ground tends to follow a very narrow interpretation of the rule of law, often front-loading support to legal drafting or the training of police, justice, and prison personnel and other common institution-building initiatives.[15]

Kavanagh and Jones are generally critical of the practical implications of both of these options, as well as of the slide from one to the other. They suggest that while thick accounts might be apt for some post-authoritarian transitions, neither thick nor thin

> seem[s] entirely suitable for the contexts where the UN has its largest operational practice, i.e. in low-income, low-institutional countries that have emerged from civil conflict ("post-conflict settings"), nor do they fit into the timeframes that characterize UN engagements whether in post-conflict or traditional development settings.[16]

A 'thick' conception is unrealistic in such settings, they argue, because the complex social, political, economic and cultural preconditions of its realisation are lacking. Indeed, also often missing are formal institutions of particular sorts that work in particular ways, just what the thin conception dreams about. For the problem is not merely an absence but a counter-presence, not just that certain instruments that the UN wishes for are missing, but that others are often locally preferred by practised virtuosos who have neither interest nor talent to learn new instruments, and no taste for new tunes.[17]

I would add that, aside from these crucial issues of implementation, the problems confronting thick and thin are not merely pragmatic but conceptual; nor is the slide from one to the other accidental. Starting with thick, as legal philosopher Raz has argued, the closer the ROL comes to incorporating whatever it is we take to be 'the good' or 'human rights', or any other capacious hold-all of normative ambition, the less we have need for the concept of the ROL at all. After all, since we already have the former concepts, what is added by another that seems to speak of something else, but is interpreted to mean the same? Nothing, but something is taken away: any specific content to the ROL.[18]

Apart from this paradoxical combination of conceptual thickening with weightlessness, there is another problem with purporting to drive or guide practical activities by highly abstract and ambitious values. Thus Philip Selznick, one of the founders and leading figures in the sociology of institutions, often drew attention to the perhaps unintended but predictable consequences of purporting to guide practical activity by 'unanalyzed abstractions':[19] an 'intimate association of utopianism and opportunism'.[20] The association, he insisted, is not by chance. Rather, the inflated nature of proclaimed goals leads their partisans, if not inexorably then at least naturally enough, to opportunism. For the link is structural:

> words like 'democracy' and 'socialism' [...] are not useful guides to decision-making. Insofar as they fail to specify how and at what cost ideals are to be fulfilled, they are utopian 'unanalyzed abstractions', and they invite opportunism....
>
> Wherever purpose is overgeneralized, endemic opportunism is likely to appear.... When purposes are abstract, yet decisions must be made, more realistic but *uncontrolled* criteria will govern. Thus do the polarities of opportunism and utopianism meet and embrace.[21]

This switch from utopianism to opportunism is plain enough in the UNSC's peacekeeping and sanctions practice where, as Farrall documents, on the one hand the UNSC 'frequently emphasises the importance of the rule of law' yet on the other 'when it comes to sanctions decision-making, the Council's practice tends to undermine the rule of law'.[22] But even in attempts to generate the ROL in national arenas, ad hoc-ery and aimlessness are common. For UN agencies speak in very high tones, which their practices do not and arguably cannot reach. That is built into the very concepts they employ, or at least the ways they employ them; into the ways they think.

Nor, however, is it helpful to scale back one's ambitions and settle for rule-of-law-lite, as advocated by partisans of 'thin'. What is gained by defining down a concept that bears so much normative resonance, in terms that ignore any interrogation of what its point might be, simply to focus on the characteristics of institutions and practices? Particularly when it is not clear whether the characteristics chosen relate as much to what law does and should do in the world, as they do to promoters' unevenly informed intuitions and hunches about these matters. Also, given the focus of thin accounts on state institutions, what of the exercise of power by non-state forces – social networks, prominent (dominant?) families, clans, religious leaders, Mafia bosses or assorted 'fellowships of dirty togetherness', as the Polish sociologist Podgórecki used to call them?[23] If, whatever the law says, they are free to act arbitrarily, capriciously, does it make sense to insist that nevertheless the ROL exists because purported institutional underpinnings of a legal order are present, or standard practices have been mimicked?[24]

Moreover, and paradoxically, accounts that purport to be thin as a rake are often rather plumper than intended, particularly where – as is frequently the case in well-intentioned first-world interventions in benighted third-world countries – they embody parochial suggestions as to what features of familiar legal orders are likely to generate ROL-friendly results anywhere and everywhere. When packages of legal bric-a-brac are asked to travel, it often turns out that they work very differently or not at all where they land.[25] It might also turn out that institutions and practices of sorts not known in the homes of confident rule-of-law exporters perform adequately in their own homes, or can be made to do so, even if they look quite strange to visitors.

Whether they do or not should be a matter of investigation, not overbearing legalistic assumption, and either way it is folly to ignore them. Too often, however, imported assumptions about the working of legal institutions, based on distant histories, traditions, institutions and practices, have been smuggled in and then on-sold under the guise of universal 'best practice'. For example, most such efforts focus on tinkering with state legal structures, even though a figure widely cited (if drawn from God knows where) – of 80 per cent of total cases being handled by traditional or customary legal systems[26] – might suggest that this is not the best route to effective legal transformation. What is? We just don't know.[27] Again, many interventions to bolster 'rule of law' in authoritarian states actually work to strengthen (e.g. police training) and/or legitimate (e.g. training of judges, who remain in thrall to their paymasters) the very sorts of regimes they purport to challenge.[28] When such reforms fail to 'take', is it because the ROL is a false ideal, or because what has been exported is not apt to generate it?

3 Begin with the end

After some 30 years of intensive and expensive rule-of-law promotion, then, the brutal assessment that 'we know how to do a lot of things, but deep down we don't really know what we're doing'[29] remains plausible, or at least eminently arguable. Partly that stems from the intractability of the problems with which rule-of-law reformers deal. But partly, too, it has to do with how they/we think. If the ROL comes to be a concept that it is mandatory to use, but that has no clear or specific content, then it will add nothing at all, either in principle or in practice, to what we do. And if the ROL might have signified something worth having, that is a shame.

No one is in a position to lay down what such a contested phrase as the ROL must mean. But given that the ROL is an intrinsically normative concept, it makes sense to *begin* by seeking to identify some conception of the end or ends one thinks it serves, rather than with any immediate enumeration of its purported institutional features.[30] The proper place to start, I believe, is with the question of *why* (what might one want the ROL *for*?) not *what* (what is it made up of?). And that matters because no sensible answer to the second question can be given until one comes to a view on the first. Moreover, even with the first question answered, what counts in one place as a sensible answer to the second might not be sensible somewhere else. Societies differ, so do their institutional traditions, practices, and capacities, and so do the patterns of practice, expectation and culture in which they are always embedded. So we will need to learn something, not necessarily to be found in the works of the usual suspects, about these things.

How would we know whether or not rule-of-law initiatives were successful, if we didn't have any idea what success would involve? If just having a court-house is the end-state we want from building one, then fine, but if contributing to the ROL is the point of the exercise then we must already have some conception of what sort of achievement the ROL is.

To speak of the ROL is to characterise a valued state of affairs in the world, to which law is thought to contribute. The aspiration or ideal is satisfied to the extent that some purpose or goal for law is realised. Of course, the ROL is a relative and variable achievement, not all or nothing. But one can say it exists in good shape in so far as a certain sort of valued state of affairs in society exists, not simply because certain institutions, recognisable by donors, are in place. If we value that ideal we should of course seek to identify what might be necessary to generate it. But that is a second step. Without some principle of selection, even if only tacit, we won't find a bunch of legal bits and pieces waiting 'out there' and recognisable as the ROL.

My contention is, then, that to understand what the ROL requires we start by reflecting first on its *point* rather than by starting, as is typical of thin accounts, with an enumeration of purportedly defining legal-institutional *features*, whether they be particular institutions such as common law courts (Dicey),[31] particular formal qualities of rules, such as prospectivity, clarity, etc. (Fuller)[32] or particular ways of organising familiar legal institutions, such as courts, police and prosecutors' offices. One might well *come* to such features, among others, in any attempt to pin down how to fulfil the ends of the ROL in particular circumstances, but only where one is persuaded that they can help in this end. It is never enough that we have them at home, not even that they work in particular ways at home.

In relation specifically to the UNSC and the ROL, there is the particular problem that a lot of those institutions typically thought of in connection with the ROL in domestic circumstances don't exist in the international arena. But, as I argue below, even were it otherwise, that would not warrant an account of the ROL that *begins* with the specification of what are (hoped to be) *means* for its attainment.

The conceptual starting-point I commend has in common with thick accounts a normative component. However, this approach diverges from thick accounts by asking what might *distinguish* the ROL from other things we value in a polity – what is the distinctive vocation of the ROL? Unless that question is asked, the empty conceptual duplication of which Raz warns will soon follow, and soon after that it will be hard to resist the allures, of which Selznick warned, of opportunism.

4 Law and power

If we start by asking what are specific, distinguishing, ends of the ROL, where should we look first? My suggestion is where law meets power. That of course is in no way an original suggestion. Indeed, it is highly traditional. As Waldron has pointed out, 'the lead idea of the Rule of Law is that somehow respect for law can take the edge off human political power, making it less objectionable, less dangerous, more benign and more respectful'.[33] My only amendment to this passage would be to stress that if political power needs such tempering, so too should other forms of power, including non-state power. In many countries, powerful clan leaders are more powerful than politicians, businessmen trump legislators, local beats central. It is what power can do, rather than where it is located, that matters. The ROL has to do with the tempering and channelling of power's exercise, and its specific vocation is to combat *arbitrary* exercise of power, that is to say, to play a role in rendering power answerable to others than those who directly wield it, and responsive to the needs and claims of those whom it affects. This is not the only thing in the world that matters, or what necessarily matters most. It does, however, matter greatly, when power is exercised, that this not be done arbitrarily. There are other things we want, but at least we should secure this, since a great deal else and good flows from it. Wild power is a terrible thing; it needs to be tamed. Not paralysed or eliminated; just made reliably and respectfully non-arbitrary.

This candidate for the immanent value of the ROL reflects a recurrent and central theme in ROL traditions.[34] Unpredictable exercise of power is one way of treating power's targets arbitrarily; one of the horrors of Stalin's regime in the 1930s is that millions of people had no way of knowing, or ensuring against (e.g. by behaving legally) arrest, deportation or worse. Another form of arbitrariness is the exercise of power, whether predictable or not, that takes no account of the interests or perspectives of those whom it would affect. Once the system got going, many Jews had a very good idea what would happen to them; no surprises there. The arbitrary choice to liquidate them having been made, there was simply nothing they could do to affect it. What makes both forms arbitrary is the fact that the act of power 'is subject just to the *arbitrium*, the decision or judgement of the [power-wielding] agent; the agent was in a position to choose it or not choose it, at their pleasure'.[35] Conversely, those subject to such power cannot in the first case take account of it in choosing how to act ahead of time nor manifest their voice and perspective in the second.

Rule of law is in relatively good order in so far as some possible behaviours, central among them the exercise of political, social and economic power, are effectively tempered and channelled, so that non-arbitrary exercises of such powers are relatively routine, while other sorts, such as lawless, capricious, wilful exercises of power routinely occur less. The role of law in the ROL is to contribute to this state of affairs, though it will not be able to do it alone.

Arbitrariness is a specific and obnoxious vice when added to power. Of course it is the *combination* that is lethal. If my acts do not have potential to harm, then I can be as arbitrary as I please; indeed, my surprising eccentricities might be part of my charm. But we don't often find surprise as charming in those who have power over us. There are many other vices which depend on the *substance* of the law, but arbitrary power is vicious enough even without them and moreover can be vicious even when the substance is fine. Arbitrary power is a free-standing vice.

Where arbitrariness is linked with significant power, it tends ineluctably to: threaten the *liberty* of anyone subject to it; generate reasonable and enduring *fear* among them; and deprive citizens of reliable sources of expectations of, and *coordination* with, each other and with the state. And as Fuller and Waldron[36] have emphasised, it threatens the *dignity* of all who find themselves mere objects of power exercisable at the whim or caprice of another.[37]

These are four good reasons to value reduction of the possibility of arbitrary exercise of power. To the extent that the ROL can help deliver such reductions, this is reason to value it. This is not, of course, merely a negative matter of removing evils, but can be expressed positively. A world in which arbitrariness is routinely and reliably curbed is one in which freedom, confidence, coordination and dignity are less threatened than otherwise. That takes it some great and positive distance from many available alternatives. There are many other goods, but most of them are immeasurably harder to attain without institutionalising constraints on arbitrariness in the exercise of power.

5 Ends and means

The ideal I start with is not a recipe for detailed institutional design. It is rather a value, or interconnected cluster of values, that should inform the criteria by which such design is assessed, and which might be – and have been – pursued and institutionalised in a variety of ways. So specifying the ultimate values that the ROL is to secure is not yet to describe how these values are to be achieved. And perhaps such specification can never be achieved with any combination of generality and precision. In different societies, with different histories, traditions, circumstances and problems, these (and other) values have been secured in different ways. And there are many ways to fail, too. Nevertheless, starting with generally specified commitments – e.g. hostility to arbitrary power – one can seek to elaborate more specific conditions and intermediate and more concrete principles – e.g. don't put all power in the same hands; generate power to balance power, etc. From these, in turn, one can seek to generate specific practical and institutional recommendations, in particular circumstances, with particular ways and means derived from and adapted to those circumstances. These intermediate principles can help in appraising whatever normative and institutional setups one has, and suggesting modifications or alternatives to them. They are variably fulfilled, and fulfilled in various ways, in different societies and times.

On the one hand, ideals of the ROL have been better served in some nations and by some institutions than others. Institutional possibilities are not infinite, institutions have consequences, different institutions have different consequences, learning can and does occur and you have to start somewhere. So it would be absurd to ignore what Selznick, following John Dewey, called the 'funded experience' of generations,[38] among them truisms that have proved valuable again and again. One of these is that only power can tame power.

One is, therefore, often warranted in starting with presumptions in favour of institutional models which have worked elsewhere. On the other hand, one should be wary of too swiftly converting presumptions into prescriptions, particularly prescriptions that are highly specific, let alone that hold out particular institutions as universal models to be emulated. Here it is important to keep the point(s) of the ROL in mind. One should not conclude from institutional variety that new contexts are simply '*sui generis*'[39] (as all contexts are in part but not completely), pursuit of the ROL requires reflection on how some generally valuable goods might be achieved in particular contexts. Problems and predicaments will vary, and so too will the best ways to meet them. Wherever you are, the ROL should be approached with a combination of its point(s) in mind, more specific principles derivable from those grounding values, and acquaintance with various attempts to secure and institutionalise such ends, *together with* a great deal of reflected-upon local knowledge.

6 The Security Council and the rule of law

But what has this to do with the UNSC, an institution at once more powerful than many states and quite different from them? And what to do with the ROL in relation to it, when it does so many things, some having to do with advancing the ROL in places under its authority, and others having to do with the way it pursues its own Charter- and self-appointed tasks.

Thinking in the ways I have sketched might aid reflection on the UNSC's professed commitment to the ROL both as to how it might be made good in the often tortured societies which it oversees and in its modes of oversight themselves.

On the one hand, this approach avoids the empty expansiveness of thick accounts, while on the other it dodges the aimlessness of thin formal accounts. One starts with a conception of what the ROL is good for that doesn't collapse it into whatever else we would like, and that provides criteria for what one should seek to do and to have in order to accomplish such an end. One avoids recipes but not purposes.

Of course, while it is not vacuous, it is also not precise. It is a starting point, from which it is still necessary to explore middle-range proposals – more concrete and specific – as to what institutions, practices and particular values need to achieve to aid in taming arbitrariness. It helps that we are not starting from scratch here, but we don't have ways both specific and universalisable to institutionalise and realise these values. For reaching those concrete solutions depends on respect for and complex appraisal of the particular and variable contexts in which power is being exercised – appraisal in light of rule-of-law principles but not simply deducible from them.

I interpret Farrall's 'pragmatic rule-of-law model' for the UNSC in this way.[40] His five principles – transparency, consistency, equality, due process and proportionality – are all middle-level principles of the sort I have in mind, and I would happily interpret them as particular instantiations of non-arbitrary exercise of power. Kleinfeld has a partially overlapping list.[41] The important point is, on the one hand, that they be particularisations of values which might be at the same time precious but too general without more to give specific practical guidance, and on the other hand, that they not be *too* particular and specific. The more precise and concrete they become the less they are likely to be generalisable. To fill in those crucial ground-level institutional and other blanks, our general prescriptions need to be explored for particular implications and interwoven with specific contexts. Or, as Farrall explains his approach:

> It is grounded on the basic premise that underpins almost every approach to the rule of law; namely, that the primary goal of the rule of law is to prevent the misuse and abuse of political[42] power. But the emphasis of this model is somewhat unconventional. Rather than requiring the introduction of new mechanisms which would seek to impose external regulation of the Council's actions in accordance with an ideal model of the rule of law, the aim here is to infuse the existing Security Council decision-making process with greater awareness of and adherence to basic rule of law principles.[43]

A lot is often made of the peculiarity of the international domain, and in it of the UNSC, in lacking many of the institutions we routinely associate with the ROL: state monopoly over force, independent tribunals with enforcement powers, separation of powers and so on. The rule-of-law tradition, after all, was developed within states and largely concerned with the exercise of power within them. As noted above, many institutions typically thought of in relation to the ROL in the domestic arena don't exist in the international one, and some international institutions, such as the veto power of the permanent members of the UNSC, are inimical to the ROL.

However, many of what we take to be rule-of-law institutions don't exist, or don't work as we might anticipate, in many domestic arenas as well. In both domains, it is appropriate to work from both ends, one normative and the other factual, to guide the generation of institutions that connect them.

One further, and for the moment final, implication of this approach is that realising 'basic rule of law principles'[44] is likely to depend upon much besides law – domestic or international.[45] If we value the immanent end(s) of the ROL (whatever we conclude it or them to be), we cannot assume, without further investigation, that any particular assemblage of legal institutions or practices will generate such ends or, conversely, that such ends can nowhere be generated in quite other ways, ways of which we haven't thought, which might be simply beyond our ken.

7 Conclusion: law and the rule of law

There is nothing original or even lonely in nominating opposition to arbitrariness as a fundamental concern of the ROL. However, taking the point seriously and starting with it rather than lists of legal hardware has a number of implications that have not always been noted. I conclude by mentioning three. These implications would follow, moreover, whether or not you agree with my specification of the point of the ROL, just so long as you think it makes sense to begin thought about the ROL with consideration of what its distinctive vocation might be.

One is that the salience of features of any particular legal institutions and formal and procedural characteristics usually nominated to constitute the ROL depends on how successfully they support the attainment of the ROL in the wider society. To the extent they do, they have aided us in identifying what the law needs to be like to serve the end of the ROL – at least in *that* society. To the extent that they do not, however, it is not at all clear why rule-of-law practitioners fix on them so, still less try to extend them to places where they might merely have parodic roles. The challenge for anyone seeking the ROL anywhere is not primarily to emulate or parody practices that seem to have worked elsewhere, but to find ways of reducing the possibility of arbitrary exercise of power, whatever that takes, here.

A second implication is that if the arbitrariness of the exercise of power is the target and the danger one fears, there is no reason a priori to limit one's attention to state power. If non-state power is arbitrarily exercised by oligarchs, Mafiosi, warlords, tribal elders, Al-Qaida, business executives or university administrators, it too has the potential to bring with it all the vices of arbitrariness mentioned above. So the ROL is opposed to arbitrariness in the exercise of significant power, whoever is doing the exercise. In every case, one is involved in the pragmatic exercise Farrall advocates, though of course in some domains it is likely to be more strenuous exercise than in others.

Finally: taking the ROL seriously may not only require different legal rules and practices from those we know, particularly in places we don't know, but also recognition that many of the most significant sources of, goods generated by and dangers to the ROL are to be found elsewhere than in or even near the obvious institutional centres of official law.[46] That is true both nationally and internationally. Sources of power are many. There are numerous circumstances in which arbitrariness flows as much or more from extra-state exercises of power, sometimes aided by suborned official agencies, sometimes opposed to them. Moreover, possible constraints on it may come, or fail to come, from many domains of social life, and from many agencies other than legal ones. Not only might this occur, but it already does, in spades and all around us. That this is so adds greatly to the complexity of the concept of the ROL. It also adds to the precious value of the thing itself.

Notes

1 See Martin Krygier, 'The Rule of Law after the Short Twentieth Century: Launching a Global Career', in Richard Nobles and David Schiff (eds), *Law, Society and Community: Essays in Honour of Roger Cotterrell* (Aldershot, Ashgate, 2014).
2 See United Nations, 'United Nations and the Rule of Law', www.un.org/en/ruleoflaw.
3 Jeremy Matam Farrall, *United Nations Sanctions and the Rule of Law* (Cambridge, Cambridge University Press, 2007), p. 22.
4 UN Doc. A/63/226 (6 August 2008), *Strengthening and Coordinating United Nations Rule of Law Activities: Report of the Secretary-General*, p. 6.
5 To the point where, as Sannerholm and Wall point out in their chapter in this collection, UN ROL assistance is now often criticised for being supply-driven.
6 Farrall, *UN Sanctions and the Rule of Law*, p. 24.

7 Simon Chesterman, 'Taking Stock: The UN Security Council and the Rule of Law', keynote address, dialogue with UN Member States on the rule of law at the international level, New York, 28 October 2010, p. 2.
8 Security Council Report, *Cross-cutting Report on the Rule of Law* (28 October 2011), www.securitycouncilreport.org/atf/cf/{65BFCF9B-6D27-4E9C-8CD3-CF6E4FF96FF9}/XCutting Rule of Law 2011.pdf, p. 13.
9 Philip Alston, 'The Rule of Law and the UN Security Council', paper presented at the Workshop of the ANU Centre for International Governance and Justice and the Australian Government's Australian Civil-Military Centre, *Strengthening the Rule of Law through the United Nations Security Council*, New York, 14 June 2013; Balakrishnan Rajagopal, 'Invoking the Rule of Law in Post-Conflict Rebuilding: A Critical Examination' (2008) 49(4) *William and Mary Law Review* 1347–76, 1359.
10 See Martin Krygier, 'The Rule of Law: An Abuser's Guide', in András Sajó (ed.), *The Dark Side of Fundamental Rights* (Utrecht, Eleven International Publishing, 2006), pp. 129–61.
11 Parts of this section draw upon my paper, Martin Krygier, 'Rule of Law (*Rechtsstaat*)', in James D. Wright (editor-in-chief), *International Encyclopedia of the Social & Behavioral Sciences*, 2nd edition, vol. 20 (Oxford, Elsevier), 780–7.
12 For discussion, see Natarajan's chapter in this collection.
13 Camino Kavanagh and Bruce Jones, *Shaky Foundations: An Assessment of the UN's Rule of Law Support Agenda* (New York, New York University Center on International Cooperation, 2011), p. 8.
14 UN Doc. A/66/749 (16 March 2012), *Delivering Justice: Programme of Action to Strengthen the Rule of Law at the National and International Levels: Report of the Secretary-General*, para. 4.
15 Kavanagh and Jones, *Shaky Foundations*, p. 27.
16 Ibid., p. 8.
17 Ibid., pp. 24–5.
18 Joseph Raz, 'The Rule of Law and its Virtue', in *The Authority of Law* (Oxford, Oxford University Press, 1979), chapter 11, p. 211.
19 Philip Selznick, *The Moral Commonwealth* (Berkley, CA, University of California Press, 1992), pp. 249–50.
20 Ibid., p. 249.
21 Ibid., pp. 249–50.
22 Farrall, *UN Sanctions and the Rule of Law*, p. 15.
23 A. Podgórecki, *Polish Society* (Westport, CT, Praeger, 1994), pp. 51, 115, 131–2.
24 I develop this argument in Martin Krygier, 'Inside the Rule of Law' (2014) 3(1) *Rivista di Filosophia del Diritto* 77–98, 91–6.
25 See Martin Krygier, 'Four Puzzles about the Rule of Law: Why, What, Where? And Who Cares?' in James E. Fleming (ed.), *Getting to the Rule of Law: Nomos L* (New York, New York University Press, 2011), pp. 64–104.
26 Stephen Golub, 'A House Without a Foundation', in Thomas Carothers (ed.), *Promoting the Rule of Law Abroad: In Search of Knowledge* (Washington, DC, Carnegie Endowment for International Peace, 2006), p. 116.
27 See David M. Engel and Jaruwan S. Engel, *Race, Custom, and Karma: Globalization and Legal Consciousness in Thailand* (Stanford, CA, Stanford Law Books, 2010).
28 See Mark Fathi Massoud, *Law's Fragile State: Colonial, Authoritarian, and Humanitarian Legacies in Sudan* (Cambridge, Cambridge University Press, 2013).
29 Thomas Carothers, 'The Problem of Knowledge', in T. Carothers (ed.), *Promoting the Rule of Law Abroad: In Search of Knowledge* (Washington, DC, Carnegie Endowment for International Peace, 2006), pp. 15–28, 15.
30 I have argued this at length and often. See 'Four Puzzles' and, most recently, 'Still a Rule of Law Guy' (2013) 34(1) *Recht der Werkelijkheid* 47–55.

31 Albert V. Dicey, *Introduction to the Study of the Law of the Constitution* (London, Macmillan, 1948).
32 Lon Fuller, *The Morality of Law*, 2nd edition (New Haven, CT, Yale University Press, 1969).
33 Jeremy Waldron, 'Is the Rule of Law an Essentially Contested Concept (in Florida)?' (2002) 21 *Law and Philosophy* 137–64, 159.
34 See John Phillip Reid, *Rule of Law: The Jurisprudence of Liberty in the Seventeenth and Eighteenth Centuries* (DeKalb, IL, Northern Illinois University Press, 2004).
35 Philip Pettit, *Republicanism: A Theory of Freedom and Government* (Cambridge, Cambridge University Press, 1997), p. 55.
36 See Fuller, *The Morality of Law*; and J. Waldron, 'The Rule of Law and the Importance of Procedure', in J. Fleming (ed.), *Getting to the Rule of Law: Nomos L* (New York, New York University Press, 2011), pp. 3–31.
37 I discuss these four reasons more extensively in 'Four Puzzles', pp. 78–81.
38 P. Selznick *Law, Society, and Industrial Justice* (New York, Russell Sage Foundation, 1969), p. 8.
39 Cf. Ruti Teitel, *Transitional Justice* (New York, Oxford University Press, 2000), *passim.*
40 Farrall, *UN Sanctions and the Rule of Law*, pp. 183–246. I might say that the overlap between my approach and Farrall's is not the fawning of a contributor to his editor. We came to these overlapping approaches quite independently, and only later discovered our affinities.
41 Rachel Kleinfeld, *Advancing the Rule of Law Abroad: Next Generation Reform* (Washington, DC, Carnegie Endowment for International Peace, 2012).
42 I would expand this to include social and other sources of power.
43 Farrall, *UN Sanctions and the Rule of Law*, p. 39.
44 Ibid.
45 For discussion, see Natarajan's chapter in this collection.
46 For more on this, see Krygier, 'Four Puzzles'.

3 Big rule of law℠ ™(pat.pending)

Branding and certifying the business of the rule of law

Veronica L. Taylor

Introduction

The normative content of the rule of law (ROL) continues to be energetically contested.[1] Debates generally proceed on the basis that the ROL – however defined – is a public good. The unstated assumption is that producing this public good is fundamentally a responsibility of the sovereign state, which has the right and (some argue) the obligation to shape, animate and enforce law domestically, while submitting itself to domestic and international legal authority and challenge. When a state's capacity or willingness to do so is lacking – or perceived as such by other states – those other sovereigns, acting alone or in concert, project their preferred versions of the ROL into 'weaker' states.[2] This process of projecting the ROL norms through diplomacy, official development assistance, military interventions and humanitarian assistance is both an international phenomenon (when legitimated by international law and sponsored by international multilateral organisations),[3] and a mode of transnational governance, 'somewhere beyond the reach of the nation-state and below the legal regime of international law and the authority of international organisations'.[4]

Scholars of globalisation of law have pointed out that 'the rule of law' is but one of many 'global scripts' that are promoted and institutionalised within and through transnational organisations.[5] These scripts are inscribed in legal technologies such as conventions and treaties, best practices and standards, legislative guides and model laws, international court rulings and rules of global regulatory bodies. Halliday, Carruthers and Block-Lieb point to these as the international and transnational 'soft law' and regulation that form the basis of models that are promoted to recipient states for domestic adoption.[6] The creation of this hybridised form of governance goes by many names, but here I use 'rule-of-law promotion'.

This chapter explores rule-of-law promotion as both a practice and a product:[7] the co-production of 'rule-of-law' products and services that become commodities for distribution and sale. It also seeks to show how public/private co-production of the ROL as a branded and certified product is designed to bolster the normative appeal of this type of transnational policy intervention. Viewed in this way, the ROL as a product is distinct from the ROL as a concept, or norms embedded in global scripts; as reformed legal or political institutional arrangements; or as a 'legal technology' of the kind described above – although I acknowledge that these domains overlap and are often mutually constitutive.[8]

Section 1 of this chapter provides a quick guide to how rule-of-law promotion works as a production process and distribution chain within a globalised rule-of-law industry. One industrial attribute of the 'scaling-up' of rule-of-law promotion since the 1990s is a shift towards standardisation. Section 2 describes some techniques for standardising rule-of-law products and services. Section 3 then considers how rule-of-law promotion outcomes are measured and evaluated, and how the sets of indices for measurement and evaluation themselves become rule-of-law commodities. A less remarked-upon aspect of rule-of-law promotion has been the way in which rule-of-law 'products' have been transformed into private property – what I call 'Big Rule of Law'. Section 4 explains this by describing the branding and certifying of, and trading in, rule-of-law products. In conclusion, the chapter reflects on the purpose branding and certification serves within the rule-of-law industry, and their effects. It argues that branding and certification of rule-of-law 'products', while in tension with justice-oriented versions of the ROL, is both a logical extension of, and a necessary legitimating tool for, the hybrid regulatory character of twenty-first-century rule-of-law promotion.

1 A quick guide to the rule-of-law industry

1.1 Concepts that inform the production of the rule of law

The rule-of-law 'revival' that unfolded as socialist regimes in Eastern and Central Europe began to disintegrate from the late 1980s onwards[9] was not simply a revisiting of earlier, formalist ideas of how legal institutions might effectively constrain the state.[10] Underpinning rule-of-law promotion in the 1990s was a widely shared belief in the ascendancy of western liberal democracy over socialism and the assumption that newly democratising or independent states would – and should – adopt the political, legal and economic organisational forms of their funders.[11]

Krygier argues that such reform menus that accompanied these interventions were overly prescriptive, and fundamentally misrepresented the 'rule of law' concept, pointing to the need to curb arbitrary exercises of power (by the state and others).[12] By this he means not the replication of institutional arrangements in Anglo-American or Western European states, but the context-specific use of multiple pathways and institutions to check abuses of power.

Santos' important empirical contribution was to show how competing ideas of the ROL were mobilised in the service of rule-of-law promotion.[13] His study shows different divisions of the World Bank deploying vastly different concepts of the ROL simultaneously as the foundations for different policy interventions aimed at legal reform. The concepts being operationalised ranged from Dicey's separation of powers and submission of the state to law, to Hayek's realisation of market transactions with minimal interference from the state, through Weber's substantive change in norms and personnel shaping institutions, to Sen's emphasis on institutions and their representatives delivering distributional equity to citizens.[14]

With the exception of the last category, what these formulations of the ROL omit is an articulated concept of justice. Whether the ROL as a concept ought to include a richer, fuller set of justice norms is a complex normative debate.[15] Formulations of rule-of-law programming, such as 'law and justice reform', 'security sector reform' (SSR), and 'rule-of-law promotion' itself, all display a tension between technocratic and substantive justice concerns. For instance, in SSR discourse, 'justice' denotes a technical 'sector' and is an analogue for criminal law, procedure, adjudication, sanctions and corrections, regardless of whether the processes and outcomes of these are just.[16] The potential slippage between the externally funded justice 'fix' and the substantive realisation of justice locally varies with each rule-of-law intervention, but it is not unusual for the formal, technical face of the ROL to dominate the more complex, indeterminate negotiation of 'justice'.

The malleability of the ROL as a concept lends great latitude to how rule-of-law promotion is implemented in practice. Thus international and transnational actors can develop a discourse of absence of the ROL in target states, despite a landscape full of state and non-state law.[17] That malleability extends to the production of 'rule of law'; promoters are creating a market (a perceived need or demand) and a product simultaneously. These rule-of-law products may be generic (and cost-effective), or customised (context-specific,[18] in ways that I have called 'responsive rule of law'[19]). Thus they may contribute to the realisation of justice, or human rights, or social equity in a particular location, but they need not. Cultivating the belief that rule-of-law promotion and its products are effective, however, is important, in order to maintain the narrative of 'lack' and that 'more is needed'.[20] This is the work of rule-of-law marketing, indicators, branding and certification; all ways to convince the buyer that the ROL works and is valuable.

1.2 The production of the rule of law

The work of rule-of-law promotion takes many forms: a reform programme, an individual project, a new piece of legislation or regulation, training in new legal concepts or processes, technical assistance to a legal or justice agency, or public information campaigns to communicate new legal concepts, procedures or rules. Rule-of-law promotion is generally an exchange for value. We confuse the issue by calling the financiers of rule-of-law promotion 'donors', regardless of whether they are providing a grant, loan or contribution in kind of equipment or services, and whether or not the funding is tied to procurement of goods and services from their own economy. We imagine that multinational organisations and national agencies are giving away their 'surplus' production of legal knowledge and professional services to nation-states that 'lack' law reform, modern statutes, legal training, legal information technology, legal publishing, legal professionals, government regulatory agencies or efficient legal processes. More accurately, the rule-of-law producers are creating ROL for sale, or investing in rule-of-law processes in anticipation of a future gain, which may be peace (thus eliminating the need for military intervention), economic growth or trade.[21]

The real value of the rule-of-law intervention may be market access, a favourable climate for foreign investors (sometimes at the expense of domestic business) and/or political access to lobby for these results. In situations where membership of a multilateral organisation is at stake (the World Trade Organization or the European Union, for example), the price of entry is the complete overhaul of the regulatory laws and institutions of the aspiring member state, while technical legal assistance is the accelerant. This reflects a persistent belief among international and transnational policy-makers that 'western' law is both desirable and necessary to support market transactions and trade, and thus drive economic growth.[22]

We can understand financial investment in policy areas that seem tangential to trade, such as human rights training, or access to justice for the poor, as being part of an overall strategy to make ROL attractive and to temper the apparent contradiction between strengthening a nation-state's law and legal institutions in order to make its markets more permeable, and improving the quality of justice for that state's ordinary citizens. The industrial parallels would be with the branding and marketing of products with aspirational or morally uplifting labels such as 'free range', 'organic' or 'fair trade', which makes them slightly more costly, but also more saleable because of the added normative appeal. As Marxist philosopher Slavoj Žižek points out in relation to consumption more broadly, 'feel good' activities such as charity and recycling appear to address contradictions in the liberal capitalist system (poverty and waste) without actually resolving the contradictions that give rise to the problem, and thus are fundamental to the ongoing 'saleability' of the capitalist political and economic system.[23]

Some anthropologists claim, persuasively, that the development 'project' in the field has become the development *product*.[24] By this they mean that, instead of being a means to effect a development outcome, the project itself is the goal. Funding agency and host-state partners collude in design, delivery and assessment of the project in ways that satisfy their very different objectives. On the funding side, this includes satisfying the home office's political need to have 'deliverables' from the project, whether or not these correlate with meaningful change for host-state counterparts. For host-state partners, a 'project' is often simply synonymous with 'budget support'.

If this is the case for development projects in general, then the ROL might also be embodied in its practice, packaging and branding – in addition to, and quite distinct from, its normative (product) claims. Thus a training course in human rights for judges in Afghanistan could be understood (by the participants and by their foreign trainers alike) as constituting something called 'the rule of law', regardless of how each of them understands that concept, and independently of whether the judge trainees ever apply human rights principles in their courts, or behave in ways that are consistent with having an independent and incorruptible judiciary.[25]

1.3 Market participants and funding

Thus far I have discussed rule-of-law promotion exchanges as if the sovereign state were negotiating directly with a bilateral or multilateral funder or provider of rule-of-law assistance. But the actual delivery of 'rule-of-law promotion' is through agents: a crowded marketplace that I have called the 'rule-of-law bazaar'.[26] Aggregated totals for aid flows in 2013 are estimated at US$135 billion, despite ongoing debates about how to value aid flows to include new national providers of funding, exclude interest payments on loans and calculate the real value of financial transfers to host states.[27]

Market participants range from state-owned enterprises through to self-employed individuals. In between we encounter international NGOs, state agencies, local NGOs, militaries, churches and corporations. The degree of privatisation of rule-of-law promotion varies with the identity of the funding states and the sponsoring organisation.[28] Among these actors there is considerable blurring of profit and non-profit lines. Rule-of-law NGOs typically receive significant funding from multilateral or government agencies, as well as corporations, whether disclosed or undisclosed.

The financing of the rule-of-law industry is supply-driven in the sense that it is directed towards aims that the funding provider regards as politically or economically important. Host states are consulted and concur in these allocations, but by definition do not control them. Profit and non-profit entities then compete for a share of the available funds. The result is that rule-of-law promotion across the world has a bifurcated character: discursively, it declares allegiance to one or more of the normative aims of the ROL (and the political or ideological beliefs that inform these), while in practice it pursues those aims through transactions that prioritise commercial contracts, the relationships that underpin these, market share, accumulation of assets and profit.

1.4 Industrial regulation

A distinguishing feature of the rule-of-law industry is that it is multi-nodal. There is no single international forum or agency that oversees the production and distribution of the ROL by public and private entities. So I use 'industry' in a heuristic sense – whether it fully meets the criteria for a discrete services industry, or comprises sub-sections of other service industries, are questions beyond this chapter's scope. The formal contours of the regulation of the ROL are found at the next level down, in the interlocking networks of outsourced procurement and employment contracts that link international financial institutions, bilateral aid providers, host-state agencies, local and international implementers of projects and individual consultants.

At the same time, financiers, producers, distributors and hosts together form epistemic communities and professional networks, and individuals move fluidly within these networks, taking with them their knowledge, contacts, professional practices and their sense of 'how we do' rule-of-law promotion. This affects rule-of-law products because emerging research suggests that individual reputations and prestige are, along with perceptions of organisations, one of the ways in which local participants and partners evaluate programmes and projects.[29]

2 Standardising 'the product'

Evaluation of the rule-of-law product is made easier through standardisation. As post-industrial economies in the global North turned to new public management and sought efficiencies in public spending through outsourcing, they also embraced standardisation, often through the use of technology. In development assistance, and in other fields of public expenditure, this takes the form of procurement contracts, internal reporting, costing mechanisms, personnel roles and titles, modes of organising the workplace and styles of public reporting of outcomes – all designed to be uniform within agencies and across host states.[30] These forms of standardisation are all embedded within rule-of-law promotion. However, one of the most visible attempts to standardise rule-of-law promotion is the adoption of indices by which to measure host legal system compliance with selected forms of the ROL.

Measuring the ROL is a mode of validation – establishing a 'lack' in a system that then requires an intervention, or the 'proof' that some kind of change has occurred (ideally attributable to an intervention) and that the desired features of the ROL have appeared or increased in the target location.[31] Examples of such tools are the World Bank's *Doing Business* indicators[32] and Transparency International's Corruption Perceptions Index (CPI).[33] Davis, Kingsbury and Merry describe 'the indicator culture', a strategy of global governance in which the indicators in use mimic one another as they focus on external evaluation of formal legal institutions and institutional efficiency.[34] Parsons and his collaborators identify 53 governance indicator tools that currently address different aspects of the ROL.[35] All of the existing indicator products have methodological problems. As Parsons concedes, these are exacerbated by the common practice of combining different types of indicators to produce standardised measures that 'mask the complex realities of institutional performance, obscuring the kind of detailed, disaggregated information that is necessary to understand and respond to the specific problems that may be hampering the delivery of justice'.[36] I argue that these standardisation tools seek to erase complex realities in favour of a clear normative result, because simplified representations of national legal systems are more easily digested and manipulated within a globalised template.[37]

In line with this argument, Davis, Kingsbury and Merry draw attention to how indicators are buoyed by the rise of quasi-science: how they create apparent certainty, transparency and commensurability with regard to a contested and loosely defined concept, 'the rule of law'.[38] Perry-Kessaris also observes that the rise of indicators has a disempowering effect on many communities. Indicators are framed in the language of mathematics, and so to participate in the measurement discourse you have to be literate in the mathematical language, steeped in methodology and able to understand and manipulate the metric outcomes from the indicators. By definition this excludes ordinary citizens who might have much to say about how they experience the 'rule of law' or its absence.[39] Perry-Kessaris also points to how indicator products privilege institutions' contributions to economic growth, rather than their responsiveness to citizens or achievements in social inclusion or economic distribution.[40]

3 Indicators as commodities

Rule-of-law indicators are themselves a commercial product.[41] BizCLIR, for example, is a diagnostic tool for designing procurement of rule-of-law interventions to strengthen business laws and legal institutions in the host state.[42] A private sector contractor developed these indicators for the United States Agency for International Development (USAID), which acts as a distribution channel for the product to its operations around the world.

Another way of commercialising indicators is to embed them in procurement contracts and specify them as part of a design for a rule-of-law intervention. So, for example, in a USAID-MCC Solicitation from 2007[43] that focused on strengthening Indonesia's court system, anti-money laundering authority and Anti-Corruption Commission, the performance of the contractor is assessed in part by reference to externally developed indicators.[44] In this project, five such indicators are built into the contract performance targets: Transparency International's *CPI*, the World Bank Institute's *Control of Corruption Indicator*, Freedom House's *Freedom in the World* rating, the Global Competitiveness Report, and Transparency International's *Global Corruption Barometer*.

3.1 The World Justice Project's Rule of Law Index®

A more recent evaluative product is the World Justice Project Rule of Law Index®. The World Justice Project (WJP) is a non-profit entity. Among its funding sources are multinational corporation GE and other corporate sponsors.[45] The 47 indicators used in the WJP Index are clustered around eight themes: constraints on government powers, absence of corruption, open government, fundamental rights, order and security, regulatory enforcement, civil justice and criminal justice, with 'informal justice' representing a ninth and less developed cluster.[46]

By now we have a number of evaluative tools like this in the rule-of-law policy space that refer to each other and look remarkably similar. Why? One explanation may be that it is a branding phenomenon. Informationally, indices and assessment 'tools' and 'toolkits' help establish an organisation's profile in the rule-of-law industry. This is most obvious in the WJP case: the Rule of Law Index® is not only a 'brand name' but also a registered trademark. It seems unlikely that people are going to steal the WJP's (fairly predictable) formal indicators of 'rule of law'. So why register the Index? It may be a proxy for value – to reassure financial contributors to the WJP that the organisation takes a corporate, professional approach to its work and has a technology that 'works'.

But there is an apparent contradiction between promoting the ROL as a public good, distributing it to partners in developing economies through whole or partially publicly funded channels, and holding private a technology for doing so.

Methodologically this tool falls into the category Davis and Merry criticise heavily. You can see the final outcome in the 2014 WJP report:[47] an aggregated number across all of the questions asked, which first ranks the target state globally out of the total number of states surveyed, then ranks it regionally, then ranks it against other states in a similar indicator group. We then get graphic representations of how the state does, relative to those comparators in areas such as access to justice, open government and regulatory enforcement. The focus is on the institutions of the state, almost exclusively the formal justice sector.

How the final numbers are arrived at is quite an opaque process. The methodology and the questionnaires used have now been published.[48] So we could, theoretically, replicate the results. I have participated in the project as an expert, but it is not clear how the experts are selected, or whether they are held constant over different waves of the survey.

However, to forestall the very obvious criticisms of the methodology, the Index's developers have sought an imprimatur from a group of European scientists. An opinion piece from that group[49] validates the instrument from a social science perspective; this is a quality assurance label from a scholarly research group.

3.2 The UN's Rule of Law Indicator Toolkit

We can contrast the privatised approach of the WJP with the UN Rule of Law Indicator Toolkit of 2011.[50] This is an open-access toolkit that assumes rigorous social science methods, including familiarity with the target state, linguistic competence and ethical approaches to research in fragile or transitional settings. The UN questions have much more normative content relating to gender and human rights, although there is no real consideration of informal or non-state justice here. The focus is still fairly narrow: an exhaustive series of questions to be asked of judges, police and prosecutors. This is curious, given the breadth of the definition of the ROL now adopted and promulgated within the UN system;[51] what is being measured is only a small subset of that definition.

3.3 Better evaluative approaches

What these instruments have in common is that they generate, indirectly, profiles of rule-of-law deficits in the target state.[52] The WJP and UN Rule of Law instruments simply seek to evaluate, on the basis of perceptions, how justice institutions are working on a given day and in a given state. They work ahistorically – none ask 'How did this situation come about?'. In the WJP approach, the resulting profiles are then used to make explicit or implicit comparisons across states.

The UN instrument alone seeks to take a longitudinal approach. It supposes the indicators will be applied in a state over time so that you can chart progress or change in the formal justice institutions' adoption and performance of the ROL. It is explicitly designed *not* to compare states. Nonetheless, even with these enhancements, it does oversimplify the depiction of the host state by assuming implicitly (and perhaps deliberately) that the UN is the only rule-of-law actor affecting that nation-state. Trying to isolate the influence of the UN and its projects on formal institutions would be methodologically impossible where – as is typical – many external actors are seeking to influence the target state's legal institutions. As with the WJP instrument, it also leaves out any consideration of non-state actors or the role of any supporting institutions such as the media, education institutions, civil society, or indeed any other private regulatory actors.

These indicator products focus on formal legal systems and the agencies of the state, while erasing or de-emphasising competing systems of normative ordering. What is not measured, or indeed acknowledged, in such indicators is legal pluralism – the legitimacy and widespread use of informal justice, non-state justice, customary justice and religious forms of law. This chasm between a national legal system's depiction through indicators and how everyday legal pluralism appears to different observers in reality, calls into question the utility of indicators in a profound way.[53]

By contrast, the Vera Institute has a tool that combines strategic indicators (high-level policy goals such as reducing violence in society), institutional indicators (measuring outputs of institutions such as number of criminal convictions) and activity indicators (for example, arresting suspects).[54] This work has informed the UN Rule of Law Toolkit[55] and the promising new direction in participatory indicator design devised by Stone *et al.*,[56] which explicitly acknowledges the power dynamics inherent in 'measuring' local legal systems.

This 'bottom-up' approach is consistent with Braithwaite's recommendations about responsive regulation,[57] and with the proposal of Kavanagh and Jones for strengthening the UN's own rule-of-law capacity, through looking to the immediate self-defined needs of the citizenry as a guide.[58]

4 Branding and certification

What we see so far is an attenuated relationship between the actual nature of legal systems and how they are represented through rule-of-law indicators. Research suggests that there is a rather weak causal relationship between rule-of-law interventions and outcomes of the kind that would satisfy such indicators.[59] What remains strong, however, is a desire on the part of financiers to reinforce the idea that rule-of-law interventions 'work'.

4.1 Branding rule-of-law products

One way to increase the appeal of a product is to brand it. This may explain why many foreign aid providers now have some form of 'brand architecture'. In the case of Australia's Department of Foreign Affairs and Trade, 'law and justice' interventions are delivered by a bouncing red kangaroo (Figure 3.1).[60]

Australian
Aid

Figure 3.1 Logo for the former Australian development agency 'AusAID'.

The Australian government explanation for this is unapologetic: '[t]he Australian Aid Identifier represents *the product* we deliver – Australian aid' (emphasis added).[61] In the United States, the genesis of USAID's branding is explained as a direct result of desired diplomatic outcomes:

> Clear evidence of the value of the increased visibility of *foreign aid* [original emphasis] came in the aftermath of the 2004/2005 U.S. tsunami relief effort, the first time USAID's new 'brand identity' was used publicly.... [I]n 2004, favourable opinions of the U.S. were at record lows in many Muslim countries. But, in early 2005, favourability of the U.S. nearly doubled in Indonesia (from 37 to 66 per cent) thanks to the massive delivery of – for the first time 'well branded' – U.S. foreign assistance.[62]

In both cases, all projects – including rule-of-law promotion projects – that are funded by a government agency are required to use the agency's brand. USAID specifies that 'competing logos or identities, such as the contractor's, are excluded'.[63] This is significant, because where the contractor is a long-term, highly regarded organisation in the host state, its prestige and attractiveness to local partners may well outstrip that of the nation-state providing the funding. So here branding is also performing a regulatory function, with the funder (USAID) compensating for its reliance on a chain of external implementers by insisting that they present themselves visibly as USAID's agents.[64]

Brands are not necessarily durable. National aid agencies AusAID and CIDA[65] have been recently disestablished as agencies and brands by the Australian and Canadian governments, respectively. Perhaps paradoxically, the strength and value of the brand in each case is demonstrated by the need to completely obliterate it. In each case, a conservative government sought to de-emphasise the development assistance aspect of aid, and to reorient its aid programme more explicitly in the direction of delivering trade benefits and pursuing national (financing) state interest.[66]

The rule-of-law industry is crowded with branded 'products' that nest under, or go beyond, national agencies' brand architecture. Examples include *J4P* (World

Bank: 'Justice for the Poor'); *E2J* (USAID, 'Educating and Equipping Tomorrow's Justice Reformers');[67] and *P2P* (USAID, 'People to People Peacebuilding').[68] Some of the appeal of such 'acronym brands' is undoubtedly cultural – the deep attachment that bureaucracies and industries have to special internal language and codes. But there are other, more prosaic factors at work here as well.

In the USAID context, TCBoost (Worldwide Support for Trade Capacity Building project) is an example of a co-branded rule-of-law product.[69] TCBoost is a 'rapid response mechanism' with 'pioneering analysis, practical tools, and customized training' that provides 'USAID/Washington, USAID missions, and trade hubs access to expert assistance in determining the needs of developing-country partners and stakeholders and in designing and implementing projects that meet those needs'.[70] As we read further about TCBoost's 'products', we find that these are produced through a joint venture by DAI/Nathan Group and their subcontractors. Thus TCBoost, like BizCLIR above, is simultaneously a USAID project, and a privately owned and developed product embedded within USAID's brand architecture.

In these examples we see branding working in multiple ways – informationally, by signalling to consumers where the funding originates; as a regulatory device, by affiliating distribution agents with the funding agency and allowing the funder to assume the benefits of any prestige or goodwill generated by the agent; and aspirationally, by suggesting to consumers that the branded product is in some way more desirable than its unbranded (but substantively indistinguishable) forerunner or competitor product.

4.2 Certifying rule-of-law products

A catchy brand name is one thing, but how does a potential 'consumer' know that the product is worth purchasing, or that it will live up to its claims? Our consumers could be the citizens of a state where formal law reform is being implemented – the ultimate beneficiaries of the intervention. However, it seems more likely that the principal 'consumers' to whom these rule-of-law brands are directed are state agencies in both the funding and host states, corporate sponsors of the organisation producing the product (where this is a non-profit) and foreign investors who are seeking to be assured that state X is superior to state Y in the quality of its ROL.

One way to increase trust in a brand and help legitimate its claims is through certification.[71] The usual requirement for certification is a trustworthy, independent third party that informs the consumer that the standards claimed for the product or service by its makers are being met. Certification is not the same as an endorsement, which comes from paid supporters or close associates. The WJP Index's videotaped 'endorsements' of its product by global luminaries and members of its epistemic community illustrate this.[72] Typical certification benchmarks include whether the promoting body has a comprehensive understanding of the product and the field (technical competence); whether there is buy-in from diverse stakeholders (inclusivity); whether the promoting body has standing to endorse the system (legitimacy); ability to avoid brand confusion (a degree of exclusivity); and promoters' resources to make certification 'stick' (dissemination strategies and compliance capacity).[73]

How do our rule-of-law brands and certification systems match up to these criteria for effective certification? Arguably they fall short in under-inclusiveness of the 'product' category and in industry-wide buy-in.

A typical threshold requirement for a strong system of certification is that you actually certify the *whole product category*, rather than a single product. When third parties endorse the WJP's Rule of Law Index®, they are endorsing it, not as an actual measure of the ROL, but as a product in the category of (industrially produced) rule-of-law indicators and toolkits. These products ignore historical narratives and omit normative concerns such as justice, non-state legal pluralism, religious values and resistance. They create 'one-dimensional' profiles[74] of a state's 'rule of law' and tell linear stories about whether this is improving or not. This kind of packaging is appealing in its simplicity and promised ease of use. If we actually took them into a conflict-affected state with competing systems of governance, weak state apparatuses and very rudimentary capacity to provide formal legal services, they would be unreliable guides to reality and reform. However, that the product under-describes the complexities of contemporary legal and regulatory systems in the states being 'measured' is irrelevant. What they do – and do very well – is to inscribe certain ideological positions into the operational concept of the ROL and suggest that rule-of-law promotion should privilege reforms that track these positions. What matters is that we recognise the evaluative 'product': the branding and certification work together to enhance our belief in the legitimacy and effect of the product.

A second threshold requirement for certification in other industries is buy-in from diverse stakeholders. This matters because part of norm formation through certification is intense debate – including with outliers and dissenters – about what constitutes the standard. The WJP mobilised formidable energy in its initial rollout of the Index, and continues to heavily promote the 'launch' of its annual Index reports. The 2014 launch video features suited men of a certain age. Though arguably not a representative sample of stakeholders in rule-of-law norms in the real world, this is part of the certification effort to stake a claim to the most 'authentic' rule-of-law product and alert consumers to the (assumed) dangers and deficits of competing ideas or processes.

Where – as here – an industry has weak governance systems, it may be difficult to firm up buy-in from a sufficient number of industry actors in order to create a binding system of certification. When – as with the ROL – types of certification proliferate, this tends to dilute their impact – consumers become wary and sometimes cynical about product claims. Moreover, there may be little or no penalty for failing to comply with the standards being declared.

5 Conclusion

Transforming rule-of-law services or technologies into branded 'products' – the process of creating what I have called 'Big Rule of Law' – is a four-fold regulatory move. It represents an attempt to harness globalised regulatory tools such as soft law and technical assistance; to deploy these in ways to shape or contest the production of the ROL (itself a regulatory space); to borrow from the prestige and legitimacy of science by suggesting that objective, measurable certainties lie at the heart of rule-of-law policy interventions; and to harness business know-how by branding and attempting to certify rule-of-law promotion as a kind of consumer product.

The test of a branded product, however, is whether the branding and certification works in practice. From a marketing standpoint, the branded rule-of-law products may represent elements of rule-of-law promotion, even while simultaneously under-describing the actual complexities of contemporary legal and regulatory systems. Attempts to 'certify' rule-of-law products, however, become problematic in a diffuse industry that has no central source of authority.

Some empirical questions that remain are whether the rule-of-law products reviewed here will gain traction – whether their producers convince funders and consumers to support them in practice – and whether the results are meaningful. Which branded products and evaluative tools become embedded in project design may be less a question of objective quality and more a question of how branding and certification helps to influence decision-makers within the rule-of-law industry.

One possible outcome of the rise in rule-of-law branding and certification is that these products and evaluative tools actually increase rule-of-law ritualism – the danger that we become mesmerised by the technocratic promise of the products, rather than their actual effect. The products and evaluative tools threaten to 'become' the ROL in ways that draw attention and resources away from the substantive behavioural changes that most rule-of-law interventions seek: internalisation of new norms by actors on the ground and the actual achievement of normative objectives, however framed.

The creation and dissemination of commodified rule-of-law is costly. We could spend that time and energy in the service of real change on the ground – but this is an altruistic view that assumes rule-of-law promotion to be a form of development assistance. Increasingly, we must conclude that rule-of-law promotion is also something else entirely – a mode of public/private co-production of branded and certified commodities designed to bolster the normative appeal of the transnational policy interventions that we call rule-of-law promotion.

Notes

1 See the contribution to this volume by Martin Krygier; and Michael Zürn, André Nollkaemper and Randall Peerenboom, *Rule of Law Dynamics* (Cambridge, Cambridge University Press, 2012).

2 See Ugo Mattei and Laura Nader, *Plunder: When the Rule of Law is Illegal* (New York, Wiley-Blackwell, 2008).

3 On development assistance as foreign policy, see Carol Lancaster, *Foreign Aid: Diplomacy, Development, Domestic Politics* (Chicago, University of Chicago Press, 2006).

4 See Gunnar Folke Schuppert, 'New Modes of Governance and the Rule of Law', in

Michael Zürn, André Nollkaemper and Randall Peerenboom, *Rule of Law Dynamics* (Cambridge, Cambridge University Press, 2012), pp. 90–107.
5 Eve Darian-Smith, *Laws and Societies in Global Contexts: Contemporary Approaches* (Cambridge, Cambridge University Press, 2013).
6 Terence Halliday, Susan Block-Lieb and Bruce Carruthers, 'Rhetorical Legitimation: Global Scripts as Strategic Devices of International Organizations' (2010) 8(1) *Socio-Economic Review* 77–112.
7 See Bruno Latour, *The Making of Law: An Ethnography of the Conseil d'État* (Cambridge, Polity Press, 2009), p. 81.
8 See Patrick McAuslan, *Bringing the Law Back In* (London, Ashgate, 2004).
9 Thomas Carothers, 'Rule of Law Revival' (1998) 77(2) *Foreign Affairs* 95–106.
10 See Albert V. Dicey, *Introduction to the Study of the Law of the Constitution* (London, Macmillan, 1959).
11 See Francis Fukuyama, *The End of History and the Last Man* (New York, Free Press, 1992).
12 See Martin Krygier's contribution to this volume.
13 See Alvaro Santos, 'The World Bank's Uses of the "Rule of Law" Promise in Economic Development', in David Trubek and Alvaro Santos (eds), *The New Law and Economic Development: A Critical Appraisal* (New York, Cambridge University Press, 2006), pp. 253–300.
14 Ibid. Regarding Sen, see also David Trubek and Alvaro Santos (eds), *The New Law and Economic Development: A Critical Appraisal* (New York, Cambridge University Press, 2006), and Amartya Sen, *Development as Freedom* (Oxford, Oxford University Press, 1999).
15 See Peter Cane (ed.), *The Hart-Fuller Debate in the 21st Century* (Oxford, Hart Publishing, 2010).
16 See Whit Mason, 'Introduction', in Whit Mason (ed.), *The Rule of Law in Afghanistan: Missing in Inaction* (Cambridge, Cambridge University Press, 2011), pp. 1–12.
17 For a recent survey of this discourse in relation to Mindanao in the Southern Philippines, see Imelda Deinla and Veronica Taylor, 'Towards Peace: Rethinking Justice and Legal Pluralism in the Bangsamoro' (2015) *RegNet Research Paper No. 2015/63*: http://ssrn.com/abstract=2553541.
18 Benjamin van Rooij and Penelope Nicholson, 'Inflationary Trends in Law and Development' (13 December 2013): http://ssrn.com/abstract=2367357.
19 See http://regnet.anu.edu.au/responsive-rule-law/home.
20 Mattei and Nader, *Plunder*.
21 See Lancaster, *Foreign Aid*.
22 Stephen Humphreys, *Theatre of the Rule of Law: Transnational Legal Intervention in Theory and Practice* (New York, Cambridge University Press, 2010); Michael J. Trebilcock and Ronald J. Daniels, *Rule of Law Reform and Development: Charting the Fragile Path of Progress* (Cheltenham, Edward Elgar, 2008).
23 See Slavoj Žižek, *Trouble in Paradise: From the End of History to the End of Capitalism* (London, Penguin, 2014). Thanks to ANU colleague Shane Chalmers for this point and recommending the following illustrative clip: www.youtube.com/watch?v=hpAMbpQ8J7g.
24 See Emma Crewe and Elizabeth Harrison, *Whose Development? An Ethnography of Aid* (London, Zed Books, 1998).
25 See Tania Murray Li, *The Will to Improve: Governmentality, Development, and the Practice of Politics* (Durham, NC, Duke University Press, 2007).
26 Veronica Taylor, 'The Rule of Law Bazaar', in Per Bergling, Jenny Ederlof and Veronica Taylor (eds), *Rule of Law Promotion: Global Perspectives, Local Applications* (Uppsala, Iustus Förlag, 2010), pp. 325–58.
27 Development Initiatives, *Investments to End Poverty: Real Money, Real Choices,*

Real Lives (Bristol, Development Initiatives, 2013): http://devinit.org/wp-content/uploads/2013/09/Investments_to_End_Poverty_Chapters_0–6.pdf.

28 On the less privatised delivery of rule-of-law promotion in Japan, see Veronica Taylor, 'New Markets, New Commodity: Japanese Legal Technical Assistance' (2005) 23(2) *Wisconsin International Law Journal* 251–81.

29 See Anna Bosch, 'Local Actors in Rule of Law Assistance in Indonesia: Owners, Partners, Agents?' (University of Washington, PhD dissertation in progress, unpublished); Cynthia Alkon, 'The Flawed U.S. Approach to Rule of Law Development' (2013) 117 *Pennsylvania State Law Review* 797–872.

30 See Andrew Natsios, *The Clash of the Counter-bureaucracy and Development* (Washington, DC, Center for Global Development, 2010): www.cgdev.org/content/publications/detail/1424271.

31 Elin Cohen, Kevin J. Fandl, Amanda Perry-Kessaris and Veronica Taylor, 'Truth and Consequences in Rule of Law: Interferences, Attribution and Evaluation' (2011) 3(1) *Hague Journal on the Rule of Law* 106–29.

32 See The World Bank Group, 'About Doing Business': www.doingbusiness.org/about-us.

33 See Transparency International, 'Corruption Perceptions Index: Overview': www.transparency.org/research/cpi/overview.

34 Kevin Davis, Benedict Kingsbury and Sally Engle Merry, 'Indicators as a Technology of Global Governance' (2012) 46(1) *Law and Society Review* 71–104.

35 Jim Parsons, Besiki Kutateladze, Monica Thornton, April Bang and Aminou Yaya, 'Justice Indicators for Post-Conflict Settings: A Review' (2010) 2(2) *Hague Journal on the Rule of Law* 203–17; Jim Parsons, 'Developing Clusters of Indicators: An Alternative Approach to Measuring the Provision of Justice' (2011) 3(2) *Hague Journal on the Rule of Law* 170–85.

36 Ibid., 171.

37 Veronica Taylor, 'The Law Reform Olympics: Measuring Technical Legal Assistance in Transition Economies', in Tim Lindsey (ed.), *Law Reform in Developing and Transitional States* (London, Routledge, 2007): http://ssrn.com/abstract=893682.

38 Davis *et al.*, 'Indicators as Technology of Global Governance'.

39 Amanda Perry-Kessaris, 'Prepare Your Indicators: Economics Imperialism on the Shores of Law and Development' (2011) 7 *International Journal of Law in Context* 401–21.

40 Ibid.

41 Taylor, 'Law Reform Olympics'.

42 USAID, 'BizCLIR': egateg.usaidallnet.gov/bizclir.

43 Millennium Challenge Corporation (a US government agency created in 2004).

44 Taylor, 'Rule of Law Bazaar'. The Millennium Challenge Corporation (MCC) USAID/Indonesia, 'Scope of Work', *MCC Threshold Country Program for Indonesia: Control of Corruption Proposals Submission* (Solicitation Number: Indonesia 07-003) closing date 16 February 2007.

45 The World Justice Project, 'Supporters': worldjusticeproject.org/supporters.

46 The World Justice Project, 'Informal Justice': worldjusticeproject.org/factors/informal-justice.

47 The World Justice Project, *WJP Rule of Law Index® 2014* (Washington, DC, The World Justice Project, 2014): worldjusticeproject.org/sites/default/files/files/wjp_rule_of_law_index_2014_report.pdf.

48 Juan Carlos Botero and Alejandro Ponce, 'Measuring the Rule of Law' (30 November 2011): http://ssrn.com/abstract=1966257.

49 See *Independent Assessment of the European Commission's Joint Research Centre*: http://worldjusticeproject.org/rule-of-law-index.

50 DPKO and OHCHR, *The United Nations Rule of Law Indicators: Implementation Guide and Project Tools* (New York, United Nations, 2011).

51 See the UN Secretary-General's definition: UN Doc. S/2004/616 (23 August 2004),

The Rule of Law and Transitional Justice in Conflict and Post-conflict Societies: Report of the Secretary-General.

52 A third instrument is the *Regulatory Guillotine*™ developed by Scott Jacobs and his business associates. I discuss this instrument in an extended version of this chapter available on SSRN: http://papers.ssrn.com/sol3/cf_dev/AbsByAuth.cfm?per_id=80146.

53 See Miranda Forsyth, *A Bird That Flies with Two Wings:* Kastom *and State Justice Systems in Vanuatu* (Canberra, ANU E-Press, 2009); Martha Marie-Kleinhans and Roderick Macdonald, 'What is a *Critical* Legal Pluralism?' (1997) 12 *Canadian Journal of Law and Society* 25–46.

54 Jim Parsons, Monica Thornton, Hyo Eun (April) Bang, Ben Estep, Kaya Williams, and Neil Weiner, 'Developing Indicators to Measure the Rule of Law: A Global Approach', in *Report to the World Justice Project* (New York, Vera Institute of Justice, 2008): www.altus.org/pdf/dimrol_en.pdf.

55 DPKO and OHCHR, *The United Nations Rule of Law Indicators.*

56 Christopher Stone, 'Problems of Power in the Design of Indicators of Safety and Justice in the Global South', *Indicators in Development: Safety and Justice Series* (Cambridge, MA, Program in Criminal Justice Policy and Management, Harvard Kennedy School, 2011): dash.harvard.edu/bitstream/handle/1/8160719/Stone_Indicators-ProblemsofPower.pdf?sequence=1.

57 John Braithwaite, 'The Essence of Responsive Regulation' (2011) 44 *University of British Columbia Law Review* 475–520.

58 Camino Kavanagh and Bruce Jones, *Shaky Foundations: An Assessment of the UN's Rule of Law Support Agenda* (New York, New York University Press, 2011), p. 25.

59 Elin Cohen and Kristina Simion, *Research Report: Evaluations and Learning in Rule of Law Assistance* (Stockholm, Folke Bernadotte Academy, 2013).

60 Australian Government Department of Foreign Affairs and Trade, 'The Department of Foreign Affairs and Trade Logo and the Australian Aid Identifier': aid.dfat.gov.au/about/Pages/logo.aspx.

61 Ibid.

62 USAID, 'Branding': www.usaid.gov/branding.

63 USAID, 'Frequently Asked Questions': www.usaid.gov/branding/assistance-awards/frequently-asked-questions-marking-requirements-assistance-awards.

64 Thanks to ANU colleague Christoph Sperfeldt for making this point.

65 Canadian International Development Agency.

66 See, e.g. Julie Bishop, Foreign Affairs Minister, Australia, 'The New Aid Paradigm' (Policy Speech, 2014): http://foreignminister.gov.au/speeches/Pages/2014/jb_sp_140618.aspx.

67 See University of Washington School of Law, Asian Law Center, 'Educating and Equipping Tomorrow's Justice Reformers (E2J) Project in Indonesia': www.law.washington.edu/AsianLaw/Research/Projects/IndonesiaE2J.aspx.

68 USAID Office of Conflict Management and Mitigation, *People-to-People Peacebuilding: A Program Guide* (Washington, DC, USAID, 2011): www.usaid.gov/sites/default/files/documents/1866/CMMP2PGuidelines2010-01-19.pdf.

69 USAID, 'About TCBoost': egateg.usaidallnet.gov/tcboost/about.

70 Ibid.

71 Thanks to University of Washington colleague, Professor Jane Winn for suggesting this idea.

72 The World Justice Project, 'Endorsements': worldjusticeproject.org/endorsements.

73 See Michael Conroy, *Branded! How the 'Certification Revolution' is Transforming Global Corporations* (Gabriola Island, Canada, New Society Publishers, 2007), pp. 10–19.

74 ANU colleague Shane Chalmers points out that this recalls Herbert Marcuse, *One-dimensional Man: Studies in the Ideology of Advanced Industrial Society* (Boston, MA, Beacon Press, 1991).

4 Accounting for the absence of the rule of law

History, culture and causality

Usha Natarajan

Introduction

In considering how to strengthen the rule of law (ROL) through the United Nations (UN) Security Council (UNSC), it may be helpful to begin with a definition of the ROL. Numerous definitions exist and these are oftentimes characterised as either 'thick' or 'thin' conceptions of the ROL, with thick definitions encompassing broader substantive conceptions of justice, such as consistency with human rights or other ethical standards, and thin understandings delineating a more basic, formal, narrower notion.[1] This chapter utilises the concept in the thinner sense, understanding the ROL as that which asks that all entities, including states and international organisations, remain accountable to laws that are publicly known.[2] The ROL, even when defined narrowly as in this chapter, is beneficial because it creates order and predictability and ensures equal treatment, thereby helping to guard against abuses of power and protect the weak from the strong.

With regard to the UNSC, strengthening the ROL is usually understood on two levels, the domestic and international.[3] The former entails the UNSC ensuring that its impact within nations through the authorisation of the use of force, sanctions, peacekeeping, peacebuilding and so on promotes rather than undermines a domestic rule-of-law culture. The latter requires the acts of the UNSC itself, including decisions to use force, administer sanctions and undertake peacekeeping and peacebuilding missions, be governed by law. In the first case, the underlying assumption is that the UNSC's decisions are capable of promoting and undermining a rule-of-law culture within states. In the second case, the usual assumption is that the UNSC is lacking in a rule-of-law culture. I agree with these assumptions, but argue in this chapter that this is not the whole story. The solutions proposed by commentators to strengthen the ROL, whether within states or in the UNSC itself, are often regulatory and institutional reform, checks and balances and judicial review. My argument here is that such reforms are at best a partial solution and may be ineffective or even counterproductive if the complex relationship between the UNSC and the ROL is not more fully contextualised and understood.

At the outset, two points must be made. First, regulatory and institutional reform cannot bring about a rule-of-law culture in the absence of a broader enabling environment. The ROL is usually affirmed as a universal value.[4] If we assume this to be true,[5] how then do we account for the triumph of a rule-of-law culture in some states and not in others? By rule-of-law culture, I mean a society's recognition that respect for law is a basic standard of human behaviour, where citizens and public officials are broadly committed to law as a restraint on private and government coercion and arbitrariness.[6]

In states now considered epitomes of the ROL, there is a complex history to the emergence of a rule-of-law culture. In the UK, for example, it involved, among other things, a gradual transition from an absolute monarchy to a more parliamentary and democratic kingdom, alongside the expansion and contraction of the British Empire, the acquisition and the emancipation of slaves, the gradual expansion of suffrage, the scientific and industrial revolutions and so on. While the role of law and legal reform was very important, it alone cannot adequately explain the emergence of a rule-of-law culture in the UK. In places where ROL is lacking today, the reason is not only a lack of legal, institutional or regulatory safeguards. Other reasons include being on the receiving end of a history of conquest, empire-building, enslavement and disempowerment; cultural and racial discrimination; exploitative networks of global resource extraction, consumption, waste and environmental degradation; and mass migration and the establishment of colonial settlements. Often the practice of empire allowed for movement towards a thriving rule-of-law culture in the centres of power at the expense of – or actively undermining – such cultures in the peripheries. Such dynamics are not entirely absent from the international system in the postcolonial era, albeit with actors and power-centres evolving in new ways.

There are hazards when examining historical reasons for the ROL flourishing in some places and not in others. One hazard is that tracing the ongoing relevance of past dynamics is not a straightforward process. The ROL is not merely a vehicle for the west's neo-imperial adventures in the third world. It is used by a whole host of contemporary actors for various contradictory purposes and even in its thinnest sense holds anti-imperial potential. Power operates more diffusely in the postcolonial era,[7] and the concept of the ROL itself plays a role in disguising and distorting operations of power. Indeed, it is ideally suited to do so. Another hazard is the risk of falling into an unstated assumption of social evolutionism, namely that the ROL is a hard-won western achievement, and the west must exercise patience in its efforts to help others catch up. This is a false narrative as the path the west followed to prosperity, peace and order rendered such a path impossible for others.

The second point, in some ways related to the first, is that the assumption that legal and institutional reform is lacking may be incorrect. There may be enough law, thoughtfully and beautifully crafted law, or even too much law. Many of the issues lately raised regarding the UNSC and the ROL were debated when the UN Charter was written and have also been grappled with in the decades since. Reform proposals have been implemented regarding both the UNSC and the UN more generally. Sanctions regimes and peacekeeping operations have been subject to various reforms, particularly in recent decades. Given the UNSC's continual attention to rule-of-law issues since the end of the Cold War, it is worth considering why its ability to promote and abide by the ROL remains the subject of unabated concern two decades later. It may be because some phenomena characterised as rule-of-law problems and dealt with through a regulatory and institutional reform framework are actually problems of another nature.

The UN Charter envisioned a balance between the different parts of the UN. While the UNSC is the most powerful part of the UN in many ways, its mandate was meant to be narrow compared with the UN General Assembly's all-encompassing mandate. The UNSC was not intended to uphold the ROL in the sense that the International Court of Justice should. Nor was it designed to function impartially or provide equal treatment; it institutionalises unequal representation through granting permanent membership and veto power to some states. The Charter also does not identify a clear mechanism to ensure that the UNSC remains governed by the Charter, thus giving the UNSC a high degree of power, discretion and flexibility in interpreting its mandate. Thus, there are aspects of the UNSC that inherently undermine the ROL, even in its thinnest sense.

If the goal is to minimise such aspects, one way would be to consider revitalising the General Assembly (UNGA). Its mandate has been actively undercut, both by the Bretton Woods institutions on economic issues,[8] and the UNSC's expansive reading of its peace and security mandate.[9] Seen in this context, the UNSC's interest in promoting the ROL in the domestic realm faces a paradox: the UNSC's increasing mandate in the domestic realm undermines the ROL in the international realm. The UN Secretary-General (UNSG) recognised this danger at the first UNSC summit meeting after the Cold War in 1992, when several state representatives raised the importance of the ROL.[10] He pointed out,

> democratization at the national level dictates a corresponding process at the global level. At both levels, it aims at the rule of law. For national societies, democracy means strengthening the institutions of popular participation and consent, political pluralism and the defence of human rights, including those of minorities. For global society, it means the democratization of international relations and the participation of all States in developing new norms of international life.[11]

The UNSC could be urged to construe its own mandate as narrowly as possible in its own interests, so that it will be perceived as fairer and more legitimate. Such a perception would be a powerful tool in service of the UNSC's ultimate purpose of keeping the global peace.[12] But self-rule is not the ROL. In any case, the UNSC, its extraordinary powers and its undemocratic character, are themselves creatures of international law. Therefore, it is of limited usefulness to frame inconsistent UNSC action as a rule-of-law problem. It is rather a question of legal preferences, and whether different international laws would bring us nearer to equal treatment than the current arrangement.

To illustrate the two aforementioned points, the first part of this chapter examines attempts to assess and promote the ROL domestically, looking at some recent developments in Tunisia and Egypt and arguing that the reasons for movement towards or away from a rule-of-law culture are not entirely confined to either the domestic or the legal realm. Consequently, tinkering in those realms alone cannot produce such a culture. The second part considers the ROL in the international context through the case of Iraq, arguing that it is not an absence of law, legal institutions or law reform that allows powerful states to operate as they wish. Rather, it is the proliferation of specific types of laws, institutions and reforms that create and maintain unequal international relations.

The analyses in the first and second sections together illustrate that the ROL in the domestic and international realms is intimately connected, and assessing both side-by-side allows for a fuller understanding of the manifold operations of rule-of-law discourse. The Arab region is particularly helpful for such an examination, as a region dominated by authoritarian regimes governing without the ROL, as well as the subject of long-standing attention from the UNSC and other international bodies.

1 Promoting domestic rule of law

When the UNSC authorises action within states for extended periods through peacekeeping and peacebuilding operations it consistently highlights the importance of promoting the ROL. One of the reasons this is easier said than done is that the idea of the ROL allows for flexible multiple usages by a wide range of actors, all agreeing that the ROL is vital, but each diagnosing in different ways what is lacking or needed. The idea itself is of limited usefulness in discerning between these different diagnoses. Thus invoking it merely enables a retreat from controversy.

The following section illustrates this dynamic through two brief examples in Tunisia and Egypt. It goes on to argue that, of the various actors invoking the ROL, the most influential have prioritised domestic law reform of a particular kind, placing insufficient emphasis on non-legal and international factors.

In the Arab region, public attention to domestic rule-of-law issues has intensified over the last three years. The uprisings across the region since December 2010 were provoked not only by rising unemployment and food and fuel prices, but also by unequal distribution of power, wealth and opportunities. In a region dominated by authoritarian regimes, there was no ROL to ensure accountable and consistent action, and even benevolent state behaviour could prove capricious. Given this, the concept of the ROL and its increased touting by international organisations in the post-Cold War era should have been an invaluable ally to those striving for equal treatment in the region. In actuality it has been less straightforward.

Until immediately before the Arab uprisings, the international community was praising many Arab states for their economic and human development progress. Arab states led the world in terms of improvements in human development over the past 40 years.[13] This was due to some of those states successfully channelling their natural resource wealth into social welfare schemes and infrastructural and institutional development, including in the legal sector. In 2010, the World Economic Forum singled out Tunisia as the best economy in Africa, largely because of its business-friendly legal environment, with simple and predictable economic, financial and labour regulations.[14] Yet Tunisia was also where the Arab uprisings began when a street vendor, Mohammed Bouazizi, self-immolated in despair after many years of police bullying and extortion of bribes from him and other such vendors. In December 2010, Tunisia's legal environment for businesses was simultaneously ideal and hopeless, depending on who was asked and what type of business they had.

For foreign investors, Tunisia provided laws that were predictable, clear, accessible, non-retroactive and of equal application. The international organisations that lauded Tunisia in 2010 conceived of the ROL primarily in terms of laws that enable specific sectors of the market to prosper. The ROL in this minimalist sense is not concerned with equal treatment of citizens, but rather with commercial and financial sector conditions that allow trade partners and investors to predict the outcome of their transactions. Governments need not be generally accountable, responsible or fair for actors in such markets to prosper. Indeed, such actors prefer having their discretion preserved with regard to issues such as health, environmental or labour standards.

Many Arab states, including Algeria, Egypt, Jordan, Morocco, Tunisia and the financial sectors of the Gulf countries, promoted such cosmetic, sector-specific reforms over the last two decades. Arguably, these reforms exacerbated domestic inequalities of power and wealth, contributing to the discontent that led to the Arab uprisings and creating in Egypt and Tunisia instability so severe that it eventually eroded even this minimal ROL. Rather than leading to a deeper rule-of-law culture, as Baviera states, such reforms instead cloak greedy and ruthless governments with an aura of international legitimacy for a time, 'turning the stern gaze of the "international community" elsewhere and giving local actors an even steeper hill to climb'.[15]

Most Arab citizens are familiar with the slippage between 'rule *of* law' and 'rule *by* law' discourse in authoritarian states, where the power of law and legal institutions helps to structure and maintain systemic quotidian injustice. Nevertheless, in post-revolutionary states such as Tunisia and Egypt, it is to the ROL that people are turning for deliverance. There is a renewed faith particularly in constitutionalism and reform of legislatures, courts and police, as the primary means of effectively constraining state power. However, before the revolution, Egypt had a constitution that guaranteed separation of powers, civilian control of the military, an independent judiciary and international human rights. It had laws against corruption and abuse of power. It had laws guaranteeing transparent governance and a free press. It had a constitutional court and systems of judicial review. Indeed, the international community lauded some of these protections as movement towards a rule-of-law culture in Egypt.[16] President Mubarak's regime rendered these protections inoperative through emergency provisions in the constitution, ruling Egypt under a 'state of emergency' for many decades. In these circumstances, how should Egypt move towards a rule-of-law culture? Will more or different laws and institutions help? Would stricter provisions for recourse to a state of emergency have prevented the executive from undermining the ROL? Or would it have found a way to manipulate these laws as well?

To answer these questions, one has to go beyond legal and institutional structures and consider other barriers to the ROL in Egypt. It is beyond the scope of this chapter to enter into the myriad factors that have played a role in maintaining an authoritarian regime in Egypt. Suffice to say, they have not been purely domestic or legal. For instance, Egypt's geostrategic location, its control of the Suez Canal, its role in the ongoing impasse between Israel and the occupied Palestinian territories and its influential position in the Arab world are just some of the reasons why the US, Saudi Arabia, the United Arab Emirates and various other states support Egypt's powerful military and enable its rule. It is difficult to envision any domestic law reform in the constitutional, judicial, or security sector that could offset the impact of external factors on Egypt's inability to move towards a rule-of-law culture. This is not to say that domestic law reforms are irrelevant, but rather to contextualise what can be expected from them, and ensure such reforms do not serve to distract attention from other cogent factors.

As Baviera states, one of the reasons for the discouraging outcomes of many domestic rule-of-law initiatives is the idea's lack of precise theoretical bases. She describes three widely embraced but different philosophies of the ROL: the ROL as fairness, in the positivist sense of law as distinct from politics; the ROL as justice, based on moral values and promoting the common good; and the ROL as legitimacy, where law rules instead of force or arbitrary power.[17] The broad philosophical scope of this one idea ensures that it commands virtually universal approbation, but also allows actors to invoke those aspects that best suit their purposes, allowing them to posit a universalist justification for what might otherwise appear to be policy prescriptions.[18] As Shalakany states in the context of Egypt, the ROL is capable of being everything to everybody, and thus makes for some strange bedfellows.[19]

The types of reforms undertaken in Tunisia and Egypt in the name of the ROL, both before and since the uprisings, reflect an increasingly technocratic understanding of the concept. Recasting controversial political ideas as technocratic and culturally neutral renders them more manageable as exportable commodities, ostensibly infinitely replicable without affecting local mores.[20] Despite the invocation of the ROL as a universal ideal, rule-of-law initiatives do not usually encompass the legal conventions of developing societies. In any case, most postcolonial states no longer have a coherent set of indigenous legal practices to resurrect that remain applicable to the new cultural configurations of the modern nation-state.[21] They inherited the partially integrated legal systems and institutions left by departing colonisers and were either encouraged or forced to develop them. Functioning within these regimes required highly technical training. More importantly, it required an awareness of the underlying mores shaping the system, as such awareness confers capacity to play the game, manipulate the rules and win. Obtaining such expertise or access to it can be expensive.[22] International organisations' contemporary efforts to promote the ROL largely extend this process of reproducing western legal and institutional arrangements and expertise, with a particular focus on criminal law when it comes to war-torn states. Such processes may or may not contribute to evolution of a domestic rule-of-law culture, but they inevitably empower lawyers and create a legal elite, while disempowering those beyond the reach of such expertise.[23]

Western states' increasing interest in promoting the ROL, human rights, democracy and sustainable development in the non-western world through the UNSC is evidenced in a trend over the last two decades of linking the use of force with humanitarian aims. Reasons for this trend are manifold but arguably one is the need for western states to craft a new self-image in the post-Cold War era and articulate what they stand for in the absence of the Soviet threat.[24] Foreign policy that cannot be presented in the context of ideological aims can look to be grounded solely in the self-interest of political elites.[25] Thus, there is benefit in reformulating commitment to larger, shared moral purposes.[26] As Ignatieff observes,

> when policy was driven by moral motives, it was often driven by narcissism. We intervened not only to save others, but to save ourselves, or rather an image of ourselves as defenders of universal decencies. We wanted to show that the West 'meant' something.[27]

Articulating morality abroad as opposed to at home entails less accountability if interventions fail to achieve their declared aims.[28] The excuse of 'we tried, but they failed' is always available.[29]

2 Observing the international rule of law

The dynamics examined in the previous section with regard to UNSC efforts to promote the ROL within states also have ramifications for the UNSC's relationship with the international ROL. The Arab region provides a useful lens for considering the operation of rule-of-law discourse regarding the UNSC, as the region has been the subject of peacekeeping and peacebuilding missions, extensive sanctions regimes and various authorised and unauthorised international uses of force. The region's geostrategic importance, its extensive fossil fuel resources, and its symbolic importance for major world religions, have ensured that it has remained the subject of continual international attention. Contemporary Arab systems of law, governance, economy and development reflect the impact of French and British League of Nations mandates, as well as the legacy of colonial powers' considerable private corporate, trade and cultural influences. The region aptly illustrates that rule-of-law issues in domestic and international spheres cannot be understood separately. The following section explores these dynamics in the Iraqi context.

When the US and some of its allies formed a 'Coalition of the Willing' to invade Iraq in 2003 and institute regime change, the Coalition states' use of force was widely opposed in the UNSC, including by some of their traditional allies.[30] The act provoked anti-war protests worldwide, including mass demonstrations within Coalition states.[31] International law scholars and practitioners criticised it in academic literature and mass media.[32] While opposition was expressed in political, economic and moral terms as well, the dominant critique was legal: it was an illegal use of force in violation of the UN Charter and customary international law. However, for the purposes of this section, legality or lack thereof is not the material point. Rather, it is the use of rule-of-law discourse on both sides of the debate that is illuminative as to the relationship between the UNSC and the ROL.

Coalition states argued the invasion was justified by Iraqi President Saddam Hussein's repeated violations of international law – failing to disarm weapons of mass destruction as per the 1990 war ceasefire conditions, committing aggression against his neighbours and human rights abuses against his own citizens. The Coalition's primary legal argument was that the resolution permitting the 1990 war provided ongoing UNSC authorisation to intervene in Iraq.[33] However, the majority of states and scholars perceived the use of force as illegal absent a specific authorisation from the UNSC in 2003. For them, this was the UNSC's redeeming moment, as it was functioning as it ought to by refusing to authorise an illegal use of force despite the considerable pressure from Coalition states to procure a last-minute resolution. Thus, in this instance, they saw the UNSC as observing the international ROL.

While the UNSC's stance was ultimately futile, as it could not stop the invasion, allegations as to illegality were for the most part not levelled at the UNSC but at the Coalition. However, for those who favoured the invasion, it was the other way around: the UNSC was criticised as incapable of upholding its own resolutions requiring disarmament in Iraq.[34] Certain parties on both sides defined the problem as an inability to compel permanent members of the UNSC to obey the ROL. In so doing, both sides misrepresented the UNSC's relationship to the ROL. Undertaking a fuller examination of international interventions in Iraq, a more complete picture emerges, illustrating how rule-of-law discourse systematically draws attention to some operations of power while camouflaging others.

International law and international institutions played a definitive role in creating and shaping modern Iraq. From the seventeenth to the early twentieth century, the territory of Iraq was part of the Ottoman Empire. Upon defeat in the First World War, this empire was dismantled and its territories divided among victorious Allied powers. The UK and France drew borders in the region, including the borders of modern Iraq, to enlarge colonial spheres of influence and exploit known oil resources.[35] The legal principle of *uti possedetis juris* maintains these borders by declaring the inalterability of colonial frontiers.[36] While intending to minimise conflict, the principle also contributed to some of the ailments of modern Iraq, as the three Ottoman provinces joined to create Iraq had never constituted a single entity before. The borders of the Arab provinces of the Ottoman Empire – now constituting Syria, Lebanon, Jordan, Palestine/Israel, Iraq, Kuwait and the Gulf states – have produced extraordinary stresses including ethnic and political strife. The legitimacy of each of these states is repeatedly questioned by its neighbours, and sometimes its own citizens. All of Iraq's major conflicts, including the 1980–1988 Iran–Iraq war,[37] the tensions between Sunni,

Shia, Kurdish and Christian populations,[38] and the 1990 Kuwait invasion, are partially attributable to the preservation of colonial frontiers.[39]

France and the UK did not administer the region directly as part of their empires, but through the League of Nations Mandate System, which aimed to guide territories towards eventual independence.[40] In reality Britain undermined Iraq's ability to self-govern.[41] Prior to Iraqi independence in 1932, Britain's primary concern was to install an Iraqi ruler favourable to British interests,[42] and negotiate an Anglo–Iraqi treaty that gave Britain valuable oil concessions and access to military bases.[43]

Since Iraq's independence, western powers have hindered evolution towards representative government. In 1941, a popular and elected government replaced the monarch Britain had installed, and this government revoked permission for British troops to land at Basra. Britain invaded, defeated the newly formed Iraqi army, reoccupied the country and reinstalled the monarch that would do its bidding.[44] During the Cold War, all the UNSC permanent members at various times militarily and financially supported the authoritarian regime in Iraq.[45] The brutal nature of Saddam Hussein's regime was well documented.[46] Despite this, and even after the UN condemned the use of chemical weapons by both sides in the Iran–Iraq war, the US continued to sell Iraq materials and knowledge that helped develop weapons of mass destruction.[47] The big powers courted Hussein at various times as a tool of regional influence from the 1960s until Iraq's invasion of Kuwait, at which point the Cold War had ended and regional interests changed.[48]

The 1990 Iraqi annexation of Kuwait led the UNSC to authorise a US-led coalition to expel Iraqi forces from Kuwait.[49] The resulting air bombing had repercussions for Iraqi civilian infrastructure, including electricity and water supply, sewage treatment, agricultural production, food distribution and public health systems, to an extent that continues to be felt in efforts to rebuild Iraq.[50] When Iraq was expelled from Kuwait in 1991, the ceasefire resolution tightened the UN sanctions regime against Iraq.[51] Iraq has been 'in a class by itself' as the recipient of 'the longest, most comprehensive, and most severe multilateral sanctions regime ever imposed'.[52] Hundreds of thousands, if not millions, died as a direct result,[53] with particularly dire effects on women and children.[54] Prior to this, Iraqis had already suffered through a decade-long war with Iran. Thus, Iraqi society plummeted from relative affluence to poverty in the 1990s, and is yet to recover.

The ceasefire resolution also prescribed other measures to discipline Iraq after its expulsion from Kuwait, including UN observers monitoring a demilitarised zone inside the Iraqi border and weapons inspectors overseeing destruction of weapons of mass destruction.[55] Later, no-fly zones were enforced in Iraq's north and south, after the UNSC condemned the suppression of Kurds and Shiites.[56] Iraq was divided, monitored, supervised and subjugated and the ceasefire resolution mentioned no deadline. The UN explicitly and implicitly gave the US and its allies authority to carry out disciplinary procedures in the 1990s. Accordingly, it was the US and its allies, not the UN, that determined when, where and how to enforce the resolutions. From 1991 to 2003, the US, UK and France bombed Iraqi territory at their discretion, and implemented no-fly zones, without seeking additional resolutions.[57] It was in this context that the Coalition states argued the 2003 invasion was justified, on the basis of a long-standing understanding that they could indefinitely discipline Iraq.

Despite stepping outside UNSC authorisation for the 2003 invasion, the Coalition soon placed Iraq in a peacebuilding situation familiar to the UNSC. Thousands of aid workers and private contractors joined Coalition forces, addressing issues great and small with a view to building a liberal democracy, including removing Baath party adherents, privatising state-owned industries, establishing banks, amending intellectual property laws, rebuilding infrastructure, writing the constitution and privatising the oil industry.[58] The UNSC to some extent legitimated the invasion *ex post facto*. A series of resolutions purported to govern the subsequent occupation,[59] declaring the territorial integrity and political autonomy of Iraq and simultaneously granting wide interim governing powers to the Coalition without specifying a time limit.[60] While UNSC resolutions referred to the laws of occupation, they established no accountability mechanisms for Coalition behaviour.[61] They declared the Coalition could distribute proceeds of the Iraqi oil trade,[62] using them to benefit Iraqis. But benefit was to be assessed by the Coalition, allowing use of oil money to pay western corporations to repair Iraqi infrastructure that Coalition forces destroyed.[63] The Coalition was required to promote the welfare of the Iraqi people; the Coalition saw this mandate as sufficient to transform Iraq into a free-market economy.[64] Initial acts included abolition of barriers to foreign investment and trade and facilitating Iraq's eventual entry into the World Trade Organization, including constitutional guarantees to move Iraq towards economic liberalisation.[65] In fact, as with Tunisia and Egypt, Iraq undertook superficial, selective, market-oriented reforms. A decade later, such reforms have not produced a sea-change in governance towards respect for human rights and the ROL. Death and insecurity are rife,[66] corruption is rampant[67] and despite Iraq possessing vast natural resource wealth, large sectors of the population remain mired in poverty.[68]

This overview illustrates the complex roles international law and institutions have played in Iraq. Since the British and French first drew the borders of modern Iraq, there has been no lack of applicable international law. It has been regularly invoked by all parties over the last century, asserted alternatively as a reason for intervention, non-intervention, particular types of intervention and so on. In recent times, freed from its Cold War impasse, the UNSC functioned roughly as the Charter intended, at times authorising the use of force, at times denying it. The legality debate fixated on whether there was UNSC authorisation for the invasion, suggesting that if authorisation existed then the violence that ensued would have somehow been more just.[69] Rule-of-law discourse tends to draw attention to when the law is breached, rather than when it is obeyed, thus distracting from systemic injustices enabled by law. As mentioned in this chapter's introduction, the Charter institutionalises immense unregulated power in an unrepresentative institution. When compared with diffuse self-selected ‘coalitions of the willing’, power operates in more structured, regularised and relatively predictable ways within the UNSC, but both arrangements ensure that states, peoples and institutions will not be treated equally.

As with the example of Tunisia and domestic law in the previous section, international law’s role in Iraq could be described as either dysfunctional or efficient, depending on which histories we choose to highlight. If dysfunctional, then we could suggest more or better international laws: judicial and other types of oversight, more consistent and effective uses of force, sanctions, peacekeeping and peacebuilding. On the other hand, if international law has significantly shaped the modern Iraqi state, then the problems of contemporary Iraq are not because states failed to follow international law but because they adhered to it all too well. In the Arab world, the latter view often triumphs, as a history of problematic international interventions has created suspicion of international law and institutions. This was evidenced by the bombing in 2003 of the UN Headquarters in Baghdad, even though most UNSC members and the UNSG himself had spoken out firmly against the invasion. While such prejudices may be overturned through international legal and institutional reform, there is also a risk that reforms instead further entrench an international system of unequal sovereigns.

3 Conclusion

The ROL is in some ways an enchanted idea, giving authority to those who invoke it and act in its name.[70] In some instances, such enchantment acts as a substitute for moral assessment of the propriety of action.[71] While the powerful can use the ROL to institutionalise their power, the concept is also wedded to equal treatment and is therefore useful in struggles against power. One way to guard against the former tendency and promote the latter may be to situate rule-of-law discussions in broader historical, political, economic and cultural contexts so as to avoid the pitfalls of past reform efforts and move towards a more equitable and just system of international relations. Reform efforts through the UNSC may not be as effective as we would wish unless they are read alongside trends in, and implications of, other areas of international law and policy such as trade, economics, migration and the environment. Advocacy may be more effective if we more holistically assess the complex causalities involved in journeys towards or away from rule-of-law cultures in each individual situation. If we diagnose more broadly the things that undermine a rule-of-law culture both in the UNSC and within states, then the types of reforms that rationally follow may be different. Or expectations may have to be adjusted as to what law reform proposals may achieve. Alternatively, if a particular justice outcome is what is really desired, then it may be more effective to advocate for particular laws than a rule-of-law culture more generally.

Notes

1 Brian Tamanaha, *On the Rule of Law: History, Politics, Theory* (Cambridge, Cambridge University Press, 2004), pp. 91ff.; UN Doc. S/2004/616 (23 August 2004), *The Rule of Law and Transitional Justice in Conflict and Post-conflict Societies: Report of the Secretary-General*, para. 6. See also Martin Krygier's chapter in this collection.
2 See Charles Sampford's chapter in this collection.
3 See generally the contributions to this collection.
4 See, e.g. Mark Lyall Grant, United Kingdom Permanent Representative to the UN, *The UN's Response to the Arab Spring: One Year On* (14 February 2012): webarchive.nationalarchives.gov.uk/20130217073211/http://ukun.fco.gov.uk/en/news/?view=PressS&id=730248882. See also Sampford's chapter in this collection.
5 While this assumption is accepted for the purposes of this chapter, considerable debate exists as to whether the ROL is a universal value. See Tamahana, *On the Rule of Law*, pp. 137–41; Maxwell Chibundu, 'Globalizing the Rule of Law: Some Thoughts at and on the Periphery' (1999) 7 *Indiana Journal of Global Legal Studies* 79–116; and Elisabetta Baviera, *A Closer Look at the Rule of Law* (Kenya, lawanddevelopment.org, 2004): www.lawanddevelopment.org/docs/ruleoflaw.pdf.
6 On the correlation between the ROL and its socio-cultural milieu, see particularly the scholarship of Martin Krygier including 'The Rule of Law', in Michel Rosenfeld and András Sajó (eds), *Oxford Handbook of Comparative Constitutional Law* (Oxford, Oxford University Press, 2012), pp. 233–49; and 'The Rule of Law: Legality, Teleology, Sociology', in Gianluigi Palombella and Neil Walker (eds), *Relocating the Rule of Law* (Oxford, Hart, 2009), pp. 45–69. See also Philip Selznick, 'Legal Cultures and the Rule of Law', in Martin Krygier and Adam Czarnota (eds), *The Rule of Law after Communism: Problems and Prospects in East-Central Europe* (Aldershot, Ashgate, 1999), pp. 21–38.
7 See generally Eve Darian-Smith and Peter Fitzpatrick, *Laws of the Postcolonial* (Ann Arbor, MI, University of Michigan Press, 1999).
8 Antony Anghie, *Imperialism, Sovereignty and the Making of International Law* (Cambridge, Cambridge University Press, 2005), pp. 245–72.
9 See, e.g. UN Doc. SC/10172 (11 February 2011); UN Doc. S/PV.3977 (12 February 1999); UN Doc. S/PV.4046 (16 September 1999); UN Doc. SC/9000 (17 April 2007).
10 UN Doc. S/PV.3046 (31 January 1992).
11 Ibid., p. 8.
12 See, e.g. Simon Chesterman, *The Role of the Security Council in Strengthening a Rules-based International System: Final Report and Recommendations from the Austrian Initiative 2004–2008* (Vienna, Austrian Ministry for European and International Affairs, 2008), p. 7.
13 See, e.g. UN Development Programme, *Human Development Report* (New York, UN, 2010), p. 29.
14 World Economic Forum, *The Global Competitiveness Report 2010–2011* (Geneva, WEF, 2010), p. 15.
15 Baviera, 'A Closer Look', p. 13.
16 See, generally, Nathalie Bernard-Maugiron, 'Legal Reforms, the Rule of Law, and the Consolidation of State Authoritarianism under Mubarak', in Saïd Arjomand and Nathan Brown (eds), *The Rule of Law, Islam, and Constitutional Politics in Egypt and Iran* (Albany, NY, State University of New York Press, 2013), pp. 179–206.
17 Baviera, 'A Closer Look', pp. 3–4.
18 Chibundu, 'Globalizing the Rule of Law', pp. 83–4; Morton Horwitz, 'The Rule of Law: An Unqualified Human Good?' (1977) 86 *Yale Law Journal* 561–6.
19 Amr Shalakany, '"I Heard It All Before": Egyptian Tales of Law and Development' (2006) 27 *Third World Quarterly* 833–53, 833.
20 See, generally, David Kennedy, 'The Forgotten Politics of International Governance' (2001) 2 *European Human Rights Law Review* 117–25.

21 Chibundu, 'Globalizing the Rule of Law', p. 89.
22 Ibid.
23 See, e.g. Shalakany, 'I Heard It All Before', tracing the effect rule-of-law reforms had in empowering Egyptian legal elites.
24 This context is changing and evolving as Russia reemerges as a threat to western states, especially in light of recent developments in the Crimea.
25 David Chandler, 'The Other-regarding Ethics of the "Empire in Denial"', in David Chandler and Volker Heins (eds), *Rethinking Ethical Foreign Policy: Pitfalls, Possibilities and Paradoxes* (London, Routledge, 2007), pp. 161–83, 162, 167.
26 David Chandler, 'Rhetoric Without Responsibility: The Attraction of "Ethical" Foreign Policy' (2003) 5 *British Journal of Politics and International Relations* 295–316.
27 Michael Ignatieff, *Warrior's Honor: Ethnic War and the Modern Conscience* (New York, Henry Holt, 1998), p. 95.
28 Hans Morgenthau, *Politics among Nations: The Struggle for Power and Peace*, revised edition (New York, McGraw-Hill, 1993), p. 49, observing that the distance of the international sphere enables values and higher aims to be more easily articulated.
29 Ignatieff, *Warrior's Honor*, p. 9.
30 UN Doc. S/PV.4709 (19 February 2003).
31 Antiwar.com, 'February 2003 Antiwar Demonstrations': www.antiwar.com/feb03 demos.html.
32 See, e.g. Richard Falk, 'What Future for the UN Charter System of War Prevention?' (2003) 97 *American Journal of International Law* 590–8; Vaughan Lowe, 'The Iraq Crisis: What Next?' (2003) 52 *International and Comparative Law Quarterly* 859–71; 'Letter: War Would Be Illegal', *Guardian* (London), 7 March 2003, p. 29; 'Joint statement: Howard Must Not Involve Us in an Illegal War', *The Age* (online), 26 February 2003: www.theage.com.au/articles/2003/02/25/10460640312 96.html; Henry Michael, 'Canadian Law Professors Declare US-Led War Illegal', *World Socialist Website*, 22 March 2003: www.wsws.org/articles/2003/mar2003/ lawy-m22.shtml.
33 UN Doc. S/2003/351 (21 March 2003); UN Doc. S/2003/352 (20 March 2003); UN Doc. S/2003/350 (21 March 2003).
34 *Remarks by the President after Visit with Employees at Nebraska Avenue Homeland Security Complex* (19 September 2002): www.whitehouse.gov/news/releases/ 2002/09/20020919-7.html; Ruth Wedgwood, 'The Fall of Saddam Hussein: Security Council Mandates and Pre-emptive Self-defence' (2003) 97 *American Journal of International Law* 576–85; Abraham Sofaer, 'On the Necessity of Pre-emption' (2003) 14 *European Journal of International Law* 209–26.
35 In December 1917, the newly established Bolshevik regime in Russia published the overthrown Czarist government's secret treaties. Among these were the *Sykes–Picot Accords* – agreements between Britain, France and Russia to partition the Middle East among them. These agreements eventually became the basis for the post-war division of the region between Britain and France.
36 *Frontier Dispute (Burkina Faso* v. *Republic of Mali)*, Judgment [1986] ICJ Rep. 554, 565 describes *uti possedetis juris* as a general principle which is logically connected with the phenomenon of obtaining independence.
37 Thom Workman, *The Social Origins of the Iran–Iraq War* (Boulder, CO, Lynne Rienner, 1994), p. 23; Majid Khadduri, *The Gulf War: The Origins and Implications of the Iraq–Iran Conflict* (New York, Oxford University Press, 1988); Daniel Pipes, 'A Border Adrift: Origins of the Iran–Iraq War' (1983): www.danielpipes. org/164/a-border-adrift-origins-of-the-iraq-iran-war.
38 Rashid Khalidi, *Resurrecting Empire* (Boston, MA, Beacon Press, 2004), pp. 40–4.
39 'Press Release by the Press Office of the Embassy of the Republic of Iraq, London, 12 September 1990', in Elihu Lauterpacht, C.J. Greenwood, M. Weller and D. Bethlehem

(eds), *The Kuwait Crisis: Basic Documents, Volume 1* (Cambridge, Cambridge University Press, 1991), p. 73.

40 *Covenant of the League of Nations*, opened for signature 28 June 1919, [1919] UKTS 4 (entered into force 10 January 1920), art. 22.

41 See further, Usha Natarajan, 'Creating and Recreating Iraq' (2011) 24 *Leiden Journal of International Law* 799–822.

42 Khalidi, *Resurrecting Empire*, p. 99.

43 Frank Tachau (ed.), *Political Parties of the Middle East and North Africa* (Westport, CT, Greenwood Press, 1994), p. 175.

44 See Georg Schwarzenberger, *Power Politics: A Study of World Society* (London, Stevens and Sons, 1964), p. 179; Khalidi, *Resurrecting Empire*, p. 24.

45 See, e.g. Akbar Ahmed, *Postmodernism and Islam: Predicament and Promise* (Oxford, Psychology Press, 2004), p. 135; Stephen Pelletiere, 'A War Crime or an Act of War?', *New York Times* (New York), 31 January 2003, p. A27; Patrick Tyler, 'Both Iraq and Iran Gassed Kurds in War, US Analysis Finds', *Washington Post* (Washington, DC), 3 May 1990, p. A37; Ewen MacAskill and Nick Watt, 'Anger Over Straw's Dossier on Iraqi Human Rights', *Guardian* (online), 3 December 2002: www.guardian.co.uk/Iraq/Story/0,2763,852522,00.html.

46 Susan F. Kinsley, *Whatever Happened to the Iraqi Kurds?* (Human Rights Watch, 11 March 1991): www.hrw.org/reports/1991/iraq; Adam Jones, *Case Study: The Anfal Campaign (Iraqi Kurdistan), 1988* (Gendercide Watch, undated): www.gendercide.org/case_anfal.html.

47 US Senate Committee on Banking, Housing, and Urban Affairs, *Riegle Report* (7 October 1994): www.gulflink.osd.mil/medsearch/FocusAreas/riegle_report/riegle_report_main.html; Nathaniel Hurd, *US Diplomatic and Commercial Relationships with Iraq, 1980–2 August 1990* (Campaign on Sanctions Against Iraq (CASI), 15 July 2000): www.casi.org.uk/info/usdocs/usiraq80s90s.html; Alan Friedman, *Spider's Web: The Secret History of How the White House Illegally Armed Iraq* (New York, Bantam Books, 1994).

48 Schwarzenberger, *Power Politics*, pp. 181–8; Ahmed, *Postmodernism and Islam*, pp. 129–30; US National Security Archive, *The Saddam Hussein Sourcebook* (18 December 2003): www.gwu.edu/nsaarchiv/special/iraq/index.htm.

49 SC Res. 678 (29 November 1990).

50 Middle East Watch, *Needless Deaths in the Gulf War: Civilian Casualties During the Air Campaign and Violations of the Laws of War* (New York, Human Rights Watch, 1991); Laurence Freedman and Efraim Karsh, *The Gulf War 1990–1991: Diplomacy and War in the New World Order* (London, Faber and Faber, 1993), pp. 318–19 and 321; Rajiv Chandrasekaran, *Imperial Life in the Emerald City* (New York, Vintage Books, 2006).

51 SC Res. 687 (3 April 1991).

52 David Cortright and George Lopez, *The Sanctions Decade: Assessing UN Strategies in the 1990s* (Boulder, Co, Lynne Rienner, 2000), p. 8.

53 Eric Hoskins, 'The Humanitarian Impact of Economic Sanctions and War in Iraq', in Tomas Weiss, David Cortright, George Lopez and Larry Minear (eds), *Political Gain and Civilian Pain: Humanitarian Impacts of Economic Sanctions* (New York, Rowman and Littlefield, 1997), pp. 91–148, 122.

54 Lori Buck, Nicole Gallant and Kim Nossal, 'Sanctions as a Gendered Instrument of Statecraft: The Case of Iraq' (1998) 24 *Review of International Studies* 69–84; Cortright and Lopez, *Sanctions Decade*, p. 46; UN Children's Fund, *Iraq Survey Shows 'Humanitarian Emergency'* (12 August 1999): www.unicef.org/newsline/99pr29.htm.

55 SC Res. 687 (3 April 1991).

56 SC Res. 688 (5 April 1991).

57 Wedgwood, 'Fall of Saddam Hussein', 579; Yoo, 'War in Iraq', 570.

58 See, generally, *Orders and Regulations of Coalition Provisional Authority*: www.casi.org.uk/info/cpa.html; Chandrasekaran, *Emerald City*.

59 SC Res. 1472 (28 March 2003); SC Res. 1483 (22 May 2003); SC Res. 1511 (16 October 2003).
60 SC Res. 1483 (22 May 2003).
61 James Gathii, 'Historical Dispossession Through International Law: Iraq in a Historical and Comparative Context', in Branwen Gruffydd Jones (ed.), *Decolonising International Relations* (New York, Rowman and Littlefield, 2006), pp. 131–52, 131.
62 SC Res. 1483 (22 May 2003), paras 13 and 20.
63 See, e.g. Dave Whyte, 'The Crimes of Neo-Liberal Rule in Occupied Iraq' (2007) 47 *British Journal of Criminology* 177–95; Darren Atkinson, 'Selling Iraq: Reconstruction, Privatisation and Empire in Denial', in Regional Centre on Conflict Prevention, *Conflict in Focus* (Amman, Jordan Institute of Diplomacy, 2007), p. 18; International Crisis Group, *Reconstructing Iraq* (Amman, 2 September 2004); US Government Accountability Office, *Rebuilding Iraq: US Mismanagement of Iraqi Funds* (Washington, DC, US House of Representatives, 2005).
64 Gathii, 'Historical Dispossession', p. 142.
65 *Constitution of the Republic of Iraq* (2005), arts 25, 26, 110.
66 At the time of writing (29 March 2014), there are already 2,927 civilian casualties this year: *Iraq Body Count*: www.iraqbodycount.org.
67 Transparency International, *Iraq Country Profile*: www.transparency.org/country#IRQ.
68 Iraq country data in UNDP, *Human Development Report* (New York, UNDP, 2013), p. 143.
69 Lori Damrosch and Bernard Oxman, 'Agora: Future Implications of the Iraq Conflict: Editors' Introduction' (2003) 97 *American Journal of International Law* 553–7.
70 See Rachel Kleinfeld, 'Competing Definitions of the Rule of Law', in Thomas Carothers (ed.), *Promoting the Rule of Law Abroad: In Search of Knowledge* (Washington, DC, Carnegie Endowment for International Peace, 2006), pp. 31–74, 32.
71 Dale Stephens, 'The Accommodation, Disjunction and Felt Experience of Law in Military Operations', *ARC Linkage Project on Strengthening the Rule of Law Through the United Nations Security Council Workshop Paper Series*, Working paper No. 5.1 (Canberra, ANU, 2012), p. 16.

5 The rule of law begins at home

Charles Sampford

Introduction

During the last decade there has been growing agreement that the rule of law (ROL) is critical in both domestic and international affairs. At the 2005 United Nations (UN) World Summit, member states unanimously recognised the need for 'universal adherence to and implementation of the ROL at both the national and international levels'.[1] This resolved an impasse in which some western states were pressing for improvements in the ROL in developing states and others were pressing some western states to adhere to the international ROL – especially with regard to interventions and other missions involving the deployment of troops.

This was an inspiring compromise – to pursue both rather than none. However, we should remain inspired without becoming naive. One of the problems of this welcome consensus is that the term 'rule of law' is subject to a range of interpretations/perspectives/dimensions that are affected by context as well as theory. Even within the UN, the variety of interpretations is considerable and influenced by the perceived missions of various UN agencies.[2]

Peacekeeping missions now typically involve police, military and civilian components from a range of states. Indeed, integrated missions can also draw in staff members from non-government organisations (NGOs) and UN agencies, who might have different conceptions of what the ROL means and, more importantly, what it requires. Peacekeeping missions raise issues of both international and domestic law and so form one of the intersecting points of the 'domestic rule of law' and the 'international rule of law' (i.e. the ROL in, respectively, national and international affairs). Such overlapping ROL issues should be addressed concurrently and consistently rather than divorced at the risk of making the missions and the participants appear hypocritical.

In this chapter, I draw on my work on the ROL going back 21 years,[3] including an Australian Research Council (ARC) linkage project[4] with (then) Lt. Col. Mike Kelly.[5] Kelly took what I saw as a Hayekian justification for the ROL in peacekeeping missions – if you state clearly, firmly and convincingly in advance how you will use force then others will adapt their behaviour to avoid that which will generate that use of force.[6] I therefore argue that the ROL in this sense must start when the first 'blue helmet' puts a foot on the ground, not after the first elected president takes office. This means that in international affairs the ROL must start when the mission is planned and then authorised. The UN Security Council (UNSC) and the states taking part in peacekeeping missions need to plan for what they are going to do to assist the host state to develop its own ROL (and its integrity system generally). They need to plan how the ROL will be applied to what they do. And they must ensure that the mandate is, itself, subject to the international ROL. If the mission participants are not prepared to subject themselves to the ROL, the chances of the ROL emerging in the communities that are the subject, and intended beneficiaries, of peacekeeping missions are remote. In this sense, the ROL begins at home – in the UNSC and in the states that take part in these missions. The fact that there are differences of view about the meaning of the ROL does not excuse the UNSC and participating states from subjecting themselves to both the non-contentious aspects of the ROL *or* the ROL as they understand it.

The chapter proceeds in five sections. Section 1 examines the core elements ascribed to the ROL in the domestic context. Section 2 explores how these elements are reflected in the international ROL. Section 3 then applies these elements of the ROL to peacekeeping missions. Section 4 examines the ROL problems in the UNSC. Finally, Section 5 examines two ways to promote and respect the ROL in the UNSC. It advocates two approaches. The first is to promote voluntary acceptance of judicial review and formal accountability by the UNSC and its insistence that these principles must be accepted by any state that expects UNSC authorisation to act. The second approach envisages a 'Coke moment' – named after the English judge who insisted that James I could not be a legislator and judge as well as king.

1 The 'domestic' rule of law

Domestically, the ROL is a majestic phrase with many largely reinforcing and supportive meanings. It is alternatively characterised as a fundamental value/ideal, an ethic for lawyers and officials, the basic principles of constitutionalism and a set of institutions that supports its attainment. While these multiple meanings and dimensions may occasionally serve to confuse, they are generally congruent and mutually supportive in that the partial achievement of each supports the fuller achievement of all. This reflects the multifaceted nature of the ROL. However, it is important to keep the meanings and dimensions distinct to avoid confusion.

The differences of meaning do not seem to be essentially cultural. I previously carried out a project for the Open Society Institute comparing governance values in western and Islamic states. Our findings were that Islamic/western comparison showed that there was no fundamental difference, with 'congruent', if not necessarily identical, meanings. However, there are differences within cultures based on emphasis and position. Liberal Muslims and liberal westerners have a great deal in common. Indeed, fundamentalist Muslims and fundamentalist Christians have more in common than either dare admit. All cultures have rule-of-law traditions (howsoever called) and contrary traditions.

1.1 'Thick' and 'thin' theories of the rule of law

One of the biggest distinctions different supporters of the ROL have is more a matter of classification – of what is included within the ROL and what is listed under different governance values. Some of the most popular definitions of the ROL mix an expression of an ideal or value with the institutional prerequisites for the achievement of that ideal. Developing ideas found in Hayek, Fuller[7] and others, Raz listed eight basic elements of the ROL: (1) laws should be prospective, open and clear; (2) laws should be relatively stable; (3) law-making should be guided by open, stable, clear and general rules; (4) independence of the judiciary must be guaranteed; (5) principles of natural justice should be observed; (6) courts should have review powers (of the exercise of power by others); (7) courts should be easily accessible; and (8) discretion of crime-policing agencies should not be perverted.[8] An overlapping principle is that sanctions (especially involving the use of force) should only be applied to others according to clear rules publicised in advance.

I have characterised this as a 'thin' theory of the ROL.[9] This is contrasted with 'thick' theories of law propounded by those who seek to incorporate within the ROL other governance values/virtues concerning the content and provenance of law, that is, human rights and democracy.

Those who adhere to such thin theories are generally just as supportive of democracy and human rights but prefer to keep those 'governance values' or 'virtues of law' distinct, recognising that they can sometimes conflict and that they are rarely introduced at the same time (with the ROL generally coming first). They also recognise that it may be possible to secure agreement to the development of the ROL before agreement can be reached on democracy (and how it is to be interpreted and institutionally implemented) or what rights are to be incorporated into the content of law.

Chapter V of the International Forum for the Challenges of Peace Operations refers to the ROL and human rights separately – recognising their separate and mutually reinforcing importance, but also their distinctiveness.[10] They quote the UN Secretary-General's (UNSG's) 2004 definition of the ROL as 'a principle of governance in which all persons, institutions and entities, public and private, including the State itself, are accountable to laws that are publicly promulgated, equally enforced and independently adjudicated'.[11] This is a classic 'thin theory'. It is interesting that they leave out the last phrase in the UNSG's 2004 definition: 'consistent with international human rights norms and standards'. This is a bit 'thicker'.

This theoretical/philosophical list does not reflect the degree of embeddedness involved in a state subject to the ROL. In such states, the ROL is also seen as: (1) a fundamental governance value; (2) a basic constitutional principle requiring the separation of powers; (3) an ethic for officials, that is, the law should bind officials and officials can only derive their power and authority from law, with all such power held in trust to be used only to the extent permitted and for the purposes authorised; (4) a set of institutions including independent legislatures and courts and an independent bar; and (5) the core of nascent integrity systems. Within sovereign states, each of these dimensions is mutually supportive.

1.2 The rule of law as a fundamental governance value

ROL is now seen as one of the fundamental values underlying modern 'liberal democratic' states – along with human rights, democracy, citizenship and the famous trinity of *liberté, egalité, fraternité*. This was not always so. The Treaty of Westphalia was, in many senses, a tyrants' charter – made largely by and for the absolutist rulers of the day. It recognised a set of formally independent and equal states whose sovereigns were recognised on the basis of their ability to effectively control the territory of a state. Brutal enforcement of their rule was proof of sovereignty rather than a disqualification for it. Internally, absolute rule was frequently justified as the only way of avoiding the chaos of a state of nature in which the life of man would be nasty, brutish and short.[12] Once life and civil peace were secure, more was demanded of those states by *philosophes*, lawyers and revolutionaries who saw themselves as citizens in whose interests sovereigns should rule according to the above-mentioned values. As they sought and gained concessions, the institutionalising of those values gradually civilised the post-Westphalian state. The ROL was the first of these values and many states were substantially *Rechtsstaats* long before they saw even a modicum of democracy and human rights. The ROL is not only the most long-standing of enlightenment values; it is generally the least controversial.

1.3 The rule of law as a basic constitutional principle requiring the separation of powers

Rule of law underlies and is supported by basic constitutional principles such as constitutional rule and the separation of powers. However, it does not require a formal or written constitution and the concept clearly pre-dates such instruments. Such constitutional principles generally would be seen to require a separation of judicial power from legislative and executive power, with that judicial power determining what texts are recognised as laws, how these laws are interpreted and to whom the laws apply.

1.4 The rule of law as an ethic for officials exercising power

Rule of law is primarily addressed to lawyers and officials rather than citizen obedience.[13] The ROL is the central ethical principle for judges and the legal profession more generally. But it is also central to most officials, including civil servants, the military and elected officials. All such power is held in trust to be used only to the extent permitted and for the purposes authorised.[14] The domestic ROL was built by the efforts of lawyers, soldiers, politicians and dedicated NGOs from the *philosophes*, to unions, to the modern NGO.

Chapter V of the Forum Draft and the UNSG's definition of the ROL make both individuals and states accountable to law. The accountability of individuals to law is not a common requirement in ROL definitions, with good reason. Although the ordinary criminal law should apply to all, there are a number of laws that are addressed to officials – about what their power is and the purposes for which it is entrusted to them. Civil disobedience is appropriate for individuals within a society under the ROL, but not for officials.

This is particularly true in relation to the use of force – and why acceptance of the ROL is a critical element in the ethics/honour of the military, and those who deploy the military. Note that this is not just a matter of officials of the state – despite the Weberian notion that the state has a monopoly of violence, even legitimate violence. In the seventeenth century, the ROL was as much about controlling the use of force by the local barons and bands of mercenaries as royal officials. Now we should look at other sources of power – corporations, warlords and private military companies. This is where the Forum Draft rightly refers to the importance of 'all institutions and entities (public and private)' being held accountable.[15]

1.5 The rule of law as a set of institutions

Those who value the ROL recognise that it can never operate effectively as a purely normative phenomenon (be it value, ethic or principle). It requires institutions to make it effective so that the ROL may be partially defined in terms of common institutional supports for it – legislatures, courts, police, corrections, independent bars and NGOs.

1.6 The rule of law and nascent integrity systems

Since the late 1990s, it has become increasingly accepted that the way to avoid corruption and other abuses of power is an 'integrity system' – a set of norms (formal and informal), institutions and practices that serve to promote integrity (or 'good governance') and inhibit corruption. All effective integrity systems involve some basic institutional arrangements associated with the ROL – especially courts and a legal profession that are not indebted to the holders of political power and can review the actions of powerful institutions to determine whether or not they are within power. These institutions are the oldest and longest-standing elements of the integrity systems of western states. They are supported by newer institutions of democratic governance (parliaments, parliamentary committees) and oversight (ombudsperson, auditors-general, anti-corruption commissions, media and NGO watchdogs), which make ROL mechanisms more effective. Integrity systems are far less developed in international affairs and, naturally, in the states in which peace missions occur.

2 The international rule of law

How much experience of the ROL at the domestic level can apply to building the international ROL is a big question. A few points might usefully be made at this stage. At the international level, there are strong arguments for keeping to a 'thin' theory of the ROL and treating democracy and human rights as other values. The application of 'democracy' to international affairs is particularly problematic. Even here, this is more a matter of classification and tactics than a fundamental value difference for most supporters of the international ROL. However, as in the early stage of the development of domestic ROL, it may only be possible to secure widespread agreement on the international ROL, leaving democratisation of international institutions and the universal implementation of human rights to other and later battles.

On the other hand, human rights are already written into the content of international law in the most emphatic way – not only civil and political rights but also economic, social and cultural rights. Thus if international action is to be subject to the ROL in the thin sense, it will necessitate the application of human rights. Most other meanings and dimensions can be extended to the international ROL, although their realisation internationally is much more limited than in most established democracies. This does not detract from their usefulness, however, because they indicate areas where progress might be made towards an international ROL. I have discussed these areas at length elsewhere,[16] but here I will highlight ethics for officials and institutions.

2.1 Ethics for officials

As seen above, the domestic ROL is built into the ethics of key officials of sovereign states operating under the ROL – not just judges, prosecutors and lawyers, but soldiers, civil servants and elected officials. Codes of ethics for international officials are relatively new and rare, with most being enacted over the last 20 years, and the Burgh House principles for international judges being 11 years old.[17] Most would be imbued with ethical principles from their home states which may well emphasise the domestic ROL but will say little about the international ROL and may suggest that loyalty to domestic sovereign power is more important. I have argued elsewhere that international lawyers and soldiers engaged in UN missions should be at the forefront of developing and promulgating codes of ethics to govern their behaviour which respect international and domestic applications of the ROL.[18]

2.2 Institutions

The largest problems for the international ROL lie in the lack of institutions that create, interpret and enforce international law. This lack of effective institutionalisation inhibits the development of the ROL in its other senses.

The lack of an overarching and specialised legislature may complicate efforts to develop widely recognised and legitimate new international law, but it is not a fundamental problem for the ROL.[19] It makes change difficult but all that is needed is a set of clearly agreed sources, the means by which those sources generate authoritative legal texts and the hierarchy of sources in cases of conflict.

There is a court, the International Court of Justice (ICJ), which can provide authoritative interpretations of those texts and of any conflicts between them. The ICJ is harder to stack than any national appellate court. The problem is the lack of compulsory jurisdiction and the limited number of cases that can therefore be heard before it.[20] This makes it much harder for the law to give clear guidance to those who want to be bound. However, as Cassese suggests, the relative weakness of central global institutions means that other institutions and practices may take on a greater role[21] – including self-regulation and standard setting by non-state actors, civil society,[22] business and legal communities.[23]

3 The rule of law in peacekeeping missions

Traditionally, peacekeeping missions were largely directed at ending mass violence. Democracy and the ROL were initially seen as the business of the relevant state or states in which, or between whom, the mission operated.

Early peacekeeping missions aimed to separate the warring parties and it was assumed that the relevant sovereign states would protect their citizens once the main threat had passed. Over the last 20 years many peacekeeping missions have been deployed to states that lack either the capacity or will to protect civilians and in some cases these states have constituted a major threat to civilians on their territory. In other missions the combatants have targeted civilians. Accordingly, it has been recognised that 'keeping the warring parties apart' does little or nothing to protect civilians and 'protection of civilians' (POC) has become a key part of missions.

When the holding of elections became part of UN mandates, the assumption seems to have been that security would come first, followed by elections, with the ROL left to the incoming regime. During the 1990s, Kelly and others emphasised that for missions' success, as well as their legitimacy, the ROL had to start with the first troops moving in, not after the first elections.

All of the domestic elements of the ROL are highly relevant to peacekeeping missions. Peacekeeping missions must initially pursue a thin theory of the ROL, which can be expanded as stability is established. Missions must respect human rights in their own activities but generally cannot force the incorporation of human rights into the content of local laws.

That said, peacekeeping missions should seek to incorporate as many dimensions of the ROL as possible. The areas of function and focus listed in the discussion of the domestic ROL above might be seen as applicable to the constitution of the mission itself – to make the mission effective, to serve as an exemplar and to help establish more effective governance measures.

The mission will naturally seek to advise and assist the host state to strengthen the ROL in its territory. It will advise on the ROL principles and administer them. It will promote the ROL as a governance value, a basic constitutional principle and an ethic for key officials. It will also help to develop a set of institutions that support the ROL, as well as integrity systems, including in particular the legal elements that support POC. But the ROL must not just be the subject of the mission. Indeed, it should be built into the peacekeeping mission itself. The mission is not just there to preach the ROL, but to practise and enforce it in its domestic and international forms.

Standard ROL principles therefore should be built into all peacekeeping missions. Thus the rules under which missions operate should be prospective, open and clear, and these rules should be relatively stable. Rule-making by the mission should be guided by open, stable, clear and general principles. An independent judiciary is essential to judge the mission's actions. That judiciary must be accessible and have review powers. Principles of natural justice should apply. Policing and prosecutions should not be one-sided. Sanctions, especially the use of force, should only be applied according to clear rules publicised in advance.

The mission should also have clear authority, generally from the host state, as national laws are important for the authorisation, limitation and governance of civil–military cooperation – as well as providing the substantive laws which should generally rule. In rare cases where authority is not given by the host state, it must be given by the UNSC or a body established by a treaty, which the host state has signed.

These caveats apply to the original authority for the mission itself. However, it should be clear that the mission has clear continuing authority. While the most serious risk is the use of force under a stale mandate (as in Iraq in the late 1990s), UNSC mandates for peacekeeping missions also constitute authority to act. It should be easier to insist on this principle with peacekeeping, setting the precedent of Chapter VII interventions.

Authority and actions that officials take under the mission should be subject to independent adjudication not just of the International Criminal Court (ICC) but also the ICJ. Even if a state does not sign up to compulsory ICJ jurisdiction, it should commit itself to accepting the ICJ's jurisdiction for its actions under the mandate. I know that this is unlikely now, but good international citizens should have nothing to fear and their actions will be more effective for standard ROL reasons.

The mission's dealings with the host state must be subject to international law. The mandate (which provides the effective 'constitutional' basis for the mission) should include the ROL as a basic principle. The ROL should be a core part of the ethic of every group of officials within the mission – including military, police and civilian components from all states contributing to the mission. The conduct of police and military forces during the mission should comply with relevant human rights norms.

The various institutional components of the mission should mutually support each other in respecting and furthering the ROL within their mission – and recognise the relationship between the ROL and POC.[24] Truly independent prosecutors before strictly independent tribunals should initiate trials of those accused of perpetrating the violence against the civilians in need of protection. Where these are not before permanent tribunals, the funding and selection of tribunal members should be from neither belligerents nor peacekeepers. These points apply to UNSC-authorised missions and in cases of bilateral agreements between a host state and one that provides assistance.

4 Rule-of-law problems in the UNSC

The UNSC has no credibility in authorising missions to build the ROL within a state if it is not subject to the ROL itself. It may make a distinction between the domestic ROL and international ROL. But the UN General Assembly (UNGA), including all member states of the UNSC, have signed up to both at the 2005 UN World Summit. The states attempting to carry out those mandates will have limited credibility (and deserve less) if they do not subject their own action to the ROL.

4.1 Integrity

This is a matter of ethics and integrity. For Singer, the key ethical question is 'how should I live my life?'[25] This involves asking hard questions about your values, giving honest and public answers, and living by them. If you do, you have integrity. If you do not, the first person you cheat is yourself because you are not the person you want to be. This is a reasonably standard individualist approach to ethics. But I have long argued that this can and should be applied to institutions. Institutions must also ask themselves hard questions about their values, give honest and public answers and structure themselves so that they will collectively live by them. If an institution does this, it has institutional integrity. If it does not, it is not only hypocritical but is not the institution it claims to be and wants to be.

I have separately contrasted integrity with corruption. If corruption is the abuse of entrusted power for personal or party political gain, it is not possible to know whether there is an abuse without knowing what the correct use is. That use is determined by the above process of establishing institutional integrity, sometimes with ratification by the body to which the institution is accountable. Integrity here means the 'use of entrusted power for publicly justified and official endorsed purposes'.[26]

4.2 Effectiveness

For reasons that would be equally recognised by either Hayek or Fuller,[27] a peacekeeping mission will be more effective if others know in advance how that mission will use its power. I would argue that the ROL must begin when the UNSC writes a mandate and various member states accept that mandate and agree to take part. It must be recognised that hypocrisy has a cost not just in credibility but also in effectiveness.

There may be a reluctance to authorise a mission where one of the permanent five (P5) members is also one of the states participating (directly or indirectly) in that mission. In such circumstances, there is an asymmetry between authorisation and accountability. If a P5 member responds to the mandate and interprets the mandate very broadly (and mandates tend to be broad and non-specific), the P5 member can veto any subsequent UNSC clarification contrary to its interpretation. This effectively means that there is no accountability where a P5 member is authorised to act. This outcome might be convenient for the mission and its P5 members, but it will have a chilling effect on future authorisations. If other states (including those on the UNSC and those who elect them) think that the mandate has been abused, such states may be wary about issuing further authorisations. Indeed, in the lead-up to the Kosovo war the extraordinarily extensive interpretation by the US and UK of Resolution 678 (1990), concerning Iraq, might have been an impediment to securing UNSC approval for the proposed multilateral humanitarian intervention.[28] On the other hand, if the ICJ or some other body exercises judicial review, then P5 members would be more likely to be authorised to engage in a range of peace missions because it will be clearer what the mission is and is not permitted to do. To put it another way, other states can have greater confidence that states engaged in peacekeeping will do what they say they want to do and not more.

Of course, we have to remember the practical realities of peace missions. They cannot be overly planned and overly prescribed. The mandate must set out clear limits, which can be the basis of subsequent legal determination. While higher authorities must establish those limits, they should delegate the detail to commanders. The commanders of UN missions cannot bring every issue back from the 'front line' for political decision-making. This is true even when the ultimate executive power is wielded by a cabinet of a united people, ruled by a government enjoying support from a wartime coalition comprising virtually the whole of the legislature (for example, the United Kingdom during the Second World War). Such a body faces issues of knowledge, real-time decision-making and division between those who make decisions about the mandate and those who issue orders. This is even more true of a body with very different members and views and a veto to exercise.

5 Promoting and respecting the rule of law in the UNSC

In the case of UNSC-authorised peacekeeping, policy, doctrine and interoperability protocols need to be developed based on previous missions and in advance of new missions. A commander must be appointed and take on the role of planning the mission, setting rules of engagement with military lawyers and then issuing orders. Force commanders should be given broad authority to secure the identified goals with the limitations on means being established by international humanitarian law and the Rome Statute[29] rather than detailed restrictions (some of which may be imposed by spoilers).

How can we move towards this outcome? There are broadly two ways of building the ROL into the issuing and review of UNSC mandates: the integrity route and what I call the 'Coke moment'.

5.1 The integrity route

The UNSC should make a general commitment that all mandates will be subject to judicial review, to resolve disputes as to what actions are within power, and to only issue mandates to those who agree to accept, for the purposes of that mission, the ICJ's compulsory jurisdiction and give an equivalent undertaking to the ICC.

I do not anticipate the UNSC being able to make this general commitment at this stage. However, a good start could be made with peacekeeping operations. A group of at least seven states on the UNSC (preferably more and preferably with the backing of the UNGA) could sign an 'integrity pact', jointly agreeing that no new peacekeeping missions will, in fact, be authorised unless the mandated states accept the above jurisdictions. In future elections to the UNSC, acceptance of this principle would be a condition of securing the votes of other states. This process would have a number of consequences. One, not all states need agree to be so limited initially – just those states that engage in peacekeeping. Two, it may be necessary to operate without those states which do not accept these conditions. Three, other states may need to build up forces to take the place of those who will not agree to the restriction. However, this situation is less of a problem for peacekeeping than peace enforcement and responsibility to protect (R2P) action. Peacekeeping is not as demanding, and in any case, the UNSC is unlikely to authorise major wars or even R2P pillar three[30] operations in the immediate future. By the time support for a major operation is present, there will be a weight of precedents in peacekeeping that will be hard to resist. Indeed, experience with mandates subject to the ROL may mean that P5 and other states with significant militaries are not so concerned about such mandates. Four, this gradual approach may mean that more people will suffer. But attempt to move too quickly to the ends sought, and we may stir too many forces in response. Sometimes the longer game produces more lasting success. Given the justified reticence to provide a UNSC mandate authorising force, the enforceable limitation of the use of force to the mandate may make other UNSC members more willing to vote for such mandates.

5.2 The coming 'Coke moment'

While it is time for the UNSC to adopt the integrity route and the majority of states to sign an integrity pact, the catalyst may not come from the top. Coke is generally held as a Common Law hero whose battles with James I and Francis Bacon in and out of court would make a good film and a better play. James thought he should be able to be king and also act as a legislator and a judge. Coke told him he did not have those powers.[31] With this and another of his decisions,[32] Coke helped to set the framework for the ROL in England.

The UNSC, like James I, needs to be told that it cannot act as executive, legislature and judiciary. The judges who tell it as much need not fear the UNSC in the same way as Coke had good reason to fear James. The verbal response could be ferocious (reflecting the attacks on Kofi Annan when his caution slipped and he stated what most international lawyers agreed – that the invasion of Iraq was contrary to international law). But there is no Tower of London in the UN compound.

There are a number of ways in which it might be addressed. Some are practical if fanciful – such as New Zealand suing Australia in the ICJ for breach of clause one of the ANZUS Charter for invading Iraq. There is also the possibility of a member of NATO suing the UK over one of several acts that are in breach of similar provisions in that treaty. The ICJ could be more definitive in a re-run of *Lockerbie*.[33] Another way could be if state-based or regional courts start issuing advisory opinions, declarations or injunctions with regards to the obligations the UNSC is trying to impose on them. The issue has already been raised in *Nada* v. *Switzerland*.[34] If high-quality reputable national and regional courts seek to determine issues of UNSC power, they will carry great moral weight. This action is likely to stimulate the need to go to the ICJ for a more definitive view. Until then, it might at least curtail the issue of mandates.[35]

6 Conclusion

That much-underrated General and President, Dwight D. Eisenhower, who commanded united nations forces in Europe before there was a formal UN, once said:

> The time has come for mankind to make the rule of law in international affairs as normal as it is now in domestic affairs.... Plainly one foundation stone of this structure is the [ICJ and...] the obligatory jurisdiction of that Court ... we will all have to remind ourselves that under this system of law one will sometimes lose as well as win. But ... if an international controversy leads to armed conflict, everyone loses.[36]

That was 14 years after the foundation of the UN and the ICJ. Forty-six years later that view was unanimously endorsed at the UN World Summit. The time is overripe for the UNSC to take to heart the unanimous declaration of the UNGA. While the UNGA should be more authoritative, Eisenhower's views should be more poignant and silence those who want to issue new and infinitesimally lesser mandates for the use of force without subjecting them to the international ROL he thought so critical. As argued in this chapter, it can start with the easiest of mandates – those for peacekeeping. And it should start at home, with the UNSC itself. If not, we will have to await a 'Coke moment' and I call on all aspiring Cokes to brew the broth.

Notes

1 GA Res. 60/1 (24 October 2005), *2005 World Summit Outcome*, para. 134.
2 For example, consider: Office of the UN High Commissioner for Human Rights (OHCHR), *Rule of Law Tools for Post-conflict States: Truth Commissions* (HR/PUB/06/1, 2006): www.refworld.org/docid/46cebc3d2.html; UN Development Programme (UNDP), *Strengthening the Rule of Law in Conflict- and Post-Conflict*

Situations: A Global UNDP Programme for Justice and Security (2008–2011): www.unROL.org/files/ROL_final_apr09.pdf.

3 Charles Sampford, 'What's a Lawyer Doing in a Nice Place Like This? Lawyers and Applied Ethics' (1998) 1 *Legal Ethics* 35–50; Charles Sampford, 'Challenges to the Concepts of "Sovereignty" and "Intervention"', in Burton M. Leiser and Tom D. Campbell (eds), *Human Rights in Philosophy and Practice* (Aldershot, Ashgate, 2001), pp. 325–50, 335; Charles Sampford, 'Get New Lawyers' (2003) 6 *Legal Ethics* 185–205; Charles Sampford, 'More and More Lawyers But Still No Judges' (2005) 8 *Legal Ethics* 16–22; Charles Sampford, *Retrospectivity and the Rule of Law* (Oxford, Oxford University Press, 2006).

4 'Preserving and Restoring the Rule of Law in the Asia Pacific'.

5 Michael J. Kelly, *Peace Operations: Tackling the Military, Legal and Policy Challenges* (Canberra, Australian Government Publishing Service, 1997); Michael J. Kelly, *Restoring and Maintaining Order in Complex Peace Operations: The Search for a Legal Framework* (London, Kluwer Law International, 1999).

6 See Fredrich von Hayek, *The Road to Serfdom* (Chicago, IL, University of Chicago Press, 1944).

7 See Lon Fuller, *The Morality of Law* (New Haven, CT, Yale University Press, 1964).

8 Joseph Raz, *The Authority of Law: Essays on Law and Morality* (Oxford, Clarendon Press, 1979).

9 As far as I know, I was the first person to distinguish between these versions of the ROL (applying Rawls' distinction between 'thick' and 'thin' theories of justice). I prefer this to 'formal' and 'substantive' meanings of the ROL. The 'thick theory' does include prescriptions as to the content of law. But what is substantive is the content added, not the ROL itself.

10 International Forum for the Challenges of Peace Operations, 'Chapter 5: Strengthening Rule of Law with Respect for Human Rights', in *International Forum for the Challenges of Peace Operations: Considerations for Mission Leadership in United Nations Peacekeeping Operations* (Stockholm, Edita Västra Aros AB, 2010), pp. 97–118, 97, 100.

11 UN Doc. S/2004/616 (24 August 2004), *The Rule of Law and Transitional Justice in Conflict and Post-conflict Societies*, s. iii–viii.

12 Thomas Hobbes, *Leviathan* (Cambridge, Cambridge University Press, 1991), p. 89.

13 Mathieu Deflem, 'Global Rule of Law or Global Rule of Law Enforcement?' (2006) 603 *Annals of the American Academy of Political and Social Science* 240–51.

14 Jeremy Waldron, 'The Rule of International Law' (2006) 30 *Harvard Journal of Law and Public Policy* 15–30.

15 International Forum for the Challenges of Peace Operations 'Chapter 5', p. 69.

16 See Sampford, *Retrospectivity and the Rule of Law*, pp. 257–88; Charles Sampford, 'Reconceiving the Rule of Law for a Globalizing World', in Spencer Zifcak (ed.), *Globalisation and the Rule of Law* (London, Routledge, 2005), pp. 9–31.

17 Existing codes of conduct include: The Study Group of the International Law Association on the Practice and Procedure of International Courts and Tribunals, in association with the Project on International Courts and Tribunals, *The Burgh House Principles on the Independence of the International Judiciary* (2004); International Civil Service Commission, *Standards of Conduct for the International Civil Service* (2013), which updated the International Civil Service Advisory Board, *Standards of Conduct in the International Civil Service* (1954), and forms the basis of the standards of conduct applying to UN staff members (see UN Doc. ST/SGB/2002/13 (1 November 2002), *Secretary-General's Bulletin on the Status, Basic Rights and Duties of United Nations Staff Members*); the UN Department of Peacekeeping Operations, *Ten Rules: Code of Personal Conduct for Blue Helmets* (1997); UN Doc. ST/SGB/2008/5 (11 February 2008), *Secretary-General's Bulletin on the Prohibition of Discrimination, Harassment, including Sexual Harassment, and Abuse of Authority*; and UN

Doc. ST/SGB/2003/13 (9 October 2003), *Secretary-General's Bulletin on Special Measures for Protection from Sexual Exploitation and Sexual Abuse.*

18 Charles Sampford, 'Professions Without Borders: Global Ethics and the International Rule of Law', in Vesselin Popovski (ed.), *International Rule of Law and Professional Ethics* (Aldershot, Ashgate, 2014), chapter 6.

19 I acknowledge that some see the UNSC entering a legislating phase, performing the function of a 'world legislator'. See Paul C. Szasz, 'The Security Council Starts Legislating' (2002) 96 *American Journal of International Law* 901–5; and Vesselin Popovski and Trudy Fraser (eds), *The Security Council as Global Legislator* (London, Routledge, 2014). However, the UNSC is not designed as a legislator and, in my own essay in the last mentioned volume ('The Coming Coke Moment') I argue strongly against the idea that it should act as such.

20 If states do not agree to be bound by the ICJ, then it has no jurisdiction even over crimes such as genocide. See *Armed Activities on the Territory of the Congo (New Application: 2002) (Democratic Republic of the Congo* v. *Rwanda)*, Provisional Measures, [2002] ICJ Rep 219, 245–6.

21 Sabino Cassese, 'Administrative Law Without the State?' (2005) 37 *New York University Journal of International Law and Politics* 663–94. See also Terence Halliday, *Global Legislators: The Production of Commercial Laws for the World* (forthcoming).

22 Gordon Christenson, 'World Civil Society and the International Rule of Law' (1997) 19 *Human Rights Quarterly* 724–37.

23 Walter Dellinger and Samuel Fried, 'Promoting the Rule of Law Abroad' (2003) 20 *World Policy Journal* 79–85.

24 On the relation between the ROL and POC, see Thomson's chapter in this collection.

25 See Peter Singer, *Practical Ethics*, 3rd edition (Melbourne, Cambridge University Press, 2011).

26 See Noel Preston, Charles Sampford and Carmel Connors, *Encouraging Ethics and Challenging Corruption* (Sydney, Federation Press, 2002); Charles Sampford, Arthur Shacklock, Carmel Connors and Fredrik Galtung (eds), *Measuring Corruption* (Aldershot, Ashgate, 2006).

27 See Hayek, *The Road to Serfdom*; Fuller, *The Morality of Law.*

28 SC Res. 678 (29 November 1990).

29 *Rome Statute of the International Criminal Court*, opened for signature 17 July 1998, 2187 UNTS 90 (entered into force 1 July 2002).

30 GA Res. 60/1 (24 October 2005), *2005 World Summit Outcome*, paras 138–40; UN Doc. A/63/677 (12 January 2009), *Report of the Secretary-General Implementing the Responsibility to Protect.*

31 *Prohibitions del Roy* (1607) 77 ER 1342, 12 Co. Rep. 64; and *Case of Proclamations* (1611) 12 Co. Rep. 74.

32 *Dr. Bonham's Case*, 8 Co. Rep. 114 (Court of Common Pleas [1610]).

33 *Questions of Interpretation and Application of the 1971 Montreal Convention Arising from the Aerial Incident at Lockerbie* (*Libyan Arab Jamahiriya* v. *United Kingdom*), Provisional Measures, ICJ Rep. (1992), 3; *Questions of Interpretation and Application of the 1971 Montreal Convention Arising from the Aerial Incident at Lockerbie* (*Libyan Arab Jamahiriya* v. *United States of America*), Preliminary Objections, ICJ Rep. (1998), 115.

34 *Nada* v. *Switzerland* [2012] ECHR 1691. For discussion, see de Wet's chapter in this collection.

35 For further discussion of these points, see Charles Sampford, 'The Coming Coke Moment', in Vesselin Popovski and Trudy Fraser (eds), *The Security Council as Global Legislator* (London, Routledge, 2014).

36 Dwight Eisenhower, *Remarks Upon Receiving an Honorary Degree of Doctor of Laws at Delhi University* (11 December 1959): www.eisenhowermemorial.org/speeches/1959.

6 Humanity, law, force

Gerry Simpson[1]

> History is not something that one understands, it is something one endures – if one is lucky.
>
> Hayden White, 'Against Historical Realism'[2]

> [O]utside the Commonwealth is the empire of passions, war, fear, poverty, nastiness.
>
> Thomas Hobbes, *On the Citizen*[3]

Introduction

In this chapter, I explore the relationship between humanitarianism, hegemony and the rule of law (ROL). The chapter begins by assessing recent efforts to rethink the relationship between the United Nations (UN) Security Council (UNSC) and the ROL through projects of global administrative law, constitutionalisation and legitimacy (this discussion is footnoted with some brief thoughts on the special meta-problem of interpretation). A familiar question is then posed, namely, are these problems of legitimacy, force and authority – in any respects – novel? This question invites a consideration of the arrangements of authority developed in earlier moments of post-war reconstruction (the Congress of Vienna in 1815, the Atlantic Charter in 1941) and describes, in particular, the historical antecedents of a contemporary practice of going *beyond* institutional (or constitutional) limits in order to promote a general system of security, or a more substantive conception of the good.

The chapter continues with some thoughts on 'humanity' and humanitarianism in the context of the UNSC and the use of force, and argues that, increasingly, humanitarianism seems to be conditioning, qualifying or provoking UNSC action in ways that might prove awkward for some versions of the 'rule of law'. In particular, I ask what it would mean (for law or for legitimacy) to act in the name of humanity when using violence, one of the great social evils, to prevent or abate great social evil (say, mass governmental killing). How has the invention of a juridically constituted 'humanity' (by Raymond Poincaré, the French President, in his opening address at the Versailles Peace Conference of 1919),[4] opened up the possibility of experimental forms of redemptive violence? Here, the relationship between the legitimation (of empire) and the legitimacy (of law) is likely to be illustrative.

I end by remarking on the capacity of the ROL to consolidate existing structural inequalities and support the activities of elites. The ROL, in an international society in which such inequalities are deeper and less easily ameliorated, is likely to be, what I call, the rule of humanity's law. The latter – pervasive and increasingly ascendant – underpins a system in which punitive security measures and humanitarian self-confidence sit side-by-side.

1 The Council and the rule of law: some proposals

E.H. Carr said:

> When modern writers on international politics find the highest moral good in the rule of law, we are equally entitled to ask, What law? And Whose law? The law is not an abstraction. It cannot be understood independently of the political foundation on which it rests and of the political interests which it serves.[5]

We know this already. We now seem to be at the stage where there is an effort to work out how to understand legitimacy or the ROL in relation to institutions we also know are dominated by coalitions of Great Powers, and which were established in order that these Powers act decisively, and in ways only moderately mediated by any concern for lawfulness. So we find ourselves going back and forth between worldliness and indignation. This is why it seems possible to say that the UNSC is fatally flawed, dominated by a duplicitous elite and subject to a veto that runs against the grain of law altogether, while at the same time calling on the UNSC to intervene in Syria or Libya, or demanding that the UNSC operate in conformity to an existing ROL.

There are several projects related to the latter demand for normative or procedural oversight of this apparently 'political' organ. I want to just provide a brief, prelusive sketch of these here.

I will begin with the overarching idea of a global administrative law whereby a set of process-oriented norms (often derived from the public law of western democracies) is applied in international (or inter-governmental) institutions or domestic bodies with international aspects.[6] The study of the emerging practice of subjecting sites of global governance to forms of administration and governance outside the parameters of treaty-making and judicial review has been initiated in a project developed at New York University Law School early this century, but with precursors found as early as the late-nineteenth century.[7] The UNSC can be understood here as an institution exercising administrative power either directly or through its committees. One possibility arising from this is that there might be administrative or judicial oversight of – or various procedural rules capable of being applied to – UNSC decision-making.[8] Drawing on 'domestic' cases such as *Kadi* and *Al Jedda*, and following on from international decisions in *Tadic* and *Lockerbie*, proponents of this view argue that an outline for a possible new order has emerged (or, at least, an old system has fragmented) where UNSC decisions become subject to forms of judicial or administrative scrutiny either at the (usually) local or the international level.[9] This scrutiny, often related to the assertion of individual rights, was negligible in *Lockerbie*, weak in *Tadic*, diffident at the House of Lords in *Al Jedda* and intrusive in *Kadi* and at the European Court of Human Rights in *Al Jedda.*[10]

An associated, but perhaps more radical, thought is that the international institutional order is undergoing a process of *constitutionalisation* or has already constitutionalised.[11] Looked at from the perspective of UNSC limits, this project might be based on the belief that the UN Charter can be read as a founding document from which certain basic rules of behaviour can be read down[12] or that somehow the UNSC can be imagined as a constitutional body with executive,[13] legislative[14] and judicial functions.[15] Tom Franck was one of the earliest advocates of this approach:

> As in a state where a constitution defines and legitimates the exercise of political power, so too at the UN the legitimacy of the exercise of power by the Security Council depends upon the public perception that it is being exercised in accordance with the Charter's applicable defining rules and standards.[16]

This constitutionalism runs against the grain of a more traditional way of thinking of the UNSC's powers as untrammelled and this has led to a debate – between those we might think of as textualists and others who might be regarded as constitutionalists – about how to interpret the UNSC's powers under Article 39 of the UN Charter. It is sometimes surprising how this disagreement plays out. Recently, I asked a group of military officers from around the Pacific what they thought constituted a 'threat to the peace'. Every one of them came up with a variation of the constitutionalist reading. One variation focused on either the practice of the UNSC (a Common Law version, if you like, in which the UNSC was bound by the precedents of its own – often originally unprecedented – activity; thus a 'threat to the peace' was aggression, international conflict, human rights violations, international terrorism). Another variation emphasised the existence of constitutional norms directing UNSC action (for example, behaviour that breached fundamental norms of international law or principles embedded in the UN Charter).

Yet, many international lawyers will say a threat to the peace is anything the UNSC says it is. This, of course, is the anti-constitutional, textualist reading (sometimes described as 'realism'). This debate is often understood as a disagreement between 'law' and 'politics'. The debate, though, cuts across these divisions. Textualists focus on the wording of Article 39 but also want to widen the UNSC's range of authority unhindered by legal constraints. Constitutionalists want the UNSC to be guided by the principles of the Charter read *against* the bare legal text of Article 39. As Justice Weeramantry put it in his famous dissent in *Lockerbie*: '[does] the Security Council discharge its variegated functions free of all limitations, or is there a circumscribing boundary of norms or principles within which its responsibilities are to be discharged?'[17] In the end, constitutionalism and global administrative law might be thought of as ways in which the ROL is strengthened by recourse to deeper principles of social organisation.

But, for a while now, international lawyers have been wrestling with the problem of law and ethics, not through the ROL as such, but with reference to the language and symbols of legitimacy, a structure of argument that draws on moral and legal norms to reason creatively about hard cases. This move has come about partly as a result of the sense that when it comes to war (and especially humanitarian interventions), ethical imperatives push lawyers in one direction, legal rules in the other.[18] Legitimacy seems to promise some in-between-point where ethics and law are in happy balance or harmony.[19] Interventions can be described as illegal – or barely legal – but legitimate. The Kosovo intervention in 1999 is a good example of this. A number of international lawyers (Simma, Cassese, Chinkin) recoiled from the prospect of simply declaring the intervention illegal and wanted to somehow qualify this with the language of legitimacy.[20] The appeal is rather obvious. International law is, in a way, a retreat from ethics so it is impossible and nostalgic to return to the romantic fantasy of some transcendental position from which to judge the justness of war. At the same time, the legal rules seem unsatisfactory. Legitimacy offers a *via media*.

But what might legitimacy mean? On one hand, legitimacy has associations with proper process or just authority: an illegal act undertaken after, or in the context of, a proper process might qualify as more legitimate than one committed 'in isolation'. So, for example, the interventions in Kosovo and Iraq, though widely regarded as illegal, might compare favourably to, say, the German invasion of Poland in 1939 (where there was little in the way of legal or institutional context).[21]

In the case of both Kosovo and Iraq, the UNSC was 'seized of the matter' and had passed several resolutions purporting to deal with the situation under Chapter VII.[22] There was in both cases a threat to the peace identified in a series of UNSC resolutions and apparently posed by a transgressor state (in the Kosovo case, Serbia; in the Iraq case, Saddam Hussein's regime).[23] What was absent, of course, was a clearly legible authorisation to use force. And this lack adds a further complication to the application of the ROL to UNSC action: *What* has the UNSC actually authorised? In particular, had it implicitly authorised the North Atlantic Treaty Organization (NATO)'s offensive against Belgrade in 1999 (in, say, Resolution 1160 (1998))? Had it prospectively authorised Anglo-American action in 2003 (in Resolution 1441 (2002))? And had it authorised a comprehensive strategy of regime change in Libya in 2011 (in Resolution 1973 (2011))? These were questions of interpretation and meta-interpretation: there were debates about what the resolutions meant but also about how one might go about finding out what the resolutions meant. The existence of this context was an argument *against* legality in the case of Iraq (if the UNSC was seized then how could it be lawful for NATO or a Coalition of the Willing to act unilaterally?) but *for* legitimacy in the case of Kosovo (at least the UNSC *was* seized and the action took place in the context of repeated condemnations by the UNSC). This argument about the *relevance* of context and the interpretation of UNSC resolutions might account for the fact that legal argument in both cases was vigorously pursued through academic journals, official statements and in public debates.[24]

Legitimacy, though, can sometimes be taken to refer to something more substantive than institutional context and often this is related to the plausibility or force of some ethical argument for or against the intervention. Here I turn to the question of *humanitarianism*, another idea that shapes UNSC action as well as action outside the UNSC's strict authority. Increasingly, humanitarianism seems to be conditioning, qualifying or prompting UNSC action. Indeed, it is hard to imagine any more the UNSC acting simply to restore or maintain international peace and security. Humanity has usurped security as the dominant metaphor, even while security continues to be the central organising principle in many UNSC resolutions. So the 'responsibility to protect' (R2P) and the 'protection of civilians' (POC) doctrines have become frames for understanding or provoking UNSC action, as well as adding authority and legitimacy to that action. This can work the other way too: the greater the appeal to humanitarianism the more likely that post-intervention chaos or reckless conduct will undermine the legitimacy of the original claim.[25]

These may be familiar enough problems but have they, perhaps, always been familiar? I now want to consider some precursors in the hope of shedding light on the current scene. The thought I would like to pursue is that the role of Great Power condominia is often organised around a relationship between a public law idea of constitutionality or administrative propriety, and a more flexible standard of legitimacy that will sometimes permit extra-curricular action to protect the background values of the system. This, rather than the tired clichés about law and politics, might be a better way to think through recent dilemmas of UNSC action.

2 Historical antecedents of a contemporary practice

2.1 Vienna, 1815[26]

At the beginning of 1814 (towards the end of the Napoleonic Wars), in the French town of Langres, the four victorious Powers (Great Britain, Prussia, Russia and Austria) signed a Secret Protocol in which they appointed themselves as guarantors and architects of the post-war reconstruction. Article 1 stated that 'the relations from whence a system of real and permanent Balance of Power in Europe is to be derived, shall be regulated at the Congress upon the principles determined upon by the *Allied Powers themselves*' (my italics).[27]

The Langres Protocol provided the basis for a Congress of Vienna in which these same powers initiated a European public law project that was to culminate a century and a half later with a global UN Charter. The Congress – a response to Napoleonic revolution, conquest and imperial ambition – sought to restore

Europe to some sort of equilibrium by institutionalising the balance of power, partially restoring the sovereignty of middle and minor powers and introducing a novel form of Great Power management.[28] This was the essence of the Concert system that was to operate, though with diminishing effect, until the Great War.

The Congress of Vienna is not a particularly celebrated marker in the history of international law. It seems distinctly pre-modern in its lack of an institutional architecture, in its failure to create any judicial organs and in its overall lack of solidity (though there had been proposals to establish a bureaucracy or 'office of Europe' with von Gentz, Metternich's adviser, as the first 'Secretary-General of Europe').[29] And, of course, it was, famously, in Talleyrand's phrase, 'the Congress that was not a Congress'.[30] The small and middle powers did not meet. Vienna was Dumbarton Oaks (the Four Power meetings in 1945) without its San Francisco (the plenary conference to draft the UN Charter).[31] The Great Powers determined the future of Europe in secret protocols prior to the Congress and in the Austrian Foreign Minister, Metternich's apartment in Vienna. They established a Central or Directing Committee composed exclusively of the big four Powers. As one writer put it, 'This committee is the core of the congress, the congress exists only when the committee is in being, and it is terminated when the committee dissolves itself'.[32]

Metternich's apartment, it might be said, is now situated on the East River.[33] So the Congress brought into being, or at least juridified, the idea of an 'international community' acting as the guardian of peace, good government and the international ROL.

But the Concert of Europe, itself, and especially in its early incarnation, was emblematically arranged around a relationship between the constitutional norms developed at Vienna and an informal security arrangement that deviated from the central commitments of the Congress.[34] This latter was the Holy Alliance, or the 'pact of love'.[35] After 1815, the Eastern Powers (Austria, Prussia and Russia) engaged in a regional security effort, disparaged by the other Great Powers of the time, to promote a particular, and highly interventionist, conception of international order whereby constitutional reform and revolution in other states would be met with military reaction by the Eastern Powers (and, in certain circumstances, France). The idea was to insert 'a salutary fear into the revolutionists of all lands'.[36] All of this was underpinned by a commitment to a very particular vision of international order based not on the formal arrangements found at Vienna but on 'the precepts of [the] Holy Religion; namely, the precepts of Justice, Christian charity and peace'.[37] Sovereignty was found not in states but in heaven, the source of 'infinite wisdom' (a precursor to doctrines founded on 'infinite justice' developed just under a century later).

The early interventions by the Holy Alliance in 1821 in Naples and Piedmont (unwanted but also unopposed by the UK) were not to be repeated, however.[38] There was a very hostile reaction, on the part of the UK and the US, to the interventionist decisions made at the 1822 Congress of Verona. Both Wellington, the Commander of the Allied Army that defeated Napoleon at Waterloo, and Canning, the British Foreign Secretary, reiterated the British opposition to meddling in the internal affairs of sovereign states. The British regarded the problem of Bonapartism as one of territorial aggrandisement and not internal revolution. Canning, in particular, was an advocate of sovereign equality. 'Our business', he said, 'is to preserve the peace of the world and therefore the independence of the several nations which compose it.'[39] The Americans, meanwhile, responded with the Monroe Doctrine, which concluded, 'It is impossible that the Allied Powers should extend their political system, to any portion of our continent, without endangering our peace and happiness.'[40] In the end, the Holy Alliance was short-lived. The constitutionalists of South America and Spain could not be pacified and, ultimately, the conservative regimes of Europe were, themselves, overthrown by the revolutions of mid-nineteenth-century Europe.

This relationship between the Holy Alliance's discretionary violence and the existing security apparatus later turned out to be archetypal. As with subsequent policies of interventionism, the Holy Alliance was rationalised from the inside as the logical extension of the already existing international order coupled with the idea that the moral weight of action, grounded in some overarching normative order, could be sufficient to outweigh certain 'technical' objections to an interventionist policy.

The Eastern Powers argued that the Holy Alliance was a natural consequence of the adherence of European powers to the Second Treaty of Paris. This treaty was aimed at destroying the influence of revolutionary politics on international relations. The powers of the Holy Alliance believed that the desirable consequence of this aim was the future suppression of revolutionary practices within domestic contexts. Why fight a future Napoleon on the battlefields of Europe when he could be destroyed *prior* to taking power in one of the states of Europe? The rhetoric arising out of the Holy Alliance was designed to mollify the other powers and demonstrate the link between the system brought into existence at Vienna and the specific aims of the Alliance itself. And, as I say, this relationship between institutional and extra-institutional security continues to be a theme in contemporary thinking around intervention.

The contemporary version of this is the idea that groups of states can 'enforce' UNSC resolutions, for example, or intervene in order to make good on the authentic or underlying normative structure of the system. This carries through obviously to the debates over Iraq, Kosovo and Libya, but it has its post-war roots in the relationship between institutionally authorised and extra-curricular intervention mapped out in The Atlantic Charter off the coast of Newfoundland in 1941.

2.2 Newfoundland, 1941

On Sunday, 3 August 1941, Winston Churchill boarded a train in London and began travelling north. Only a very few people knew of his whereabouts. The London Blitz was still in progress though the Battle of Britain had been won, and just over a month previously Hitler had launched his invasion of Russia (on 22 June, the same day as Napoleon's march on Moscow). These two invasions, we might say, established an international system based on condominium in 1815 and legal hegemony in 1945.

Churchill had chosen to embark on his daring journey across the Atlantic in order to discuss the system of collective security that is the primary subject of this book.[41] Roosevelt had the easier trip up the Eastern Seaboard in his yacht, *The Potomac*. The Atlantic Charter, then, was not drafted in the middle of the Atlantic but rather off the coast of North America. In a way, of course, this anticipates the arrangement of forces at the UN itself.[42]

Churchill seems to have written the preliminary draft himself.[43] There is a somewhat stronger institutional tenor in the original. Churchill, for example, speaks of an 'effective international organization' while the Charter talks more loosely of a general system of security (Principle 8). Even this was accepted only reluctantly by Roosevelt. This tension over collective security was to become a familiar aspect of the post-war regime. It is striking that even Roosevelt was unenthusiastic about the prospects of a more fully realised UN. This anticipates decades of opposition to the organisation culminating in the antipathy of the US Ambassador to the UN, John Bolton, towards the UN.

This relationship between 'effective organisation' (Vienna, Churchill, the French at the UNSC in 2003) under the ROL and 'a general system of security' (the Holy Alliance, Roosevelt, the US at the UNSC in 2003) has survived into recent times. Kosovo and Iraq, in a way, each represent aspects of this struggle. The UK and US argued in relation to both Kosovo and Iraq that they were acting under a general system of security because the UN had proved ineffective. Iraq could be re-read, then, not as a retreat from law to politics but rather as a continuation of themes present in 1815 and 1941. Indeed, the Churchill/Roosevelt discussions resemble in some ways Tony Blair's meetings with George Bush at Bush's Crawford ranch and at Camp David (though it's hard to imagine Churchill saying of Roosevelt: 'The President had immense simplicity in how he saw the world. Right or wrong, it led to decisive leadership').[44]

3 Humanity and the rule of law

This chapter has traced two broad themes. The first rotated around the question of how the ROL might be developed or implemented in such a way as to constrain institutionally authorised intervention (and, in the case of legitimacy discourse, permit unauthorised war). The second theme, drawing on this latter point, considered the historical antecedents of a contemporary practice of going beyond institutional limits altogether in order to promote a general system of security or a more substantive conception of the ROL through which particular values might be advanced.

Let me conclude by sketching some thoughts about the ROL itself and, in particular, the way in which 'humanity' might be deployed to support interventions under and/or beyond the ROL.

In the abstract, the ROL, for all its virtues in a stable, liberal democracy, is a form of rule that is likely to favour entrenched elites over resistance groups, vested interests carrying out lawful activity over civil disobedients, official actors over unofficial actors and property owners over protestors. In the international system, where the distribution of power, goods and advantage is so vastly, indefensibly and asymmetrically skewed, where the law is largely written by and on behalf of a powerful minority of states and where institutions are funded by, established at the behest or instigation of (or, at least, with the tacit approval of), and, often, directed by, sovereign elites, it is little wonder that the ROL is regarded either as illusory and distant (in its radical guise) or concrete and violent (in its existing instantiation). China Mieville, in one of the most important sentences ever written about international law, reminds us that 'death, destruction, poverty, torture: this *is* the rule of law'.[45] In other words, Hobbes was wrong: the empire of passions is *inside* the Commonwealth.

But these are not very pervasive images of the ROL. In fact, they seem almost impolite. Indeed, the idea or rhetoric that mobilises some of its practitioners and supporters is that of acting in the name of humanity as a way of underpinning a commitment to intervention as an apparently neutral act of (rule of) law-enforcement (whether institutional or extra-institutional) or as a way of bypassing excessively formalistic and passive versions of the international ROL.[46] Certainly, humanity is invoked a great deal in contemporary doctrines ('crimes against humanity', 'responsibility to protect'), in the preambular statements of institutions and in the rhetorical justifications of its practitioners. War and intervention are now justified as the work of 'humanity' rather than some sectional interest or other.[47] The ROL is now, at times, the rule of 'humanity's law'.[48]

But this rule of humanity's law is likely to be less inclusive than classic liberal notions of the ROL with their formal commitments to equal application. Indeed, some of its most energetic practices are dedicated to punishing 'inhumane' acts (acts committed by individuals who have lost their humanity?) and acting on behalf of humanity against those who are deemed to have stepped outside or defied humanity (e.g. certain sorts of terrorists, whether they have committed inhumane acts or not). Its favoured penalties, indeed, often come in the form of extreme violence applied to these outsiders (historically, the quartering of pirates, the beheading of tyrants; more recently, the hanging of war criminals and the waging of humanitarian wars). Raymond Poincaré, announcing the latest incarnation of humanity's law against the idea of a concert of sovereign equals, stated at the beginning of the Versailles Peace Conference, 'Humanity can place confidence in you, because you are not among those who have outraged the rights of humanity.'[49]

At the same time, the category 'enemies of mankind' was revived through the idea – first found in the League of Nations – of humanity acting as a unified political agent, or concatenation of Great Powers (in the name of the international community) against outlaw or aggressor nations. This transformation, disentangled by Carr and lamented by Schmitt, made war into a form of 'pest control'.[50]

And so, we have a continuation of themes present at Vienna and elsewhere, where substantive conceptions of the common good pursued through looser security systems either prevail over the formal arrangements of institutionalism or are used to modify (or substantiate) the commitments found in those arrangements.

ROL becomes at once a formal-legal mechanism for organising the indefensible arrangements of economic and political life on the planet (Mieville), a way of bypassing formal rules in favour of a more strongly ideological interventionism in the name of humanity (Blair's humanitarian interventions, Bush's eradication of evil) and a means by which institutions are commandeered in the name of 'the rule of humanity's law' (for example, responsibility to protect) and remade in its image.[51]

In this way a legal order designed to prevent recourse to force has begun to open up normative space for improvisational uses of force. As I have said elsewhere, the policing wars of the contemporary era (whether undertaken under UNSC auspices or not) sometimes are regarded as having transcended the prohibition against force altogether.[52] International lawyers meanwhile engage in efforts to restrain force through procedure (constitutionalism, administration), promote or critique it through a turn to ethics (legitimacy) or justify it in both its institutional and extra-institutional variants as the work of 'humanity'.

Notes

1 I want to thank my colleague at the London School of Economics and Political Science, Devika Hovell, for helping me clarify many of these ideas in a course I taught with her at Melbourne Law School in 2013, and for alerting me to the extensive literature on the UNSC and the idea of public law. Hannah Douglas (Melbourne Law School JD, 2015) assisted with research on this paper.

2 Hayden White, 'Against Historical Realism' (2007) 46 *New Left Review* 89–110, 110.

3 Richard Tuck and Michael Silverthorne (eds), *Hobbes: On the Citizen* (Cambridge, Cambridge University Press, 1998), p. 115.

4 Raymond Poincaré, 'Opening Statement at Paris Peace Conference', 18 January 1919, in Charles F. Horne (ed.), *Source Records of the Great War, Vol. VII* (National Alumni, 1923).

5 Edward H. Carr, *The Twenty Years' Crisis, 1919–1939* (New York, Palgrave, 2001), p. 179.

6 A small selection might include Nico Krisch, 'Global Administrative Law and the Constitutional Ambition', in Petra Dobner and Martin Loughlin (eds), *The Twilight of Constitutionalism* (Oxford, Oxford University Press, 2008), pp. 245–66; David Dyzenhaus, 'The Rule of Administrative Law in International Law' (2005) 68 *Law and Contemporary Problems* 127–66.

7 Benedict Kingsbury, Nico Krisch and Richard Stewart, 'The Emergence of Global Administrative Law' (2005) 68 *Law and Contemporary Problems* 15–61. For earlier work see Paul Reinsch, 'International Administrative Law and National Sovereignty' (1909) 3 *American Journal of International Law* 1–45.

8 Jose Alvarez, 'Judging the Security Council' (1996) 90 *American Journal of International Law* 1–37 catalogues some of these early proposals to think of the international legal order in terms of, say, a separation of powers. For a discussion of other institutions, see Daniel Esty, 'Good Governance at the Supranational Scale: Globalizing Administrative Law' (2006) 115 *Yale Law Journal* 1490–562.

9 The concern in some of these cases was about the substance of the decisions (how they related, for example, to other norms) rather than the transparency, legality and

participation associated with such decisions. See Kingsbury *et al.*, 'The Emergence of Global Administrative Law', 29.

10 *Questions of Interpretation and Application of the 1971 Montreal Convention arising from the Aerial Incident at Lockerbie (Libyan Arab Jamahiriya* v. *United States of America) (Preliminary Objections)* [1998] ICJ Rep. 115; *Prosecutor* v. *Tadic (Jurisdiction)* (International Criminal Tribunal for the former Yugoslavia, Appeals Chamber, 2 October 1995), paras 1–64; *Al-Jedda* v. *Secretary of State for Defence* [2007] UKHL 58; *Kadi and Al Barakaat International Foundation* v. *Council of the European Union and Commission of the European Communities*, Joined Cases C-402/05 P and C-415/05 P [2008] ECR I–6351; *Al-Jedda* v. *United Kingdom*, Appl. No. 27021/08 *(Judgment)* (European Court of Human Rights, Grand Chamber, 7 July 2011). See, too, Devika Hovell, 'A Dialogue Model: The Role of the Domestic Judge in Security Council Decision-making' (2013) 26 *Leiden Journal of International Law* 1–19; Anthea Roberts, 'Comparative International Law? The Role of National Courts in Creating and Enforcing International Law' (2011) 60 *International and Comparative Law Quarterly* 57; Grainne de Burca, 'The European Court of Justice and the International Legal Order after Kadi' (2009) 51 *Harvard Journal of International Law* 1–49; Kingsbury *et al.*, 'The Emergence of Global Administrative Law', 46–7; and de Wet's chapter in this collection.

11 Andreas Paulus, 'The International Legal System as a Constitution', in Jeffrey Dunoff and Joel Trachtman (eds), *Ruling the World? Constitutionalism, International Law and Global Governance* (Cambridge, Cambridge University Press, 2009), pp. 69–109; Michael Doyle, 'The UN Charter: A Global Constitution?' in Dunoff and Trachtman (eds), *Ruling the World?*, pp. 113–32. Striking some important notes of caution, see Deborah Cass, *The Constitutionalization of the World Trade Organization: Legitimacy, Democracy, and Community in the International Trading System* (Oxford, Oxford University Press, 2005); Michael Wood, '"Constitutionalization" of International Law: A Sceptical Voice', in Kaiyan Homi Kaikobad and Michael Bohlander (eds), *International Law and Power: Perspectives on Legal Order and Justice* (Leiden, Martinus Nijhoff, 2009), pp. 85–98.

12 Bardo Fassbender, *The United Nations Charter as the Constitution of the International Community* (Leiden, Martinus Nijhoff, 2009), pp. 77–115.

13 Georges Abi-Saab, 'The Security Council as Legislator and as Executive in its Fight against Terrorism and against Proliferation of Weapons of Mass Destruction: The Question of Legitimacy', in Rüdiger Wolfrum and Volker Röben (eds), *Legitimacy in International Law* (Berlin, Springer, 2008), pp. 109–30; Steven Wheatley, 'The Security Council, Democratic Legitimacy and Regime Change in Iraq' (2006) 17(3) *European Journal of International Law* 531–51.

14 Stefan Talmon, 'The Security Council as World Legislature' (2005) 99 *American Journal of International Law* 175–93.

15 Oscar Schachter, 'The Quasi-Judicial Role of the Security Council and the General Assembly' (1964) 58 *American Journal of International Law* 960–5.

16 Thomas Franck, *Fairness in International Law and Institutions* (Oxford, Clarendon Press, 1995), p. 221.

17 *Questions of Interpretation and Application of the 1971 Montreal Convention arising from the Aerial Incident at Lockerbie (Libyan Arab Jamahiriya* v. *United Kingdom) (Provisional Measures, Order of 14 April 1992) (Dissenting Opinion of Judge Weeramantry* [1992] ICJ Rep. 50, p. 61 (quoted in ibid., p. 244).

18 See, for an early example, Antonio Cassese, '*Ex Iniuria Ius Oritur:* Are We Moving Towards International Legitimation of Forcible Humanitarian Countermeasures in the World Community?' (1999) 10 *European Journal of International Law* 23–30.

19 For a general outline, see Allen Buchanan and Robert Keohane, 'The Legitimacy of Global Governance Institutions' (2006) 20(4) *Ethics and International Affairs* 405–37; David Caron, 'The Legitimacy of the Collective Authority of the Security

Council' (1983) 87 *American Journal of International Law* 552–88; Ian Hurd, 'Legitimacy, Power and the Symbolic Life of the UN Security Council' (2002) 8 *Global Governance* 35–51.

20 Bruno Simma, 'NATO, the UN and the Use of Force: Legal Aspects' (1999) 10(1) *European Journal of International Law* 1–22; Christine Chinkin, 'The State that Acts Alone: Bully, Good Samaritan or Iconoclast' (2000) 11(1) *European Journal of International Law* 31–41; Antonio Cassese, 'A Follow-up: Forcible Humanitarian Countermeasures and Opinio Necessitas' (1999) 10(4) *European Journal of International Law* 791–800. See, too, Ian Brownlie, Christine Chinkin, Christopher Greenwood and Vaughan Lowe, 'Memoranda on Kosovo to House of Commons Foreign Affairs Committee' (2000) 49 *International and Comparative Law Quarterly* 876–943.

21 I don't want to suggest that the German invasion of Poland took place in isolation. Clearly, there was a context that included the way in which the Munich Agreement had failed to fully comprehend German expansionism, but it would be unreasonable to read Munich as having *authorised* the invasion.

22 For general discussions see Olivier Corten, *The Law against War: The Prohibition on the Use of Force in Contemporary International Law* (Oxford, Hart Publishing, 2010); Christine Gray, *International Law and the Use of Force*, 3rd edition (Oxford, Oxford University Press, 2008) especially chapters 1, 2 and 4; Christopher Greenwood, 'New World Order or Old?' (1992) 55 *Modern Law Review* 153–78 (on the 1991 Iraq War). For a classic statement, see Thomas Franck, *Recourse to Force: State Action against Threats and Armed Attacks* (Cambridge, Cambridge University Press, 2002).

23 See Efthymios Papastravidis, 'Interpretation of Security Council Resolutions under Chapter VII in the Aftermath of the Iraq Crisis' (2007) 56 *International and Comparative Law Quarterly* 83–118; Alexander Orakhelashvili, 'The Acts of the Security Council: Meaning and Standards of Review' (2007) 11 *Max Planck Yearbook of United Nations Law* 143–95; Michael Byers, 'Agreeing to Disagree: Security Council Resolution 1441 and Intentional Ambiguity' (2004) 10 *Global Governance* 165–86; Ian Johnstone, 'Security Council Deliberations: The Power of Better Argument' (2003) 14(3) *European Journal of International Law* 437–80; Jules Lobel and Michael Ratner, 'Bypassing the Security Council: Ambiguous Authorizations to Use Force, Cease-Fires and the Iraqi Inspection Regime' (1999) 93(1) *American Journal of International Law* 124–54; Michael Wood, 'The Interpretation of Security Council Resolutions' (1998) 2 *Max Planck Yearbook of International Law* 73–95.

24 In the case of Iraq, two book-length accounts have emerged: Marc Weller, *Iraq and the Use of Force in International Law* (Oxford, Oxford University Press, 2010); and Charlotte Peevers, *The Politics of Justifying Force: The Suez Crisis, the Iraq War and International Law* (Oxford, Oxford University Press, 2013). Official assessments of the legality of the war are found variously in United Kingdom (UK) Attorney-General, Lord Goldsmith, *Opinion on the Legality of Military Action against Iraq* (7 March 2003): news.bbc.co.uk/1/shared/bsp/hi/pdfs/28_04_05_attorney_general.pdf; UK Attorney-General, Lord Goldsmith, *Published Advice on the Legality of the Iraq War* (17 March 2003): www.guardian.co.uk/world/2003/mar/17/iraq2; *Chilcot (Iraq) Inquiry Hearings* (26–27 January 2010): www.iraqinquiry.org.uk and www.iraqinquiry.org.uk/transcripts/oralevidence-bydate/100126.aspx, especially Elizabeth Wilmshurst, Michael Wood and Peter Goldsmith; UK Deputy Legal Adviser to the Foreign Office, *Letter of Resignation* (18 March 2003): news.bbc.co.uk/2/hi/uk_news/politics/4377605.stm; Australian Attorney-General's Department and Department of Foreign Affairs and Trade, 'Memorandum of Advice to the Commonwealth Government on the Use of Force against Iraq' (2003) 4 *Melbourne Journal of International Law* 178–82. For an acerbic re-arrangement of neo-conservative rhetoric, see Eliot Weinberger, *What I Heard About Iraq* (New York, Verso, 2005), pp. 67–75 and pp. 9–20; for a critical approach, see John Strawson, 'Provoking International Law:

War and Regime Change', in Fleur Johns, Richard Joyce and Sundhya Pahuja (eds), *Events: The Force of International Law* (Oxford, Routledge, 2011), pp. 267–80; for a cry of despair, see Philippe Sands, *Lawless World* (London, Penguin, 2005); for a cry of despair about cries of despair, see Costas Douzinas, *The End of Human Rights* (Oxford, Hart Publishing, 2000).

25 For discussion of Iraq, see Natarajan's chapter in this collection; for further discussion of legitimacy, see Bellamy's and Heathcote's chapters in this collection.

26 This section is drawn from my book, Gerry Simpson, *Great Powers and Outlaw States* (Cambridge, Cambridge University Press, 2004) and from an essay of mine entitled 'International Law in Diplomatic History', in James Crawford and Martti Koskenniemi (eds), *Cambridge Companion to International Law* (Cambridge, Cambridge University Press, 2013), pp. 25–46.

27 'For all practical purposes, Europe meant the four states which were considered … to be Great Powers': Gordon Craig, *Europe Since 1815* (New York, Holt, Rinehart and Winston, 1971), p. 11.

28 Rene Albrecht-Carrie, *The Concert of Europe* (New York, Walker, 1968); Carsten Holbraad, *The Concert of Europe* (New York, Barnes and Noble, 1970).

29 Harold Nicolson, *The Congress of Vienna* (New York, Harcourt Brace Jovanovich, 1974); David King, *Vienna 1814* (New York, Harmony Books, 2008), p. 310.

30 Alan Palmer, *Metternich, Councillor of Europe* (London, Orion, 1977), p. 139.

31 Genevieve Peterson, 'The Equality of States as Dogma and Reality II: Political Inequality at the Congress of Vienna' (1945) 60 *Political Science Quarterly* 532–54.

32 Paul Sweet, *Wilhelm von Humboldt, II* (Columbus, OH, Ohio State University Press, 1980), p. 180.

33 Clemens W.L. Metternich, *Memoirs of Prince Metternich* (New York, Charles Scribner's Sons, 1881); Guglielmo Ferrero, *The Reconstruction of Europe: Talleyrand and the Congress of Vienna 1814–1815* (New York, G.P. Putnam's Sons, 1941); Palmer, *Metternich.*

34 Ian Clark, *The Hierarchy of States: Reform and Resistance in the International Order* (Cambridge, Cambridge University Press, 1989).

35 King, *Vienna 1814*, p. 308.

36 William P. Cresson, *The Holy Alliance* (New York, Oxford University Press, 1922).

37 The text of the Holy Alliance (from which these quotes are taken) is found in Walter Alison Phillips, *The Confederation of Europe* (New York, Fertig, 1966), pp. 305–6.

38 Robert S. Castlereagh, *Correspondence* (London, John Murray, 1853).

39 Letter from George Canning to Henry Wellesley, 16 September 1823, reproduced in Augustus G. Stapleton, *George Canning and his Times* (London, John W. Parker and Son, 1859), p. 374.

40 'Monroe Doctrine', *President Monroe's Speech to Congress* (2 December 1823).

41 For example, Henry V. Morton, *Atlantic Meeting* (London, Methuen and Co., 1943). I discovered recently that Churchill left the UK from a small town at the northernmost tip of Scotland, called Thurso. It also happens to be where I was born and grew up. In fact, I could see from my bedroom window the harbour from where Churchill had set out to create the UN.

42 The Atlantic Charter was never signed. Approval was sought through an exchange of telegrams (so the Congress of Vienna did not meet, and the Atlantic Charter was not signed).

43 Winston Churchill, *The Second World War, Volume III: The Grand Alliance* (Boston, MA, Houghton Mifflin, 1950), p. 386.

44 Tony Blair, *A Journey* (London, Random House, 2008), p. 394.

45 China Mieville, *Between Equal Rights* (London, Pluto Press, 2006), p. 319.

46 *The Responsibility to Protect: Report of the International Commission on Intervention and State Sovereignty* (Ottawa, International Development Research Centre, 2001), pp. i–18; Cassese, '*Ex Iniuria Ius Oritur*'; UN Doc. A/59/565 (2 December 2004), *A*

More Secure World: Our Shared Responsibility – Report of the Secretary-General's High-level Panel on Threats, Challenges and Change. For a highly critical view, see Tom Hazeldine, 'The North Atlantic Counsel' (2010) 63 *New Left Review* 17–33.

47 For a representative sample of the literature on humanitarian intervention, see Francis Kofi Abiew, *The Evolution of the Doctrine and Practice of Humanitarian Intervention* (Leiden, Martinus Nijhoff, 1999); Simon Chesterman, *Just War or Just Peace? Humanitarian Intervention and International Law* (Oxford, Oxford University Press, 2001); Anne Orford, *Reading Humanitarian Intervention: Human Rights and the Use of Force in International Law* (Cambridge, Cambridge University Press, 2003); Nick Wheeler, *Saving Strangers: Humanitarian Intervention in International Society* (Oxford, Oxford University Press, 2000); Sean Murphy, *Humanitarian Intervention: The United Nations in an Evolving World Order* (Philadelphia, PA, University of Pennsylvania Press, 1996); Aidan Hehir, *Humanitarian Intervention: An Introduction* (New York, Palgrave MacMillan, 2010); Brendan Simms and D.J.B. Trim (eds), *Humanitarian Intervention: A History* (Cambridge, Cambridge University Press, 2011); Davide Rodogno, *Against Massacre: Humanitarian Interventions in the Ottoman Empire, 1815–1914* (Princeton, NJ, Princeton University Press, 2011).

48 Ruti Teitel's phrase, of course. See Ruti Teitel, *Humanity's Law* (Oxford, Oxford University Press, 2011).

49 Papers relating to the Foreign Relations of the United States, *The Paris Peace Conference Papers 1919* (1942) p. 159.

50 Carr, *The Twenty Years' Crisis*; Carl Schmitt, *The Nomos of the Earth* (New York, Telos Press, 2003), p. 123. See, for a lengthier elaboration of these themes, Gerry Simpson, 'Atrocity, Law, Humanity', in Conor Gearty and Costas Douzinas (eds), *Cambridge Companion to Human Rights Law* (Cambridge, Cambridge University Press, 2012), pp. 114–33.

51 Robert Cooper, a former adviser to Tony Blair, said,

> The challenge … is to get used to the idea of double standards. Among ourselves, we operate on the basis of laws.… But when dealing with more old-fashioned kinds of states … we need to revert to the rougher methods of an earlier era – force, preemptive attack, deception.

See Robert Cooper, 'The Postmodern State', in Mark Leonard (ed.), *Reordering the World: The Long-term Implications of September 11th* (London, Foreign Policy Centre, 2002).

52 Gerry Simpson, 'Warriors, Lawyers, Humanitarians' (2008) 27 *Australian Yearbook of International Law* 143–63.

Part II

The Security Council, peacekeeping and the rule of law

7 Rule-of-law assistance in UN peace operations

Securitisation, sectorisation and goal displacement

Richard Zajac Sannerholm and Frida Wall

Introduction

For the United Nations (UN), the rule of law (ROL) is now a central element in the maintenance of peace and security.[1] Justice and the ROL, together with security and democracy, are seen to be mutually reinforcing imperatives in fragile post-conflict, peace- and state-building processes.[2]

This chapter explores the relationship between policy guidance and practice, and examines what type of rule-of-law assistance the UN provides in peacekeeping operations and special political missions and peacebuilding offices (hereinafter political missions and offices). It draws on data collected for the Folke Bernadotte Academy (FBA) research project on the UN and rule-of-law assistance in Africa between 1989 and 2010. It is in Africa where most UN peacekeeping and special political missions are found, and also where a majority of the UN's rule-of-law assistance is undertaken. Looking at the UN's experience in Africa allows for inferring patterns, trends and practices to the organisation's work and responsibility elsewhere. The data are recorded from all UN Secretary-General's (UNSG) reports on each peace operation between 1989 and 2010, creating a comprehensive dataset on UN rule-of-law assistance. The dataset covers seven broad areas based on the UN definition of the ROL from 2004, in addition to supporting policy, strategic and operational documents: (1) justice reform, (2) constitutional reform, (3) law reform, (4) the ROL in public administration reform, (5) legal awareness[3] and access to justice reform, (6) police reform and (7) corrections reform.[4]

Based on this dataset, the chapter argues that despite an increase in volume of UN rule-of-law assistance there is a 'goal displacement' – that is, a discrepancy between how the ROL is formulated in policy and the concretisation and application of the concept in practice. This goal displacement reveals the extent to which the UN is failing to deliver rule-of-law assistance that is varied and situational and that can address long-term peacebuilding and development priorities early on in peace operations. The significant increase in rule-of-law assistance also raises issues about how to organise knowledge management processes to measure the impact and effectiveness of the assistance – in response to increasing pressure from UN member states to do so – and identify future trends, challenges and demands.[5]

War-torn societies are often described as lacking the ROL. The question of rule-of-law assistance in war-torn societies is about the function of law itself, raising questions about whether the ROL can be constructed by building and strengthening a combination of parts, or in accordance with a design or plan. How law functions plainly varies depending on a number of general factors, with history, culture, tradition, and social norms leaving a mark on legal and administrative systems. War-damaged societies also typically display a layered complexity of law exacerbated by the conflict: 'formal' state law exists together with customary and/or religious law. Moreover, the formal legal system is often disputed and disrupted. The deleterious effects of conflict run wide and deep and the legal and administrative systems of these devastated countries often suffer from a lack of the most basic equipment, as well as more serious difficulties such as a lack of educated personnel. Empirical studies also show that the state of the ROL prior to conflict substantially impacts assistance efforts after conflict, and also that how conflicts end matters for predicting successful reform efforts.[6] Thus helping states to achieve the institution of the ROL is challenging for the UN as a whole, not least in those environments where UN peace operations are deployed.

1 Rule of law: supply and demand

ROL has gradually emerged as a key objective in UN peace operations, with a more defined 'rule-of-law policy' starting to take form after 2000.

Since 1989 there has also been a general increase in UN peace operations. Parallel with this growth has been the corresponding and significant expansion of rule-of-law assistance (see Figure 7.1), as operations have evolved towards

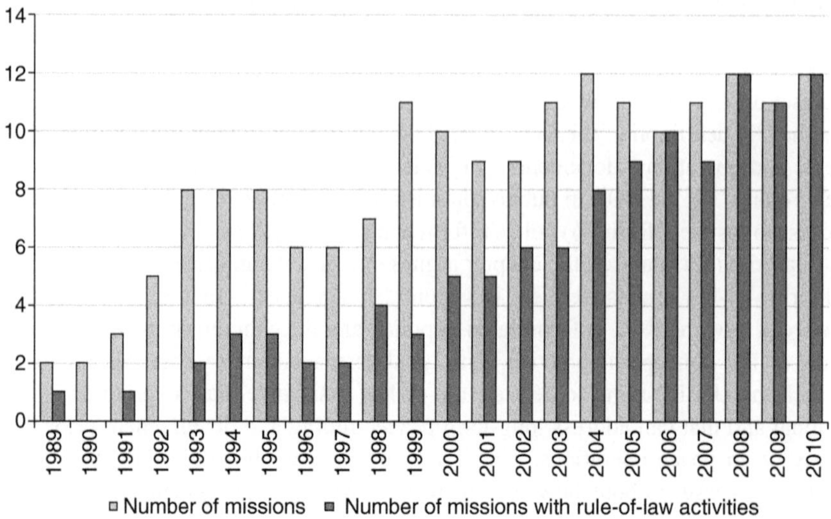

Figure 7.1 Total number of UN peace operations and missions providing rule-of-law reform assistance in Africa, 1989–2010.[7]

multidimensional interventions with larger and more complex civilian mandates. During the 1990s, more than half (12 out of 21) of the UN peace operations in Africa were involved to a varying degree in rule-of-law assistance (i.e. in one or more of the areas mentioned above). From 2000 onwards, the proportion of such operations providing rule-of-law assistance increased to a large majority (19 out of 24). It is notable that in 2006, and 2008–2010, all such operations were involved in at least one rule-of-law area.

The increase in volume over the past decade has prompted organisational changes within the UN, particularly with the establishment of the Office for Rule of Law and Security Institutions, the Rule of Law Coordination and Resource Group, the Standing Police Capacity, and the Justice and Corrections Standing Capacity.

In line with this trend, in 2012 the UNSG also launched the Global Focal Point (GFP) for Police, Justice and Corrections,[8] with the aim of streamlining rule-of-law issues by designating Special Representatives of the UNSG, or in non-peace operation settings, the Resident Coordinator, as the person responsible and accountable for guiding and overseeing rule-of-law activities. The GFP comes at a time when member states have been applying pressure to show results, effective management of resources and enhanced communication with in-country donors. There are high expectations of what the GFP will accomplish, and one of the main challenges lies in setting up GFP structures in peace operations and non-peace operation settings, while avoiding duplication of in-country expertise.

While these organisational changes are a positive step, there does not seem to have been a correlating increase in financial resources and personnel allocated to rule-of-law assistance. According to a 2014 briefing to the Special Committee on Peacekeeping Operations, the UN had approximately 750 corrections and justice personnel in authorised field presences (14 Department of Peacekeeping Operations (DPKO) and Department of Political Affairs (DPA) missions and offices).[9] Corrections and justice personnel represent 0.35 and 0.28 per cent, respectively, of all staff in DPKO and DPA operations. Justice and corrections amount to 0.84 per cent of the total peacekeeping budget.

That demand from member states and the UN itself to focus on the ROL in post-war transitions is not properly matched with capacity to supply such assistance presents a serious challenge. There are limited human resources with rule-of-law expertise within the UN and in some areas, such as constitutional reform, the scarcity of capacity is striking.[10]

Compounding this capacity problem, rule-of-law assistance generally, not just for the UN, is often criticised for being supply- and donor-driven and for failing to meet the specific demands, concerns and problems of different crisis, conflict and post-conflict societies.[11] In a 2004 report, the UNSG emphasised that UN entities and international partners should avoid employing ready-made models to address national rule-of-law problems.[12] The 2008 *Guidance Note of the Secretary-General: UN Approach to Rule of Law Assistance* makes clear that when rule-of-law assistance is donor-driven, it results in the uneven and contradictory development of rule-of-law institutions and short-term, superficial gains.[13]

This raises critical questions about the capacity of the UN to deliver rule-of-law assistance. Does it have sufficient capacity to handle simultaneously the high volume of rule-of-law assistance in many different conflict and post-conflict environments? More specifically, what is the capacity of the DPKO and DPA to provide rule-of-law assistance that is comprehensive, timely and adjusted to country conditions? The increased focus on and number of UN Security Council (UNSC) mandates for providing rule-of-law assistance also requires the DPKO and DPA to work more closely together where there is a drawdown of operations or handover of DPKO responsibilities to the DPA. It is unclear what this increase means for the UN's capacity to effectively, and with sustained quality, ensure policy coherence and take on new responsibilities in rule-of-law assistance.

2 UN rule-of-law policy

Following the UN's increased responsibility for rule-of-law assistance in peace operations, and particularly after its experience in Kosovo and Timor-Leste, the need grew for a comprehensive and guiding definition of 'the rule of law'. In 2004 the UNSG launched a common definition for the whole organisation, defining the ROL as 'a principle of governance in which all persons, institutions and entities, public and private, including the State itself, are accountable to laws'.[14] The definition also provides that laws should be publicly promulgated, equally enforced and independently adjudicated, and consistent with international human rights standards.[15] The definition is ends-based and generally in accord with how the ROL is portrayed in legal doctrine and scholarly works.[16]

The UN's definition is also systemic and sets out to encompass not only courts and judicial institutions, but also police agencies, corrections institutions and administrative functions. The definition includes both substantive justice (the aims and outcomes of justice) and procedural justice (the process by which those aims and outcomes are achieved). In this sense the UN definition is 'thick' or 'material'.[17] The emphasis is not only on having proper procedural guarantees, but also on the content of laws and regulations adhering to certain international standards.[18] These are seen as representing universally applicable principles, bringing 'a legitimacy that cannot be said to attach to exported national models'.[19]

Overall, the UN policy that has evolved is comprehensive and positions the ROL as a means for sustainable peace, security and development, as well as an end in itself. In this way the UN's rule-of-law agenda comprises many different elements, while accentuating the systemic relevance of the ROL in all state and individual interactions.[20]

When it comes to UNSC mandates for peace operations there is a variety of practice in terms of how the ROL is described. On a general level, mandates mention the ROL as an end together with other political objectives such as democracy, good governance and justice. In these resolutions, broad narratives of the ROL appear more as political encouragement than as an operational directive.[21]

However, linking the ROL with security and law and order is more often done in specific directives, detailing strategies and focal areas, often concerning the support of police, correctional reform[22] or reforming the security sector so that it can and will protect citizens and respect the ROL and the constitution.[23] Another central thrust in UNSC mandates is to emphasise the judiciary as a key agency. Extending support to judicial reform as a rule-of-law strategy takes many different forms, including establishment of court-monitoring programmes,[24] calling for training and specialisation of national lawyers and judges[25] and judicial independence.[26]

At the most practical level, UN staff have at their disposal a number of guidelines and manuals on various rule-of-law areas. Not all of the guidelines and manuals concern peace operations. Some contain guidance on UN rule-of-law assistance on a global level, including long-term development.[27] The Office of the High Commissioner for Human Rights (OHCHR) has established a toolkit for rule-of-law assistance consisting of seven sets of instruments on issues such as mapping of the justice sector, seeking prosecution initiatives and monitoring.[28] The DPKO, UNDP and the UN Office on Drugs and Crime (UNODC) have also developed similar guidelines and manuals.[29]

There is no apparent hierarchy between the different material, and it is difficult to assess to what extent they are actually used in peace operations.[30] The fact that some of the guidelines and manuals are formulated for development cooperation, and others for post-conflict peace operations, might well impede ready access and use across the two fields. Making this guidance material part of daily operations requires not only knowledge of their existence, but the training and capacity-building of UN judicial officers, UN police and other categories of staff involved in rule-of-law assistance. This is an area that remains underdeveloped in the UN system.[31]

Thematically the guidelines and manuals chiefly cover 'justice-chain' actors (judiciary, police and corrections). Where guidance in other rule-of-law areas has been developed, for example on access to justice or legislative reform, the topical orientation is often towards criminal justice matters. While relevant to most sectors and organisational divisions of the UN system for peace operations, constitutional assistance and public administration are notably fragmented and less supported than other rule-of-law areas. Constitutional reform is an area where both staff resources and policy guidance are limited. Existing policy covers the area only superficially while highlighting the pressing need to develop strategic guidance on methods to support national actors.[32] Similarly, there is both staff shortage and weak policy guidance in the area of public administration, specifically where it relates to the ROL in terms of ensuring support to judicial functions, legality in government decision-making and accountability for grievances.[33]

3 Patterns and trajectories

Considering the growing prominence of the ROL as an objective of peace operations, it is important to identify those areas where assistance is provided and consistent with overall policy. While the type of rule-of-law assistance has varied over time, the trend is for justice-chain institutions to stand for a significant portion of rule-of-law assistance in peacekeeping and peacebuilding (see Figure 7.2).

The justice chain includes rule-of-law actors such as judges, prosecutors, defence lawyers, law clerks, court bailiffs, police personnel and correction personnel in DPKO- and DPA-led operations.[34] Much of the support to the justice chain takes the form of mentoring, monitoring and advice – sometimes through co-location of UN personnel to different national institutions. The methods of doing business also include technical assistance for the development of national justice plans and strategies and conducting assessments of justice-chain actors and institutions, or capacity building and professionalisation through training.[35] Police personnel are the recipients of most training initiatives, followed by judicial personnel and corrections officers. Much of the support to the justice chain appears to focus on 'quick wins' or 'quick impact' projects, aimed at demonstrating a break with the past by, for example, redeploying police in order to enhance security or increasing access to justice by establishing mobile courts.[36]

It is important to recognise that the main contribution to rule-of-law assistance in DPKO- and DPA-led operations is by way of UN personnel, with limited

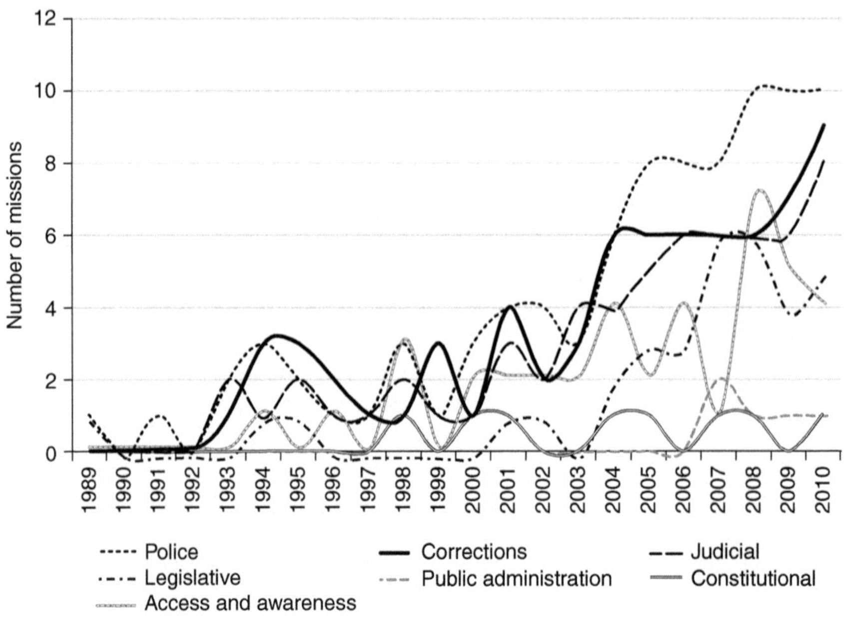

Figure 7.2 UN peace operations involved in rule-of-law reform in Africa, 1989–2010.[37]

funding for projects and programmes. This means that UN rule-of-law assistance in peace operation contexts essentially depends on transmitting good ideas, advice and technical expertise through meetings and workshops with national counterparts.

The justice-chain pattern is possible to identify over time and across different peace operations, starting with the early operations in Namibia, Angola and Mozambique, and reinforced by later operations in countries such as Liberia, Sierra Leone and Sudan. Reform outside the justice chain, in fields such as legislation, constitutions or access and awareness, was infrequent during the 1990s. The predominant focus on the justice chain might be explained by the fact that political missions and offices were not in effect until the late 1990s and that a more comprehensive policy on the ROL was still in the making (for example, the 2004 UN rule-of-law definition), as were organisational changes such as the UN Peacebuilding Commission.

From the mid-2000s, however, the number of peace operations reportedly engaging in rule-of-law assistance increased dramatically. This also coincided with an expansion of rule-of-law areas, increasing the prevalence primarily of access to justice and legal awareness and legislative reforms.

A general pattern that emerges on examining the different reform areas over time is that rule-of-law assistance in relation to public administration is only reported in isolated instances. The UN Mission in Sudan (UNMIS) supported training initiatives organised by the Ombudsperson's office and provided logistical support to harmonise administrative divisions, while the UN in Sierra Leone assisted the Anti-Corruption Commission. Besides these, and a few other reported instances of developing codes of conduct for public officials and supporting decentralisation processes, reform of public administration receives limited attention.

While access to justice and legal awareness and legislative reform increased around the year 2000, projects and programmes in these areas tend to underpin initiatives in the justice sector. For instance, typical activities UN peace operations undertake in the area of legislative reform encompass technical assistance and advice on legislative topics, analysis of specific areas of law and advice on the process of law-making, including capacity-building of national legislative assemblies.[38]

Thematically, legislative reform supported by peace operations is primarily focused on criminal justice, including criminal law and criminal procedure law, and specific initiatives such as human trafficking and narcotics. Other subject-matter areas include counter-terrorism, national intelligence and security, and laws on juries, bail, legal aid, police and corrections.

On access to justice and legal awareness, public events, workshops and seminars seek either to inform the broader public about proposed or actual changes in the legal and administrative framework, build trust and confidence or explain and facilitate discussions on the role of certain actors in the criminal justice sector.[39] In terms of institutional reform, some of the activities deal with support to bar associations and women lawyers' organisations.[40] Some activities also focus on establishing mechanisms for reviewing backlogs of cases and pre-trial detainees.[41]

Table 7.1 Number of UN peace operations in relation to rule-of-law areas[42]

Rule-of-law areas	*All UN operations (36 missions)*	*PKO operations (22 missions)*	*Political missions and offices (14 missions)*
Police	28	17	11
Corrections	22	14	8
Legal access and awareness	21	11	10
Judicial	20	12	8
Legislative	15	7	8
Constitutional	7	1	6
Public administration	5	1	4

Examining the number of peace operations that have been engaged in a specific activity demonstrates that police reform is the single rule-of-law reform area that most peace operations have supported over time (see Table 7.1). Considering all UN peace operations, 28 out of 36 (78 per cent) were at some point during their deployment engaged in police reform.

4 Transitions between peace operations

How to ensure smooth transitions from peacekeeping to peacebuilding or from a UN mission drawdown – that is, to handing over responsibilities to national authorities – is a key challenge confronting the UN.[43] The UN continues to face increasing complexity in peace operation settings, making it important that peacekeeping, peacebuilding and development are interlinked so that initial reforms undertaken by peacekeeping operations serve to support later peacebuilding activities. It is also critical that the UN from the very start assist in a gradual build up of national capacities to handle the ROL and justice responsibilities.[44]

The 2013 UN Guidance Note on transitions and national capacity states the importance of adapting capacity development to the national context and of prioritising what is feasible.[45] Looking at rule-of-law assistance specifically, it is therefore appropriate to examine if there is a difference when there are successive operations in one country, particularly from an adaptability and prioritisation perspective.

Of specific interest is the question of whether the activities of peace operations that are first on the ground differ in scope from those of subsequent operations. One plausible assumption is that there would be a complementary relationship between peace operations – for example, that the same type of activities would be carried out in order to continue and complete previous initiatives. But it is also reasonable to assume that as the situation changes in the host country (for example, in terms of stability, political maturity, economic and social development, etc.),[46] the type of rule-of-law assistance would also change from a more narrow initial justice and security sector focus to include aspects of legislative and constitutional reform, access and legal awareness, and governance-related rule-of-law challenges more generally.

About half of all peace operations follow a previous operation: 10 out of 22 peacekeeping operations and 11 out of 14 political missions and offices in the period 1989–2010 were built on previous ones or were deployed during an existing operation. During their deployment, first-time peace operations concentrated primarily on assistance to the justice chain. More modest assistance was directed towards legislative reform and enhancing access to justice and legal awareness. Very little or no attention was accorded to constitutional reform or public administration.

The transition from peacekeeping to peacebuilding is also of particular interest. Political missions and offices are rarely deployed as the first peace operations on the ground, as indicated above, but follow a peacekeeping operation in most cases. The transition from peacekeeping to peacebuilding is problematic for practical and financial reasons. Peacebuilding offices often lack access to funds, staff and expertise in the area of the ROL, and cannot easily draw on the resources of the DPKO.[47] Similarly, a handover from the DPKO or DPA to UN Country Teams might also pose risks in terms of the Country Team not having secured the necessary funding to continue rule-of-law activities established by an operation.

Reform relating to access and legal awareness, police, corrections and the judicial sector is pursued in both peacekeeping operations and special political missions and offices, with some variations. A major difference, however, is that peacekeeping operations give very little or no attention to constitutional, legislative or public administration reforms compared with political missions and offices. For example, a number of political missions or offices have engaged in constitutional reform and public administration, while only one out of 22 peacekeeping operations focused on constitutional reform (MONUC in the Democratic Republic of the Congo),[48] and one on public administration (UNMIS in Sudan). This indicates that political missions and offices continue in large part the rule-of-law assistance of peacekeeping operations, but also that there exists a broader scope of assistance in terms of the number of reform areas included. The more comprehensive rule-of-law agenda seen in political missions and offices might suggest a division of labour by default between different operation types, where long-term, structural and political activities are more feasible in less unstable environments and under peacebuilding mandates.

The differences between peacekeeping and peacebuilding might imply a conscious transition strategy. Moreover, the DPKO does not have an explicit mandate to work on constitutional reform, whereas this reform area is typically seen to fall within the DPA's responsibilities. Also, political missions and offices lack the financial strength, the capacity to deploy personnel rapidly and the logistics of peacekeeping operations. In consequence, political missions and offices are more dependent on support from UN Country Teams and other UN entities present in the host country, which might explain the extension of rule-of-law assistance to areas outside the justice chain.[49]

At the same time, the practice of transferring the responsibility for non-justice chain areas to peacebuilding means that many rule-of-law areas are not addressed immediately after a conflict settlement has been brokered and an international force deployed, but rather depend upon a would-be future transition to a political mission, or on structures and mechanisms to ensure support from the UN Country Team being in place while the peacekeeping operation attends to justice-chain challenges.

5 Implications of the focus on criminal justice reform

The securitisation and sectorisation, illustrated in Figure 7.3, suggests that the UN has a tendency to concentrate its practice rather narrowly, and this is a pattern that has evolved over time. It is important to recognise that this approach has spurred the development of practical guidelines and manuals. While this might ensure a higher level of quality, it might also make it harder to depart from a well-established trajectory and facilitate the discharge of responsibilities in broader rule-of-law areas.

The path dependency might mean that the UN employs a ready-made model of the ROL, rather than being informed by rule-of-law challenges and demands in specific post-conflict environments. If so, this represents a misconception of the overarching UN policy. The limited attention paid to the ROL as a 'principle of governance', for instance in relation to public administration, is also a striking contrast to growing insights that administrative agencies (i.e. property rights agencies, supervisory and audit institutions and civic registration and licensing offices) also have a key role to play in overcoming civil conflict. A majority of peace agreements address public administration and governance, including issues such as civil service reform, re-organisation of public administration, anti-corruption policies and strategies for revenue collection.[50]

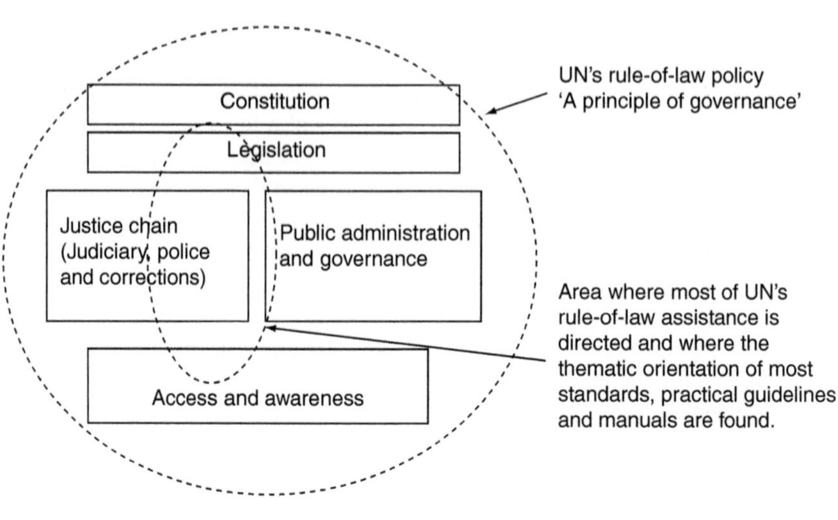

Figure 7.3 Scope and reach of UN peace operations and rule-of-law assistance in Africa.

The 2011 World Development Report emphasises the need to ensure rule-based, accessible and accountable administrative organisations, particularly at the local level – both for conflict prevention and for recovering from conflict.[51] The need to extend rule-of-law assistance to areas outside the justice sector is not unknown to UN agencies working in post-conflict environments, but it seems difficult to realise this insight. The OHCHR toolkit on mapping the justice sector notes the critical importance of addressing rule-of-law concerns in public administration 'since even more people have contact with these agencies (and their history of discriminatory practices and corruption) than they do with the formal judiciary'.[52]

A 2012 UNSG report raises the importance of addressing rule-of-law challenges in areas outside the justice chain – for instance, in relation to property and housing, civic records and corruption.[53] Broadening the present rule-of-law focus to move beyond law and order, however, depends on the organisational capacity of UN entities involved in post-conflict rule-of-law assistance, primarily the DPKO and DPA, where personnel capacities are already constrained. To that end the UNSG's proposed programme of action includes a call to UN member states to nominate civilian justice experts to support the organisation's rule-of-law assistance.[54]

To grasp this opportunity, the UN should also consider the need to develop a standing capacity on legislative, public administrative and constitutional reform areas similar to that of existing capacities for police, justice and corrections. A broadening of present-day rule-of-law assistance might also necessitate additional guidance (manuals, tools, etc.) on how to work in such areas, in order to ensure consistency of policy and practice. Similarly, a GFP arrangement might strengthen the UN's capacity and flexibility in non-justice chain reform areas.

In 2011, the UNSC also stressed the importance of clarity of roles and responsibilities between peace operations and UN Country Teams 'for the delivery of prioritised support to a country consistent with its specific peacebuilding needs'.[55] Nevertheless, there are tensions between the DPKO and 'development' entities within the UN system, particularly the UNDP, which might affect assistance to rule-of-law areas without a clear entity-address.[56] There are considerable overlaps in many rule-of-law reform areas between the DPKO, DPA and other UN entities, most notably with regard to police reform, judicial and legal reform and corrections reform.[57] There also seems to be a deeper conceptual difference between UN entities on peacekeeping and peacebuilding. As the DPKO and DFS study notes, 'peacekeepers approach early peacebuilding tasks as technical responses occurring in a long-term, development context, where peace generally prevails', instead of framing peacebuilding initiatives within the general priorities of peacekeeping operations.[58] For post-conflict peace operations specifically, planning tools such as the Integrated Mission Planning Process and other similar mechanisms have also been developed to further integration and 'One UN' approaches, but their implementation seems to be inconsistent.[59]

6 Concluding remarks

The UN's approach to rule-of-law reform assistance has evolved markedly over the last decade. Although the UN has made considerable efforts and progress in terms of policy formulation, organisational restructuring and development of tools, manuals and frameworks, the data on what type of assistance the UN actually provided from 1989 to 2010 raise serious questions about comprehensiveness, adaptability, capacity and context-adjusted support. Based on these data, this chapter demonstrates that there is a discrepancy between the high-level UN policy formulation on the ROL and how the organisation's agencies implement the concept.

From a policy perspective, the UN employs the term 'the rule of law' in a general way to provide a sense of direction. Thus the term is broad enough to encompass peace, security and development, the primary pillars of the UN as set out in its Charter. It is also broad enough to allow for different member states to engage in a dialogue on a variety of issues linked to the ROL. While this makes for good diplomacy, it has clear drawbacks when it comes to operationalising the term as a concept in peace operations – for example, the tendency to fall back on established practice in the criminal justice chain while only marginally including other governance related rule-of-law challenges.

The UN is now, more than ever, called upon to provide rule-of-law assistance to countries emerging from crisis and conflict. This confirms that the ROL is today firmly established as both a means and an end in the UN's maintenance of international peace and security. At the same time, the fact that more peace operations are engaged in rule-of-law assistance than ever before in Africa and elsewhere raises several questions. Most important is the question of whether the UN has the institutional and human resources to handle the increase, the capacity to maintain a high level of quality and the ability to adapt to new challenges and demands in post-conflict transitions.

It is clear that in the current form of rule-of-law assistance through peacekeeping and peacebuilding, sufficient capacity and ability to adapt are in demand. The call for rule-of-law assistance to increase, from member states and within the UN itself, vastly surpasses the organisation's ability to undertake complex reform efforts. Recent initiatives, for instance the GFP arrangement, mark steps taken in the right direction towards more effective use of different experiences and comparative advantages in the UN rule-of-law family. The GFP and similar efforts need to be supported by member states if the UN is to meet the demand for delivering quality rule-of-law assistance. In addition, engaging more UN agencies in peace operations should also be employed as an opportunity to further broaden the thematic scope of rule-of-law assistance delivered. This means not only improving how assistance is undertaken, but also what that assistance looks like and how it responds to the demands that really matter – that is, the hopes and aspirations, challenges and threats of governments and individuals in war-torn societies.

Notes

1 The UNSC has included rule-of-law components in almost all thematic and country-specific resolutions since 2003. See Security Council Report, *Cross-cutting Report on the Rule of Law* (28 October 2011), p. 15.
2 GA Res. 67/1 (30 November 2012), *Declaration of the High-level Meeting of the General Assembly on the Rule of Law at the National and International Levels.*
3 Legal awareness refers to public information campaigns, sensitisation workshops and seminars seeking to inform legal professionals and civil servants as well as the broader public about changes in the legal and administrative framework.
4 See Richard Zajac Sannerholm, Frida Möller, Kristina Simion and Hanna Hallonsten, *UN Peace Operations and Rule of Law Assistance in Africa 1989–2010: Data, Patterns and Questions for the Future*. The FBA project on rule-of-law assistance in UN peace operations is currently ongoing, and will include all UN peace operations between 1989–2013. A synthesis report is expected in 2014.
5 UN Doc. S/2013/341 (11 June 2013), *Measuring the Effectiveness of the Support Provided by the United Nations System for the Promotion of the Rule of Law in Conflict and Post-conflict Situations.*
6 Stephan Haggard and Lydia Tiede, 'The Revival of the Rule of Law in the Wake of Civil War' (2012) 4 *Hague Journal on the Rule of Law* 120–34.
7 Sannerholm *et al.*, *Rule of Law Assistance in Africa*, p. 30.
8 UN Secretary-General, *Decision No. 2012/13: Rule of Law Arrangements* (11 September 2012).
9 Data presented at DPKO/OROLSI Annual Meeting of Heads of Justice and Correction Components in UN Peace Operations, New York, 22–24 April 2014, where the authors participated.
10 UN Doc. A/65/747–S/2011/85 (22 February 2011), *Civilian Capacity in the Aftermath of Conflict: Independent Report of the Senior Advisory Group*, p. 7. See also UN Doc. A/67/312–S/2012/645 (15 August 2012), *Civilian Capacity in the Aftermath of Conflict: Report of the Secretary-General*, p. 12.
11 See, e.g. Matteo Tondini, 'From Neo-Colonialism to a Light Footprint Approach: Restoring Justice Systems' (2008) 15 *International Peacekeeping* 237–51; Barbara Oomen, 'Donor-Driven Justice and Its Discontents: The Case of Rwanda' (2005) 36 *Development and Change* 887–910; and Rule of Law Unit, Executive Office of the UN Secretary-General, *New Voices: National Perspectives on Rule of Law Assistance* (New York, United Nations, 2011), p. 14.
12 UN Doc. S/2004/616 (23 August 2004), *The Rule of Law and Transitional Justice in Conflict and Post-conflict Societies: Report of the Secretary-General*, p. 21.
13 *Guidance Note of the Secretary-General: UN Approach to Rule of Law Assistance* (New York, United Nations, 2008).
14 UN Doc. S/2011/634 (12 October 2011), *Rule of Law and Transitional Justice in Conflict and Post-conflict Societies*, p. 4.
15 Ibid. Since 2006 the UNSG has reported annually on the ROL at the national and international levels.
16 See, e.g. the contributions in Gianluigi Palombella and Neil Walker (eds), *Relocating the Rule of Law* (Oxford, Hart Publishing, 2009). For discussion of the conceptualisation of the ROL, see Krygier's chapter in this collection.
17 For a discussion of 'thin' or 'thick' interpretations of the ROL, see Brian Tamanaha, *On the Rule of Law: History, Politics, Theory* (Cambridge, Cambridge University Press, 2004), pp. 91ff.
18 *Rule of Law and Transitional Justice in Conflict and Post-conflict Societies*, p. 5. Most of these standards relate to the justice chain (judiciary, police and corrections): for example, UN Doc. A/CONF.121/22/Rev.1 at 59 (1985), *Basic Principles on the Independence of the Judiciary*; GA Res. 40/33 (29 November 1985), *United Nations*

Standard Minimum Rules for the Administration of Juvenile Justice; and Eighth UN Congress on the Prevention of Crime and the Treatment of Offenders, *Guidelines on the Role of Prosecutors* (1990).

19 *Rule of Law and Transitional Justice in Conflict and Post-conflict Societies*, p. 5.

20 The UNSG and different UN entities have made several attempts to provide concrete guidance by describing specific components, tasks and functions in rule-of-law assistance. See, e.g. *Guidance Note of the Secretary-General: UN Approach to Rule of Law Assistance*, and DPKO and DFS, *Policy: Justice Components in United Nations Peace Operations* (1 December 2009).

21 See, e.g. SC Res. 1040 (29 January 1996), para. 2; SC Res. 1345 (21 March 2001), para. 5; SC Res. 1711 (29 September 2006), para. 9; SC Res. 1265 (17 September 1999), preamble; and SC Res. 1483 (22 May 2003), preamble.

22 SC Res. 1542 (30 April 2004), preamble; SC Res. 1812 (30 April 2008), para. 13; and SC Res. 1870 (30 April 2009), para. 19.

23 SC Res. 1756 (15 May 2007), para. 8; SC Res. 1746 (23 March 2007), para. 10; and SC Res. 1806 (20 March 2008), para 15.

24 SC Res. 1168 (21 May 1998), para. 4.

25 SC Res. 1867 (26 February 2009), para. 9.

26 See SC Res. 1778 (25 September 2007), para. 2(g); SC Res. 1493 (28 July 2003), para. 11; SC Res. 1536 (26 March 2004), para. 5; and SC Res. 1706 (31 August 2006), para. 8.

27 Most are developed by a specific entity or the Secretariat. Some, however, are developed by specific peace operations. See, e.g. UN Verification Mission in Guatemala, *Manual for Public Prosecutors* (October 1996).

28 OHCHR, *Rule-of-Law Tools for Post-conflict States: Truth Commissions, Mapping the Justice Sector, Prosecution Initiatives, Monitoring Legal Systems, Vetting* (New York and Geneva, United Nations, 2006); OHCHR, *Rule-of-Law Tools for Post-conflict States: Reparations Programmes, Maximizing the Legacy of Hybrid Courts* (New York and Geneva, United Nations, 2008).

29 DPKO and OHCHR, *The UN Rule of Law Indicators: Implementation Guide and Project Tools* (2011); DPKO and DFS, *Guidelines on Methodology for Review of Justice and Corrections Components in United Nations Peace Operations* (2009); UNODC, *Criminal Justice Assessment Toolkit* (2006); DPKO, *DPKO Best Practice Guidelines: Executive Corrections Management in UN Peacekeeping* (2003); DPKO, *United Nations Police Handbook* (2005); DPKO, *Handbook for Judicial Affairs Officers in United Nations Peacekeeping Operations* (2013); DPKO, *Rule of Law Training Programme for Judicial Affairs Officers in United Nations Peacekeeping Operations: Instructor's Manual* (2013). For recent publications, see UNDP, *Why, What and How to Measure? A User's Guide to Measuring Rule of Law, Justice and Security Programming* (New York, United Nations, 2014); UNDP and FBA, *User's Guide for Assessing Rule of Law in Public Administration* (2015).

30 Camino Kavanagh and Bruce Jones, *Shaky Foundations: An Assessment of the UN's Rule of Law Support Agenda* (New York, NYU Center on International Cooperation, 2011), p. 61.

31 UN Doc. A/65/747–S/2011/85 (22 February 2011), *Civilian Capacities in the Aftermath of Conflict*, p. 18.

32 *Guidance Note of the Secretary-General: United Nations Assistance to Constitution-making Processes* (New York, United Nations, 2009), p. 3; see also Executive Office of the UNSG, *Inventory: United Nations Capacity in Peacebuilding* (New York, United Nations, 2006), p. 76.

33 See Per Bergling, L. Bejstam, J. Ederlöv, E. Wennerström and R. Zajac Sannerholm, *Rule of Law in Public Administration: Problems and Ways Ahead in Peace-building and Development* (Stockholm, Folke Bernadotte Academy, 2008).

34 DPKO, *Handbook on United Nations Multidimensional Peacekeeping Operations* (2003), p. 83.
35 See, e.g. UN Doc. A/60/612 (21 December 2005), *Performance Report on the Budget of the United Nations Operation in Burundi for the Period from 1 July 2004 to 30 June 2005*; and UN Doc. S/2011/73 (15 February 2011), *Report of the Secretary-General on Developments in Guinea-Bissau and on the Activities of the United Nations Integrated Peacebuilding Office in that Country.*
36 See UN GFP for the Police, Justice and Corrections Areas in the Rule of Law in Post-conflict and other Crisis Situations, *Resource Note: Sector Planning for Police, Justice and Corrections in Post-crisis and Transition Situations* (2013), pp. 8ff.
37 Sannerholm *et al.*, *Rule of Law Assistance in Africa.*
38 See, e.g. UN Doc. A/63/588 (30 June 2010), *Performance Report on the Budget of the United Nations Mission in Liberia for the Period from 1 July 2007 to 30 June 2008.*
39 See, e.g. *Report of the Secretary-General on Developments in Guinea-Bissau.*
40 See, e.g. UN Doc. A/61/716 (25 January 2007), *Performance Report on the Budget of the United Nations Operation in Burundi for the Period from 1 July 2005 to 30 June 2006.*
41 See, e.g. UN Doc. A/60/645 (30 July 2007), *Performance Report on the Budget of the United Nations Mission in Liberia for the Period from 1 July 2004 to 30 June 2005.*
42 Sannerholm *et al.*, *Rule of Law Assistance in Africa.*
43 See UN Inter-Agency Team on National Capacity Development, *United Nations Guidance Note for Effective Use and Development of National Capacity in Post-conflict Contexts* (29 July 2013).
44 UN Doc. A/66/311–S/2011/527 (19 August 2011), *Civilian Capacity in the Aftermath of Conflict.*
45 *UN Guidance Note for Effective Use and Development of National Capacity in Post-conflict Contexts*, p. 3.
46 See, e.g. UN Secretary-General, *Policy on UN Transitions in the Context of Mission Drawdown or Withdrawal* (4 February 2013).
47 UN Doc. A/66/340 (12 October 2011), *Review of Arrangements for Funding and Back-stopping Special Political Missions*, p. 10. Special political missions have started to benefit from the ability to receive support from the UN Peacebuilding Fund: see *United Nations Political Missions: Report of the Secretary-General* (2013).
48 UN Organization Mission in the Democratic Republic of the Congo.
49 See *Policy on UN Transitions*; and for recent UN transition experiences, see Megan Price and Lina Titulaer, *Beyond Transitions: UNDP's Role before, during and after UN Mission Withdrawal* (The Hague, Netherlands Institute of International Relations, Clingendael, 2013).
50 Astri Suhrke, Torunn Wimpelmann and Marcia Dawes, *Peace Processes and State-building: Economic and Institutional Provisions of Peace Agreements* (Bergen, Chr. Michelsen Institute, 2007), pp. 23–4.
51 World Bank, *World Development Report: Conflict, Security, and Development* (Washington, DC, 2011). See also Dough Porter, Deborah Isser and Louis Alexander-Berg, 'The Justice–Security–Development Nexus: Theory and Practice in Fragile and Conflict Affected States' (2013) 5(2) *Hague Journal on the Rule of Law* 310–18, on the importance of addressing justice grievances and not justice sector problems.
52 *Rule-of-Law Tools for Post-conflict States: Mapping the Justice Sector*, p. 14.
53 UN Doc. A/66/749 (16 March 2012), *Delivering Justice: Programme of Action to Strengthen the Rule of Law at the National and International levels*, pp. 8ff.
54 Ibid.
55 UN Doc. S/PRST/2011/4 (11 February 2011), *Statement by the President of the Security Council.*
56 Jones and Kavanagh, *Shaky Foundations*, p. 61, though over the years the DPKO and UNDP have attempted to enhance their joint programming: see UN Doc. A/66/133

(8 August 2011), *Strengthening and Coordinating United Nations Rule of Law Activities*, p. 17.

57 *Inventory: United Nations Capacity in Peacebuilding*, pp. 9f.

58 DPKO and DFS, *Peace: Keep It. Build It.* (2011), p. 15.

59 Jones and Kavanagh, *Shaky Foundations*, pp. 63–4. See also *United Nations Integrated Mission Planning Process (IMPP) Guidelines Endorsed by the Secretary-General* (13 June 2006).

8 Human rights *vis-à-vis* the rule of law

Unruly cousin or bedrock of the family?

Annemarie Devereux[1]

> Whereas it is essential, if man is not to be compelled to have recourse, as a last resort, to rebellion against tyranny and oppression, that human rights should be protected by the rule of law.
>
> Universal Declaration of Human Rights (1948)

> [We note] with deep regret and concern the systematic violations of human rights and fundamental freedoms and the general absence of rule of law in the Congo.
>
> United Nations Security Council Resolution 161 (1961)

Introduction

The inter-linkages between human rights and rule of law (ROL) have long been recognised within United Nations (UN) documents, even if the precise relationship between the two concepts has not always been clear. The first excerpt above, from the Universal Declaration of Human Rights (UDHR),[2] envisages human rights being protected by the ROL. The second excerpt, from UN Security Council (UNSC) Resolution 161 (1961) concerning the Congo,[3] contains the first reference to the ROL to be found in a UNSC resolution. Varying interpretations might be given to its expression of concern with 'the systematic violations of human rights and fundamental freedoms and the general absence of the rule of law in the Congo'. Human rights might be seen as part of the ROL, separate from the ROL or, alternatively, intersecting with the ROL.

The exact relationship between human rights and the ROL continues to be debated within the academic community. In this chapter I argue that human rights are critical to the conceptualisation, design and implementation of effective rule-of-law assistance, as illustrated by the policies and practice of UN peace missions[4] in such areas as transitional justice, constitutional assistance and broader technical assistance in the rule-of-law space. At the same time, challenges remain at both the conceptual and operational levels. The chapter concludes by suggesting some steps that could be taken to optimise the coherence and effectiveness of this human rights-based approach to the ROL.

1 Human rights and the rule of law within the academic discourse

The place (if any) of human rights within the concept of the 'rule of law' is vigorously contested. Historically, the concept of the ROL was employed primarily to evaluate legal systems operating within particular domestic country settings. Yet it has come to be applied also in discussions of actions at an international level. While many theorists and practitioners agree on some core principles of the ROL, there remains no one agreed definition. Indeed, the ROL concept tends to be used in a manner that might be variously described as reflexive and fluid, aspirational and pragmatic. In exploring the ROL, some legal philosophers have sought to explain how power relations should be governed in a nation, while others have been concerned to establish the superiority of a particular legal system.[5] In the area of international assistance, the increasing usage of rule-of-law programmes in blueprints for action has led one commentator to compare the ROL to a 'product sold on late night television', in which the ROL is 'touted as able to accomplish everything from improving human rights to enabling economic growth to helping win the war on terror'.[6] Notwithstanding critiques that the concept remains undefined and ubiquitous, most commentators accept the ROL as an important foundational concept for states.[7]

Within academia, the place of substantive human rights guarantees remains a particular friction point between those advocating a 'thin', primarily procedural, definition of the ROL, focusing on the establishment and operation of rule-of-law institutions/systems, and those proposing a 'thick' definition incorporating qualitative notions such as consistency with human rights.[8] Balakrishnan Rajagopal's concern about the relationship between the two concepts is quite distinct: seeing ROL discourse as coming to be a 'convenient substitute for human rights', used to avoid the transformative and emancipatory implications of human rights themselves.[9]

While debate concerning the place of human rights *vis-à-vis* the ROL continues to rage, UN doctrine and practice has embraced human rights as being at the heart of the ROL. The results, examined further in Section 2 of this chapter, suggest that it would be artificial and counterproductive to attempt to divorce the concepts, and that explicitly basing rule-of-law assistance programmes on human rights law and standards provides a strong foundation for such programmes.

2 Current UN definitions and policies

The key definition of the ROL used by the UN is that found in the 2004 report of the UN Secretary-General (UNSG) to the UNSC entitled *The Rule of Law and Transitional Justice in Conflict and Post-conflict Societies*.[10] Acknowledging the multiplicity of definitions in existence, this report presented an understanding of the ROL as:

> *a principle of governance* in which all persons, institutions and entities, public and private, including the State itself, are accountable to laws that

> are publicly promulgated, equally enforced and independently adjudicated, and *which are consistent with international human rights norms and standards*.[11]

The report elaborated supportive measures also required by the ROL:

> It requires, as well, measures to ensure adherence to the principles of supremacy of law, equality before the law, accountability to the law, fairness in the application of the law, separation of powers, participation in decision-making, legal certainty, avoidance of arbitrariness and procedural and legal transparency.[12]

Human rights are thus integrated into the very definition of the ROL, and are visible (or implicit) in the supportive measures through references to, for example, equality before the law, accountability, fairness and participation. Under this approach, the ROL is to be regarded as more than a set of functioning institutions such as the courts or criminal justice-related institutions.[13] The ROL potentially relates just as much to ensuring that laws regulating protests comply with human rights standards, as it does to having clear, public laws on a particular subject.

The UNSG has continued to submit reports on the ROL, with the latest generic report to the UNSC dating from 2011.[14] The 2011 UNSG's report on *The Rule of Law and Transitional Justice in Conflict and Post-conflict Societies* explicitly incorporates human rights issues within its discussion of the ROL, with coverage of such areas as transitional justice and accountability for grave human rights violations, children's rights and women's rights.[15] By analysing the human rights of stateless persons as part of rule-of-law work and promoting dialogue on the realisation of family and land rights, the report also brought some aspects of economic, social and cultural rights into the dialogue. A similar approach has been taken by the UNSG in his reports to the UN General Assembly (UNGA) on *Strengthening and Coordinating United Nations Rule of Law Activities*.[16]

Turning to operational guidance, the increasing integration of human rights within the UN rule-of-law framework is evident in the burgeoning number of texts designed to govern UN rule-of-law activities.[17] The umbrella document containing key policy guidance for all UN actors is the 2008 *Guidance Note of the Secretary-General: UN Approach to Rule of Law Assistance*. The introduction to this note states that '[a]ll human rights, the rule of law and democracy are interlinked and mutually reinforcing'.[18] Indeed, the first 'guiding principle' identified is to base rule-of-law assistance on international norms and standards, in particular international human rights law, international humanitarian law, international criminal law and international refugee law. The note asserts that these 'universally applicable standards' incorporate a legitimacy that 'cannot be said to attach to exported national models reflecting the values or experience of donors and assistance providers'.[19] Thus, there is no cultural cringe to be attached to unashamedly basing assistance on such standards. Specialist human rights standards are cited, such as the Standard Minimum Rules for the Treatment of Prisoners, and the Basic Principles on the Independence of the Judiciary.[20] National human rights bodies and independent commissions on human rights, which are consistent with the Paris Principles, are categorised as rule-of-law institutions.[21] Transitional justice processes and mechanisms also receive explicit attention.[22] The focus given to national ownership and national reform constituencies resonates with recognition of individuals' right of participation in public affairs, and a rights-based approach to development.[23] Particular mention is made of the need to take initiatives aimed at involving those marginalised within a community. Attention is called not only to equal access to justice, but also to a 'system of governance that promotes a culture of legality, legal empowerment and ensures the public is aware of and educated in the full range of its rights and responsibilities'.[24] Thus the 2008 Guidance Note incorporates what might be termed a human rights-based approach to the ROL.

3 UN practice: the contribution of a human rights-based approach in select areas

In practice, human rights can and do make a difference to rule-of-law programming. Taking a human rights-based approach is not necessarily going to make the UN popular in all instances, but it does assist the UN with devising informed, principled programmes that can contribute to the long-term strengthening of the ROL. Without limiting the areas of contribution, I would draw attention to the role of a human rights perspective in shaping responses to six questions. First, *why* the UN is providing assistance in this field. Second, *who* to speak to in the course of planning and implementing programmes. Third, *what* initiatives to carry out and what standards to use to assess/evaluate institutions, laws and programmes. Fourth, *when* to provide particular assistance. Fifth, *where* to focus energy. And sixth, *how* to carry out activities.

There is myriad subject matter to choose from in relation to the world of 'human rights and the ROL'. This chapter focuses upon three topics in particular, namely: (1) transitional justice; (2) constitutional processes; and (3) monitoring, training and technical assistance (in relation to human rights). In each area, the impact of a human rights-based approach is highlighted, leading to the conclusion that it would be artificial to segregate human rights from the conceptualisation and implementation of rule-of-law assistance programmes.

3.1 Transitional justice

'Transitional justice' in this context is an umbrella term used to refer to both judicial and non-judicial mechanisms that assist a country to address, recover and move forward from a period of gross human rights violations. It is intended to cover the full range of potential initiatives, including investigations and prosecutions, truth-seeking initiatives, reparations programmes and institutional reform.[25] As the UNSG's 2011 report on the *Rule of Law and Transitional Justice in Conflict and Post-conflict Societies* noted, appropriate transitional justice initiatives help to nurture or rebuild eroded trust in the system of governance and law following conflict, including through promoting accountability.[26] Conversely, if transitional justice takes place outside the rule-of-law framework, it can undermine other efforts within the rule-of-law area. The issue arises most prominently in relation to holding persons accountable for international crimes through the instigation of investigations and prosecutions. To state it baldly, how can you re-establish trust in a justice system if that system does not deal equally with all? How can you expect respect for a legal system that prosecutes a murderer today, but does not hold someone responsible for crimes against humanity that caused hundreds of deaths last year? As the then UN High Commissioner for Human Rights, Navi Pillay, stated at the UNGA:

> Judicial training workshops, co-mentoring judges and lawyers and assisting in the reform of the criminal procedure code will only make a difference when the State takes seriously its legal obligations to meaningfully investigate and punish past and ongoing crimes and atrocities.[27]

At a policy level, the 2010 *Guidance Note of the Secretary-General: UN Approach to Transitional Justice* adopts a human rights- and victim-centric approach to transitional justice. Baseline standards are drawn from international human rights, humanitarian and criminal laws and the guidance provided in soft-law instruments.[28] Certain 'red lines' are also identified. For example, the UN will not endorse provisions in peace agreements that include amnesties for genocide, war crimes, crimes against humanity and (other) gross violations of human rights.[29] Nor will it establish or provide assistance to tribunals that impose the death penalty.[30] Equipping UN mediators with relevant human rights and transitional justice expertise is identified as a key action to assist with the integration of human rights into peace processes.[31]

Adopting a human rights-based approach within this work affects the content of advocacy and assistance in relation to both process and substance. First, a human rights-based approach underlines the importance of national consultations, so that the affected community, in particular victims of violations, can voice their opinions about appropriate transitional justice initiatives. Thus in several countries, such as Afghanistan, Burundi, Guinea, Nepal, Tunisia and Uganda, the UN has assisted with the design and implementation of consultation programmes.

Second, a human rights-based approach supports a holistic approach to transitional justice, emphasising the plurality of measures needed to 'come to terms with a legacy of large-scale past abuses, in order to ensure accountability, serve justice and achieve reconciliation'.[32] Transitional justice mechanisms are viewed as complementary, rather than mutually exclusive. The choice to work on truth-seeking (for example through a Truth and Reconciliation Commission (TRC)) should not preclude the pursuit of prosecutions, or vice versa. An emphasis on victims' rights to truth, justice and reparations inevitably extends the focus of efforts beyond traditional rule-of-law institutions to, for instance, truth commissions and reparations programmes.

While respecting the importance of states developing transitional justice mechanisms that fit their national context, the UN plays a particular role in advocating compliance with international norms and standards and promoting this comprehensive approach to transitional justice. Human rights officers in OHCHR field presences,[33] for instance, are often engaged in providing assistance in relation to prosecutions, truth seeking, reparations and institutional reform. Assistance is provided to national actors investigating and prosecuting international crimes and other gross human rights violations, by sharing material from investigations (where this can be done without infringing confidentiality or endangering witnesses).[34] Technical assistance is often commonly provided with respect to establishing relevant legal frameworks and programmes (e.g. laws dealing with international crimes, or victim and witness protection systems) and specialist advice provided with respect to topics such as the integration of women and children's rights.

In some cases, assistance extends to providing personnel to work with national authorities. The UN, for instance, played a significant role in assisting prosecutions of persons named by the 2006 UN Independent Special Commission of Inquiry for Timor-Leste by providing funding for an international prosecutor.[35] In the Democratic Republic of the Congo (DRC), the UN's Joint Human Rights Office has provided personnel for Joint Investigation Teams to gather information that will assist in the opening of criminal investigations and prosecutions.[36] Human rights field presences have also been involved in providing cooperation to international and hybrid tribunals. In recent years, referrals to the International Criminal Court (ICC) have attracted particular controversy, yet where a state fails to act or its efforts show that it is unwilling or unable to properly investigate and prosecute international crimes, international justice has an important role to play.

Truth and Reconciliation Commissions are the most common form of national strategy for seeking truth following conflict. They allow for a much broader investigation into the causes of a conflict, the nature of violations, the needs of victims and the means of institutional reform than the criminal justice system alone permits.[37] From a human rights perspective, it is important to consider whether the conditions are ripe for a TRC (particularly whether violence has ended and there is sufficient security for witnesses, as well as adequate community and government support for a Commission).[38] A prospective TRC should also be established in accordance with international standards, including with respect to the TRC's terms of reference, mandate and powers, and selection process for Commissioners.[39] Recent contexts in which technical assistance has been provided in relation to the design and/or functioning of truth commissions include Brazil, Honduras and Côte d'Ivoire, or in relation to the follow-up of commission's reports, Togo.[40]

The provision of reparations to victims of human rights violations is one of the most neglected topics in state rule-of-law schemes, often due to concerns about the financial implications of reparations schemes.[41] OHCHR's work focuses on respect for victims' right to a remedy. Its programmes stress, *inter alia*, the need to consult with victims in relation to the design and roll-out of any scheme, usage of an appropriate definition of victims, the integration of gender considerations,[42] and the need for any scheme to be developed and implemented transparently.

The UN is increasingly involved in mobilising funding for reparation programmes. In Sierra Leone, for instance, the human rights component of the United Nations Integrated Office in Sierra Leone (UNIOSIL) was a member of the government-organised reparations taskforce. It also supported an application to the UN Peacebuilding Fund that allowed the reparations programme to commence. In the DRC, the UN High Commissioner for Human Rights deployed a High-level Panel to hear directly from victims of sexual violence about their needs and their perceptions of remedies available to them.[43]

The nature of institutional reform necessary to respond to the violations that have occurred and to prevent repetition will vary from context to context. It might include, for instance, embedding civilian control over the military or strengthening accountability mechanisms, including the courts. In many cases, there may be a need to vet those exercising public power to exclude officials who perpetrated human rights or humanitarian law violations. The United Nations Stabilization Mission in Haiti (MINUSTAH), for instance, undertook a comprehensive vetting exercise as part of a broader programme of police reform. Between 2006 and 2010, MINUSTAH personnel completed 3,500 background checks of police and handed the information over to national authorities. Vetting resumed in 2011 following the interruption caused by the earthquake and the damage to the vetting database.[44] In this context the concern of a human rights approach is twofold. First, accurate human rights information is necessary in order to carry out the substantive vetting inquiry. At the same time, however, a human rights perspective helps to ensure due process to those involved.

3.2 Constitutional processes

If it is decided that a new constitution is needed,[45] the process for developing an appropriate constitution is often critical for human rights protection. The constitution-making process prompts dialogue about the nature of governmental power, the constraints on that power and the community's expectations of one of the key determinants of the relationship between the government and individuals, namely human rights.

The 2009 *Guidance Note of the Secretary-General: United Nations Assistance to Constitution-making Processes* (2009) explicitly exhorts UN actors to encourage compliance with international human rights and other norms and standards.[46] It unambiguously states:

> The UN should be the advocate of the standards it has helped to develop. Accordingly, the UN should engage national actors in a dialogue over

> substantive issues, and explain the country's obligations under international law and the ways in which they could be met in the constitution.[47]

In directing UN officials to speak out about human rights-related issues associated with a constitution, it provides authority for strong advocacy and combats an occasional hesitancy from senior UN officials motivated by fear of 'interfering' with a sensitive sovereign process. The document does not state who should engage in the advocacy and the task often falls to OHCHR/the High Commissioner for Human Rights or other specialised agencies to raise human rights questions, particularly those deemed 'sensitive'. Recent contexts in which OHCHR has advocated inclusion or consistency with international norms include Egypt, Fiji, Libya, Somalia and Tunisia.[48]

The Guidance Note is also important for its stress on supporting inclusivity, participation and transparency.[49] UN human rights field officers are increasingly promoting 'participatory constitutionalism', that is, a process which is open to the participation of all, but explicitly acknowledges and seeks to address pre-existing marginalisation and discrimination on bases such as sex, race, age and disability. For instance, concrete steps towards participatory constitutionalism that the author has been involved in vary from advocacy for outreach activities by the Constituent Assembly in Timor-Leste to hosting key conferences to bring together decision-makers and civil society actors to discuss human rights matters in Timor-Leste and Nepal.

3.3 Monitoring, training and the provision of technical assistance

In order to develop properly targeted assistance within the rule-of-law sphere, it is vital to have solid analyses of gaps and weaknesses in the existing system. These assist with the planning of interventions, as well as the monitoring of the effectiveness of assistance provided. Human rights standards offer a helpful normative framework for assessing the functioning and impact of institutions, including traditional rule-of-law institutions. For instance, human rights components of UN missions regularly monitor police practices in relation to detention and the use of force, court proceedings, correctional services and the state's response to alleged human rights violations (including any alleged discriminatory application of laws and programmes). The importance of human rights indicators in this assessment process for the justice sector is reflected in OHCHR and DPKO's joint work in developing UN Rule of Law Indicators to measure the progress of institutions of criminal justice in post-conflict states.[50]

Monitoring generally leads to both formal and informal dialogue with national authorities, as well as public reporting, which also catalyses further pressure for change.[51] On a daily basis, UN human rights officers monitor many aspects of rule-of-law institutions and raise concerns directly with authorities. To take the example of criminal justice systems, human rights officers monitor such issues as the arbitrary detention of persons, torture or ill-treatment, access to lawyers, unfair trials and inhumane conditions of detention. In some cases the effect of monitoring and public reporting is immediately apparent. In 2011 the human rights component of the United Nations Assistance Mission in Afghanistan (UNAMA) released a report on the treatment of conflict-related detainees by the National Directorate of Security (NDS) and Afghan National Police (ANP). As a result, the Afghan Government and the International Security Assistance Force (ISAF) made changes to their policies, including introducing a system for tracking detainees handed over by ISAF to the Government. The Government also established an internal oversight commission of the NDS.[52]

In keeping with an emphasis on ensuring feedback from affected communities, in some contexts UN human rights components support 'grass roots feedback' on the justice system. From 2011, the United Nations Integrated Peacebuilding Office in Sierra Leone (UNIPSIL) Human Rights and Rule of Law Section sponsored justice coordination fora at the district level that allowed those involved in the justice sector (whether government representatives, lawyers or civil society) to raise concerns and propose responsive strategies. The problems that have been addressed through these fora include the ill-treatment of detainees and the inaccurate determination (sometimes deliberate inflating) of the ages of those accused, thus leading to the inappropriate treatment of minors.[53]

Taking a human rights-based approach to rule-of-law technical assistance means prioritising the reform of laws, institutions and programmes that have a particular impact on individuals' human rights. Law reform-related advice might be given, for instance, in the fields of criminal law, family law, inheritance law, the establishment of a national human rights institution and transitional justice, among other topics. In Timor-Leste, the human rights component of various missions have provided critical advice on shaping human rights-friendly police standard operating procedures, and in advocating more rigorous systems of accountability. Most UN mission human rights components also provide training on international human rights standards to officials such as judges, lawyers, police, corrections staff, parliamentarians and national human rights commissioners, as well as civil society representatives.

4 Addressing outstanding challenges

Significant progress has been made in integrating human rights into UN rule-of-law discourse and practice, yet a number of challenges remain. This section offers reflections on steps that might be taken to strengthen the UN's policy coherence and operational effectiveness.

4.1 Avoiding the reduction of rule-of-law conceptualisation to institutional programming

The temptation to treat the 'rule of law' as a purely technical task involving specific institutional strengthening programmes must be resisted. The emphasis on institutional mandates in recent years has been understandable, given the desire to improve coordination between UN actors.[54] However, in the long term, it will be important for the UN to retain the holistic approach to the ROL embodied in the 2004 UNSG's report,[55] and so encourage greater awareness of the interlinking features of a properly functioning ROL. This includes paying attention to the oft-neglected topic of the 'rule of law culture',[56] through instituting specific programmes to bolster a shared belief that power should be constrained by predetermined laws and processes.

4.2 Accepting the need for prioritising, sequencing and incremental change while retaining the commitment to human rights

In any country context where ROL challenges are great, but resources are limited, change is likely to be incremental. Prioritising and sequencing of actions to fit the evolving situation will be necessary. However, recognising the need for gradual, planned action does not necessarily equate to abandoning the more substantive notion of the ROL.[57] In particular, it does not mean that human rights considerations should be deferred until 'a later time'. To take a concrete example: if a state was rehabilitating the justice sector (re-opening courthouses and managing case-loads) in circumstances where it had resources to support only 50 per cent of cases, preference could still be given to a plan that re-opened half of the courts initially, rather than limiting the courts to hearing certain types of cases (such as only criminal justice matters, and not family law matters, an outcome likely to have a particular gendered impact).

4.3 Addressing nervousness around the political sensitivities in the human rights field

Undoubtedly, highlighting gaps in a country's human rights practice and calling for reform can create tensions with national authorities. Perceived political sensitivities around human rights topics may engender a certain nervousness among officials. However, failure to speak out about human rights issues itself risks the long-term impact of the UN's rule-of-law assistance programmes, and is inconsistent with abiding UN principles. The leadership and staff of peace missions should be encouraged to take further initiatives to strengthen the shared commitment to human rights. But they should also be assured that they will enjoy the necessary institutional backing to take 'difficult' stances.

4.4 Ensuring access to human rights information

Gaining an accurate picture of the human rights situation in a particular country context is vital for informed UN action. The involvement of human rights actors in teams conducting initial and periodic assessments and planning exercises is thus to be welcomed. In relation to the UNSC in particular (given this volume's focus on its operations), there are further initiatives that could be taken to strengthen access to relevant information to help inform deliberations. For instance, the UN High Commissioner for Human Rights could be given a standing invitation to address the UNSC in both formal and informal deliberations. In addition, greater use could be made of the reports of International Commissions of Inquiry – including integrating recommendations/follow-up of the reports into ongoing UNSC considerations of country contexts.

4.5 Expanding consideration of human rights matters in rule-of-law initiatives

The UNSC might give consideration to expanding its scope of action with respect to human rights matters. One topic noted earlier in this chapter as oft-neglected by the UNSC in its resolutions is that of victims' rights to reparation for human rights violations. While the UNSC has referred to the need for reparations in some cases,[58] it is not a regular feature of resolutions.

The more active law-making role the UNSC has employed in other contexts might be considered in relation to situations of egregious human rights violations. To take a somewhat controversial example, it is interesting to ask whether the UNSC might be convinced to take similar steps as it has in the context of counter-terrorism. Looking at the terms of UNSC Resolution 1373,[59] for instance, is it possible to envisage the UNSC appealing to member states to: ratify human rights treaties; investigate and prosecute those responsible for egregious violations; cooperate with each other in relation to investigations; and refrain from providing safe haven to those responsible for violations?[60]

4.6 Ensuring application of human rights principles in all aspects of UN operations

In order to be effective in its human rights and rule-of-law operations, it is critical that the UN can speak from a position of credibility. The handling of topics such as sexual exploitation and abuse by peacekeepers or UN civilian staff and the operationalisation of its Human Rights Due Diligence Policy for support to non-UN security forces are of particular importance in this field. It is likewise important for inter-governmental bodies, including the UNSC, to act in accordance with human rights principles, including due process, in deciding how to exercise their powers.

5 Conclusion

UN discourse and practice has adopted a substantive view of the ROL that sees human rights as a means of judging whether the ROL exists. While much UN rule-of-law work focuses on traditional rule-of-law institutions such as the police, courts and prisons, there are signs of a broadening approach (for example, through embracing a holistic approach to transitional justice including truth commissions and reparation schemes). Debate may usefully continue regarding issues such as the appropriate rule-of-law architecture and the appropriate sequencing of rule-of-law initiatives. However, it would be counterproductive to suggest that UN rule-of-law work could be divorced from a human rights perspective. Human rights provide the basis for how to look at an effective operating justice system, as well as more broadly, the exercise of power by institutions that enjoy the trust of the community and exercise their power in accordance with agreed pre-determined limits. While the sensitivity of some human rights topics means that some actors might still see human rights as an 'unruly cousin', increasingly there is recognition within the UN that human rights form a vital part of the bedrock for effective rule-of-law assistance.

Notes

1 This chapter was revised when the author was a visitor at the Centre for International Governance and Justice, ANU, and at the Faculty of Law, QUT.
2 *Universal Declaration of Human Rights*, adopted by GA Res. 217A/III (10 December 1948), preamble.
3 SC Res. 161 (21 February 1961), preamble.
4 In addition to examples from operations involving a peacekeeping component, some examples in this chapter are drawn from political missions administered by either the UN Department of Peacekeeping Operations (DPKO) or the UN Department of Political Affairs (DPA). Within this chapter, examples are drawn primarily from the work of the UN Office of the High Commissioner for Human Rights (OHCHR) field presences, reflecting both the author's familiarity with this work from her professional background, and OHCHR's key responsibility for human rights within the UN system.
5 Dicey, for instance, whose conception of the ROL is widely quoted, was concerned to demonstrate the superiority of the English system over French constitutionalism. Dicey proposed three elements for the ROL, namely (1) that government is based upon and abides by law (as opposed to the exercise of wide, arbitrary or discretionary powers of constraint); (2) that all are subject (equally) to the law (administered by the courts); and (3) that courts will be the bodies to determine rights: see Albert V. Dicey, *Introduction to the Study of the Law of the Constitution* (London, Macmillan, 1915), chapter IV.
6 Rachel Kleinfeld, 'Competing Definitions of the Rule of Law', in Thomas Carothers (ed.), *Promoting the Rule of Law Abroad: In Search of Knowledge* (Washington, DC, Carnegie Endowment for International Peace, 2006), pp. 31–74, 31.
7 Note, for instance, Michael Oakeshott's pithy statement:

> The rule of law breaks no bread, it is unable to distribute loaves and fishes (it has none), and it cannot protect itself against external assault, but it remains the most civilized and least burdensome conception of a state yet to be devised.

Quoted by Kleinfeld, 'Competing Definitions', p. 31.
8 Within the Australian context, contrast the views of Charles Sampford, 'Reconceiving the Rule of Law for a Globalising World', in Spencer Zifcak (ed.), *Globalisation and the Rule of Law* (London, Routledge, 2005), pp. 9–31, with those of Spencer Zifcak, 'Globalizing the Rule of Law: Rethinking Values and Reforming Institutions', in the same volume at pp. 32–64. See also Krygier's discussion of the debate over 'thin' and 'thick' concepts of the ROL in his chapter in this collection.
9 Balakrishnan Rajagopal, 'Invoking the Rule of Law: International Discourses', in Agnes Hurwitz and Reyko Huang (eds), *Civil War and the Rule of Law: Security, Development and Human Rights* (Boulder, CO, Lynne Rienner Publishers, 2008), pp. 47–70, 53.
10 UN Doc. S/2004/616 (23 August 2004), *The Rule of Law and Transitional Justice in Conflict and Post-conflict Societies: Report of the Secretary-General* ('2004 UNSG Rule of Law Report').

11 2004 UNSG Rule of Law Report, para. 6 (emphasis added).
12 Ibid.
13 In practice, there is often a tendency for 'rule-of-law institutions' to be equated with criminal justice-related institutions, though see, for instance, the *Guidance Note of the Secretary-General: UN Approach to Rule of Law Assistance* (April 2008) ('Guidance Note on Rule of Law Assistance'), which refers *inter alia* to 'Institutions of justice, governance, security and human rights', p. 1.
14 In 2013 the UNSG submitted a report to the UNSC on the ROL, but it was more specific in nature: See UN Doc. S/2013/341 (11 June 2013), *Measuring the Effectiveness of the Support Provided by the United Nations System for the Promotion of the Rule of Law in Conflict and Post-conflict Situations*.
15 UN Doc. S/2011/634 (12 October 2011), *The Rule of Law and Transitional Justice in Conflict and Post-conflict Societies: Report of the Secretary-General* ('2011 UNSG Rule of Law Report').
16 See UN Doc A/69/181 (24 July 2014), *Strengthening and Coordinating United Nations Rule of Law Activities*.
17 Other examples include guidelines such as documents entitled *Justice Components in UN Peace Operations*, and the *Guidelines on the Methodology for Review of Justice and Corrections Components in UN Peace Operations*.
18 Guidance Note on Rule of Law Assistance, 'Introduction', p. 2. The same language appears in, for instance, UN Doc. A/RES/67/1 (30 November 2012), *Declaration of the High-level Meeting of the General Assembly on the Rule of Law at the National and International Levels*, para. 5.
19 Guidance Note on Rule of Law Assistance, p. 2. See, too, Guiding Principle 4, which addresses advancing human rights and gender justice.
20 Ibid., p. 5.
21 Ibid., p. 6. The Paris Principles refer to the *Principles Relating to the Status of National Institutions*, adopted by GA Res. 48/134 (20 December 1993).
22 Ibid., p. 7.
23 For a useful guide on this topic, see UN Doc. HR/PUB/06/8, OHCHR, *Frequently Asked Questions on a Human Rights-based Approach to Development Co-operation* (New York and Geneva, United Nations, 2006).
24 Ibid.
25 2004 UNSG Rule of Law Report, para. 8; *Guidance Note of the Secretary-General: United Nations Approach to Transitional Justice* (March 2010) ('Guidance Note on Transitional Justice'), pp. 7–10.
26 2011 UNSG Rule of Law Report, para. 17.
27 General Assembly Interactive Thematic Debate on the Rule of Law and Global Challenges, New York, 11 April 2011.
28 UN Doc. A/RES/60/147 (21 March 2006), *Basic Principles and Guidelines on the Right to a Remedy and Reparation for Victims of Gross Violations of International Human Rights Law and Serious Violations of International Humanitarian Law*; UN Doc. E/CN.4/2005/102/Add.1 (8 February 2005), *Updated Set of Principles for the Protection and Promotion of Human Rights through Action to Combat Impunity*.
29 Guidance Note on Transitional Justice, p. 4.
30 Ibid. Senior UN officials have also made representations concerning the imposition of the death penalty: note, for instance, the High Commissioner for Human Rights' submission of amicus briefs to the Iraqi High Tribunal: see www.un.org/apps/news/story.asp?NewsID=21147.
31 The role of UN mediators in relation to ensuring parties to a negotiation understand the demands of international law, including on the issue of amnesties, is detailed further in *UN Guidance for Effective Mediation* (New York, United Nations, 2012), pp. 16–17.
32 Guidance Note on Transitional Justice, p. 2.

33 'OHCHR field presence' is used as a generic term to describe the different forms of OHCHR-supported operations, ranging from OHCHR country/stand-alone offices, to components of UN peace missions, to regional offices and human rights advisers, to UN Country Teams. From 2006 to 2012, OHCHR was designated as the global 'lead entity' within the UN for transitional justice.
34 This includes sharing information drawn from 'mapping exercises', such as those conducted by OHCHR in the DRC and Nepal and regular field investigations. Information from international commissions of inquiry can also assist national and international prosecutions.
35 UNMIT did note, however, that progress had been slow in relation to the prosecutions: as of January 2012, seven cases had proceeded to final judgment, with another four cases closed. UN Doc. S/2012/43 (18 January 2012), *Report of the Secretary-General on the United Nations Integrated Mission in Timor-Leste*, para. 33.
36 Support was also provided for court hearings, with Congolese courts in 2011 delivering 276 judgments, leading to 22 convictions for serious crimes under international law, including war crimes and crimes against humanity: OHCHR Report 2011, p. 55.
37 As to national contexts in which OHCHR has been active in assisting truth commissions, see OHCHR Report 2011, pp. 56–7.
38 UN Doc. HR/PUB/06/1 (2008), *Rule of Law Tools for Post-conflict States: Truth Commissions*, p. 2.
39 Ibid., particularly parts II and III. See also UN Doc. A/HRC/24/42 (28 August 2013), *Report of the Special Rapporteur on the Promotion of Truth, Justice, Reparation and Guarantees of Non-recurrence, Pablo de Greiff*, part IV.
40 OHCHR Report 2013, p. 44.
41 De Greiff has concluded that the international community rarely provides significant resources for reparations schemes because of a view that reparations should not be the equivalent of a (victims of) crime insurance scheme, but instead need to be linked to acknowledged responsibility for the violations: Pablo de Greiff, 'Addressing the Past: Reparations for Gross Human Rights Abuses', in Agnes Hurwitz and Reyko Huang (eds), *Civil War and the Rule of Law: Security, Development and Human Rights* (Boulder, CO, Lynne Rienner Publishers, 2008), pp. 163–92, 182.
42 For a useful outline of key considerations concerning reparations, see UN Doc. HR/PUB/08/1 (2008), *Rule of Law Tools for Post-conflict States: Reparations Programmes*.
43 OHCHR Report 2011, p. 57. As to the pilot project on access to justice, reparations and remedies for victims of sexual violence in South Kivu, see OHCHR Report 2012, p. 69.
44 *UN Police Magazine*, January 2012, p. 10.
45 See Michele Brandt, Jill Cottrell, Yash Ghai and Anthony Regan, *Constitution Making and Reform: Options for the Process* (New York, Interpeace, 2011), p. 36, on the importance of asking whether a new constitution is needed.
46 *Guidance Note of the Secretary-General: United Nations Assistance to Constitution-making Processes* (2009) ('Guidance Note on Constitution Making'), p. 4.
47 Ibid.
48 OHCHR Report 2013, p. 32.
49 Guidance Note on Constitution Making, p. 4.
50 The UN Rule of Law indicators are available online: www.un.org/en/events/peacekeepersday/2011/publications/un_rule_of_law_indicators.pdf.
51 For a recent study of the impact of monitoring activities, see Liam Mahony and Roger Nash, *Influence on the Ground: Understanding and Strengthening the Protection Impact of United Nations Human Rights Field Presences* (Brewster, MA, Fieldview Solutions, 2012).
52 OHCHR Report 2011, p. 51. As to the further follow-up on the UNAMA report, see OHCHR Report 2012, p. 35, and OHCHR Report 2013, p. 34.
53 OHCHR Report 2011, p. 51. See further, *2gether: Joint Newsletter of the UN Joint*

Vision Programme 2: Access to Justice and Human Rights (Sierra Leone, December 2011), p. 4.

54 In relation to the focus on reforming the institutional arrangements for reform of the ROL, see UN Doc. S/2013/341 (11 June 2013), *Measuring the Effectiveness of the Support Provided by the United Nations for the Promotion of the Rule of Law in Conflict and Post-conflict Situations*, paras 11–19.

55 2004 UNSG Rule of Law Report.

56 See Jane Stromseth, David Wippman and Rosa Brooks, *Can Might Make Rights? Building the Rule of Law after Military Interventions* (New York, Cambridge University Press, 2006), p. 310; Thomas Carothers, 'The Rule of Law Revival', in Thomas Carothers (ed.), *Promoting the Rule of Law Abroad: In Search of Knowledge* (Washington, DC, Carnegie Endowment for International Peace, 2006), pp. 3–14, 12; Rachel Kleinfeld, *Advancing the Rule of Law Abroad: Next Generation Reform* (Washington, DC, Carnegie Endowment for International Peace, 2012), pp. 90–107; Annemarie Devereux, 'Strengthening the Rule of Law in Post-Conflict Societies: Is it time to Jettison the Lawyers?', ANZSIL Annual Conference, 28–30 June 2007 (copy on file with author).

57 The suggestion that the UN abandon the 'thick' approach to the ROL in most post-conflict environments has been made, for instance, by Camino Kavanagh and Bruce Jones, *Shaky Foundations: An Assessment of the UN's Rule of Law Support Agenda* (New York, NYU Center on International Cooperation, 2011), p. 7.

58 In relation to the DRC in 2000, the UNSC expressed the view that the Governments of Uganda and Rwanda should make reparations for the loss of life and property damage they had inflicted on the civilian population in Kisangani, and requested the UNSG to submit an assessment of the damage as a basis for such reparations: SC Res. 1304 (16 June 2000), para. 14. In relation to Timor-Leste, the UNSC encouraged national authorities to make further progress in finalising draft laws on reparations: SC Res. 2037 (23 February 2012), preamble.

59 SC Res. 1373 (28 September 2001).

60 For further consideration of this and other steps that the UNSC might take, see Annemarie Devereux, 'Strengthening Human Rights Policy Coherence within Security Council Approaches to the Rule of Law: Recommendations for Action', Working Paper No. 6.3, Regulatory Institutions Network (Canberra, ANU, 2012).

9 The UN and 'rule-of-law constitutions'

Laura Grenfell

> I do think it would be helpful to get the United Nations in to help write a constitution [for Iraq].... I mean, they're good at that.
>
> George W. Bush, September 2003[1]

Introduction

Should the United Nations (UN) assist post-conflict states in writing their constitutions? If so, how? In 2012 the UN boasted that it was 'assisting 150 Member States on various aspects of the rule of law, ranging from advice and assistance in constitution-making processes to reforming justice and security institutions'.[2] This suggests that a shift has taken place at the UN. As recently as 1999, when the UN Security Council (UNSC) outlined the mandate for the UN Transitional Administration in East Timor (UNTAET), there was no specific mention of a constitution-making process or the rule of law (ROL).[3] Yet since 2011 the UNSC has specifically added rule-of-law promotion and constitution-making assistance to mission mandates, such as those regarding South Sudan and Libya.[4] This shift implies that the UN is no longer concerned that such assistance may be perceived as constituting interference with the sovereign affairs of post-conflict states.[5] Indeed, in 2009 the UN Secretary-General (UNSG) published a Guidance Note on constitutional assistance to post-conflict states, which formally articulated the UN's policy guiding this form of assistance.[6] This built on a 2008 Guidance Note, which explained the UN's approach to promoting the ROL.[7]

This chapter explores the extent to which the UN is able to offer constructive constitutional assistance to post-conflict and transitional states. It begins by examining the two UN Guidance Notes that recommend a set of processes and ingredients, such as international human rights and international humanitarian law norms, which may assist states to ensure that their new constitutions will establish and strengthen the ROL. I refer to the combination of these processes and ingredients as a 'rule-of-law constitution', but this is not to suggest that such constitutions automatically achieve any degree of success in establishing or strengthening the ROL. Drawing on Timor-Leste's experience, the chapter argues that post-conflict states readily adopt 'rule-of-law constitutions' in order to bolster their external legitimacy. It is now more than a decade since Timor-Leste adopted such a constitution to herald its independence, but this post-conflict state is still struggling to establish the ROL.[8] Timor-Leste's experience illustrates that post-conflict constitutions entrenching a raft of international norms may not necessarily assist a state in strengthening the ROL unless they also enjoy internal legitimacy and build national identity by recognising shared national norms.

The chapter concludes by making some suggestions as to how the UN might offer more constructive constitutional assistance to post-conflict states. It argues that if the international community wants to offer constitutional assistance, 'constitution-making' should be reconceptualised to include the long-term process of reconciling international and national norms.

1 UN policy on constitutional assistance and the rule of law

In 2006 the UNSG stated that the ROL was central to the work of the UN[9] and established a Rule of Law Assistance Unit which, among other things, carries out the role of constitutional assistance. In 2009 the unit issued a Guidance Note entitled *UN Assistance to Constitution-making Processes*, which outlined the UN's guiding principles for constitutional assistance. The articulation of a UN policy on constitutional assistance and the ROL was important as the UN had previously taken an ad hoc approach when offering assistance to more than a dozen constitution-making processes, including that of Timor-Leste.[10]

The first guiding principle states that while constitution-making is a 'key opportunity' for peacebuilding in post-conflict states, '[p]riority attention should be given to situations in which UN [constitution-making] assistance will likely strengthen the rule of law and democratic institutions and practices'.[11] This indicates that the UN understands constitution-making as a primary site for rule-of-law promotion, although it acknowledges that not all of its efforts will be constructive. This is reiterated by the UNSG's 2008 Guidance Note entitled *UN Approach to Rule of Law Assistance* which, in its detailing of a framework for strengthening the ROL, gives primary consideration to:

> a constitution [which...] incorporates internationally recognized human rights, provides for their applicability in domestic law ... provides for non-discrimination [...and] the equality of men and women ... limits the powers of government and its various branches ... and empowers an independent and impartial judiciary.[12]

These two policy documents confirm that the main means by which the UN aims to strengthen the ROL through constitution-making is to offer expert advice and access to resources. Furthermore, they can be read as setting out certain ingredients or criteria for a 'rule-of-law constitution', to which post-conflict states in particular should aspire if they wish to avoid a relapse into conflict.

If the UNSG's Guidance Notes are read as mapping the UN's understanding of the recipe for successful constitution-making and consequent rule-of-law promotion, then on its face the UN's involvement with the 2002 Timor-Leste Constitution was a textbook model. The Constitution repeatedly articulates the ROL as a state objective (the preamble, Articles 1 and 6). It also entrenches an extensive bill of rights, including guarantees of equality and non-discrimination, and it enshrines the separation of powers (Article 69) and the independence of the courts and judges (Articles 119 and 121). The Constitution also elevates international law, as a source of law, to a position superior to the laws made by Timor-Leste's own Parliament (Article 9). Furthermore, Article 23 provides that '[f]undamental rights enshrined in the Constitution [...] shall be interpreted in accordance with the *Universal Declaration of Human Rights*'. During the drafting process, Timorese leaders voiced their support for such international norms. For example, Bishop Belo announced: 'It is our dream to build a society founded on the values enshrined in the [UDHR]. These are the values that guided and inspired our struggle for independence.'[13] The then Timorese Foreign Minister José Ramos-Horta added that upon independence, Timor-Leste intended to accede to 'the greatest possible number of international human rights treaties'.[14]

Thus, in terms of substance, Timor-Leste's constitution-making appears successful in laying a foundation for the ROL. Some of this adherence to international human rights standards can be attributed to UN influence, direct and indirect, although there is contention as to the extent of UNTAET's direct influence on the substance of the Constitution.[15] The Constitution's repeated invocation of the ROL can be traced partly to the lusophone constitutional models provided by Portugal and Mozambique. However, the Timor-Leste Constitution goes further by articulating the objective of the Timorese state as being a 'State based on the rule of law' (Article 6), possibly due to the influence of the UN or the World Bank.

2 Adopting 'rule-of-law constitutions' as a means to attaining international legitimacy

What leads post-conflict states to embrace and entrench international norms in their constitutions? One factor may be the genuine belief, on the part of the drafters, that the standards set out by international law can assist the state in establishing the ROL and prevent the state from relapsing into conflict. Another factor is popular demand: for example, constitutional consultations held in Timor-Leste indicated much entrenched support for human rights, particularly the rights of women and minorities. A third factor is the desire of a newly independent state to affirm its legitimacy and sovereignty at the international level, specifically its intent to be part of the international community. According to Barkin, '[s]ince the emergence of the state system, sovereignty has always been seen by the society of states to require a certain constitutional structure'.[16] In other words, states believe that to enjoy external sovereignty in the international community, they are required to establish a certain relationship between the state and its population. Since the Treaty of Westphalia the nature of this relationship has changed, but in the post-Cold War twenty-first century it appears that the dominant norm in this regard involves the limitation of state power by the ROL.

The process of constitution-making is thus in part a matter of establishing external legitimacy. In this sense the international community has indirect influence over constitution-making processes, particularly those of post-conflict states. Barkin observes that '[s]tates' need for certain institutional structures to legitimate themselves [on the international stage] can act as a significant constraint on states' final authority over their internal affairs'.[17] He reasons that:

> States that do not honour dominant constitutional norms, and that as a result are not seen as fully legitimate by the community of states, are likely to be excluded to some degree from regular patterns of discourse within this community.[18]

While Barkin is referring more narrowly to international human rights norms, he could just as easily be referring to broader rule-of-law norms. He notes that to many, 'the international normative structure [...] may look like a form of cultural imperialism, the imposition of Western values internationally'.[19] However, Barkin observes that '*all international normative structures* can be interpreted as having a strong culturally imperialist element'.[20]

The application of Barkin's theory to constitution-making shows that in drafting and adopting 'rule-of-law constitutions', states are acting to shore up their external legitimacy. A 'rule-of-law constitution' has various important international functions: it can signal a break with the state's past; it can ease the process of state recognition or admission into regional bodies;[21] it can facilitate trade relations and aid; and it can flag to foreign investors and international financial organisations that the state is suitable for investment. Barkin's theory underlines the constitutional conformity that is implicitly required by the international community. The UN's 2009 Guidance Note makes these requirements more explicit by effectively setting them out as the ingredients of a 'rule-of-law constitution'.

However, the constitutional embrace of international norms alone does not help a state to establish or strengthen the ROL. Constitutions must also enjoy internal legitimacy. Unlike external legitimacy, which is largely based on whether the substance of a constitution complies with international standards, the internal legitimacy of a constitution relies on both the substance of the constitution and the process of constitution-making. The following section considers the tension in this double-legitimacy act.

3 The challenge of securing internal legitimacy

3.1 The tension in the UN's constitutional-assistance role

The UNSG's Guidance Notes recognise the tension inherent in the UN's role as an international organisation offering constitutional assistance to a sovereign state. While the 2009 Guidance Note reiterates the mantra that constitution-making processes must be 'nationally owned and led', it also shows that the UN believes that it has a role to play in constitutional assistance.[22] The Note describes constitution-making as a 'sovereign national process' and advises that sensitivity is important to avoid the perception of a foreign-imposed constitution.[23] It acknowledges that actors who seek to spoil and delegitimise a constitutional process can too easily characterise the process as a foreign product.

The UN's role, according to the 2009 Guidance Note, is '*to speak out* when a draft constitution does not comply with these [international human rights] standards, especially as they relate to the administration of justice, transitional justice, electoral systems and a range of other constitutional issues'.[24] All of these aspects are related to the ROL. The Note states that 'the UN should engage national actors in a dialogue over the substantive issues'.[25] Thus it can be presumed that the UN would feel compelled to 'speak out' where a drafting body intends to entrench substantive constitutional norms that are incompatible with the version of the ROL it is promoting. Indeed, this has occurred. In late 2012 the UN High Commissioner for Human Rights and a group of other UN human rights experts noted that Egypt's draft Constitution espoused respect for the ROL and human rights principles, while at the same time enshrining Islam as the principal source of legislation. They expressed particular concern regarding the Constitution's lack of substantive anti-discrimination protections, its weak protection of the independence of the judiciary, the absence of a provision incorporating international law into the domestic legal order, and the fact that almost no women were represented in the Constituent Assembly.[26]

The 2009 Guidance Note does not explicitly address situations like that in Egypt, where a state seeks to constitutionally entrench a non-secular normative legal system that is potentially incompatible with the understanding of the ROL set out in the 2009 Guidance Note. Instead it broadly states that UN constitutional assistance must be 'tailored to the specific country context'.[27] In the past there has been some uncertainty about whether systems of customary law are compatible with the modern concept of the ROL, because they can empower non-state actors who are politically unaccountable and draw their legitimacy from custom rather than democratic processes. Furthermore, systems of customary law have been characterised as contrary to international human rights standards, particularly in relation to women's rights, and hence cast as illegitimate. Indeed, in some UN fora, states such as Australia have questioned whether customary law can be considered law.[28]

As this chapter explains below, these attitudes are shifting. However, confusion currently clouds the question of whether the ROL can be considered compatible with *shariah* or Islamic law (a slightly narrower concept than *shariah*). Islamic law and *shariah* are subjected to similar concerns as customary law, relating chiefly to their approach to women's human rights and their empowerment of non-accountable and unelected actors, such as members of the clergy. In addition, the sacred nature of the law under Islam, which does not lend itself to open criticism, and the failure of that law to fully guarantee individual rights call into question its compatibility with the ROL. Further doubt is cast by the fact that it is difficult to identify a single Muslim country that currently can be said to have an effective system incorporating the ROL.[29]

The 2009 Guidance Note recognises that constitution-making presents an 'opportunity to create a common vision of the future of a state'.[30] However, it does not recognise that there may be a schism between the international human rights standards to which most post-conflict states aspire and national normative systems. Constitution-making is partly a process of attempting to identify national norms so as to develop a sense of shared national identity.[31] In many post-conflict or transitional states, these national norms hinge on customary or religious legal normative systems such as *shariah.* The process of state-building can be particularly difficult where the concept of the state has little resonance for many parts of the population. This may be because the state has been oppressive or non-existent. Many individuals may feel a stronger allegiance to other, non-state structures such as customary or religious authorities. The concept of the ROL and its attributes may also be alien, especially where state institutions are weak and non-state institutions are strong. One way for a constitution to enjoy legitimacy with these parts of the population is to articulate the state's relationship with these non-state structures and authorities. This relationship may lead to tensions but these need to be debated and reconciled in non-violent spaces in order to avoid a relapse into conflict.

Constitution-making involves a sensitive process of identity formation. One view is that a successful constitution can ultimately replace other forms of identity, which makes the constitutional articulation of other forms of identity irrelevant.[32] For Fukuyama the US Constitution is an example of this.[33] Another view is that a constitution must include extant traditional elements of collective identity in order to generate its own legitimacy. On this point, von Bogdandy *et al.* observe, '[i]n many environments a strategy of constitutional nation-building deliberately ignoring such [traditional elements of identity] is unlikely to be successful'.[34] They argue 'by incorporating into the constitutional text some of the *traditional elements of collective identity* (such as institutions or symbols), constitutional nation-building is able to filter, formalise, and direct the nation-building process towards democracy and the rule of law'.[35]

Bogdandy *et al.* do not consider the problem of potential incompatibility between these 'traditional elements of collective identity' and the ROL.[36] However, they imply that where a constitution does incorporate these traditional elements, it is more likely to be successful in being able to steer a state towards the ROL because the process of 'filtering' and 'formalising' these traditional elements connects them with the state.

In offering constitutional assistance, the UN must tread carefully in order not to stifle or delegitimise processes by which constitutional drafters identify such 'traditional elements of collective identity', through public consultations, for example, and articulate those elements in the constitutional text. The next section reflects on the UN's experience in assisting Timor-Leste's constitution-making. It argues that the failure of the Timorese constitution-making process to incorporate into the constitutional text sufficient 'traditional elements of collective identity' has, at least at a sociological and cultural level, affected the internal legitimacy of Timor-Leste's Constitution.

3.2 Timor-Leste's experience

The UN policy on constitutional assistance emphasises that the problems of achieving internal legitimacy for constitutions can be overcome if a drafting body follows a proper process that is 'nationally owned and led' and 'inclusive, participatory and transparent'.[37] While the process in Timor-Leste was largely nationally owned and led, it was not particularly inclusive or participatory. One problem was that UNTAET initially imposed an overly short time frame of three to six months for public consultation.[38] In 2001 a coalition of Timorese non-governmental organisations (NGOs) addressed a letter to the UNSC concerning the drafting of the Timorese Constitution. The letter stated:

> A Constitution is a complex document embodying fundamental choices about the type of country an independent East Timor will be. This Constitution has to be a *living document*, which *reflects how the East Timorese as a people see themselves*, relate to each other, and finally, after many centuries, govern themselves....
>
> A three-month process would rob the East Timorese of their right to contribute to the future of their country and it will alienate them from the very *document that should voice their aspirations.*[39]

The limited consultation and the lack of a feeling of local ownership over the process also drew the attention of the UN High Commissioner for Human Rights, who commented:

> [T]here is a popular perception that, to a larger extent, the drafting process has focussed on the prepared drafts of political parties, rather than incorporating comments or suggestions from ongoing consultations or the public hearings. As a result, there appears to be a limited sense of ownership of the process amongst civil society and already a questioning of the responsiveness of the [elected Constituent] Assembly to its constituents.[40]

While Aucoin and Brandt argue that UNTAET's 'overtly hands-off policy' successfully ensured that the UN was not viewed as interfering with the substance of the drafting process,[41] it is documented that UNTAET and the UN High Commissioner for Human Rights did 'speak out' by communicating to the elected drafting body, known as the Constituent Assembly, their concerns on substantive issues such as the absence of an explicit provision guaranteeing security of judicial tenure and the fact that human rights were extended only to citizens rather than to all persons.[42]

Another problem was that the only genuine public consultation process was conducted by the UN, whose findings the elected Constituent Assembly dismissed as illegitimate on the basis that the Assembly did not lead the consultations. In this sense the UN's consultation process did little more than raise the expectations of the population.

The failure of the Constituent Assembly to conduct a proper public consultation process of its own might explain why the Constitution identifies few national norms encapsulating a shared sense of Timorese culture or identity.[43] For example, the Constitution does not mention traditional leaders or give explicit recognition to customary law. This is noteworthy, given that the popular consultations the UN conducted (which the Assembly subsequently delegitimised) indicated that there was strong local support for including aspects of local customary law in the Constitution.[44] Against this backdrop it appears that the drafters of the Constitution made a conscious choice to entrench international norms and ignore local norms. International norms such as social and gender equality, as well as the ROL, enjoy primacy in the Constitution over local *adat* norms, which favour authority based on descent, gender and age.[45]

The Constitution's silence on local norms has arguably weakened its internal legitimacy, which has in turn undermined the establishment of the ROL in Timor-Leste. Timorese academic Trindade claims that many Timorese view the Constitution 'as illegitimate'.[46] He contends that the Constitution is 'a tool of alienation for most East Timorese and does not reflect the needs of the people'.[47] Trindade reports that a traditional elder commented, 'our constitution is not strong here, it must be accepted by all and be blessed by elders – converted into a sacred object (*sasan lulik*) and be part of our culture'.[48] Trindade supports this suggestion that the Constitution be transformed through ritual into a national sacred object.[49] He also recommends the establishment of a council of *luirai* (elders) to ritualise and inaugurate the elected national leaders because, he argues, 'in the eyes of the Timorese [the *luirai*] are still the legitimate leaders'.[50] Trindade's views echo the sentiments of a 2001 women's petition to the Constituent Assembly, which articulated a desire for the Constitution to assist in reconciling the two paradigms of the state and the traditional.[51] Indeed, the Timorese government acknowledges the significant role played by non-state traditional authorities and mechanisms by reporting that 'a substantial proportion of conflicts are addressed through traditional justice mechanisms'.[52] Its desire for a 'special law' to link these non-state mechanisms to the state legal system indicates its understanding of the prevailing and powerful position of these mechanisms and their potential to undermine and destabilise the state's fragile institutions.[53]

It can therefore be argued that for secular government under a 'rule-of-law constitution' to enjoy internal legitimacy in Timor-Leste, the Constitution must connect with the paradigm of ritual, traditional authority. This is not simply a matter of inviting ritual leaders to conduct a few ceremonies. It also requires the creation of a space in which to pursue the process of reconciling the norms promoted by both democratic and traditional leaders. Timor-Leste's experience suggests that the internal legitimacy of 'rule-of-law constitutions' will be undermined where they ignore or sideline non-state structures or authorities that influence the daily lives of large parts of the population. For their part, established non-state power structures are likely to marginalise such a constitution by hindering its enforcement or filtering to the local level.[54]

4 Constructive forms of UN constitutional assistance

Timor-Leste's experience illustrates that the UN should be wary of conducting public consultations or setting timelines. UN constitutional assistance is most constructive when it involves offering access to experts and resources, setting out relevant international norms and applying pressure to ensure that the constitution-making process is 'transparent, inclusive and participatory'.[55] This section discusses some other ways in which the UN can provide constructive assistance.

4.1 Guidance on non-secular, 'non-rational' systems and their compatibility with the rule of law

First, the UN can open up debate, initiate programmes and provide guidance as to the relationship between the ROL and non-western systems of law such as customary law and *shariah*. As the UK's Department for International Development notes, 'in many developing countries, traditional or customary legal systems account for 80 per cent of total cases'.[56] Despite this striking fact, the prevailing attitude among international organisations appears to be that customary law and traditional leadership will ultimately wither and die and that until they do they should be sidelined because they violate international human rights standards, principles of democratic governance and the ROL. Similarly, *shariah* is treated with scepticism within international circles despite the fact that Islamic law is one of the three major legal systems of the world and is applied, at least in part, in more than 57 Muslim countries and a number of non-Muslim states.[57] Like customary law, *shariah* is also portrayed negatively in western states: at one end of the spectrum it is painted as a form of non-secularism that hinders state-building through impeding an 'environment of civic responsibility and freedom',[58] while at the other end it is dismissed as a form of extremism and barbarism associated with the Taliban in Afghanistan.

Since the beginning of the twenty-first century, some international organisations such as the UN and World Bank have shifted their attention to how customary law and other forms of informal law interact with the ROL. The shift is apparent when comparing the 2004 report of the UNSG on *The Rule of Law and Transitional Justice in Conflict and Post-conflict Societies* with the consecutive report in 2011.[59] The 2004 report offered a 'thick' definition of the ROL as encompassing international human rights norms in addition to procedural aspects such as judicial independence and access to justice.[60] It focused on formal institutions and, while it recognised the vital role played by 'indigenous and informal traditions' in offering accessible justice, it fell short of associating them with the ROL.[61] The 2011 report goes a step further by articulating just such a connection:

> In many post-conflict settings, informal justice mechanisms are the only available recourse to serve the public's justice needs. *Recognizing the potential of informal mechanisms in strengthening the rule of law*, the Organization has increased its understanding of informal justice systems.[62]

This recognition of the role that informal justice mechanisms can play in strengthening the ROL as well as peace and security is a turning point in the UN's approach to the ROL.[63] Such recognition may encourage constitutional drafters in post-conflict states to consider engaging with non-state power structures and authorities.

It is arguable that the Arab Spring has been a useful catalyst for sharpening the UN's understanding of the compatibility of the ROL with Islam. For the UN this is not a new issue, given that in the first decade of the twenty-first century it provided constitutional assistance to at least two Muslim states, namely Afghanistan and Iraq. While the 2004 Afghan Constitution does not explicitly mention *shariah*, Article 3 does provide that all laws must be compatible with the 'beliefs and provisions' of Islam. According to Thier, the word 'provisions' 'indicates something close to reliance on the established Islamic sharia'.[64] He argues that during the constitutional-drafting process, members of the international community set out *shariah* as a 'redline' that the Afghan Constitution could not cross.[65] This was also a flash point in Iraq's constitution-making process.[66]

These issues are pertinent for the UN's mission in Libya. In 2013 Libya's National Assembly voted to make *sharia* the foundation of Libya's legislation and state institutions.[67] Such commitment to *shariah* has caused concern in international circles. Indeed, there have been calls for the international community to exert influence over Libya in this regard. One scholar of Islamic law goes so far as to argue:

> [i]t is the *responsibility of the international community* to ensure that the Sharia in Libya is modelled after progressive Muslim countries such as Turkey and Malaysia who also have a great deal of Islamic law principles in their respective legal systems.[68]

Given the significant tension on this issue, the UN's responsibility is not to 'ensure' that a progressive form of *shariah* is adopted in a sovereign transitional state, but to encourage debate on the matter in the Muslim world. It can do so by providing experts and resources concerning how such non-secular systems of law relate to the ROL.[69] Islamic law scholar Esmaeli is sceptical that Islamic systems of law are compatible with a thick approach to the ROL. In his view, '[a] limited rule of law system, which is drawn from thin and formal theories, may be able to be established with an Islamic system'. He persuasively concludes that 'a rule of law concept may be developed in the Muslim world ... but it must be developed from within and it will be slow and gradual'.[70]

4.2 Reconceptualising constitution-making as opening space for reconciling divergent norms

The UN can also contribute to constitution-making by helping participants to reconceptualise the constitution-making moment as the beginning of a series of processes or spaces for reconciling competing sets of norms.[71] At the international level, several UN treaty bodies already promote such processes.

One example is the Committee on the Elimination of Discrimination against Women (CEDAW Committee) which, under the *Convention on the Elimination of All Forms of Discrimination against Women*,[72] can make concluding observations as to whether state parties need to modify or abolish customs that constitute discrimination against women. The Convention effectively enables the CEDAW Committee to consider how competing sets of norms operate and impact on the population and then make practical suggestions as to how these norms can be creatively reconciled. Unfortunately the language of reconciliation and modification is absent in the Convention: Articles 2(f) and 5(a) use the terms 'abolish' and 'elimination' in regard to harmful customary and traditional practices. In this regard the Convention's language does not fully account for the strength of non-state structures and authorities in post-conflict states. The CEDAW Committee's engagement with state parties to the Convention could be more strategic and constructive. For example, in August 2009 the CEDAW Committee concluded in regard to Timor-Leste that the 'persistence of traditional justice systems' poses an 'impediment' for women in accessing justice.[73] Arguably, the word 'persistence' implies a desire for customary law to disappear and a belief that it can be repealed by the state like a piece of legislation. In this regard the CEDAW Committee echoes the sentiments of colonial governments. Its recommendations would be more beneficial to state parties and activists alike if they focused on how harmful customary practices can be modified through the work of state and local actors.

Other UN treaty bodies, such as the Human Rights Committee, rarely make specific observations in their General Comments on informal justice mechanisms and the extent to which they breach or uphold the rights of vulnerable members of society.[74] International fora such as these should be wary of delegitimising or sidelining 'other' forms of law, whether it be customary law or *shariah* law. Instead they should become more attuned to how such law can be modified in order to recognise and harness its positive aspects.

At the national level, the constitution-making process can be used to create non-violent spaces, specifically within courts and other state institutions, in which the tension between international norms and local norms can be contested and reconciled. South Africa's 1996 Constitution takes this approach by placing customary law on a par with the common law and entrenching an extensive list of international human rights. Its Constitution opens official spaces in which customary norms and international human rights norms such as equality are incrementally reconciled at the national level. Examples are the property rights of those women married under customary law and the customary law of intestate succession, which the South African Constitutional Court has attempted to reconcile with constitutional guarantees of equality.[75] The South African Law Reform Commission has also been exploring whether other aspects of customary law and constitutional human rights can be 'harmonised'.[76] Civil society and customary leaders have contributed to the debate on these questions at the national and local level.[77] These spaces have helped South Africa take small but significant steps towards reconciling customary law and international norms.[78]

Ideally a constitution should herald, create and guide these spaces, thus reinforcing its internal legitimacy. This process of deliberation, debate and reconciliation is unlikely to happen, however, if a state sidelines shared national norms and embraces international norms and a 'rule-of-law constitution' without undertaking meaningful community consultation. The end result is likely to be a constitution whose legitimacy is widely questioned or is simply ignored.

5 Conclusion

The UNSC's 2011 resolutions on South Sudan and Libya demonstrate that peace operations are being tasked with providing constitutional assistance to post-conflict states. The UN's Guidance Notes reveal that a major aim of UN constitutional assistance is to aid post-conflict states in strengthening the ROL. While UN constitutional assistance can be useful in setting out relevant international standards, there is a danger that it can unintentionally distract constitution-making from the essential process of identifying and articulating shared national norms that are critical in giving a post-conflict constitution internal legitimacy. Such internal legitimacy is important if the constitution is to succeed in creating non-violent spaces in which political tensions can be resolved and conflicting norms reconciled.

Notes

1 Quoted in 'France Lifts Veto Threat on Iraq', *BBC News* (online), 22 September 2003: http://news.bbc.co.uk/2/hi/europe/3127798.stm.
2 'Time for UN System to Come Together to Promote Rule of Law Activities', *UN News*, 9 November 2012; UN Doc. A/66/133 (8 August 2011).
3 A survey of UNSC mandates regarding Timor-Leste shows no clear reference to promoting the ROL until 2008: SC Res. 1802 (25 February 2008), para. 5.
4 SC Res. 1996 (8 July 2011), paras 3(a)(iii) and (c) (South Sudan); and SC Res. 2009 (16 September 2011), paras 12(a)(b) and (d) (Libya).
5 See Vijayashri Sripati, 'UN Constitutional Assistance Projects in Comprehensive Peace Missions: An Inventory 1989–2011' (2012) 19 *International Peacekeeping* 93–113.
6 *Guidance Note of the Secretary-General: United Nations Assistance to Constitution-making Processes* (April 2009) ('2009 Guidance Note'). See also Vijayashri Sripati, 'UN Constitutional Assistance: An Emergent Policy Institution' (Osgoode–York Working Paper Series in Policy Research, October 2009), p. 14.
7 *Guidance Note of the Secretary-General: United Nations Approach to Rule of Law Assistance* (April 2008) ('2008 Guidance Note').
8 Democratic Republic of Timor-Leste, *Strategic Development Plan 2011–2030*, p. 178.
9 UN Doc. A/61/636–S/2006/980 (14 December 2006).
10 Michele Brandt, Jill Cottrell, Yash Ghai and Anthony Regan, *Constitution-making and Reform: Options for the Process* (Geneva, Interpeace, 2011), p. 322; Michele Brandt, *Constitutional Assistance in Post-conflict Countries: The UN Experience: Cambodia, East Timor & Afghanistan* (New York, UNDP, 2005); Jamal Benomar, 'Constitution-Making after Conflict: Lessons for Iraq' (2004) 15 *Journal of Democracy*, 81–95.

11 2009 Guidance Note, p. 3.

12 2008 Guidance Note, pp. 4–5. Some scholars express scepticism regarding the usefulness of incorporating international human rights treaties into the domestic sphere as a means of rule-of-law reform owing to their vagueness: Richard Zajac Sannerholm, *Rule of Law after War and Crisis: Ideologies, Norms and Methods* (Cambridge, Intersentia, 2012), p. 136. However, this imprecision can lend itself more readily to the process of reconciling such international norms with potentially incompatible national norms.

13 Bishop Carlos Belo, 'To Forge a Future, Timor Needs Justice for the Past', *Sydney Morning Herald* (Sydney), 28 August 2001, p. 14.

14 'Ramos Horta Addresses the UN Security Council', Ministry of Foreign Affairs Media Release, 30 January 2002.

15 Louis Aucoin and Michele Brandt, 'East Timor's Constitutional Passage to Independence', in Laurel E. Miller and Louis Aucoin (eds), *Framing the State in Times of Transition* (Washington, DC, United States Institute of Peace, 2010), pp. 245–74, 265.

16 J. Samuel Barkin, 'The Evolution of the Constitution of Sovereignty and the Emergence of Human Rights Norms' (1998) 27 *Millennium* 229–52, 230.

17 Ibid., 232.

18 Ibid., 235.

19 Ibid., 249.

20 Ibid., 250 (emphasis added). See Vijayashri Sripati, 'The UN's Role in Post-Conflict Constitution-Making Processes: TWAIL Insights' (2008) 10 *International Community Law Review* 411–20, 418.

21 Articles 6 and 49 of the Consolidated Version of the *Treaty on European Union* (Official Journal of the European Communities, C 325/7) govern the entry of new states to the EU and establish respect for the ROL as part of the criteria, known as the Copenhagen criteria.

22 2009 Guidance Note, p. 4.

23 Ibid.

24 Ibid. (emphasis added).

25 Ibid.

26 'UN Official Voices Alarm at Egypt Violence, Cites "Major" Problems with Draft Constitution', *UN News*, 8 December 2012; 'UN Experts Urge Review of Egypt's Draft Constitution to Ensure Equality and Human Rights', *UN News*, 15 December 2012.

27 2009 Guidance Note, pp. 2, 4, 6.

28 Explanation of Australia's vote against the UN General Assembly adoption of the *UN Declaration of the Rights on Indigenous Peoples* by the Hon. Robert Hill, Ambassador and Permanent Representative of Australia to the UN: UN Doc. A/61/PV.107 (13 September 2007).

29 Hossein Esmaeli, 'The Nature and Development of Law in Islam and the Rule of Law Challenge in the Middle East and the Muslim World' (2011) 26 *Connecticut Journal of International Law* 329–66, 331; Chibli Mallat, *Introduction to Middle Eastern Law* (Oxford, Oxford University Press, 2007). Esmaeli points to some Muslim countries where elements of the ROL are present but observes that there are currently no practical examples of a state where a rule-of-law system and a flexible *shariah* system co-exist: p. 366.

30 2009 Guidance Note, p. 4.

31 Michel Rosenfeld, 'Constitution-Making, Identity Building, and Peaceful Transitions to Democracy: Theoretical Reflections Inspired by the Spanish Example' (1998) 19 *Cardozo Law Review* 1891–920.

32 Francis Fukuyama, *State-building: Governance and World Order in the 21st Century* (New York, Cornell University Press, 2004).

33 Ibid., p. 154.
34 Armin von Bogdandy, Stefan Häußler, Felix Hanschmann and Raphael Utz, 'State-Building, Nation-Building, and Constitutional Politics in Post-Conflict Situations: Conceptual Clarifications and an Appraisal of Different Approaches' (2005) 9 *Max Planck Yearbook of United Nations Law* 579–613, 597.
35 Ibid. (emphasis added).
36 Although Bogdandy *et al.* offer case studies of nation-building in South Africa and Afghanistan, they do not consider the challenge of identifying 'traditional elements of collective identity' in such environments. In this sense, they could be read as presupposing the existence of such collective identity.
37 2009 Guidance Note, p. 4.
38 *UNTAET Regulation No. 2001/2 On the Election of a Constituent Assembly to Prepare a Constitution for an Independent and Democratic East Timor* (16 March 2001), section 2.3.
39 East Timor National NGO Forum Letter (17 March 2001): www.etan.org/news/2001a/03ngoconst.htm (emphasis added).
40 See UN Doc. E/CN.4/2002/39 (1 March 2002), *Situation of Human Rights: Report of the High Commissioner*, para. 46.
41 See Aucoin and Brandt, 'East Timor's Constitutional Passage to Independence'.
42 Jonathan Morrow and Rachel White, 'The United Nations in Transitional East Timor: International Standards and the Reality of Governance' (2002) 22 *Australian Year Book of International Law*, 1–47, 41–3. The Assembly ignored the first concern but responded to the second by amending the draft constitution.
43 The Assembly conducted some semblance of a brief public consultation, albeit possibly as a 'public relations' event: Brandt, *Constitutional Assistance*, p. 17.
44 See Constitutional Affairs Branch, Office of Political Affairs, UNTAET, *Executive Summary of the Constitutional Commission Public Hearings, Dili* (September 2001). See also Aisling Swaine, *Traditional Justice and Gender Based Violence* (Report for the International Rescue Society, 2003), pp. 63–4.
45 David Hicks, 'Community and Nation-State in East Timor' (2007) 23 *Anthropology Today* 13–16, 14.
46 Josh Trindade, 'Reconciling the Conflicting Paradigms: An East Timorese Vision of the Ideal State', in David Mearns (ed.), *Democratic Governance in Timor-Leste: Reconciling the Local and the National* (Darwin, Charles Darwin University Press, 2008), pp. 160–86, 167.
47 Open letter from Josh Trindade to the Prime Minister of Timor-Leste, 10 August 2006 (on file with author).
48 Josh Trindade, 'Reconciling', p. 167.
49 Ibid., pp. 181–2.
50 Ibid., p. 181.
51 'The Women's Charter' (2001) 2(5) *La'O Hamutuk Bulletin* 2.
52 Democratic Republic of Timor-Leste, *Strategic Development Plan 2011–2030*, p. 178.
53 Ibid., p. 179.
54 Kirsti Samuels, 'Post-Conflict Peace-Building and Constitution-Making' (2006) 6 *Chicago Journal of International Law* 1–20, 9.
55 2009 Guidance Note, pp. 2, 4, 6.
56 UK DfID, *Safety, Security and Accessible Justice: Putting Policy into Practice* (2002), p. 58.
57 Esmaeli, 'The Nature and Development', p. 329.
58 According to Turkey's Constitutional Court in the *Refah Partisi* case, *shariah* is the 'antithesis' of democracy which creates a 'vast environment of civic responsibility and freedom'. Turkey's decision to ban the Refah Partisi was upheld in 2003 by the European Court of Human Rights, which endorsed these words: *Refah Partisi (The*

Welfare Party) and Others v. *Turkey*, 41340/98, 41342/98, 41343/98, 41344/98, Council of Europe: European Court of Human Rights, 13 February 2003, paras 123, 40.

59 See also UN Women, *Progress of the World's Women 2011–2012: In Pursuit of Justice* (New York, United Nations, 2011).

60 UN Doc. S/2004/616 (23 August 2004) ('2004 ROL Report'). In contrast, a 'thin' approach focuses on procedural and institutional aspects such as legal predictability, and sets aside human rights norms.

61 Ibid., para. 36.

62 UN Doc. S/2011/634 (12 October 2011), para. 39 (emphasis added). See also UN Women/The UN Children's Fund (UNICEF)/UNDP, *Informal Justice Systems: Charting a Course for Human Rights-based Engagement* (September 2012).

63 In addition to the 2004 ROL Report, see UNDP, *Strengthening the Rule of Law in Conflict- and Post-conflict Situations: A Global UNDP Programme for Justice and Security 2008–2011*; 2008 Guidance Note, pp. 1, 3, 7.

64 J. Alexander Thier, 'Big Tent, Small Tent: The Making of a Constitution in Afghanistan', in Laurel E. Miller and Louis Aucoin (eds), *Framing the State in Times of Transition* (Washington, DC, United States Institute of Peace, 2010), pp. 535–62, 552; Nathan Brown, 'Bargaining and Imposing Constitutions: Private and Public Interests in the Iranian, Afghani and Iraqi Constitutional Experiments', in Said Amir Arjomand (ed.), *Constitutional Politics in the Middle East* (Portland, OR, Hart Publishing, 2008), pp. 63–76, 72.

65 Ibid. Parts of the Afghan population also articulated this 'redline'.

66 Noah Feldman, 'Imposed Constitutionalism' (2004) 37 *Connecticut Law Review* 857–89, 877–8; Brown, 'Bargaining', pp. 63–76.

67 'Libya Assembly Votes for Shariah Law', *Aljazeera* (online), 4 December 2013: www.aljazeera.com/news/africa/2013/12/libya-assembly-votes-sharia-law-2013124153217603439.html.

68 Umar Oseni, 'Sharia in Libya: Implications for Human Rights and the Rule of Law' (2011) *JURIST–Forum* 3 (emphasis added).

69 Esmaeli, 'The Nature and Development', p. 358.

70 Ibid., 366.

71 The 2008 Guidance Note arguably recognises the need to open up such spaces: p. 4.

72 *Convention on the Elimination of All Forms of Discrimination against Women*, opened for signature 1 March 1980, 1249 UNTS 13 (entered into force 3 September 1981).

73 UN Doc. CEDAW/C/TLS/CO/1 (7 August 2009), *Concluding Observations of the Committee on the Elimination of Discrimination against Women: Timor Leste*, paras 21–2. For another example, see CEDAW Committee's 2010 *Concluding Observations on Egypt*: UN Doc. CEDAW/C/EGY/CO/7 (5 February 2010), paras 21–2.

74 The Human Rights Committee's General Comment 34 on the right to a fair trial is an exception: UN Doc. CCPR/C/GC/32 (23 August 2007), para. 24.

75 *Bhe and Others* v. *The Magistrate, Khayelitsha and Others* and *Shilubana and Ors* v. *Mwamitwa* 2009 (2) SA 66 (CC); *Gumede* v. *President of the Republic of South Africa* 2009 (3) BCLR 243 (CC).

76 See, e.g. South African Law Commission, *Harmonisation: Conflicts of Law*, Discussion Paper 76, Project 90 (1998).

77 For some examples, see Laura Grenfell, *Promoting the Rule of Law in Post-conflict States* (Cambridge, Cambridge University Press, 2013), chapters 4 and 5.

78 Ibid.

10 Strengthening the local accountability of UN peacekeeping

Jeni Whalan

Introduction

United Nations (UN) peacekeepers regularly fall short of achieving their intended consequences – of fulfilling in practice the goals set out in their UN Security Council (UNSC) mandates. But perhaps the greater tragedy is the unintended, negative consequences UN peacekeeping operations have had for host societies, among them distortions of the local economy, negative impacts on humanitarian action and criminal activity.[1] Most notorious are the acts of sexual violence and abuse by blue-helmeted soldiers towards local women and children,[2] prompting substantial attention since the mid-1990s on the accountability of peacekeepers, particularly to the legal aspects of such exploitation, given the immunities and privileges on which peacekeeping deployments are based.[3]

The UN has responded with various reforms, including adopting a 'zero tolerance' policy,[4] establishing a Conduct and Discipline Unit within the Department of Peacekeeping Operations (DPKO), and calling for troop-contributing countries (TCCs) to rigorously investigate and prosecute all allegations of human rights violations by peacekeepers, and to report their findings to the UN.[5] Although welcome, these reforms represent a narrow form of accountability, limited to preventing and redressing peacekeeper misconduct through the international-level channels of the UN and its TCCs. Missing are efforts to strengthen peacekeepers' local accountability, by which I mean the right of actors in the host society to hold peacekeepers 'to a set of standards, to judge whether they have fulfilled their responsibilities in light of these standards and to impose sanctions if they determine that these responsibilities have not been met'.[6]

This chapter considers the means by which multidimensional peacekeeping operations can attain standards of accountability that are more relevant to the populations of societies in which operations deploy. It shifts the peacekeeping accountability debate in a number of important respects: from the international to the local level; from the moral to the instrumental case for local accountability; and from the advocacy of narrow, limited accountability mechanisms to a set of more broadly applicable guiding principles. The chapter argues that UN peacekeeping operations have a range of alternative options by which to enable local input, from various constituencies within their host environment, to constitute appropriate accountability standards and assess peacekeepers' performance against them. Most feasible are forms of horizontal accountability, such as an ombudsperson or community relations office within the peacekeeping operation.

The chapter proceeds in three parts. Section 1 defines 'local accountability', assesses the current status of mechanisms for holding peacekeepers to account and moves the debate on local accountability beyond questions of legal liability and redress. Section 2 establishes the case for the UNSC to focus on local accountability reforms. It recognises that making peacekeepers more locally accountable entails costs, but argues that doing so both reduces the 'unintended consequences' that rightly attract so much attention,[7] as well as providing means by which peacekeepers can better produce their *intended* consequences. Hence strengthening local *accountability* can also make peacekeeping more *effective*. Finally, Section 3 draws on a pioneering experiment conducted by the UN Transitional Authority in Cambodia (UNTAC) to address community concern about peacekeepers' misconduct, refining the UNTAC model to propose five essential features of a local accountability forum for peace operations.

1 Understanding the accountability of peacekeeping operations

The term 'accountability' is notoriously difficult to define, the more so for its close relationship to other conceptually slippery terms like 'power', 'authority' and 'legitimacy'. In essence, accountability is about the exercise of power. Accountability processes are ways of both checking power and arguing about how it should be exercised.[8] The power relationships between accountability actors therefore provide a useful starting point for accountability analysis, with the key questions being who can call a peacekeeping operation to account, and by what means? The concept of accountability is commonly understood with reference to a hierarchical relationship between the accountable actor (in this case the peacekeeping operation) and the accountability holder who calls it to account. That is, accountability always has 'direction' – it points towards those to whom an agent must give account.[9] The accountability relationship may flow from the top down, with the more powerful actor holding the less powerful to account, as in a contractual principal–agent arrangement;[10] or it may flow from the bottom up, with the less powerful capable of checking the powerful, as in democratic elections.

These two directions can be conceptualised as *upward* accountability, as when UN organs and member states hold a peacekeeping operation to account, or *downward* accountability, as when actors within the host society hold the operation to account.[11] To these are added a third accountability type: *horizontal* accountability, which refers to accountability relationships in which the accountable actor and the accountability holder have roughly equal power,[12] such as the relationship between a UN peacekeeping operation, on the one hand, and an ombudsperson or the UN's Office of Internal Oversight Services, on the other.

This schema of upward, downward and horizontal accountability is used widely in accountability literature.[13] In the context of peacekeeping, it captures not only the relationships of power between accountability actors, but also the international–domestic divide in international law and politics. In this chapter, I use the terms 'international accountability' (upward) and 'local accountability' (downward), which put the emphasis on the identity of the accountability holder and thereby help to capture the demands on peacekeeping operations to respond to dynamics at both international and local levels.

Peacekeeping operations are institutions of both international and local governance: they are created at the international level through the authority of the UNSC,[14] but operate at the local level, pursuing change within conflict-affected states.[15] This dual role suggests that we should expect the accountability of peacekeeping to have both international and local dimensions. Yet the international accountability of peacekeeping operations dramatically overshadows their local accountability: since they derive their authority, mandates and resources from international actors (that is, from the UN and its member states), to date it has been international accountability mechanisms that check their use, and abuse, of power. Peacekeeping operations are accountable to their international creators, not to the populations in the local societies that host them.

The distinction between delegatory and participatory models of accountability usefully reveals this accountability deficit. In a delegation model, an agent is held accountable by those who entrust it with powers; in a participation model, the agent is held accountable by those affected by its actions.[16] The accountability of peacekeeping operations is directed overwhelmingly to the international actors who create them, not to those in the host society affected by their actions. Thus to recognise that peacekeeping operations have an accountability deficit is not to suggest that they are *unaccountable*, but that their accountability is inadequate and skewed towards 'the bodies that appoint them',[17] rather than to the populations that are directly affected by their deployment.[18]

While peacekeeping operations have a deficit of participatory accountability, they have strong delegatory accountability, based on their UNSC mandates.[19] The UNSC's binding resolutions determine the composition, time frame and mandate of a peacekeeping operation, and constitute the set of standards against which their performance will be judged. The UNSC delegates responsibility for operational management to the UN Secretary-General (UNSG), who in turn delegates responsibility for implementing the mandate to senior mission leaders deployed in the field. The UNSC calls the operation to account through the UNSG's regular reporting,[20] against the standards its resolutions have set for the operation, subsequently adjusting the operation's mandates and resources accordingly. Individual peacekeepers, meanwhile, are held accountable by their home nation: not even the UN, and certainly not the local host state, can call individuals to account.

The accountability of peacekeeping operations does have a local face in one important respect: the consent of the host state to the operation's deployment.

By giving this consent, the host state delegates certain powers to peacekeepers, including certain privileges and immunities from local prosecution. Host-state consent is one of the touchstone norms of UN peacekeeping.[21] It can operate as a means of power through which to call peacekeepers to account, since a host state can technically revoke its consent and demand the withdrawal of an operation if it is judged to be unaccountable.

In practice, however, the power disparity between the peacekeeping operation (with the weight of the UN and its member states behind it) and the host state means that this potential accountability mechanism has rarely been used. This highlights a central problem with the practice of 'consent': its meaning is, at best, hazy, incorporating situations in which consent may be 'coerced'[22] through the threat or application of military force or other sanction. In these circumstances, consent is a weak form of accountability. Further limiting the potential of consent to hold peacekeepers accountable is the questionable capacity of the state in many host societies. Since peacekeepers are often deployed into situations characterised by a state that is weak, contested or even non-existent, or where the state itself is a cause of insecurity, host-state consent offers little opportunity for those local populations directly affected by peacekeepers to hold them to account.

In these conditions, it is useful to consider some horizontal accountability mechanisms to be alternative forms of local accountability – provided that they include channels to facilitate local input on the standards against which to judge peacekeepers' performance, and on the judgements themselves. For example, an ombudsperson for a peacekeeping operation may *exclude* local participation, such as when its standards, judgements and sanctions are determined without input from host populations. Such an ombudsperson is not a form of local accountability. But it may be designed to facilitate local participation in the process of setting standards, forming judgements and/or determining sanctions, in which case the ombudsperson would help to strengthen the operation's local accountability.

In addition to distinguishing directional quality of accountability – upward, downward or horizontal – accountability can be separated analytically into what Andreas Schedler calls its two 'basic connotations': 'answerability, the obligation of public officials to inform about and explain what they are doing; and enforcement, the capacity of accounting agencies to impose sanctions on power-holders who have violated their public duties'.[23]

Much of the academic and policy scholarship on the accountability of peacekeepers has focused on its enforcement variant, responding to evidence of egregious wrongdoing by peacekeeping personnel, including sexual assault, rape, torture, murder, deaths in custody, child prostitution, human trafficking, black marketeering, extortion and fraud.[24] As evidence of such abuses emerged, commentators focused on imposing sanctions on the individuals responsible, a response which highlights the obstacle impeding individual accountability: the privileges and immunities that have for so long been essential to secure the contributions of peacekeeping personnel from UN member states.

Under the Status of Forces Agreements that govern the deployment of peacekeepers, TCCs have exclusive criminal and disciplinary jurisdiction in respect of the acts of their military personnel.[25] The immunity of such personnel from criminal prosecution in the host state continues to thwart efforts to hold individual peacekeepers legally accountable for wrongdoing. For example, in November 2011, Haitian and US human rights organisations lodged a complaint with the head of the Claims Unit of the UN Stabilization Mission in Haiti (MINUSTAH) on behalf of 5,000 cholera victims, alleging that a cholera outbreak in Haiti was 'directly attributable to the negligence, gross negligence, recklessness and deliberate indifference for the health and lives of Haiti's citizens by the UN and its subsidiary [MINUSTAH]', and citing a number of medical studies confirming that Nepalese MINUSTAH personnel introduced the disease to Haitian waters.[26] In February 2013, the UN dismissed the claims for reparations as 'not receivable' under Section 29 ('Settlement of Disputes') of the Convention on the Privileges and Immunities, adopted by the UN General Assembly (UNGA) on 13 February 1946.[27]

Nevertheless, in other cases the UN has proved willing to respond to egregious disciplinary and conduct matters, particularly those concerning acts of sexual exploitation and abuse by peacekeeping personnel, including through UNSC resolutions.[28] Both the UNGA and the UNSC have called for TCCs to thoroughly investigate and prosecute allegations of human rights violations made against their nationals, and to report on the findings of those investigations.[29]

Other efforts to ensure that peacekeepers are not locally perceived to be 'above the law' include experiments with ombudsperson institutions in the UN Mission in Kosovo (UNMIK) and the UN Transitional Administration in East Timor (UNTAET). Each such institution could receive complaints against the operation, providing the people in Kosovo and Timor-Leste a channel through which to raise grievances such as property damage, unfair employment and physical abuse by peacekeeping personnel. The Kosovo ombudsperson could also initiate investigations.[30]

In practice, both accountability institutions had serious flaws. In Kosovo, the ombudsperson lacked independence from the operation it was to investigate: although the Organization for Security and Cooperation in Europe managed the office, the ombudsperson was 'appointed and funded by, and reported to, the Special Representative of the Secretary-General (SRSG) and UNMIK, who were the main subjects of allegations concerning human rights violation and abuses of their extensive power',[31] a situation which enabled the operation to avoid accountability for human rights violations.[32] The ombudsperson in Timor-Leste was considerably more limited in its powers than that in Kosovo; it only had a mandate to hear complaints, not to initiate investigations, and 'was generally seen as ineffective'.[33]

Yet even if these ombudsperson institutions had been better able to meet the purposes for which they were designed, they targeted only a limited form of legal accountability. Important as it is to ensure that peacekeeping operations are held legally accountable for human rights violations, as de Coning, Chiyuki and Thakur have argued,

> much more can and should be done to develop meaningful accountability towards and by the host country, not just in the context of legal accountability related to some form of wrong doing … but also through ongoing and proactive political accountability.[34]

2 The instrumental case for local accountability

Since the UNSC so often justifies the deployment of peacekeeping operations with reference to humanitarian crises and the need to protect civilians,[35] there is a compelling moral argument that host societies should have a role in determining whether peacekeepers have met appropriate standards and fulfilled their responsibilities. That is, peacekeeping operations ought to be accountable to the people they aim to assist, protect and secure. The special vulnerabilities of people affected by violent insecurity support this argument. As the Humanitarian Accountability Partnership (HAP) recognises in the *2010 HAP Standard in Accountability and Quality Management*, organisations that assist or act on behalf of people affected by conflict and crisis

> exercise significant power in their work to save lives and reduce suffering. In contrast, crisis-affected people have no formal control, and often little influence, over these organisations. As a result, it is difficult for those people to hold organisations to account for actions taken on their behalf.[36]

Yet the moral case alone is an insufficient basis on which to demand local accountability reforms in peacekeeping. Peacekeeping is already a morally compromised instrument, a pragmatic compromise solution that allows the UN to take some peace-promoting action when the UNSC is not willing to use its more robust collective security powers. Peacekeeping sits somewhere in the murky middle between pluralist and solidarist international ethics;[37] it is a halfway house between inaction and enforcement.[38] Amid this normative contestation, the practical imperative of providing some form of assistance, protection and security to populations stuck in violent conflict suggests the need to consider the practical effects of local accountability. In what follows, I therefore focus on the *instrumental* case for accountability reforms: that is, what are the benefits of making peacekeepers more accountable to local populations, and what are the trade-offs of doing so?[39]

Making UN peacekeeping operations more locally accountable may entail at least three types of cost. First, UN peacekeeping has since its earliest days been underfunded, and strengthening local accountability may divert resources away from other activities of an operation. Second, the particular contexts in which peacekeeping operations are deployed pose more specific costs. When conflict parties continue to fight for power, often through violent means, after a peacekeeping operation is deployed, vested interests have incentives to abuse local accountability processes and thereby undermine both the operation and its mandate. Under these conditions – frequently experienced by peacekeeping operations – accountability can 'divert attention towards irrelevant targets, and foster distrust'.[40] Third, since peacekeeping operations regularly lack the personnel and equipment needed to fulfil their ambitious mandates, further checking their capacity through accountability mechanisms could threaten the viability of their activities. In other words, local accountability reforms may be an 'own-goal' for peacekeeping operations: being accountable to actors in the host society restricts their autonomy,[41] which may undermine their ability to achieve their fundamental purposes of assisting, securing and protecting host populations.

A further limitation on local accountability also demands attention: in conflict-affected societies, it is not clear that agreement on basic accountability principles can be reached. Where host societies are deeply fractured by the experience of conflict, opinion may be so divided on the question of what standards peacekeepers should be held accountable to that the exercise becomes practically unfeasible.

Against these arguments stands the case that local accountability reforms can make peacekeeping operations more effective, by which I mean better able to achieve their mandated goals. Much of the scholarship on the benefits of accountability assumes a set of political conditions that do not apply in the case of peacekeeping – namely, stable representation and the rule of law.[42] But over the past decade, researchers have begun to examine the instrumental case for local accountability in conflict-affected contexts, asking whether making international organisations more accountable to affected communities improves the quality and impact of their assistance.[43] A recent study on humanitarian and development aid concluded that local accountability has four principal benefits: it can make assistance more relevant (by fostering better understanding of local vulnerabilities), more effective (by increasing trust and decreasing fraud), more efficient (by empowering communities to monitor implementation and resource allocation) and more sustainable (by increasing community ownership).[44]

The instrumental benefits of local accountability for peacekeeping operations have also received recognition. Some benefits contribute directly to effectiveness: armed with better information about the needs, preferences and perceptions of local populations, peacekeeping operations can design operating practices and policies that better fit their deployment environment, and adjust their actions according to what local populations deem appropriate. But other effects are less direct. Frédéric Mégret argues that local accountability can foster a 'culture of respect for the civilian population' and thereby increase 'the acceptability of a mission'.[45] Similarly, I have argued elsewhere that local accountability provides an influential means of legitimation for peacekeeping operations, and that this in turn can be expected to increase their effectiveness.[46] This is because the belief that a peacekeeping operation is legitimate – that the operation, its personnel and its goals are right, fair and appropriate – provides reasons for the local actor holding that belief to comply and cooperate with peacekeepers.[47]

The local accountability under discussion in this chapter is one means by which peacekeeping operations can be locally legitimised. Strengthening the local accountability of a peacekeeping operation checks its exercise of power, requiring it to justify its relations and actions towards the less powerful – as local populations typically are. But since peacekeeping operations ultimately depend for their effectiveness on the decisions and actions of local actors[48] – from political and military elites to rank-and-file soldiers and political parties to community leaders and groups – the legitimation process of local accountability can provide peacekeepers with a new means of power.[49] Importantly, *informal* processes of local accountability appear to be particularly influential: when peacekeeping personnel voluntarily provide explanations for their presence and actions, articulate standards against which their performance can be evaluated, and address the criticisms or reform demands of local actors, they are more likely to be considered legitimate.[50] Further, these informal processes might also help to constitute accountability standards appropriate to the specific context of a particular peacekeeping operation.

Being held locally to account may also help peacekeeping operations tailor their activities in ways that promote local ownership, which the UN recognises as a 'success factor' and 'critical to the successful implementation of a peace process'.[51] As Leif Wenar notes, 'An agent who knows that its affairs must be capable of withstanding scrutiny will have an *incentive* to respond to the values of those to whom they are accountable'.[52] Thus an 'accountable agent' is likely 'to put *more effort* into fulfilling its responsibilities, to be *more efficient*, to maintain *higher ethical standards*, to take *extra care in planning and acting*, and so on'.[53]

Additionally, if stronger local accountability does indeed lead peacekeepers to become more attuned to the diverse, even contradictory opinions locals are likely to have about them, the operation will also become better able to respond to, and even prevent, the escalation of local grievances. Accountability processes can be a way of mediating conflict and even achieving consensus. As an independent study on integrated UN missions commissioned by the UN Executive Committee on Humanitarian Affairs argued, 'The ability to sensitise a mission to the perceptions, expectations and attitudes of local populations is directly related to a mission's success, and effective management of the above is an important problem-solving tool'.[54] The failure to establish 'two-way communication between mission and society' thus 'allows minor incidents to take on major importance and impact, and in extreme cases, can derail a mission'.[55]

3 UNTAC's Community Relations Office: a case study in local accountability

The UNTAC was one of the UN's first big multidimensional peace operations – and one of the first to face substantial controversy over the abuse of local populations by peacekeepers.[56] Abuses ranged from traffic accidents caused by incompetent drivers to racism to serious misconduct including child molestation, sexual harassment and rape, and arms smuggling.[57] Just three months after the first UNTAC personnel arrived in Cambodia, the operation's Force Commander recognised offensive behaviour by peacekeepers as a threat to the operation's credibility and effectiveness. Responding to 'a growing number of reports of offensive behaviour by UNTAC troops on the roads, in restaurants and in respect to Cambodian women', the Force Commander directed peacekeepers to 'build confidence in UNTAC on the part of all Cambodians', noting that '[t]he hearts and minds of the Cambodian people must remain with us if we are to succeed'.[58]

In October 1992 a group of 165 Cambodians and expatriates wrote to the head of the UNTAC, SRSG Yasushi Akashi, of their 'sense of outrage at the unacceptable behaviour of some male UNTAC personnel [...] regarding mistreatment of women'.[59] They raised concerns not only about the 'frontier behaviour' of certain personnel, but also – and crucially – the lack of any mechanism of redress for women experiencing such behaviour.

In response, UNTAC created a Community Relations Office, the first such forum in UN peacekeeping history. Created to deal with UNTAC's 'image problem', the office served as a 'focal point for receiving, channelling and following up on complaints about the behaviour of UNTAC personnel'.[60] The Office enabled members of the local community to report complaints about UNTAC and was intended to 'act as an honest broker between disputing parties'.[61] The office also conducted cultural awareness-raising activities among UNTAC personnel, particularly about HIV/AIDS, sexually transmitted diseases and condom usage. Finally, it administered a voluntary fund for traffic accident victims.

In practice, it was a limited exercise. The Office's operations were restricted to Phnom Penh and managed by only one official. Further, most of the 84 complaints heard by the Office were of a monetary nature, such as claims for 'damages caused by UNTAC drivers to Cambodians and their vehicles'.[62] Rape investigations were 'rather shoddy and chaotic', with many cases '"covered up" or financially settled'.[63]

Despite its flaws, UNTAC's Community Relations Office offers a model on which efforts to strengthen local accountability can build. Its limited scope and authority constrained the Office's practical effect, but the idea is sound: a forum at the local level, with oversight of a peacekeeping operation's local-level impacts. Those impacts may include issues of legal liability, such as human rights abuses, as in the case of the ombudspersons for Kosovo and Timor-Leste, but they should also extend to political answerability on broader impacts, such as the economic effects of peacekeeping operations, their geographical distribution and their prioritisation of some tasks over those that local communities consider most important. Importantly, such a forum must look beyond wrongdoing and compensation to answerability – the obligation of peacekeepers to inform host populations about what they are doing, and explain their course of action.

Many peacekeeping operations have featured local mechanisms, specifically local claims review boards, to address third-party claims, including as early as the UN Operation in the Congo (1960–1964).[64] As Guglielmo Verdirame notes, the rulings of these local claims mechanisms are not made public,[65] which makes assessing their effectiveness in terms of local accountability very difficult. More significant for my purposes here, however, is that these mechanisms are limited to settling claims through financial compensation, but offer little to increase the *answerability* of peacekeeping operations to host populations. Similarly, while there has been substantial progress on issues of peacekeeper misconduct relating to sexual exploitation and abuse, these are issue-specific. The creation of a Conduct and Discipline Unit within DPKO and the deployment of Conduct and Discipline Teams within peacekeeping missions are welcome reforms of the past decade,[66] but are focused principally on accountability for wrongdoing, not extending the political accountability of peacekeepers via answerability.

4 Conclusion: five principles for making peacekeepers more locally accountable

This chapter has argued that peacekeeping operations should be made more locally accountable. I conclude here by articulating a set of five principles to guide practical efforts in this regard.

First, as I have argued throughout this chapter, there is a need to strengthen the answerability dimension of local accountability. Progress on peacekeepers' accountability to date has largely focused on enforcement: on ensuring that TCCs rigorously investigate alleged misconduct and impose sanctions on those found guilty. While preventing and redressing the unintended consequences of peacekeeping operations is undeniably important, strengthening their answerability can also help peacekeepers to achieve their intended aims. An accountability mechanism of the type experimented with in UNTAC provides a forum in which host populations have opportunities to ask 'uncomfortable questions' of the peacekeeping operation,[67] in addition to receiving appropriate redress for peacekeeper misconduct.

Second, local accountability institutions must have a substantial degree of independence from the peacekeeping operation itself, including their own budget and reporting requirements. The experience of the ombudsperson in Kosovo demonstrates the limits of an accountability mechanism that depends for its authority and funding on the very actors it is trying to hold to account.

Third, local accountability mechanisms must be locally accessible, capable of hearing and responding to complaints and testimonies throughout the host society, not just in the capital.[68] They should also be proactive about promoting awareness and engagement among local populations. One means by which this could be achieved is to link local accountability efforts to the communication strategies of peace operations. All multidimensional peacekeeping operations today have media outlets – usually radio, sometimes also television and social media channels – tasked with disseminating information about the mission to the host population. These public information outlets are already contributing to local accountability by making the operation's mandates, priorities and activities transparent to a wide audience. But operation media could also formally become part of a local accountability institution.

The *Handbook on UN Multidimensional Peacekeeping Operations* directs public information officers within each operation to 'play a proactive role in addressing negative public perceptions and attitudes about the mission and should initiate clear, accurate and timely public information programmes and campaigns to address them'.[69] Such information could include how to make a complaint about the operation in a local accountability forum. Finally, public outreach should be a two-way, interactive process, in which operations publicly respond to community concerns through explanation and dialogue, important for those issues that might not meet the criteria for financial settlement by local claims review mechanisms.

Fourth, there must be scope for local input into the issues and standards on which the peacekeeping operation can be called to account. In this respect, perhaps more than any other, the international accountability of peacekeepers far outstrips their local accountability, a consequence of enforcement-focused accountability practice based on pre-set standards from the international sphere. The goals, priorities, codes of conduct and performance standards of peacekeeping operations are overwhelmingly set by actors at the international level: by the UNSC, UNGA and Secretariat, and by TCCs. Yet for peacekeepers to be more locally accountable, as the UN's Taskforce on Sexual Exploitation and Abuse recognises, the 'local community in each geographical area must be engaged in designing' complaints mechanisms.[70] This process of local input should extend across all local accountability efforts.

Finally, local accountability forums must have support from both a peacekeeping operation's leadership and its international patrons. This is perhaps the most difficult of the five features to ensure in practice. However, making operations more locally accountable can, at least under some conditions, help peacekeepers to achieve their objectives. Where accountability processes help to legitimise peacekeeping operations from the perspective of local actors, peacekeepers can expect to receive more cooperation from them. If operations can encourage accountability processes that help to interpret, explain, challenge and change political life in host societies, their ambitious task of transforming conflict-affected societies into more peaceful, secure states may become a little easier. As Olsen suggests, '[u]nder some conditions, accountability processes have an integrative community-building effect; promoting a culture of cooperation, compromise and rule-following'.[71] Local accountability may have costs, but the conclusion that it may help make peacekeepers more effective provides substantial grounds for challenging the reluctance of international actors to accept such constraints on their power.

Notes

1 See Chiyuki Aoi, Cedric de Coning and Ramesh Thakur (eds), *Unintended Consequences of Peacekeeping Operations* (Tokyo, UN University Press, 2007).

2 See Róisín Burke, 'Attribution of Responsibility: Sexual Abuse and Exploitation, and Effective Control of Blue Helmets' (2012) 16 *Journal of International Peacekeeping* 1–46.

3 See UN Doc. A/51/306 (26 August 1996), *Impact of Armed Conflict on Children: Report of the Expert of the Secretary-General, Ms. Grac'a Machel, Submitted Pursuant to General Assembly Resolution 48/157*; Anne Orford, 'The Politics of Collective

Security' (1996) 17 *Michigan Journal of International Law* 373–409; UN Doc. A/57/465 (11 October 2002), *Report of the Office of Internal Oversight Services on the Investigation into Sexual Exploitation of Refugees by Aid Workers in West Africa*; UN Doc. A/59/710 (24 March 2005), *A Comprehensive Strategy to Eliminate Future Sexual Exploitation and Abuse in United Nations Peacekeeping Operations* ('Zeid Report'); Anthony J. Miller, 'Legal Aspects of Stopping Sexual Exploitation and Abuse in UN Peacekeeping Operations' (2006) 39 *Cornell International Law Journal* 71–96; Ray Murphy, 'An Assessment of UN Efforts to Address Sexual Misconduct by Peacekeeping Personnel' (2006) 13 *International Peacekeeping* 531–46; Rose Freedman, 'UN Immunity or Impunity? A Human Rights Based Challenge' (2014) 25 *European Journal of International Law* 239–52.

4 UN Doc. ST/SGB/2003/13 (9 October 2003), *Secretary-General's Bulletin: Special Measures for Protection from Sexual Exploitation and Sexual Abuse*.

5 For detailed analysis of these reforms, and their limits, see Machiko Kanetake, 'The UN Zero Tolerance Policy's Whereabouts: On the Discordance Between Politics and Law on the Internal–External Divide' (2012) 4 *Amsterdam Law Forum* 51–61.

6 Ruth Grant and Robert O. Keohane, 'Accountability and Abuses of Power in World Politics' (2005) 99 *American Political Science Review* 29–43, 29.

7 See, for example, Aoi, de Coning and Thakur, *Unintended Consequences*.

8 See John P. Olsen, 'The Institutional Basis of Democratic Accountability' (2013) *West European Politics* 36(3) 447–73.

9 Leif Wenar, 'Accountability in International Development Aid' (2006) 20 *Ethics & International Affairs* 1–23, 6.

10 Darren G. Hawkins, David A. Lake, Daniel L. Nielson and Michael J. Tierney, 'Delegation under Anarchy: States, International Organizations, and Principal-Agent Theory', in Darren G. Hawkins, David A. Lake, Daniel L. Nielson and Michael J. Tierney (eds), *Delegation and Agency in International Organizations* (Cambridge, Cambridge University Press, 2006).

11 Guillermo O'Donnell, 'Horizontal Accountability in New Democracies' (1998) 93 *Journal of Democracy* 112–26.

12 See O'Donnell, 'Horizontal Accountability'; Andreas Schedler, 'Conceptualizing Accountability', in Andreas Schedler, Larry J. Diamond and Marc F. Plattner (eds), *The Self-restraining State: Power and Accountability in New Democracies* (Boulder, CO, Lynne Rienner, 1999), pp. 13–28.

13 See, e.g. Jennifer Rubenstein, 'Accountability in an Unequal World' (2007) 69 *Journal of Politics* 616–32; Nick Devas and Ursula Grant, 'Local Government Decision-Making: Citizen Participation and Local Accountability – Some Evidence from Kenya and Uganda' (2003) 23 *Public Administration and Development* 307–16; Wenar, 'Accountability in International Development Aid'; Staffan I. Lindberg, 'Mapping Accountability: Core Concept and Subtypes' (2013) 79 *International Review of Administrative Sciences* 202–26.

14 The only operation *not* to have been created by the UNSC was the UN Emergency Force (UNEF), the operation for which the term 'peacekeeping' was invented: see Maxwell Cohen, 'The United Nations Emergency Force: A Preliminary View' (1957) 12 *International Journal* 109–27.

15 See Jeni Whalan, *How Peace Operations Work: Power, Legitimacy, and Effectiveness* (Oxford, Oxford University Press, 2013).

16 See Grant and Keohane, 'Accountability and Abuses of Power in World Politics'; Robert O. Keohane and Joseph Nye, 'Redefining Accountability for Global Governance', in Miles Kahler and David A. Lake (eds), *Governance in a Global Economy: Political Authority in Transition* (Princeton, NJ, Princeton University Press, 2003), pp. 386–411.

17 Richard Caplan, 'Who Guards the Guardians? International Accountability in Bosnia' (2005) 12 *International Peacekeeping* 463–76, 463.

18 Ibid.
19 See Whalan, *How Peace Operations Work*, p. 205.
20 The final part of a UNSC resolution creating a peacekeeping operation usually requests that the UNSG report regularly on the operation's performance. A typical example is SC Res. 2149 (10 April 2014), creating MINUSCA in the Central African Republic, which requests that the UNSG report every four months, and 'include in his reports to the Council updates on and recommendations related to the dynamic implementation [of] MINUSCA's mandated tasks', including information on finances, the security situation, political dynamics and the conduct of peacekeepers.
21 See United Nations, *United Nations Peacekeeping Operations: Principles and Guidelines* (New York, United Nations, 2008).
22 Adam Roberts and Dominik Zaum, *Selective Security: War and the United Nations Security Council since 1945* (Abingdon, Routledge for the International Institute for Strategic Studies, 2008), p. 54. See also Nicholas Wheeler and Tim Dunne, 'East Timor and the New Humanitarian Interventionism' (2001) 77 *International Affairs* 805–27.
23 Schedler, 'Conceptualizing Accountability', 14.
24 See Frederick Rawski, 'To Waive or Not to Waive: Immunity and Accountability in UN Peacekeeping Operations' (2002–2003) 18 *Connecticut Journal of International Law* 103–32; Florian Hoffman and Frédéric Mégret, 'Fostering Human Rights Accountability: An Ombudsperson for the United Nations?' (2005) 11 *Global Governance* 46–63; Jennifer Murray, 'Who Will Police the Peace-Builders? The Failure to Establish Accountability for the Participation of United Nations Civilian Police in the Trafficking of Women in Post-Conflict Bosnia and Herzegovina' (2002–2003) 34 *Columbia Human Rights Law Review* 475–527; Aoi, de Coning and Thakur, *Unintended Consequences*; Burke, 'Attribution of Responsibility'; Miller, 'Legal Aspects of Stopping Sexual Exploitation and Abuse'; Murphy, 'An Assessment of UN Efforts'; Zeid Report.
25 For a fuller discussion, see Hoffman and Mégret, 'Fostering Human Rights Accountability'.
26 'Petition for Relief', lodged by Mario Joseph, Brian Concannon Jr and Ira Kurzban on 3 November 2011: www.ijdh.org/wordpress/wp-content/uploads/2011/11/english-petitionREDACTED.pdf.
27 Correspondence from Patricia O'Brien, UN Under Secretary-General for Legal Affairs, 21 February 2013: www.ijdh.org/wp-content/uploads/2011/11/UN-Dismissal-2013-02-21.pdf.
28 See, e.g. SC Res. 1208 (19 November 1998); SC Res. 1318 (7 September 2000); SC Res. 1325 (31 October 2000); and SC Res. 1379 (20 November 2001).
29 See, e.g. UN Doc. A/55/163–S/2000/712 (19 July 2000), *Children and Armed Conflict: Report of the Secretary-General*. See, further, Hoffman and Mégret, 'Fostering Human Rights Accountability'.
30 See *UNMIK Regulation No. 2000/38, On the Establishment of the Ombudsperson in Kosovo*, 30 June 2000 (UNMIK/REG/2000/38); and UNTAET Daily Briefing, 1 June 2001: reliefweb.int/report/timor-leste/untaet-daily-briefing-01-Jun-2001. See also Jonas Nilsson, 'UNMIK and the Ombudsperson Institution in Kosovo: Human Rights Protection in a United Nations "Surrogate State"' (2000) 22 *Netherlands Quarterly of Human Rights* 389–411; Gezim Visoka, 'The "Kafkaesque Accountability" of International Governance in Kosovo' (2012) 6 *Journal of Intervention and Statebuilding* 198–212; and Caplan, 'Who Guards the Guardians?', 468.
31 Visoka, 'Kafkaesque Accountability', 206.
32 Ibid., 190.
33 Simon Chesterman, *You, The People: The United Nations, Transitional Administration, and State-building* (Oxford, Oxford University Press, 2004), pp. 149–50.
34 Cedric de Coning, Aoi Chiyuki and Ramesh Thakur, 'Unintended Consequences of

Peacekeeping', in Andrea Ricci (ed.), *From Early Warning to Early Action? The Debate on the Enhancement of the EU's Crisis Response Capability Continues* (Luxembourg, Office for Official Publications of the European Countries, 2008), pp. 167–76, 175; see also Aoi, de Coning and Thakur, *Unintended Consequences*.

35 See Victoria Holt and Glyn Taylor, *Protecting Civilians in the Context of UN Peacekeeping Operations* (New York, United Nations, 2009); Michael G. Smith, Jeni Whalan and Peter Thomson, 'The Protection of Civilians in UN Peacekeeping Operations: Recent Developments' (2011) 7 *Security Challenges* 27–38.

36 *The 2010 HAP Standard in Accountability and Quality Management* (Geneva, AP International, 2010), p. 1.

37 See Nicholas Wheeler, *Saving Strangers: Humanitarian Intervention in International Society* (Oxford, Oxford University Press, 2000).

38 Peacekeeping operations are diverse; depending on complex local and international political circumstances, operations may lean more to one or other end of these spectra. Importantly, these tensions might be evident within a single operation: for example, MONUSCO (Democratic Republic of Congo) has since 2013 contained both an enforcement element (the Intervention Brigade) and mission components with a much less coercive, more consent-based profile. See SC Res. 2098 (28 March 2013).

39 On the need for a cost–benefit test for accountability reforms, see Wenar, 'Accountability in International Development Aid', 6–9; Ngaire Woods, 'Making the IMF and the World Bank More Accountable' (2001) 77 *International Affairs* 83–100.

40 Wenar, 'Accountability in International Development Aid', 8.

41 See Grant and Keohane, 'Accountability and Abuses of Power in World Politics', 40–1.

42 Accountability scholarship has only recently begun to look at other contexts. See, e.g. Jonathan A. Fox, *Accountability Politics* (Oxford, Oxford University Press, 2007).

43 See, e.g. Wenar, 'Accountability in International Development Aid', 7–8; see also Rubenstein, 'Accountability in an Unequal World'.

44 Andy Featherstone, *Improving Impact: Do Accountability Mechanisms Deliver Results?* (Christian Aid/Save the Children/Humanitarian Accountability Partnership, 2013): www.hapinternational.org/pool/files/improving-impact-do-accountability-mechanisms-deliver-results.pdf. See also Matthew S. Winters, 'Accountability, Participation and Foreign Aid Effectiveness' (2010) 12 *International Studies Review* 218–43; Wenar, 'Accountability in International Development Aid'.

45 Frédéric Mégret, 'The Vicarious Responsibility of the United Nations for "Unintended Consequences" of Peacekeeping Operations', in Chiyuki Aoi, Cedric de Coning and Ramesh Thakur (eds), *Unintended Consequences of Peacekeeping Operations* (Tokyo, UN University Press, 2007), pp. 250–67, 252.

46 Whalan, *How Peace Operations Work*, pp. 71–3.

47 Ibid., p. 200.

48 Ibid., pp. 3–5.

49 On the compliance pull of procedural legitimacy, see Thomas Franck, *The Power of Legitimacy Among Nations* (Oxford, Oxford University Press, 1990). On the cooperation-promoting effects of procedural legitimacy, see Tom Tyler, *Why People Obey the Law* (Princeton, NJ, Princeton University Press, 2006); and Tom Tyler, 'The Psychology of Legitimacy: A Relational Perspective on Voluntary Deference to Authorities' (1997) 1 *Personality and Social Psychology Review* 323–45.

50 Whalan, *How Peace Operations Work*, p. 73.

51 UN, *Principles and Guidelines*, pp. 36, 39.

52 Wenar, 'Accountability in International Development Aid', 7–8 (emphasis in original).

53 Ibid.

54 Espen Barth Eide, Anja Therese Kaspersen, Randolph Kent and Karen von Hippel, *Report on Integrated Missions: Practical Perspectives and Recommendations, Independent Study for the Expanded UN ECHA Core Group* (May 2005), p. 35.

55 Ibid.
56 This discussion draws on Whalan, *How Peace Operations Work*, pp. 126–8.
57 Trevor Findlay, *Cambodia: The Legacy and Lessons of UNTAC* (Oxford, Oxford University Press, 1995), p. 46.
58 Correspondence, 'Behaviour of UNTAC Troops in Cambodia and Thailand' (29 June 1992), Papers of Lt. Gen. John Sanderson, Academy Library, UNSW@ADFA, Australian Defence Force Academy (hereafter 'Sanderson Papers'), MS 359, Box 31, Folder 181.
59 'Letter to Yasushi Akashi, Special Representative of the United Nations' (7 October 1992), Sanderson Papers, MS 359, Box 24, Folder 131; an open letter to Akashi along the same lines was published in the *Phnom Penh Post* on 11 October 1992.
60 'Community Relations Office Report' (16 September 1993), Sanderson Papers, MS 359, Box 24, Folder 131.
61 'Community Relations Office Report', Sanderson Papers.
62 Ingrid A. Lehmann, *Peacekeeping and Public Information: Caught in the Crossfire* (London, Frank Cass, 1999), p. 73.
63 'Community Relations Office Report', Sanderson Papers.
64 Kirsten Schmalenbach, 'Third Party Liability of International Organizations', in Harvey Langholtz, Boris Kondoch and Alan Wells (eds), *International Peacekeeping: The Yearbook of International Peace Operations* (Leiden, Brill, 2004), pp. 33–52; see also Mégret, 'Vicarious Responsibility'.
65 Guglielmo Verdirame, *The UN and Human Rights: Who Guards the Guardians?* (Cambridge, Cambridge University Press, 2011), p. 225.
66 See Burke, 'Troop-Discipline and Sexual Offences'; Nicola Dahrendorf, *Sexual Exploitation and Abuse: Lessons Learned Study, Addressing Sexual Exploitation and Abuse in MONUC* (New York, United Nations, 2006).
67 Schedler, 'Conceptualizing Accountability', p. 14.
68 The lack of accessibility is a weakness of other accountability mechanisms, such as the World Bank's Inspection Panel; see Caplan, 'Who Guards the Guardians?', 466.
69 United Nations, *Handbook on UN Multidimensional Peacekeeping Operations* (New York, United Nations, 2008), p. 48.
70 See Pillar 1 of the UN framework on Addressing Sexual Exploitation and Abuse: www.un.org/en/pseataskforce.
71 Olsen, 'Institutional Basis of Democratic Accountability', 460.

11 Robust peacekeeping, gender and the protection of civilians

Gina Heathcote[1]

Introduction

The blurred line between peacekeeping and force mandates is apparent in robust peacekeeping (the authorisation of tactical force within a peacekeeping mission) and peace enforcement (the escalation of a peacekeeping mission into a 'Chapter VII force').[2] While the United Nations (UN) Security Council's (UNSC) authorisation of Chapter VII force attracts attention, as does authorisation of peace enforcement missions, the UNSC's development of robust peacekeeping has not attracted the same level of attention. This is despite the UNSC considerably enlarging its functions through the creation of robust peacekeeping mandates. Thus in 2011 the UNSC, and much of the western world, debated the merits of intervention in Libya on the grounds of a responsibility to protect (R2P) civilians;[3] and the world watched while the peacekeeping mission in the Ivory Coast was transformed into a Chapter VII operation. Yet the use of force as robust peacekeeping in the Democratic Republic of the Congo (DRC) less than 12 months prior to the Libya and Ivory Coast authorisations received considerably less attention.[4] In this chapter, I argue that the UNSC would benefit from internal rather than external projections of the rule of law (ROL) in the context of robust peacekeeping, to better account for the risks associated with the deployment of force. I use a gender analysis as a means to interrogate the function and deployment of robust peacekeeping measures in the DRC.

In the following part of the chapter I review the emergence of robust peacekeeping as a force authorisation. In Section 2, I analyse the relationship between force mandates and sexual violence in armed conflict, in particular the UNSC's acknowledgement that widespread and systematic sexual violence may function as a trigger for the authorisation of force. I argue robust peacekeeping is in part legitimated via the threat of sexual violence and under the need for greater protection for civilians, despite the larger questions this asks of feminist accounts of force. I follow this in Section 3 with an analysis of UNSC accountability structures for perpetrators of sexual violence in armed conflict, as well as analysis of the emergence of 'gender perspectives' in UNSC resolutions to demonstrate that rather than new mechanisms for the authorisation of force there needs to be a shift to assess the deployment of force and the manner in which it is deployed within a mission. In the final section of the chapter I analyse these debates in light of a very basic articulation of the ROL.[5]

1 Robust peacekeeping and the use of force

This chapter focuses on the creation of robust peacekeeping forces in the DRC, in 2010 and again in 2013 and 2015, in order to consider the need for a rule-of-law approach to the use of force. I use robust peacekeeping as a mechanism to advance this argument as the very creation of robust peacekeeping demonstrates an expansion of UNSC power that occurs without any form of review or limit. Importantly, despite the UNSC reiterating that the DRC robust peacekeeping model is exceptional and does not create a precedent,[6] robust peacekeeping measures have also been developed in the Central African Republic (CAR) (described as a capacity for 'Urgent Temporary Measures' that can be undertaken by the UN Multidimensional Integrated Stabilization Mission in CAR (MINUSCA) peacekeeping mission).[7] This suggests a new era of forceful peacekeeping or force and peacekeeping that would benefit from attention, both of a scholarly, but also institutional form, to assess the legitimacy and success of this development.

The UN defines robust peacekeeping as 'the use of force at the tactical level with the consent of the host authorities and/or the main parties to the conflict'.[8] The UNSC authorises robust peacekeeping with the protection of civilians providing the trigger for the UNSC's escalated involvement in a matter otherwise internal to a state. While humanitarian interventions have tended to be authorised to protect civilians from government forces (as in Kosovo and Libya), robust peacekeeping operations are, by definition, with the tacit or express approval of the state and the force is (primarily) directed at non-state actors. The combination of an existing peacekeeping mandate and the consent of the host state obscure the visibility of robust peacekeeping operations, in contrast to the authorisation of a humanitarian intervention which occurs without the consent of the host state. Despite lesser attention, robust peacekeeping has the potential for increased effectiveness due to a degree of local legitimacy. This is due to the pre-existing UN presence in the form of the peacekeeping mission (or, in the case of CAR, a prior enforcement mission) and the resulting capacity to tailor the authorisation of force to the conditions on the ground. In addition, the consent of the host state can provide significant support for robust peacekeeping, where knowledge of the local infrastructure and conditions can be used to supplement the robust peacekeeping force. Nevertheless, this represents a novel use of UNSC Chapter VII powers that, to a degree, has developed through practice and, like all UNSC acts, is not subject to any form of review.

The peacekeeping mission in the DRC, MONUC,[9] was first established under UNSC Resolution 1279 (1999).[10] In May 2010, MONUC was replaced by MONUSCO,[11] with Resolution 1925 (2010).[12] The MONUSCO remit included the creation of a rapid reaction force.[13] Subsequently, with Resolution 2098 (2013),[14] the UNSC authorised an 'Intervention Brigade' with responsibility for 'neutralizing armed groups' and 'contributing to reducing the threat posed by armed groups to state authority and civilian security in eastern DRC' while making 'space for stabilization activities'.[15] Resolution 2098 also asserts that this does not create a precedent or prejudice the agreed principles of peacekeeping, establishing this as a robust peacekeeping situation rather than one of peace enforcement.[16] In elaborating the role of the Intervention Brigade, the resolution configures the mandate as primarily centred on the protection of civilians,[17] including with respect to prevention of and response to conflict-related sexual violence.[18]

In analysing robust peacekeeping, as exemplified by the UNSC's intervention in the DRC, the UNSC's approach to 'gender perspectives' in force mandates should be highlighted. Increasingly the 'civilian' is constructed through gendered narratives produced within the UNSC's agenda on women, peace and security. The UNSC's references to civilians and their protection are entwined with and bolstered by narratives about apprehending the perpetrators of sexual and gender-based violence in conflict and post-conflict states.[19] Together the protection-of-civilians (POC) focus, and the corpus of resolutions on women, peace and security that centre on the vulnerability of civilians to sexual violence, construct a population in need of saving, through force if necessary, and work to propel and necessitate force in peacekeeping missions.

In constructing the sexual and bodily vulnerability of civilians, the UNSC is able to sustain the logic of force within its mandates and to effectively mobilise soldiering as robust peacekeeping. At the same time the vulnerable gendered body of civilians actively works against recognition of women's broader roles and potential in both security and peace processes while perpetuating myths of rogue military actors using sexual violence in a specific and targeted manner. As such, robust peacekeeping requires UN peacekeepers to use force to protect civilians from sexual violence despite the persistent failure of peacekeepers to commit to this role and the risk to women and men in civilian communities from peacekeeper involvement in sexual exploitation, abuse and violence. This must then be understood as knowledge that exists on a continuum, with the UNSC's use of sexual violence as a trigger for force mandates, which I discuss in the next part.

2 Sexual violence as a trigger for the use of force

The UNSC has produced seven resolutions focused on women, peace and security, as well as developing text on gender issues within country-specific resolutions. The first of the seven resolutions, 1325,[20] was adopted in 2000, and the most recent, 2122, in October 2013.[21] Four of the resolutions focus specifically on sexual violence within armed conflict: – 1820 (2008),[22] 1888 (2009),[23] 1960 (2010)[24] and 2106 (2013)[25] – with three of these connecting the UNSC's activities to combat sexual violence with the use of force. That is, in paragraph one of the first three sexual violence resolutions the UNSC identifies systematic and widespread sexual violence as exacerbating conflict and as potentially impeding the maintenance of international peace and security.[26] The UNSC's choice of language in this thrice-repeated paragraph implicitly invokes Chapter VII action as a potential means to halt widespread and systematic sexual violence in conflict regions. In identifying sexual violence as impeding international peace and security and following this with the intention to 'where necessary, adopt appropriate steps to address widespread and systematic sexual violence',[27] the UNSC replicates the language that it has employed to authorise the use of force (euphemistically referred to as 'all means necessary') in Chapter VII resolutions. This linkage between force and the regulation of sexual violence when paired with robust peacekeeping, such as the authorisation of the Intervention Brigade in the DRC, also signals sexual and gender-based violence as a component of the authorisation of tactical force to protect civilians.

The construction of victim narratives depicting women as survivors of sexual violence at the hands of local men in conflict becomes part of the justification for the use of force in peacekeeping missions. The UNSC's production of knowledge on force and its production of knowledge on sexual violence are usually conducted separately and deal with different aspects of conflict – one (force) is the ultimate and last resort enforcement mechanism that focuses on the actions of states, while the other (regulation of sexual violence) centres on individual responsibility.[28] At the same time, through common paragraph 1 of resolutions 1820, 1888 and 1960, over the years 2008–2010 the UNSC moved towards the perception that widespread and systematic sexual violence could justify the use of force.[29] While it might be unlikely that this would occur as a straightforward Chapter VII authorisation, it is not unfeasible that a robust peacekeeping resolution could permit the use of force on the grounds of a threat of sexual or gender-based violence.

In the DRC, sexual violence perpetrated during the conflict illustrates the failure of the UNSC's development of authorisation for force linked to the prevention of sexual violence. Between 30 July 2010 and 2 August 2010, Mayi Mayi Cheka fighters, in conjunction with other armed militia, embarked on a campaign of systematic sexual violence in Luvungi and surrounding villages in the DRC's North Kivu Province.[30] Subsequently, over 300 individuals from Luvungi and surrounding villages were recorded by humanitarian medical personnel in the region as requiring treatment for sexual assaults and related injuries.[31] Although these attacks were brought to the UNSC's attention, it was not until a month later that the nearby UN forces re-commenced patrols and increased their visibility in Luvungi and surrounding villages, and questions remain about the level of protection supplied by UN peacekeepers. UN peacekeepers subsequently arrested the leaders of the Mayi Mayi Cheka group responsible for the Luvungi attacks, in October 2010.

In January 2011, in Fizi in the South Kivu province of the DRC, after a National Congress for the Defence of the People (CNDP) General was shot in a bar fight, CNDP soldiers, integrated into the DRC national army in 2009, embarked on a series of revenge attacks on the local community that resulted in 60 serious sexual attacks.[32] After the attacks, Lt. Col. Mutware Kabibi, a high-ranking officer in the Congolese army, was tried in the DRC and found guilty of leading the attacks. Although UN peacekeeping personnel did not respond to the threat or actual attacks in either the 2010 or 2011 episodes, both resulted in local trials and convictions. Lt. Col. Mutware was sentenced to a 20-year prison sentence. In both cases the prosecutions focused on commanding officers rather than individual perpetrators.[33] I return to this aspect of the prosecutions for sexual violence committed in the DRC in the following section. In addition, and importantly for this study, in both instances the UN might have deployed the Rapid Reaction Force to deal with the threat before it materialised into harm. As indicated above, in the month prior to the first set of attacks, in Kivu, UNSC Resolution 1925 had transformed MONUC (also accused of perpetrating sexual abuse in the DRC)[34] from a peacekeeping operation to a robust peacekeeping operation, MONUSCO, which was authorised to maintain a reserve force capable of rapid redeployment in the DRC.

Although MONUSCO chose not to use force to halt the threat of or actual sexual violence, it is clear that the UNSC constructed the Rapid Reaction Force, and the more recent Intervention Brigade, with the capacity for the use of force in the form of robust peacekeeping, to respond to precisely this type of scenario. As such, the selective deployment of MONUSCO's Rapid Reaction Force demonstrates the indifferent attitude of militaries to the threat of sexual violence and suggests a need for review of the construction of robust peacekeeping mandates and when robust peacekeeping forces are deployed in-mission.

In addition to considering individual and institutional accountability mechanisms for sexual-violence crimes, the linkage between robust peacekeeping, the ROL and the UNSC's women, peace and security agenda requires reflection. This illuminates the failure of the UNSC, and its subsidiary bodies, to apply internal checks to ensure the implementation of its mandates complies with ROL criteria. While developments in the UNSC to authorise force, including in the form of robust peacekeeping, can be seen as a response to changing and clearer understandings of the nature of conflict, the accountability of the UNSC for both the construction and deployment of robust peacekeeping forces remains unchecked and untouched by any conception of the ROL.[35]

3 Individual and institutional accountability for sexual violence in armed conflict

Even as the UNSC develops the capacity for robust peacekeeping to respond to context specific violence, the deployment of force to halt sexual or gender-based violence remains an unlikely military strategy. Consequently, the use of force to halt widespread and systematic sexual violence demonstrates the flaw of seeking more rather than fewer authorisations for the use of force via a women, peace and security or protection of civilians agenda. What is more, the authorisation of force depends on and reinforces the representation of women in conflict as victims of sexual violence in a manner that raises questions about whether this might be justification for the deployment of new forms of force and yet an unlikely trigger for military commanders to actually deploy their troops on the ground.

Furthermore, within UNSC resolutions there remains a distinction between the crime of sexual violence in armed conflict and the disciplinary offence of sexual exploitation and abuse. This has led to different treatment in terms of labelling and consequences for perpetrators. Sexual exploitation and abuse has been defined as

> any actual or attempted abuse of a position of vulnerability, differential power, or trust, for sexual purposes, including, but not limited to, profiting monetarily, socially or politically from the sexual exploitation of another [...or the] actual or threatened physical intrusion of a sexual nature, whether by force or under unequal or coercive conditions.[36]

The UN refers to sexual exploitation and abuse to describe violations by UN personnel, both civilian and military, and has repeatedly articulated a policy of 'zero tolerance' for such violations, indicating that the:

> United Nations standards of conduct prohibit sexual activity with prostitutes, which is the most accessible form of sexual activity for contingent members [...] and in high risk areas [...] banning all sexual relations with the local population in all or part of the mission area.[37]

Alongside these strategies, the UNSC has developed and deployed separate terminology to refer to sexual violence committed during conflict and in post-conflict communities. The term 'sexual violence' is used to refer to mechanisms for dealing with perpetrators of sexual crimes within an armed conflict or post-conflict community; and the term 'sexual exploitation and abuse' to refer to acts of UN personnel perpetrated while working on a UN mission. UNSC Resolution 2106 (2013), centred on sexual violence, requests the UN Secretary-General (UNSG) to

> continue and strengthen efforts to implement the policy of zero tolerance on sexual exploitation and abuse by United Nations personnel and urges concerned Member States to ensure full accountability, including prosecutions, in cases of such conduct involving their nationals.[38]

In contrast to the articulation of sexual exploitation and abuse to be managed by troop-contributing states, alongside a policy of zero tolerance for UN personnel, the remainder of the Resolution focuses on 'sexual violence' and appears to be directed at the parties to a conflict, in particular non-state military actors, rather than UN personnel. Similarly, in the earlier Resolution 1960 (2010), the focus throughout is 'sexual violence', with the UNSC reaffirming its intention to use necessary measures to address widespread and systematic sexual violence, reiterating the need for the UNSG to list parties responsible for such violence during armed conflict,[39] and reiterating its intention to develop targeted sanctions against those responsible for such violence.[40] By contrast, in the same resolution in operative paragraph 16, the UNSC addresses sexual exploitation and abuse, requesting the UNSG to continue 'efforts to implement the policy of zero tolerance on sexual exploitation and abuse by United Nations peacekeeping and humanitarian personnel'. Neither of these two resolutions, nor any prior resolution of the UNSC, addresses the consequences of and responsibility for sexual *violence* perpetrated by UN peacekeeping and humanitarian personnel.

The sexual exploitation and abuse threshold, while created to expand the nature of abuses that UN personnel could be found accountable for, in effect creates a two-tier structure of sexual abuse within armed conflict and post-conflict settings. Different culpability is attributed to local perpetrators, where sanctions, potential criminal charges and even the use of force may be the international response, while UN personnel are dealt with via national military disciplinary structures, often meaning little more than being sent home from the mission. This is evidenced by the DRC incidents, described above, as well as the UNSC sanctions-listing regime, which bypasses individual responsibility to pursue commanding officers responsible for acts of sexual violence by members of their contingent. Yet within UN missions, command responsibility for acts of sexual violence, sexual exploitation or abuse committed by UN personnel is not pursued.

Two sets of acts are being elaborated by the UN here. On the one hand, local perpetrators of sexual violence in conflict zones are considered as responsible for widespread and systematic attacks – thus invoking superior orders and command responsibility. In contrast, the internal discipline structures of UN missions seek to project sexual exploitation and abuse and sexual violence perpetrated by UN personnel as not a policy or 'weapon' deployed by UN personnel and not the responsibility of commanding officers or troop-contributing states. However, the continuum of UNSC procedures I wish to draw attention to connects the failure of UN command structures and the UNSC's women, peace and security framework to recognise that omissions to act to halt sexual violations perpetrated by UN troops, to the failure, of those same commanding officers, to respond to the threat of sexual violence from foreign, local or rogue forces. International law acknowledges omissions to act as potentially incurring international responsibility of a state so that the reports of peacekeeper complicity in sexual abuse, exploitation and violence during conflict indicates, at the very least, a turning of a blind eye by military hierarchies. Although these are UN missions, troop-contributing countries remain responsible for the discipline of forces. Yet the actions of MONUC troops, whose replacement by MONUSCO was in part due to persistent scandals involving sexual crimes committed by UN personnel, attracted individual responsibility rather than command or institutional/state responsibility. The experiences of the Mayi Mayi Cheka commander who was held, with others, responsible for the Luvungi attacks in 2010 and the CNDP General prosecuted for the Fizi attacks in 2011 can be contrasted with the UN procedures for responding to sexual exploitation and abuse and/or sexual violence by peacekeepers.

Thus, the attempt to develop a UNSC agenda on sexual exploitation and abuse has resulted in lesser consequences for UN personnel and a renaming of sexual violence as sexual exploitation and abuse. While the terminology of sexual exploitation and abuse may have been strategically developed to include more abuses within military disciplinary procedures, this wider term has in fact watered down the offence to one of a disciplinary rather than criminal nature. This has had the further effect of permitting sexual exploitation and abuse within peacekeeping communities to be regarded as the wayward behaviour of a handful of actors as opposed to a continuing, global problematic of military sexual cultures. I would add, the UNSC's persistent identification of women in post-conflict and transitional communities as sexually vulnerable, rather than as active community participants, fails to disrupt out-of-date understandings of post-conflict spaces, of gender and of sexuality.[41]

This institutionalised response seems to reflect the perspectives of western military leadership who are yet to publicly or effectively challenge internal sexual cultures within militaries and the destructive gender expectations and abuses that co-exist with such attitudes. Both the women, peace and security agenda and the move toward robust peacekeeping as a mechanism to protect civilians, have, then, at their core a central paradox that suggests the UNSC initiatives to protect civilians or to halt widespread and systematic sexual violence function as the perceived rationale for robust peacekeeping, and yet an unlikely site for the use of force on the ground. There is an inconsistency in troop-contributing countries (TCCs) deployed to 'protect' who do not regard violence against women, in particular sexual violence, as a 'crime' or a product of military cultures themselves, suggesting the UNSC's gender perspectives are of limited value to women in conflict communities. This is the continuum between the deployment of force to protect civilians and the means to challenge sexual violence perpetrated by UN personnel that demonstrates the peacekeeping/force confusion at the core of robust peacekeeping, indicating a need for ROL standards to provide internal review of UNSC acts.

While robust peacekeeping mandates may be preferable to humanitarian intervention because they are often able to provide a locally responsive mandate, have the cooperation of the host state and in principle will be strategically limited in time and scope, the blurring of peacekeeping and peace enforcement has made the application of the accountability components of a ROL-type measure increasingly difficult. Decisions to deploy the 'robust' aspect of peacekeeping are not assessed or reviewed. As the responses to the systematic sexual violence attacks in the DRC in 2010 and 2011 demonstrate, military understandings of a 'threat' in the field continue to dismiss the threat of widespread and systematic sexual violence as appropriately dealt with through the deployment of Rapid Reaction Forces. At the same time the UNSC has opened up the possibility of the use of force to halt widespread and systematic sexual violence, although this widening of the notion of what constitutes a threat has also not been subject to due process, review or a clear set of decision-making processes. To add to these two aspects of robust peacekeeping, the complicity of UN personnel in sexual violence and the tendency to treat these crimes as disciplinary offences raise questions about why the UNSC regards the sexual violence of non-state actors as justifying force but regards the sexual violence of members of its own operations as minor offences.

4 Raising the rule of law

Robust peacekeeping becomes an important site for understanding the limited role for the ROL in UNSC-authorised use of force. Although the ROL itself may be a contested concept,[42] it is also an emergent feature of the UNSC's own work, particularly in relation to the standards the UNSC elaborates for transitional and post-conflict communities to conform with. The UNSC has conducted debates on the ROL since 2003 and UNSC resolutions and UNSG's reports regularly refer to the ROL in relation to specific situations on the UNSC's agenda. These outward projections of the ROL as good governance and as global standards may be questioned; however, this is not the focus of this chapter.

There are two aspects connected to the absence of the ROL that I have brought out in this discussion and which relate not to transitional societies but to the decision-making structures of the UNSC itself. First, the creation of the sexual-violence trigger in paragraph 1 of Resolutions 1820, 1888 and 1960 demonstrates the lack of rule-of-law safeguards on decisions to use force or to advance force mandates, because the consultation behind the creation of this new ground for the use of force does not have a procedure for checks and balances, a similar argument can and should be made with respect to the innovation of robust peacekeeping mandates.

Second, deficiencies in peacekeeping accountability – especially with regard to sexual violence, subsumed under the 'sexual exploitation and abuse' language – raise questions about the viability of robust peacekeeping initiatives. Peacekeeping operations do not respond to the threat of or actual sexual violence within transitional and post-conflict states and accountability mechanisms within UN missions are insufficient to address sexual violence committed by peacekeeping personnel. What I have sought to demonstrate in this chapter is that this lack of accountability extends from the participation of peacekeeper personnel, while deployed, in egregious behaviour including criminal acts of sexual violence and the lesser crime but still serious issue of sexual exploitation, and exists alongside the failure of robust peacekeeping missions to respond to either the threat or actual crimes of sexual violence. The latter failure to respond at the mission level is then compounded by the UNSC's failure to develop mechanisms to review, judicially or otherwise, its own decisions, in particular decisions to authorise the use of force, including in situations of robust peacekeeping.

According to Dicey's basic theorisation, the ROL incorporates three key requirements: the law must be clearly articulated in advance; there must be equality under the law; and there must be a right to judicial review.[43] Accepting Dicey's formulation, the requirements of the ROL are not met in UNSC decisions to extend the triggers to use force, in the application of such force or with respect to the accountability of actors responsible for the deployment of force, including in robust peacekeeping situations.

Robust peacekeeping is not always sufficiently regarded or included in our discussions of the UNSC's authorisation of the use of force. While robust peacekeeping has the potential to become the mechanism through which the UNSC authorises the use of force, bypassing the larger questions and challenges raised by its other early twenty-first-century narratives on humanitarian intervention and the R2P,[44] the accountability, democratic, legitimacy and ROL components of robust peacekeeping require attention.

4.1 Accountability failures and the peacekeeping continuum

Accountability failures within the UNSC, for example with respect to the management and disciplining of peacekeeping personnel responsible for sexual violence, need to be understood as functioning on a continuum that extends from the authorisation of the use of force through to the management of UN forces. Given this continuum, a discrepancy arises when the UNSC invokes various terms prefaced by 'gender' – equality, perspectives, balancing – in peacebuilding and post-conflict initiatives as mechanisms that assist transitional societies to demonstrate their commitment to the ROL, but does not reflect the same concern in the management of UN forces. While the UNSC compels transitional societies to pay attention to gender equality, gender perspectives and gender balancing to help evidence the development of state structures that comply with the UNSC's rule-of-law requirements, it does not pay the same attention internally. This indicates that, while the UNSC recognises the role of gender justice within the re-building and the reconstruction of institutions within a post-conflict state, it does not sufficiently address the questions a full gender perspective raises about the UNSC's own working structures, decision-making spaces and agendas.

4.2 The democratic deficit in the Security Council

While other texts identify the democratic deficit in the UNSC,[45] it is important to reflect on how the UNSC's women, peace and security agenda is also a limited democratic model, in both a practical and a substantive manner. At the level of practice, consideration of which feminist voices/actors gain access to international institutional fora and how the diversity of feminist discussions can be a necessary casualty due to the need for these actors to present themselves as in agreement. At the level of substance, the consequence is that the UNSC has not welcomed important feminist understandings of the diverse interconnected issues in re-imagining security; for example, the role of disarmament in a feminist politics of peace.[46] As a result, the feminist ideas that shape the legal reform around women, peace and security become unlinked from wider feminist debates, tensions and dialogues. Furthermore, the UNSC is itself unrepresentative of regional diversity and gender diversity, limiting the production of resolutions and of action to a very narrow global mind-set.

4.3 Securing legitimacy; whose legitimacy?

Not only does this reinforce a 'benign' and seemingly acceptable model of robust peacekeeping (designed to protect civilians, women and children, vulnerable groups and sexual violence victims), the use of force as robust peacekeeping bypasses the normative role of the UN General Assembly (UNGA). There is therefore an urgent need to discuss the move towards the UNSC functioning as a quasi-legislative body that does not abide by the ROL, precisely because it is a political body (albeit with legal implications to its decisions). Understanding the UNSC as a political body with legal outcomes reminds us that the UNSC was never intended to function in a legislative capacity. Deploying gender perspectives, protection of civilian narratives or the women, peace and security mantra appears to enhance the legitimacy of the UNSC,[47] yet the gender perspectives (flawed and partial as they might be) are only applied outwardly and not inwardly, leaving the UNSC untouched by its own considerations on women, peace and security.

4.4 The gap between legitimacy and the rule of law

Understandings of legitimacy have produced volumes within the discipline of international law; however, we must remember this is distinct from the ROL. Compliance with the ROL may aid the production of institutional legitimacy, but the pursuit of institutional legitimacy does not attest to the application of the ROL. As Otto has demonstrated, the UNSC's initiatives on women, peace and security function as a mechanism for legitimating the work of the UNSC, including the authorisation of the use of force;[48] this also results in a downplaying of the need for accountability within the UNSC in the authorisation, deployment and use of force.

In 1992, Thomas Franck wrote with respect to the emergent right to democratic governance that 'the key to solving these residual problems is ... that older democracies should be the first to be volunteered to be monitored in the hope that this will lead to near-universal compliance'.[49] We must demand the application of the same leadership standards from the UNSC. The deployment of ROL criteria in transitional and post-conflict communities must be matched with the UNSC also developing checks and balances drawn from the ROL rather than pursuing legitimacy through the enlargement of its own agenda.

5 Conclusion

To finish, it seems time to ask what happens if international legal actors cease to look for 'women and children' within conflict regions, and cease with the category of civilians. If international legal tools were to respond to women, children and civilians as agents actively producing both conflict and peace within their community, we take away the justification for the use of force in humanitarian crises or in situations of robust peacekeeping. Calls for a humanitarian intervention in Syria from 2012, alongside the authorised intervention in Libya in 2011, deploy a discourse revolving around the identification of civilians, women and children to justify the use of force. In situations of robust peacekeeping the identification of the risk women face in conflict zones not only fuels the authorisation of force, it allows the military forces to disregard women in local communities as human beings who should be offered a stake in decision-making processes rather than mere protection. Women become an element of the justification for military force and women are characterised as vulnerable and in need of protection in a manner that actively works against recognition of the contribution women bring to a security situation.

In undertaking robust peacekeeping operations the UNSC deploys imagery of civilians to downplay the problems that the UNSC faces in choosing to support the goals of specific states. This can result in downplaying the violations the state itself may be responsible for, as well as the absence of clear international law permitting the UNSC to authorise the deployment of force to support governments against insurgent groups. There is a need to be cautious of authorisations of force that seek to champion one group of 'rebels' challenging state oppression (under humanitarian intervention narratives) while selectively outlawing others (in situations of robust peacekeeping).

The UNSC's women, peace and security resolutions present the conundrum that (in Dianne Otto's words) 'women's participation may be used to advance military and institutional agendas while maintaining women's marginality [...and] while enacting the formal performance of inclusivity'.[50] We must extend this finding to think beyond the legitimacy of the UNSC secured by the women, peace and security framework and acknowledge that the UNSC increasingly needs the women-as-victims narrative to justify the use of force, and to justify the robust protection of civilians, robust peacekeeping and humanitarian interventions. The development of these narratives without attention to how the rules are decided, adjudicated and applied makes a mockery of the UNSC's separate agendas on the ROL in post-conflict states and raises questions about the deployment of robust peacekeeping and the line between force and peacekeeping that is blurred along the way.

Notes

1 Thanks to participants at the ARC Workshop on the Linkage Project, *Strengthening the Rule of Law through the UN Security Council*, Canberra, June 2012, to Hilary Charlesworth, Jeremy Farrall, Marie-Eve Loiselle and Shane Chalmers for editorial support and the invitation to participate.

2 Chapter VII force is defined as UNSC operations that include the use of military force; often termed 'all necessary means' in UNSC resolutions. This is contrasted to peace enforcement missions, which commence as neutral forces with limited capabilities to use force and have their mandates adapted to use 'all means necessary' in response to changing conditions on the ground. The latter involves a peacekeeping force transformed into a military (Chapter VII) force. The distinction on the ground between the two types of forces (Chapter VII and peace enforcement operation) may be negligible, as both are, in effect, Chapter VII forces. The shift from an impartial

peacekeeping operation to an enforcement mandate, without consent of the state, and with military capacities, is different in terms of the process of authorisation only; ostensibly raising similar concerns to those identified in relation to robust peacekeeping in this chapter. Peacekeeping operations do not have a force mandate and are established with the consent of the host state.

3 SC Res. 1973 (17 March 2011), preambular para. 4: '*Reiterating* the responsibility of the Libyan authorities to protect the Libyan population and *reaffirming* that parties to armed conflicts bear the primary responsibility to take all feasible steps to ensure the protection of civilians.' For discussion, see Harrington's chapter in this collection.

4 SC Res. 1925 (28 May 2010), which authorises the creation of a Rapid Reaction Force in the DRC; see also SC Res. 2098 (28 March 2013) authorising an 'Intervention Brigade'. These tactical components of the mission are authorised to use force, yet are clearly perceived as peacekeeping forces; see SC Res. 2098 (28 March 2013), para. 9, stating 'on an exceptional basis and without creating a precedent or any prejudice to the agreed principles of peacekeeping'.

5 For a modern articulation, see Lord Bingham's speech at the Centre for Public Law, University of Cambridge, 16 November 2006 ('Bingham speech'), where he concludes: 'the individual [...] accepts the constraints imposed by laws properly made because of the benefits which, on balance, they confer. The state for its part accepts that it may not do, at home or abroad, all that it has the power to do but only that which laws binding upon it authorise it to do': www.cpl.law.cam.ac.uk/past_activities/the_rule_of_law_text_transcript.php

6 See SC Res. 2211 (26 March 2015), para. 1, which extends the mandate of the DRC Intervention Brigade until March 2016.

7 SC Res. 2217 (28 April 2015), para. 23(f).

8 UN Department of Peacekeeping Operations, *United Nations Peacekeeping Operations: Principles and Guidelines* (New York, United Nations, 2008), p. 19 ('Capstone Doctrine'). For analysis of this definition, see Thierry Tardy, 'A Critique of Robust Peacekeeping in Contemporary Peace Operations' (2011) 18(2) *International Peacekeeping* 152–67.

9 United Nations Organization Mission in the Democratic Republic of Congo (MONUC).

10 SC Res. 1279 (30 November 1999).

11 United Nations Organization Stabilization Mission in the Democratic Republic of Congo (MONUSCO).

12 SC Res. 1925 (28 May 2010).

13 Ibid., para. 4: 'Authorizes MONUSCO, while concentrating its military forces in the east of the country, to keep a reserve force capable of redeploying rapidly elsewhere in the country.' The UNSC had previously authorised a rapid reaction force; however, a lack of state logistical support led the UNSC to transform the mandate in 2010.

14 SC Res. 2098 (28 March 2013).

15 Ibid., para. 9. See also Oswald's chapter in this collection.

16 Tardy, 'A Critique of Robust Peacekeeping', 155.

17 SC Res. 2098 (28 March 2013), para. 12(a)(i).

18 Ibid., para. 12(a)(iii).

19 See, e.g. SC Res. 2098 (28 March 2013), paras 11, 12(1).

20 SC Res. 1325 (31 October 2000).

21 SC Res. 2122 (18 October 2013).

22 SC Res. 1820 (18 June 2008).

23 SC Res. 1888 (29 October 2009).

24 SC Res. 1960 (16 December 2010).

25 SC Res. 2106 (24 June 2013).

26 SC Res. 1820 (18 June 2008), para. 1; SC Res. 1888 (29 October 2009), para. 1; SC Res. 1960 (16 December 2010), para. 1.

27 SC Res. 2106 (24 Jun 2013), para. 1 alters the wording of the three prior resolutions:

the UNSC emphasises the need to take 'effective steps to prevent and respond to such acts' and 'stresses women's participation as essential to any prevention and protection response'. This leaves considerable ambiguity with regard to the UNSC's readiness to authorise force in response to sexual violence occurring within armed conflict.

28 See Roisin Burke, 'Attribution of Responsibility: Sexual Abuse and Exploitation and Effective Control of Blue Helmets' (2012) 16(1) *Journal of International Peacekeeping* 1–46.

29 See Gina Heathcote, 'Feminist Politics and the Use of Force: Theorising Feminist Action and Security Council Resolution 1325' (2011) 7 *Socio-Legal Review* 23–44.

30 United Nations Joint Human Rights Office, *Final Report of the Fact-finding Mission of the United Nations Joint Human Rights Office into the Mass Rapes and other Human Rights Violations Committed by a Coalition of Armed Groups Along the Kibua-Mpofi Axis in Walikale Territory, North Kivu from 30 July to 2 August 2010* (July 2011): www.ohchr.org/Documents/Countries/ZR/BCNUDHRapportViols MassifsKibuaMpofi_en.pdf. According to this report (summary, para. 2), rapes were carried out by a coalition of combatants from the Democratic Forces for the Liberation of Rwanda and the Mayi Mayi Cheka, as well as residual elements of a force led by Lt. Col. Emmanuel Nsengiyumva.

31 These figures vary across reports; the 'Final Report', ibid., found over 387 civilians had suffered sexual violence during the attacks.

32 Chloe Christman and Aaron Hall, 'Minerals, Militias and Rape: How Do We Make Peace a Reality in Congo?' (1 March 2012): www.womenundersiegeproject.org/blog/entry/minerals-militias-and-rape-how-do-we-make-peace-a-reality-in-congo.

33 See Chuck Sudetic, 'Congo Justice: What happened in Fizi', *Voices: Open Society Justice Initiative* (21 April 2011): www.opensocietyfoundations.org/voices/congo-justice-what-happened-fizi.

34 See Jane Rasmussen, *MONUC: Sexual Exploitation and Abuse End of Assignment Report* (25 February 2005): www.peacekeepingbestpractices.unlb.org/PBPS/Library/MONUC%20SEA%20EOA-Rasmussen%20%2825–02–05%29.pdf.

35 Cf. the chapters by Thomson and Whalan in this collection.

36 See UN Doc. ST/SGB/2003/13 (9 October 2003), *Secretary-General's Bulletin: Special Measures for Protection from Sexual Exploitation and Sexual Abuse*, para. 1.

37 See UN Doc. A/59/710 (24 March 2005), *Letter from the UN Secretary-General to the President of the General Assembly*, paras 44 and 49.

38 SC Res. 2106 (24 June 2013), para. 15.

39 SC Res. 1960 (16 December 2010), paras 3 and 4.

40 Ibid., para. 7.

41 See Olivera Simic, *Regulation of Sexual Conduct in UN Peacekeeping Operations* (Berlin, Springer, 2012).

42 For discussion see the chapters in Part I of this collection.

43 Bingham speech.

44 SC Res. 2098 (28 March 2013), paras 11 and 12(1).

45 Anne Orford, 'The Politics of Collective Security' (1996) 17 *Michigan Journal of International Law* 373–411.

46 Felicity Ruby, 'Security Council Resolution 1325: A Tool for Conflict Prevention', in Gina Heathcote and Dianne Otto (eds), *Rethinking Peacekeeping, Gender Equality and Collective Security* (Basingstoke, Palgrave Macmillan, 2014).

47 Dianne Otto, 'The Security Council's Gender Legitimacy: The Symbolic Capital of Resolution 1325', in Hilary Charlesworth and Jean-Marc Coicaud (eds), *Fault Lines of International Legitimacy* (Cambridge, Cambridge University Press, 2010), pp. 239–76.

48 Ibid.

49 Thomas M. Franck, 'The Emerging Right to Democratic Governance' (1992) 86(1) *American Journal of International Law* 46–91.

50 Otto, 'The Security Council's Alliance of Gender Legitimacy', pp. 239–76, 239.

12 Protection of civilians and the rule of law

Building synergies between the agendas

Peter Thomson

Introduction

Two agendas in the United Nations (UN) Security Council (UNSC) are essential to the effective protection of civilians in conflict situations. The first is the protection of civilians in armed conflict (POC) and the second is the rule of law (ROL). These two agendas effectively operate in the UNSC as topics for discrete consideration. While this separation of the agendas is understandable, as both are wide-ranging and substantive topics for deliberation, this UNSC practice complicates efforts to build good synergistic policy in peacekeeping operations.

Over the last decade, the POC agenda has assumed a higher priority in the work of the UNSC. This agenda contains a collection of broadly related protection items. One item is the 'protection of civilians by UN peacekeeping and other missions' (which I will refer to as 'POC/PK' agenda to distinguish it from the broader POC agenda). POC/PK relates to the mandated task of peacekeeping operations to 'afford protection to civilians under imminent threat of physical violence'.[1] It is now broadly accepted within the UN system that POC/PK is a core responsibility of peacekeeping operations.[2]

The rule-of-law agenda, for its part, is broad and ill-defined and involves numerous institutions, including a dedicated UN coordination mechanism entitled the Rule of Law Coordination and Resource Group (ROLCREG).[3] Like POC, the rule-of-law agenda has assumed a more significant place on the UNSC agenda over the last decade and the promotion of ROL is now said to be at the 'heart' of the UN's mission.[4] Increasingly there is international recognition of the importance of equipping the UN with the necessary tools to effectively promote ROL and to respond to serious human rights violations in order to create the conditions necessary for peace building and economic revival.[5]

This chapter focuses on the key links between the POC and rule-of-law agendas in peacekeeping operations. These links are most evident in the mandates given by the UNSC to peacekeeping missions themselves. They are also evident in the process for developing mission-wide comprehensive POC strategies prescribed in the *Framework for Drafting Comprehensive Protection of Civilian Strategies in United Nations Peacekeeping Operations* (POC Framework).[6] The aim of POC strategies is to build greater cohesiveness within peacekeeping missions to meet the immediate protection needs of the civilian population by drawing upon all components within the mission (including the rule-of-law component).

In order to analyse the relationship between these agendas, I examine some of the key policy documents on POC and ROL. I also draw upon recent thinking on effective ROL programming and its delivery emerging from the World Bank's ground-breaking *World Development Report 2011: Conflict, Security, and Development* (WDR11).[7] Against this background, I consider the way in which the POC/PK and ROL agendas interact and the policy and institutional links between these agendas.

In this chapter, I point to the benefits of comprehensive POC strategies. I also argue that further consideration should be given to the interaction between the two agendas and the potential impact of the POC/PK agenda on the ROL agenda. For example, there is some risk that comprehensive POC strategies may impact on those ROL programmes which require longer-term implementation, such as institutional strengthening of courts, by effectively lowering the priority afforded to such activities within the mission as a result of the higher priority afforded to POC/PK.

Another issue deserving of consideration is the move within the rule-of-law agenda towards a 'thin' (as opposed to 'thick') model for ROL in stabilisation operations. The value and utility of a more ambitious 'thick' programming have been increasingly questioned for conflict-afflicted countries with poor human resourcing. I suggest that in both POC/PK and rule-of-law agendas there is a built-in process for prioritisation. Indeed, mission priorities are established when decisions are made concerning which rule-of-law activities should be included in the POC implementation matrix, on the one hand, and within a 'thin' rule-of-law model, on the other. The conceptual links between these processes, between this new rule-of-law thinking and the POC strategising, have not been sufficiently explored. I suggest that useful links could be developed by strengthening the synergies between these agendas.

Implementing reform in these areas is no simple matter. The attempt to strengthen partnerships between the various participants in the field can prove difficult, in part because different UN agencies have differing approaches to protection and many actors are driven predominantly by their strong commitment to their particular organisation's mandate.[8]

1 The POC agenda

Protection of civilians (including POC/PK) has its roots in the humanitarian protection of civilians and the law of armed conflict, especially the Geneva Conventions and the Additional Protocols, which regulate how war is to be fought and afford certain status to civilian non-participants in armed conflict.[9] By regulating the conduct of armed conflict these laws have the effect of protecting those not taking part in the hostilities (for example, civilians, health and aid workers).

The POC landscape is complex. There is a need to recognise the differing protection roles performed, and differing understandings of protection employed, by the various relevant actors and entities.[10] This multiplicity of protection roles and understandings is reflected at the UNSC level, where several discrete processes and resolutions address protection-related issues,[11] including the well-known resolutions on women, peace and security,[12] children and armed conflict[13] and conflict-related sexual violence.[14] One of the challenges in POC/PK is therefore to develop integrated approaches in the field while doing justice to the strategic aims of the differing agendas and to build synergies, where possible, in the utilisation of the limited resources of both the mission and associated humanitarian and non-governmental actors in the field.

At the mission level, coordination is complicated by the range of activities which need to be managed in modern peace operations. As Alain Le Roy, former Under Secretary-General of the UN Department of Peacekeeping Operations (DPKO), stated:

> [t]he complex and multidimensional nature of modern peacekeeping operations requires senior mission leaders capable of managing a vast array of tasks and challenges, ranging from human rights and reconciliation efforts and the establishment of the rule of law to complex disarmament processes and the protection of civilians.[15]

The emergence of the POC/PK agenda is a reaction to the recognised failures by the UN to effectively protect civilians in countries where peacekeepers were deployed.[16] In 1994 the Rwandan genocide unfolded in the presence of a UN peacekeeping operation, the United Nations Assistance Mission for Rwanda (UNAMIR).[17] The following year reportedly 7,000 Bosnian Muslim civilians were massacred within the purview of another UN peace operation, the United Nations Protection Force (UNPROFOR).[18]

In response to these crises, the UNSC in 1999 mandated the UN Assistance Mission in Sierra Leone (UNAMISIL), using language that was to become a standard for POC/PK,[19] 'to take the necessary action … within its capabilities and areas of deployment, to afford protection to civilians under imminent threat of physical violence'.[20]

In 2002, the UNSC adopted an *Aide Memoire* as a tool for managing and analysing protection issues.[21] The *Aide Memoire*, which has been regularly updated, discusses the wider protection concerns pertaining to conflict-affected populations, especially displacement, humanitarian access, the conduct of hostilities, accountability and ROL.

Yet despite the development of such a sophisticated aid for promoting the protection of civilians, it still proved difficult for peacekeeping operations to implement the mandated task of protecting civilians.[22] In 2009, in its landmark Resolution 1894, the UNSC therefore indicated that the protection of civilians 'requires a coordinated response from all relevant mission components', and reaffirmed its practice of ensuring that mandates of UN peacekeeping and other relevant missions include provisions on the protection of civilians, and stressed that mandated protection activities should be 'given priority' in the allocation of the operation's human and financial resources.[23]

2 The POC/PK agenda

Against this background of POC at the strategic level, over recent years we have seen the UN methodically introduce operational reforms and guidance for the implementation of the POC/PK agenda. For example, useful guidance for civil affairs officers on how to support the risk assessment on POC is provided in the *Civil Affairs Handbook.*[24] Much of this recent work on the POC/PK agenda has sought to address the gaps in policy and preparedness described in the major independent study, *Protecting Civilians in the Context of UN Peacekeeping Operations: Successes, Setbacks and Remaining Challenges.*[25] The study warned that the 'chain of events to support protection of civilians'[26] – from early warning, to the development of pre-mandate planning and assessments by the UN Secretariat,[27] to the mission-level implementation of the mandates – was 'broken' and that the UNSC's intent was misunderstood. Importantly, the study identified both the need for guidance and the need for mission-wide strategies on POC to coordinate the mission's efforts to implement the mandated task to protect civilians.[28]

In 2010, the Special Committee on Peacekeeping Operations (the 'C34') addressed these criticisms by introducing several advances. These advances featured in the *DPKO/DFS Operational Concept on the Protection of Civilians in United Nations Peacekeeping Operations* (the 'Operational Concept'),[29] which proposed a three-tiered approach to protecting civilians and for the phasing of operations depending on the security context.

The first tier, entitled 'protection through political processes', recognises the need for mission leadership and personnel to promote political solutions through their engagement with the parties, including by supporting the original peace agreement and transitional arrangements. This tier also includes some rule-of-law activities, such as supporting constitution-building and transitional justice processes, as well as measures to reform the security sector, transition to elections and build support for the establishment of political parties, non-governmental organisations (NGOs) and civil society. Of course, these tasks concern key aspects of the sovereignty of the host nation and it will often be challenging for a mission to implement some of these activities, given the need for the mission to maintain the host nation's consent to its ongoing presence.

The second tier refers to 'providing protection from physical violence'. Tasks may include the well-known examples of the UN peacekeepers escorting women to markets, working with local community protection systems and assisting internally displaced persons (IDPs) by providing basic support, such as stoves, lighting, toilets and wood patrols, which can minimise the time spent outside the relative security of an IDP camp.

The third tier, where the most direct overlap occurs between POC/PK and ROL, refers to 'establishing a protective environment'. This includes the longer-term activities of promoting legal protection and supporting effective national institutions. The Operational Concept specifies that this tier applies to security sector reform (SSR) activities, rule-of-law actions aimed at the security sector and the national police and other criminal justice actors involved in protection efforts.

Following the call from the C34 in 2010 for comprehensive protection strategies to be incorporated in the overall mission implementation plans,[30] DPKO and the UN Department of Field Support (DFS) jointly released the draft POC Framework to provide guidance to mission leadership on developing comprehensive POC strategies.[31] These strategies intersect with rule-of-law programmes in three important ways. First, a dedicated POC coordination mechanism must be established to determine priorities, risk and activities,[32] for all components (including the ROL components) of the mission. The POC Framework notes that the Head of Mission (HOM), usually the Special Representative of the Secretary-General (SRSG), is responsible for both the mandate and the development of the POC strategies. The POC Framework also promotes the need for a Senior Management Group on POC.[33] It is this POC coordination mechanism that creates the opportunity for more coordinated and/or joint rule-of-law and POC activities among the relevant actors and entities.

Second, the Framework requires the mission to identify actual and potential risks to civilians in the mission's area of operation and to recommend activities to mitigate those risks.[34] What is notable about this process is that it is context-specific as it looks at the actual threats to the civilians within the mission's area of operation and how those risks can be responded to, or treated. This 'bottom-up' analysis, for reasons I will elaborate, provides a useful and practical tool for those designing rule-of-law activities for the mission. Third, the Framework requires that implementation must be 'action oriented', focused and 'concise' (in a time frame of one year).[35] These requirements are more problematic for planning rule-of-law programmes, given the length of time that rule-of-law projects generally need to be effective. It is these features of the POC Framework that raises 'red flags' about the feasibility of integrating some rule-of-law activities into a POC strategy – particularly for longer-term rule-of-law activities.

3 The rule-of-law agenda

As noted above, like POC, the rule-of-law[36] agenda has become more established both within the UN General Assembly (UNGA),[37] and the UNSC,[38] and there has been an increasing recognition that the delivery of vital services such as justice and security is critical to peacekeeping, peacebuilding and conflict resolution. The delivery of justice and security, both crucial functions of an effective state, relies on effective ROL.[39]

In 2000, the Brahimi Report called for a renewed focus on the re-establishment of ROL in post-conflict recovery.[40] In 2003, the UNSC convened its first thematic debate on ROL.[41] In 2005, the UN Secretary-General (UNSG), in his report *In Larger Freedom: Towards Development, Security and Human Rights for All*, drew critical links between the enjoyment of human rights and ROL with satisfactory development and security outcomes.[42]

The 2008 *Guidance Note of the Secretary-General: UN Approach to Rule of Law Assistance* defines broadly what the 'rule of law' means for the UN. It also provides a 'framework' for UN ROL activities at the national level, including in conflict, post-conflict and development contexts.[43] The framework is broad and ambitious, particularly for use in the post-conflict environments in which peacekeepers generally operate. The framework includes supporting a constitution, a legal framework, an electoral system, institutions of justice, governance, security and human rights, transitional justice processes and supporting civil society.

For peacekeeping operations, the range of tasks to be performed by a mission depends upon its specific mandate and component. As Simon Chesterman has observed:

> In practice, the dominant activities have tended to be training of personnel, assisting institution-building, advising on law reform issues, and monitoring, with the emphasis on criminal law processes. Less attention has been paid, for example, to land law.[44]

Different UN mission components have various responsibilities for rule-of-law activities. The resources provided to these components often do not match the demand or their importance to the success of the mission.[45] The immediate priority of ROL components in UN multi-dimensional peacekeeping operations is to begin 'basic progress ... towards the development of rule of law structures and systems.'[46] This is a 'thin' approach to the re-establishment of ROL. Peacekeeping operations are established as time-limited interventions – a first response, in a sense. Because re-establishing criminal justice systems, for example, will require longer-term support, the rule-of-law component of a mission needs to be mindful of the task of building relationships for a transition of longer-term rule-of-law programmes to other actors, including the host state, other UN member states, the UN Development Programme (UNDP) and the UN Peacebuilding Commission.[47]

The challenge of developing a strategic approach to ROL activities is complicated by the fact that several actors with differing objectives are involved. For example, the Office of the UN High Commissioner for Human Rights (OHCHR), through its human rights components in peacekeeping missions, works closely with the rule-of-law programme and has a dual reporting line of accountability both to the head of the 'peace mission' and to the High Commissioner.[48] The human rights component provides human rights advice and technical assistance designed to ensure that peace processes promote justice and equity. It also takes the lead on transitional justice mechanisms. These are generally not short-term projects. For example, developing approaches to support transitional justice mechanisms associated with a society's attempt to come to terms with a legacy of large-scale past abuses will usually take time and needs to occur at the right moment.[49]

The delivery of rule-of-law programmes in conflict and development contexts has been the subject of intense professional consideration following the release of the World Bank's WDR11. That report provides an authoritative source of empirical evidence supporting the contention that ROL and security are critical to maintaining an effective state. WDR11 provides a new direction and new tools for appropriate international responses to conflict and its causes. The central message of WDR11 is that 'strengthening legitimate institutions and governance to provide citizen security, justice, and jobs is crucial to break cycles of violence.'[50]

Connected with this central message, another key WDR11 finding is that countries with the weakest institutional legitimacy and governance are the most vulnerable to violence and instability. Violence and instability are fundamental threats to the well-being of civilians in conflict zones. Supporting the re-establishment of ROL is essential to strengthening institutional legitimacy and governance and preventing instability, which in turn strengthens human security and thus the protection of civilians.

WDR11 also emphasises the need to ensure that the solutions developed to support states are suitably adapted to their context. This point had also been recognised in the Australian Civil–Military Centre's *Rule of Law Roundtable: Towards Best Practice in Post Conflict Situations.* At that Roundtable, for example, participants learnt that the Regional Assistance Mission to the Solomon Islands (RAMSI) illustrated the importance of planning assistance based on the local environment and context: the geography of the Solomon Islands meant that the police force in that country was essentially a maritime organisation and extra maritime capacity within this context was essential.[51] More generally, western models may not take root in non-western post-conflict environments and hence there is a need to develop 'best-fit' institutions.[52]

4 The intersections between the POC and rule-of-law agendas

As mentioned in the introduction, there are two clear intersections between the POC and rule-of-law agendas at the mission level. First, the mandate itself often refers to both agendas. Second, the development of the POC strategy under the POC Framework requires rule-of-law input. Regarding mandates, each UNSC mandate contains a list of tasks for the mission. The number of tasks assigned to the peacekeeping operation often reads like a 'shopping list' and may be unrealistic for the mission to complete, given the level of resourcing provided and the challenging operational environment.

As noted above, POC/PK, when mandated, is a prioritised task in UN peacekeeping operations.[53] For example, the UNSC's 2014 resolution on the UN Mission in Liberia listed the tasks of the mission in order of priority.[54] Paragraph 10(a), and therefore priority number one, was POC/PK. Rule-of-law tasks were in paragraphs 10(c), and therefore presumably priority three of a list of six tasks.

Even though POC/PK is given priority, some ROL activities will be incorporated into the mission-wide POC strategy and therefore afforded a high priority. However, where ROL activities are not incorporated into the POC strategy, they may not gain priority for the use of scarce mission resources.

The other key intersection, the mission-wide POC strategy, has the potential to deliver better-targeted ROL programming and better coordination between all components of the mission to address violence. This strategy should help address one of the concerns mentioned in the WDR11, namely that international assistance often fails to coordinate between the military, police and justice system.[55] It is increasingly recognised that a multiagency and multidisciplinary approach is best practice in re-establishing ROL in post-conflict situations and these approaches have particular relevance for the delivery of ROL activities in peace operations. Much like the Brahimi report ten years earlier,[56] the WDR11 report states: 'A key lesson of successful violence prevention and recovery is that security, justice, and economic stresses are linked: approaches that try to solve them through military-only, justice-only, or development-only solutions will falter.'[57] Likewise, Camino Kavanagh and Bruce Jones called for creative joint operational arrangements at the field level that 'integrate rule-of-law expertise from these entities with political, security, and economic and financial expertise'.[58]

A useful intersection point between POC/PK and rule-of-law agendas is the mission's POC strategy risk analysis. As noted above, each mission element (including ROL, SSR and human rights components) is required to take part in the process of responding to the risk analysis. ROL activities can play an important part in addressing the threats faced by civilians, such as those posed by ill-disciplined local police or armed criminal gangs.[59]

The POC risk analysis developed as part of the POC strategy for the mission may also influence the development of the mission's ROL programmes and activities. This process should lead to a sharper focus by the mission on the actual *needs* of the civilian population and the threats that they face. This process can facilitate valuable 'bottom-up' community-focused interventions by all of the mission's components.[60] By supporting 'bottom-up' approaches, while maintaining key strategic 'top-down' approaches, rule-of-law programmes will be brought into line with best practice for working in fragile states.[61] In addition, focusing on community and civilian risk helps avoid supply-driven reform programmes – where organisations deliver the programmes that they have the pre-existing capacity to deliver rather than developing more adapted and responsive interventions – and ensure 'best-fit' approaches in the operation's context.[62]

More challenging is how to prioritise discrete traditional and important rule-of-law activities and programmes such as transitional justice and constitution-making, which are undoubtedly necessary in the longer term but which do not respond to a direct threat to civilians. Programmes to promote accountability, to reinforce respect for human rights and for reparations, truth-seeking, institutional reform and vetting government officials may fall within this category and are essential to building longer-term respect for ROL and justice.

In this context, it is interesting to note that there is a separate debate being undertaken within the rule-of-law community on the need to focus on confidence-building measures for interventions in post-conflict environments. Camino Kavanagh and Bruce Jones have argued:

> In post-conflict settings, in cases where institutions are weak and resources are low, the UN should refrain from using the 'thick' version of ROL as an overarching framework for initial engagement, and ensure that support to specific rule-of-law functions is accompanied by confidence building measures.[63]

While this thinking has some apparent conceptual links with the priority setting that occurs in developing a POC strategy, the concepts are far from identical. This is a critical area for a useful and constructive dialogue between those managing the two agendas as they apply in peacekeeping missions.

Building 'legitimate institutions' is now recognised as a long-term process and this will be challenging for the mission as peacekeeping operations are usually only provided with short mandates which need to be renewed – usually annually. Effective institutional reform, on the other hand, based on the WDR11 report's findings, require a much longer time frame and possibly generational change.[64] This is an ongoing challenge for the UN, which will need to establish clear pathways to manage transitions of rule-of-law programmes from peacekeeping, to peacebuilding, to post-conflict developmental phases. However, there is a risk that the POC strategising might exacerbate this problem by prioritising shorter-term activities and delaying the commencement of longer-term institutional reform efforts.

5 The need to build synergies between the two agendas

As we have seen, there is a tension between the two agendas on POC and ROL and even within each agenda there are competing interests and institutional objectives. For example, many actors play important roles in POC, including military and police components in peacekeeping, the Office of the UN High Commissioner for Refugees (UNHCR), the Office of the High Commissioner for Human Rights (OHCHR), humanitarians, the International Committee of the Red Cross (ICRC) and NGOs. There are differing interests within each of these groups and organisations in 'formulating and advancing'[65] different aspects of POC. While all are well-motivated, it is inevitable that each will try to 'advanc[e] organizational-specific interests'.[66] It has also been noted that the various UN departments apply differing definitions of 'protection', and agencies' approaches are 'coloured by their specific mandate and responsibilities'.[67] For instance, UNHCR and OHCHR tend to consider POC not as an overarching agenda but as a central dimension of their more specific tasks. The OHCHR is charged with the protection of human rights and UNHCR is primarily focused on the protection of refugees.[68] Furthermore, 'humanitarian organisations have been keen to distinguish their protection action from that of peacekeeping missions in order to safeguard humanitarian principles'.[69]

Similar issues of competing institutional interests arise in regard to the numerous UN entities that have ROL responsibilities,[70] prompting the UN to strengthen coordination of ROL work through the creation of ROLCREG.[71]

In 2009, DPKO and DFS, in *A New Partnership Agenda: Charting a New Horizon for UN Peacekeeping, United Nations* (New Horizons), acknowledged the relationship between POC/PK and ROL, but warned that fully integrating the agendas is 'as critical as it is challenging'. However, little analysis of the relationship was provided.[72]

Since the release of the Operational Concept and the POC Framework, insufficient conceptual consideration appears to have been given to the links between ROL activities of peacekeeping operations and POC/PK. For example, POC/PK was not discussed in the UNSG's *Third Report on Strengthening and Coordinating United Nations Rule of Law Activities* (save for comments by Australia and Austria, annexed to the report).[73] The report states that the UN sees coordination as 'an ongoing and critical process for the Organization', for example by developing joint programme and joint justice units,[74] but does not address the implications of the release of the Operational Concept for rule-of-law activities.

The *Aide Memoire*, prepared by the UN Office for the Coordination of Humanitarian Affairs (OCHA), touches on these issues. It includes, as 'issues for consideration', the rapid deployment of well-trained civilian police, and justice and corrections experts as a component of UN peacekeeping. The Statement by the President of the UNSC encourages senior mission leadership 'to ensure that all mission components and all levels of the chain of command are properly informed of and are involved in the mission's protection mandate and their relevant responsibilities.'[75] However, as a high-level document the *Aide Memoire* does not directly address the issues raised in this chapter about how the UN components work together in the development of the POC strategy, except for short references to a mission's POC strategies and introducing best practices.[76]

It would be beneficial for the UN to develop an officially endorsed approach that considers the impact of prioritising POC/PK on a mission's work on ROL and provides guidance on the extent to which ROL activities are to be incorporated into the POC strategy, as envisaged by the Operational Concept.

In September 2012, UNSG Ban Ki-moon established a Global Focal Point (GFP) for Police, Justice and Corrections Areas in the Rule of Law in Post-Conflict and other Crisis Situations, and prioritised 'delivery as one' by the UN in crisis and conflict settings.[77] The GFP arrangement aims to strengthen the UN's ability to fill critical civilian capacity gaps in the aftermath of conflict. These developments are to be welcomed. The GFP has the function of supporting the UN system in delivering police, justice and corrections assistance to peacekeeping, and assisting UN country teams and UN missions to develop and implement common ROL, justice and security strategies and programmes. The GFP has already supported a number of joint assessments.[78] It will be interesting to see how this coordination point links with the existing ROLCREG and whether the GFP can also address some of the issues discussed in this chapter.

6 Conclusion

Better integrating some rule-of-law field activities into the mission-wide POC strategy can have important benefits for both ROL and POC. To achieve these benefits, the POC Framework and its resultant mission-specific POC strategies should do three things. One, they should encourage better targeting of some ROL activities and more 'bottom-up' activities to address the actual threats to the civilian population at local levels. Two, they should lead to more multidisciplinary and coordinated activities that are better equipped to respond to those threats (for example, joint protection patrols). And three, they should enhance the focus on rule-of-law activities which address the actual threat to local communities.

While the two agendas are largely synergistic, there remain challenges in developing appropriate strategies under the POC Framework, and in particular ensuring the prioritisation of longer-term ROL activities such as institutional strengthening and transitional justice. For one, it is unlikely that longer-term ROL activities would be prioritised under the POC Framework, with its focus on 'action oriented' activities and with a one-year time frame for the activities on the implementation matrix. Thus there is a risk that longer-term activities will not be included as part of the mission's POC strategy matrix of activities, or more likely, that they will be pursued as a lower priority and in a non-integrated way under the rubric of differing mandate functions. This is problematic in that a blend of longer- and shorter-term rule-of-law approaches is desirable in post-conflict states. In developing the rule-of-law agenda, consideration therefore needs to be given to how a focus on 'thin' rule-of-law programming in post-conflict settings, where institutions are weak and resources are low,[79] might work synergistically with the POC strategising and phasings that are part of the POC Operational Concept. In addition, coordinated ROL activities might also be delivered under the POC strategy and supporting matrix.

There is also a risk that ROL activities pursued by the mission might be narrowed and longer-term activities not supported, given the UNSC's practise for priority tasking for POC/PK.[80] Any delay in the commencement of longer-term ROL reforms to build legitimate institutions will effectively push out the timeline for the reform of these institutions and delay the strengthening of the human resourcing and skill-base that is essential to institutional reform. Such delay might also have the unintentional effect of delaying the ability of the peacekeepers to leave with their mission accomplished. Delaying transitional justice mechanisms until better security for civilians is established may or may not be appropriate (depending on the context), but it is a decision that should be conscientiously considered by the mission and at the strategic level.

There is scope for the UNSC to provide further guidance on these issues and clarify expectations when it drafts mission mandates, even though the extent to which ROL activities will be affected may depend on the country context and the Senior Mission Leadership (SML). In particular, the UNSC could consider the links between POC/PK and rule-of-law agendas in peacekeeping operations, so that at the strategic level the links are made clearer, rather than leaving these difficult issues to be resolved at the operational level. It would also be beneficial to provide guidance to assist the SML in weighing the benefits of longer-term protection activities against the more short-term priorities of responding to civilians' need for protection, such as addressing threats to IDP camps. The Senior Management Groups on POC, where they exist, might be useful mechanisms for these discussions. These issues might also be explored in future versions of the *Aide Memoire* prepared by OCHA, taking into account the findings made in the 2012 DPKO/DFS study, *Protection of Civilians Coordination Mechanisms in UN Peacekeeping Missions*.[81]

Whatever reform is undertaken, what is clear is that effective ROL programmes are essential to effective POC/PK, to building sustainable peace and to responding to the challenges posed by repeated cycles of conflict that are faced by many fragile states.[82]

Notes

1 Cf. Hugh Breakey, *The Responsibility to Protect and the Protection of Civilians in Armed Conflicts: Review and Analysis* (Institute for Ethics, 2011), pp. 72–8: www.griffith.edu.au/__data/assets/pdf_file/0007/333844/Responsibility-to-Protect-and-the-Protection-of-Civilians-in-Armed-Conflict-Review-and-Analysis.pdf.

2 UN Department of Peacekeeping Operations (DPKO) and Department of Field Support (DFS), *A New Partnership Agenda: Charting a New Horizon for UN Peacekeeping* (New York, United Nations, 2009), p. v.

3 Alberto Cutillo, *Advancing the Rule of Law Agenda at the 67th General Assembly* (IPI Issue Brief, 2012), p. 5: www.ipinst.org/publication/policy-papers/detail/372-advancing-the-rule-of-law-agenda-at-the-67th-general-assembly.html. See also UN Doc. A/66/133 (2011) *Strengthening and Coordinating United Nations Rule of Law Activities*, para. 1.

4 See UN Rule of Law website and document depository: www.un.org/en/ruleoflaw/index.shtml.

5 The UNGA's *Declaration of the High-level Meeting on the Rule of Law at the National and International Levels* emphasised the importance of ROL as 'one of the key elements of conflict prevention, peacekeeping, conflict resolution and peacebuilding.' GA Res. 67/1 (24 September 2012), para. 18.

6 DPKO and DFS, *Framework for Drafting Comprehensive Protection of Civilian Strategies in United Nations Peacekeeping Operations* (New York, United Nations, 2010): www.refworld.org/pdfid/523998464.pdf.

7 World Bank, *World Development Report 2011: Conflict, Security, and Development* (Washington, DC, The International Bank for Reconstruction and Development/World Bank, 2011), pp. 269–88.

8 See, generally, Andreas Øien Stensland and Ole Jacob Sending, *Unpacking the 'Culture of Protection': A Political Economy Analysis of OCHA and the Protection of Civilians* (Oslo, Norwegian Institute of International Affairs, 2011), pp. 1–48; Francesco Mancini, 'Managing Partnership' (2011) 18 *International Peacekeeping* 627–33.

9 See Breakey, *Responsibility to Protect*, pp. 67–71.

10 Phoebe Wynn-Pope, *Evolution of Protection of Civilians in Armed Conflict* (Canberra, Australian Civil-Military Centre/Oxfam Australia, 2014), pp. 22–6. www.acmc.gov.au/publications/evolution-of-protection-of-civilians-in-armed-conflict.

11 See Liam Mahony and Roger Nash, *A Framework for a Holistic Approach to UNSC Resolutions on Protection of Civilians, Children and Armed Conflict, and Women,*

Peace and Security (Fieldview Solutions, 2008), pp. 7–10: www.fieldviewsolutions.org/fv-publications/Holistic_approach_to_UNSC_resolutions_on_protection-Fieldview_Solutions.pdf.

12 Commencing with the landmark SC Res. 1325 (31 October 2000).

13 See SC Res. 1612 (26 July 2005) and SC Res. 1882 (4 August 2009).

14 See SC Res. 1820 (19 June 2008).

15 Alain Le Roy, 'Foreword', in *Considerations for Mission Leadership in United Nations Peacekeeping Operations* (Stockholm, International Forum for the Challenges of Peace Operations and the Challenges Forum Partner Organizations, 2010), p. 7.

16 Michael G. Smith, Jeni Whalan and Peter Thomson, 'The Protection of Civilians in UN Peacekeeping Operations: Recent Developments' (2011) 7(4) *Security Challenges* 27–38, 27.

17 See Roméo Dallaire, *Shake Hands with the Devil: The Failure of Humanity in Rwanda* (London, Arrow Books, 2004).

18 See United Nations, *Report of the Secretary-General Pursuant to General Assembly Resolution 53/35: The Fall of Srebrenica*, UN Doc. A/54/549 (15 November 1999), p. 56.

19 SC Res. 1270 (22 October 1999). See also DPKO and DFS, *Module 2: International Legal Dimensions of the Protection of Civilians* (New York, United Nations, 2012), p. 24: http://peacekeepingresourcehub.unlb.org/PBPS/Library/Module%202%20International%20Legal%20Dimensions%20of%20the%20Protection%20of%20Civilians.pdf.

20 SC Res. 1270 (22 October 1999), para. 14.

21 The initial *Aide Memoire* was adopted on 15 March 2002 in UN Doc. S/PRST/2002/6. See UN Office for the Coordination of Humanitarian Affairs (OCHA), *Aide Memoire: For the Consideration of Issues Pertaining to the Protection of Civilians in Armed Conflict*, 5th edition (New York, United Nations, 2014).

22 Smith *et al.*, 'Protection of Civilians in UN Peacekeeping Operations', 34.

23 SC Res. 1894 (11 November 2009), para. 19.

24 DPKO and DFS, *Civil Affairs Handbook* (New York, United Nations, 2012), pp. 54ff.

25 Victoria Holt and Glyn Taylor with Max Kelly, *Protecting Civilians in the Context of UN Peacekeeping Operations: Successes, Setbacks and Remaining Challenges* (New York, United Nations, 2009). See also Alison C. Giffen, *Enhancing the Protection of Civilians in Peace Operations from Policy to Practice* (Queanbeyan, Asia-Pacific Civil-Military Centre of Excellence, 2011): http://acmc.gov.au/publications/summary-report-enhancing-the-protection-of-civilians-in-peace-operations.

26 Holt *et al.*, *Protecting Civilians*, p. 5.

27 Ibid., p. 6.

28 Ibid., pp. 7–14.

29 Unpublished; see Wynn-Pope, *Evolution of Protection of Civilians*, pp. 15, 22–6. See also Stian Kjeksrud, Jacob Aasland Ravndal, Andreas Øien Stensland, Cedric de Coning, Walter Lotze and Erin A. Weir, *Protection of Civilians in Armed Conflict – Comparing Organisational Approaches* (Norway, Norwegian Defence Research Establishment, 2011), p. 13.

30 UN Doc. A/64/19 (2010) *Report of the Special Committee on Peacekeeping Operations 2010*, substantive session, para. 146.

31 DPKO and DFS, *POC Framework*.

32 An established mechanism may be used: ibid., p. 13. See also DPKO and DFS, *Protection of Civilians Coordination Mechanisms in UN Peacekeeping Missions: DPKO/DFS Comparative Study and Toolkit* (New York, United Nations, 2012), p. 3.

33 DPKO and DFS, *POC Framework*, p. 13.

34 Ibid., p. 8.

35 Ibid., p. 5.

36 See UN Doc. S/2004/616 (23 August 2004) *The Rule of Law and Transitional Justice in Conflict and Post-conflict Societies: Report of the Secretary-General*. See also UN Doc. A/66/749 (16 March 2012) *Delivering Justice: Programme of Action to Strengthen the Rule of Law at the National and International Levels*.

37 The UNGA has considered ROL as an agenda item since 1992. On 24 September 2012, the UNGA held a one-day, high-level plenary meeting on 'the rule of law at the national and international levels'.

38 See UN Doc. S/PRST/2012/1 (20 December 2012), *Statement by the President of the Security Council*; and UN Doc. S/2011/634 (12 October 2011) *The Rule of Law and Transitional Justice in Conflict and Post-conflict Societies*.

39 UN Doc. A/66/133 (8 August 2011), para. 40; and UN Doc. S/2011/634 (12 October 2011), para. 6. See Jeremy Farrall, 'Impossible Expectations? The UN Security Council's Promotion of the Rule of Law after Conflict', in Brett Bowden, Hilary Charlesworth and Jeremy Farrall (eds), *The Role of International Law in Rebuilding Societies after Conflict: Great Expectations* (Cambridge, Cambridge University Press, 2009), pp. 134–57, 141.

40 UN Doc. A/55/305–S/2000/809 (21 August 2000), *Identical Letters Dated 21 August 2000 from the Secretary-General to the President of the General Assembly and the President of the Security Council*, p. ix and paras 39–41.

41 UN Doc. S/PV.4833 (24 September 2003), *Justice and the Rule of Law: The United Nations Role*.

42 UN Doc. A/59/2005 (21 March 2005), *In Larger Freedom: Towards Development, Security and Human Rights for All*, paras 106, 113, 129. See Security Council Report, *Cross-cutting Report on the Rule of Law* (New York, Security Council Report, 2011): www.securitycouncilreport.org/atf/cf/%7B65BFCF9B-6D27-4E9C-8CD3-CF6E4FF96FF9%7D/XCutting%20Rule%20of%20Law%202011.pdf.

43 UN Secretary-General, *Guidance Note of the Secretary-General: United Nations Approach to Rule of Law Assistance* (New York, United Nations, 2008), pp. 4–7: www.refworld.org/docid/4a54bbf64.html.

44 Simon Chesterman, *An International Rule of Law?* (New York, NYU Law School, 2007), p. 18: www.iilj.org/research/documents/chesterman.aninternationalruleoflaw.draftarticle.pdf.

45 See UN Doc. A/66/749 (16 March 2012), para. 25.

46 Dmitry Titov, 'Peacekeeping Promotes Rule of Law through Expertise and Partnerships' (2011) 2 *DPKO Justice Update* 18, 18.

47 See ibid.

48 OHCHR, *Human Rights Components of Peace Missions* (Geneva, United Nations, 2012): www.ohchr.org/EN/Countries/Pages/PeaceMissionsIndex.aspx.

49 United Nations, *Guidance Note of the Secretary-General: UN Approach to Transitional Justice* (New York, United Nations, 2010), p. 2. See also Bruce Jones, Richard Gowan and Jake Sherman, *Building on Brahimi: Peacekeeping in an Era of Strategic Uncertainty* (New York, New York Center on International Cooperation, 2009), p. 29.

50 World Bank, *World Bank Development Report 2011: Conflict, Security, and Development* (Washington, DC, World Bank, 2011), p. 2.

51 Australian Civil-Military Centre of Excellence, *Report of the Rule of Law Roundtable: Towards Best Practice in Post Conflict Situations* (Queanbeyan, ACMC, 2010), p. 8.

52 World Bank, 'Report of the Global and Regional Dimensions of Conflict and Peacebuilding', *Headline Seminar*, Addis Ababa, 10 and 12 October 2009, p. 4: http://siteresources.worldbank.org/EXTLICUS/Resources/511777-1224016350914/5474500-1257525540923/Final_Report_HS4_Regional_and_Global_Oct10_and_12_09.pdf.

53 See SC Res. 2162 (25 June 2014); SC Res. 2113 (30 July 2013); SC Res. 2155 (27 May 2014); and SC Res. 2147 (28 March 2014), para. 3.

54 SC Res. 2190 (15 December 2014), as amended by SC Res. 2215 (2 April 2015).
55 World Bank, *WDR11*, p. 29.
56 UN Doc. A/55/305–S/2000/809 (21 August 2000), para. 40.
57 World Bank, *WDR11*, p. 28.
58 See Camino Kavanagh and Bruce Jones, *Shaky Foundations: An Assessment of the UN's Rule of Law Support Agenda* (New York, New York University, 2011), p. 10.
59 This point is mentioned in the POC Framework, para. 17. However, no guidance is provided on managing the impact on the human rights Section, child protection advisers, or the humanitarian country team.
60 See World Bank, *WDR11*, p. 18. See also Kavanagh and Jones, *Shaky Foundations*, p. 28.
61 OECD Development Assistance Committee, *Principles for Good International Engagement in Fragile States and Situations* (Paris, OECD, 2007), principle 4: www.oecd.org/dacfragilestates/43463433.pdf.
62 World Bank, *WDR11*, chapter 2.
63 Kavanagh and Jones, *Shaky Foundations*, p. 9.
64 World Bank, *WDR11*, p. 37.
65 Stensland and Sending, *Unpacking the 'Culture of Protection'*, p. 8.
66 Ibid., p. 7.
67 Kjeksrud *et al.*, *Protection of Civilians in Armed Conflict*, p. 13.
68 Stensland and Sending, *Unpacking the 'Culture of Protection'*, p. 36.
69 Damian Lilly, 'Peacekeeping and the Protection of Civilians: An Issue for Humanitarians?' (2010) 48 *Humanitarian Exchange Magazine*: www.odihpn.org/humanitarian-exchange-magazine/issue-48/peacekeeping-and-the-protection-of-civilians-an-issue-for-humanitarians.
70 See Kavanagh and Jones, *Shaky Foundations*, p. 66.
71 ROLCREG is chaired by the Deputy Secretary-General and supported by the Rule of Law Unit. The Group seeks to 'ensure coherence and minimize fragmentation across all thematic rule of law areas': www.unrol.org/article.aspx?article_id=6.
72 DPKO and DFS, *A New Partnership Agenda*, p. 20.
73 UN Doc. A/66/133 (8 August 2011), Annex.
74 Ibid., para. 61.
75 OCHA, *Aide Memoire*, p. 4.
76 Ibid., pp. 45–6. The *Aide Memoire* does refer to system-wide protection, best practices and useful protection measures, such as the Joint Protection Teams, Community Liaison Interpreters, Joint Investigation Teams, Surveillance Centres and Women's Protection Advisers. Stressing the importance of continued efforts to enhance effective working between the mission's military, civilian and police components, and between the mission and humanitarian organizations in the affected region, in the implementation of its mandate. See p. 53.
77 UNDP, *Global Focal Point for Police, Justice, and Corrections* (New York, United Nations, 2013): www.undp.org/content/undp/en/home/ourwork/crisisprevention andrecovery/focus_areas/rule-of-law/global-focal-point-for-police–justice-and-corrections-.
78 In 2013 six had been completed. See *Statement by Under-Secretary-General for Peacekeeping Operations Hervé Ladsous to the Fourth Committee* (28 October 2013): www.un.org/en/peacekeeping/documents/131028-USG-Ladsous-Statement-4C-AS-DELIVERED.pdf.
79 Kavanagh and Jones, *Shaky Foundations*, p. 9.
80 See discussion of 'thick', 'thin' or 'thinner' conception of ROL in Thom Ringer, 'Development, Reform, and the Rule of Law: Some Prescriptions for a Common Understanding of the "Rule of Law" and its Place in Development Theory and Practice' (2007) 10 *Yale Human Rights and Development Law Journal* 178–208, 196.
81 DPKO and DFS, *Protection of Civilians Coordination Mechanisms*, pp. 5–10.
82 World Bank, *WDR11*, p. 2.

Part III

The Security Council, sanctions and the rule of law

13 The Office of the Ombudsperson

A case for fair process

Kimberly Prost[1]

Introduction

The Office of the Ombudsperson was established by the United Nations (UN) Security Council (UNSC) in Resolution 1904 (2009)[2] with the aim of addressing fair process concerns in the context of the use of targeted sanctions under the then Al-Qaida Taliban Sanctions regime.[3] Specifically, the Ombudsperson is mandated to receive requests for delisting from listed persons and entities, to review the same and ultimately provide the Al-Qaida Sanctions Committee of the UNSC with a report that sets out observations and a recommendation on delisting. The mandate of the Ombudsperson has subsequently been renewed on three occasions and is currently extended to late December 2017.[4]

Much has been said and written about the Office of the Ombudsperson as a concept.[5] There has also been extensive litigation surrounding the fair process issues in the use of targeted sanctions, some of which has touched upon the Ombudsperson as a mechanism in that context.[6] However, the purpose of this chapter is to consider the actual practice of the Office and how it works 'on the ground'. The chapter examines the procedure of the Office with reference to the essential components of fair process. It also considers key operational challenges and complications that arise from the tension between the competing fundamental rights at issue, namely the right to life and security and the right to fair process.

1 Ombudsperson process

From its inception, the process for the consideration of delisting petitions by the Ombudsperson has been fairly well defined in the relevant UNSC resolutions.[7] It can commence only on the basis of a request from one of the listed individuals or entities, which can be presented to the Ombudsperson directly. While petitions can be submitted by legal counsel, there is no requirement or necessity for a lawyer, and roughly half of the petitions considered in the nearly five years of operation have been without legal representation.[8] To proceed with a request, the Ombudsperson must be satisfied that the petition addresses the criteria for listing. In practice, this means that the petitioner must describe why delisting is appropriate, taking into account the narrative summary of reasons for listing, which now accompanies all names on the Al-Qaida Sanctions list. Once satisfied that the petition does indeed address the criteria for listing, the Ombudsperson will circulate it to the Committee to commence the process for considering delisting. There are then three phases of consideration, beginning with information gathering, followed by dialogue and preparation of the report, and ending with the decision phase.

The Ombudsperson has an initial four-month period to gather information, which can be extended on one occasion for an additional two months. In accordance with Resolution 2161 (2014) the Ombudsperson can shorten the period for information gathering if the Designating State or States consulted do not object to delisting.[9] This is followed by the dialogue phase, where the Ombudsperson directly engages with the petitioner. In most instances, as recommended by the UNSC, this will include a face-to-face interview. On occasion this will not take place if the case is very straightforward or it may not be possible due to security issues. In those circumstances, the engagement will be carried out through written exchanges. Within the same phase of the process, the Ombudsperson prepares a comprehensive report on the case, which is delivered to the Al-Qaida Sanctions Committee. There are two months for the entire dialogue period, although it too can be extended for an additional two-month interval. The Ombudsperson can also shorten this period by submitting the comprehensive report prior to the deadline, which often occurs.

Once the report is submitted the decision-making phase commences. Fifteen days after the Committee receives translations of the report into all official UN languages, the matter can be placed on the Committee's agenda for consideration. That consideration must be completed within 30 days of the provision of the translations. The Ombudsperson appears when the matter is discussed, to present the report and to engage with the Committee members regarding the same. She presents a summary of the key aspects of the report and her recommendation and members of the Committee can make comments or raise questions. The length and substance of the engagement with the Committee will vary depending on the size and content of the report, the issues raised and the concerns of States.

The procedure for the actual decision will vary depending upon the recommendation. Where the Ombudsperson recommends retention of the listing, consideration of the request will end and the individual and entity will continue to face the sanction measures. This decision and the reasons for it will be conveyed by the Committee to the Ombudsperson, who will then inform the petitioner.

In the case of a recommendation for delisting, upon completion of consideration of the report, the request will be circulated to the Committee members under a no-objection procedure.[10] This can result in a delisting by consensus if no member state objects. If a member state or states object, the name of the individual or entity will still come off the list in 60 days, based on the recommendation of the Ombudsperson, unless there is a consensus decision by the Committee to retain it within that 60-day period. In addition, within that same time, a member of the Committee may request that the question of whether to delist be submitted to the UNSC for a decision. In practice, to date, the Committee has not taken a consensus decision to retain a listing contrary to the recommendation of the Ombudsperson and no matter has been referred to the UNSC.

2 Meeting the fair process fundamentals

When the Office of the Ombudsperson was first established, despite the fact that the procedure was outlined within the relevant UNSC resolutions, considerable work still had to be done to flesh out how the process would work in practice. In particular, there was a need to develop procedures and approaches that could be consistently and transparently applied to maximise the fairness of the process.

The initial challenge was trying to define 'fair process' in the unique context of UNSC sanctions, given that procedural fairness is always a contextual matter.[11] The rights of individuals in a criminal case are very different from their rights in an administrative case, even domestically. And as between legal systems, the content and contours of fair process can vary significantly. This is perhaps best illustrated by contrasting the decision of the Grand Chamber of the European Court of Justice in *Kadi II*,[12] with that of the United States District Court for the District of Columbia in *Kadi* v. *Geithner*.[13] In the ECJ, procedural fairness is met only through a 'full review' of the basis for the listing of Mr Kadi. In the District Court, the decision to designate Mr Kadi is examined to determine if it was arbitrary, capricious, an abuse of discretion or otherwise not in accordance with law, a sufficient fair process protection under US law.

So in implementing the UNSC resolution establishing the Office of the Ombudsperson, it was essential to start by trying to define the fundamental elements of fair process that were applicable. The sources relied on included the UN Secretary-General's statements on the issue,[14] as well as national system concepts of fairness, due process and natural justice. Through that review, the following formulation of relevant precepts was developed.

First, the petitioners must know the case against them as far as possible. Second, they must have an opportunity to answer that case and to be heard by the decision-maker. Third, while it was evident there must be some form of independent review, no commonality of approach among legal systems as to the nature and content of that review was apparent. As a result the generic concept of an objective review that involves an effective and independent assessment of the information was adopted. Fourth, the decision to delist or not to delist must be a reasoned one. Finally, it must be an overall fair and timely process. Broadly speaking, those are the key principles identified to guide the practical implementation of the Ombudsperson process.

So the question becomes: are the procedures of the Office of the Ombudsperson, as developed in practice, in conformity with these fundamental principles?

2.1 Knowing the case

The Ombudsperson process begins with an information-gathering procedure, the aim of which is to gather as much relevant material as possible. Information is gathered with the assistance of the Monitoring Team, which aids the Committee,[15] and through independent research by the Office of the Ombudsperson. But the most significant material in most instances is that obtained from states. The resolution which outlines the mandate of the Ombudsperson – currently Resolution 2083 (2012)[16] – prescribes that the Ombudsperson will seek information from the Designating State or States (the state or states which put the individual or entity forward for listing), the state of residence, the state of nationality and any other relevant state. In accordance with the resolution, this will be done by circulating the request to these states, seeking a response. In practice, the Ombudsperson also diligently and aggressively pursues those responses by following up with states through letters, emails, calls and visits. These efforts have generally resulted in states providing responses. However, the challenge since the beginning has been with respect to the content of those responses and, in particular, obtaining substantive, detailed replies that reference the supporting information underlying the listing. The difficulties in this respect often arise from a lack of access to confidential or classified material, which is discussed in more detail below.

Importantly, however, this challenge in terms of gathering information does not impede the fairness of the process from the perspective of the petitioner. The resolutions outlining the mandate have always provided that the Ombudsperson's assessment should be premised on the information gathered in the process. It was also part of the practice from the beginning that 'undisclosed information' could not contribute to the assessment of the Ombudsperson or ultimately the Committee's decision. Resolution 1989 (2011)[17] was important in this regard because it added considerable weight to the requests for information made by the Ombudsperson. Now there is a recommendation power which – in the case of delisting – will prevail in absence of a consensus position of the Committee to the contrary or a UNSC reference and vote.[18] As a result, if a state does not provide full information in response to the Ombudsperson's request, the missing material will not form part of the case that is analysed nor will it be considered in the formulation of the recommendation. This aspect of Resolution 1989 (2011) serves as a powerful 'motivator' for the production of information by states. At the same time, a proper balance is struck in that an absence of material should not work to the detriment of the petitioner as the recommendation will be premised only on the information gathered by the Ombudsperson. The question as to whether this protection would continue to apply in cases of a consensus overturn of the Ombudsperson recommendation or a referral to the UNSC remains a matter of pure speculation at this time as no such action has been taken.

In the next part of the process – the dialogue phase – the Ombudsperson presents all information gathered to the petitioner, excluding any confidential material. As indicated above, in most instances this phase will involve a meeting and disclosure will take place either before or during that meeting. This provides an opportunity to present the petitioner with a description of the information gathered and the parameters of the case.

As discussed, there may be instances where confidential material gathered will not be disclosed to the petitioner. This obviously raises fairness issues. In practice, however, to date in those instances where such material has been gathered it has been of such a nature that it did not affect the fundamental principle of 'knowing the case'. As reflected in the Ombudsperson reports to the UNSC, in all completed cases to date, disclosure has been such that the petitioner knew the case that formed the basis of the listing though not necessarily all of the detail or underlying supporting material.[19]

2.2 *Answering the case*

The other important component of the dialogue phase is that it provides an opportunity for the petitioner to answer the case, through direct interaction with the Ombudsperson. The individual or representatives of the entity[20] are able to have an exchange with the Ombudsperson, to answer questions posed and to convey their 'answer' to the information. This exchange also allows the Ombudsperson to follow-up on issues, ask specific questions and generally assess credibility. The dialogue not only fulfils the important principle of responding to the case, but also adds to the overall fairness of the process and the perception of the same, particularly to the petitioners. On several occasions, petitioners have highlighted that, having been listed for several years, the interview process provided the first opportunity for them to answer questions and tell their 'side of the story'. This is some indication that, both in substance and in impression, the process presents as a fair one.

2.3 *Independent review*

The information gathered through the first two phases (from the states and from the petitioner) is then compiled in the comprehensive report for the Al-Qaida Sanctions Committee. What is very important in this regard is that this compilation in a single report 'levels' the information-field within the Committee. While previously only one or two states might have had information about the case, now all 15 members have access to the same information as it is available to the Committee as a whole. On the basis of the comprehensive report and the information and analysis it contains, the Ombudsperson makes her recommendation to the Committee. As indicated previously, if delisting is recommended, the person or entity will be removed either because there is no objection,[21] or in 60 days through the trigger mechanism, absent a consensus overturn or a UNSC reference. If there is a recommendation against delisting, the person will remain on the list.[22]

In combination, this process provides for an objective and independent review of the information underlying the listing. It is evidently not a judicial review given that the Ombudsperson does not occupy a judicial post. As well, there are aspects of the nature of the review that distinguish it from classic judicial review. Most significantly, the Ombudsperson assesses the gathered information with a view to whether it is sufficient to provide a reasonable and credible basis for the listing presently. The review is not of the original decision taken by the Sanctions Committee, but rather of the gathered information with a view to its current sufficiency to support the listing. This eliminates the possibility that the examination of the case will result in any form of declaration about the original listing, as is the case with judicial review. However, the distinct advantage is the Ombudsperson can take into account all relevant information, including that which post-dates the original determination. From the perspective of the petitioner, this provides an opportunity to submit additional material for consideration, to rebut inferences that may have been originally drawn, and, in appropriate cases, to advance an argument regarding changed circumstances. In this respect, the Ombudsperson procedure offers benefits which even judicial review cannot provide.

Finally, in terms of the effectiveness of the review, given that the recommendation is made on the basis of the information gathered and analysed by the Ombudsperson, evidently the full case underlying the listing, including any confidential material, is subject to an independent review.

2.4 Reasoned decision/timely process

Resolution 2161 (2014),[23] like its predecessors, mandates that when a petition is rejected, the Committee shall provide reasons for that decision. This comports with the requirement for a reasoned decision and it also provides a means to assess the overall reasonableness of the process in any particular case.

Moreover, this resolution and the one preceding it[24] enhanced the fairness of the process in terms of reasons, by providing that reasons should also be furnished in cases where a decision is made to delist. This addition in the resolution was consistent with the practice employed by the Committee since the establishment of the Ombudsperson process; reasons were provided not only for retention as mandated, but also in the case of delisting. In addition to the underlying principles, on a practical level, reasons also serve to promote consistency and transparency in the process as a whole.

However, there is still progress to be made on the question of reasons. As detailed in reports to the UNSC,[25] there are problems with significant delays in the delivery of the reasons and with the absence of detail. While the addition of a 60-day deadline in Resolution 2161 (2014) has responded in some respect to the delay issue, there remain significant problems with the substance of the reasons, a problem only exacerbated by the imposition of a deadline.[26] There are also questions as to who should originate the reasons – the Committee or the Ombudsperson – all of which are the subject of ongoing discussion and debate. Nonetheless, it can be said that the Ombudsperson process does recognise the importance of a reasoned decision and includes provision for the same.

Finally, the Ombudsperson process is designed to avoid any lengthy delay in the consideration of the delisting petition, which could reduce the efficacy and fairness of the mechanism. The whole process is governed by strict timelines that have been consistently adhered to in each of the relevant cases. Responses to requests for information are required within set periods, as is the submission of the Comprehensive Report. Based on the current regime as mandated by the UNSC, the possible time frame for the consideration of a delisting request ranges from approximately eight to 14 months, with cases taking on average just over nine months. This is an important fairness achievement of the Office of the Ombudsperson.

2.5 Cumulative fair process

A cumulative assessment of the mechanism of the Office of the Ombudsperson supports the conclusion that, in practice to date, it satisfies the fundamental requirements of a fair process and can provide an effective remedy. With a mechanism for independent review, the work of the UNSC under this sanction regime comports with fundamental rule of law and human rights precepts, as envisaged by the UN Charter. In this way the most important goal behind the establishment of the Office of the Ombudsperson has been achieved. It remains to be seen what effect that will have in terms of the views of domestic and regional courts and for the effective implementation of the Al-Qaida Sanctions regime in the longer term. The decision of the European Court of Justice in *Kadi II* indicates that regional court will continue to intervene to review the underlying material for sufficiency, even with respect to designations that flow from UNSC decisions.[27] Unfortunately, in reaching this conclusion the Court made no reference to the Office of the Ombudsperson so the decision provides no insight as to its view of the mechanism.

However, whatever the court responses, as indicated, the aim of enhancing fair process at the international level has been achieved. As well, for the individuals and entities on the Al-Qaida Sanctions list, the Ombudsperson process offers an effective and accessible avenue through which their individual cases can be reviewed in a fair and independent manner.

3 Challenges

Despite this apparent progress in the context of fair process, important operational challenges remain.

3.1 Access to information

As outlined above, one major continuing challenge – which is perhaps the most significant issue in terms of the effectiveness of the process – is to gain access to confidential or classified material that may underlie the listing. While to date there are 12 arrangements/agreements on access to confidential/classified information between states and the Office of the Ombudsperson,[28] more work is needed to expand this list, in particular in relation to those states that often possess information relevant to a delisting application.

3.2 Standard

A second challenge for the Office relates to the standard used to evaluate the case, presently formulated as 'sufficient information to provide a reasonable and credible basis for the listing'. This standard was developed from a review of applicable standards across the legal and geographic spectrum, in an effort to create a measurement appropriate to an international mechanism. While it does not come from any particular legal system as a result, it contains concepts generally familiar across legal systems. Also, it is intended to balance the individual rights to privacy, freedom of movement and property with the right to life and security and the obligation of the UNSC to maintain international peace and security, all of which are implicated in the system of targeted sanctions.

The standard, as formulated, has proven to be workable and appropriate to the specific international context. The problem, however, is one of application and the question as to what is 'sufficient' and 'reasonable and credible'. The significant challenge lies not in the standard as formulated, but in the fact that there are fundamental variations between legal systems, and even within them, as to what type and amount of information is sufficient to provide a reasonable and credible basis. The recent *Kadi* decision in the United States[29] illustrates this problem in that the US judge, operating under the applicable law, took a vastly different approach to the assessment of information to that undertaken in the *Kadi* case when it was considered by the Court of Justice of the European Union (CJEU).[30] Even taking into account that the US judge was party to information not available to the CJEU, it is still evident that there are different expectations as to sufficiency. This is but one illustration of the challenges in applying an acceptable standard at the international level.

3.3 Fairness concerns

Patently, in terms of the principles of fairness, the possibility of a consensus overturn or a UNSC override of the recommendation is a concern. However, from a practical perspective, to date those powers remain only theoretical in nature, since the Committee has not overturned any decision by consensus and there have been no references to the UNSC. Moreover, practice has indicated that it is very difficult to achieve the consensus required and there is, as well, an appropriate reluctance to utilise the UNSC reference power. Nonetheless, the question remains whether the Ombudsperson constitutes a sufficiently effective fair process mechanism when in principle the decisions of the independent reviewer are not fully binding. This was the central concern expressed by the Special Rapporteur on the promotion and protection of human rights and fundamental freedoms while countering terrorism in his 2012 report on the Office of the Ombudsperson.[31]

3.4 Transparency

While the Ombudsperson process is a robust one that meets the fundamental principles of fairness as discussed, it remains quite secretive in terms of its substantive content. The comprehensive reports prepared by the Ombudsperson are strictly confidential to the Committee. While Resolution 2161 (2014) now provides that interested states[32] can apply to obtain a copy of a particular Comprehensive Report,[33] and that has been successfully done, access is still quite limited. Most notably there is no disclosure of the reports to the petitioner or more generally to the public. There are also significant challenges in communicating substantive detailed reasons for the decisions taken, particularly in delisting cases. This is regrettable not only from a fair process point of view, but also because the lack of transparency prevents the UNSC from demonstrating the reasoned nature of the process.

3.5 Institutional protections

While remarkable steps have been taken by the UNSC to establish and strengthen the Office of the Ombudsperson, these have not been accompanied by similar progress on the part of the UN Secretariat, particularly in terms of ensuring the Office the benefits of institutionalisation. There has been no action in five years to bring the terms and conditions and administrative arrangements for the Office of the Ombudsperson into conformity with the nature of its role and responsibilities. While Resolution 1904 (2009) called for the establishment of an independent Office of the Ombudsperson,[34] no such institution has been created. It does not appear anywhere within the organisational structure of the UN. Further, the contractual arrangements used – a consultancy – create serious challenges for independence, particularly in terms of the inability of the Ombudsperson to manage staff and budgets. Further, perhaps most significantly, the unattractive nature of the contract also sends a clear message as to the lack of interest in, and prioritisation of, the fair process work of the Ombudsperson within the organisation. Finally, while the Office has operated in an independent manner over its first five years, that is attributable solely to the personalities involved. No institutional protections for the independence of the Office of the Ombudsperson have been established, which leaves it very vulnerable going forward, particularly through periods of transition. This issue has been repeatedly identified by the Ombudsperson as a matter of serious concern,[35] and will hopefully generate changes to the UN structure to allow for an institutionalised Office of the Ombudsperson for the Al-Qaida Sanctions regime.

3.6 Relationship to other sanctions regimes

One final challenge of note is the relationship between this sanctions regime and other sanctions regimes. On this issue, the question as to whether an Ombudsperson process should be available to individuals and entities targeted by other sanctions regimes is clearly one for states and the UNSC to decide. However, objectively, obvious fairness issues arise from the fact that a remedy is currently available to one set of sanctioned individuals but not to others. In this regard, the *Jim'ale* case is highly instructive. Mr Jim'ale was listed by the Al-Qaida Sanctions Committee (then the Al-Qaida/Taliban Sanctions Committee) in 2001. On

17 February 2012 he was delisted after a recommendation by the Ombudsperson to the Committee to this effect. On the very same day, he was listed under the Somalia–Eritrea sanctions regime, with no recourse to the Ombudsperson mechanism. Whatever the merits of the subsequent listing, the reality is that for one individual there was a vast disparity between the type of recourse available under one targeted sanctions regime and another. This discrepancy continues to exist for all individuals and entities listed under UNSC targeted sanctions regimes aside from that related to Al-Qaida.

4 Conclusion

The conclusion of this analysis is a positive one overall. As discussed, there remain questions as to the sufficiency of the Ombudsperson process in terms of addressing the fundamental fairness concerns surrounding the use of targeted sanctions in the Al-Qaida Sanctions regime. Furthermore, it is evident that several important challenges exist for the practical work of the Office. There are also structural questions that need to be resolved. Nonetheless, one cannot help but note the tremendous gains made in terms of fair process over the past five years. There is now a clear recourse for listed persons and entities, which addresses the fundamental components of a fair process and provides for the intervention of an objective and independent third party in the overall assessment of the information in the case. In terms of protecting rights and enhancing the credibility and strength of the regime, the Office of the Ombudsperson cannot be categorised as other than a successful undertaking by the UNSC and its Committee. Moreover, it represents an important step forward in terms of enhancing the rule of law at the international level.

Notes

1 Kimberly Prost was appointed in June 2010 as the first Ombudsperson for the Security Council Al-Qaida and Taliban Sanctions Committee. In June of 2011, with the separation of the two sanction regimes in accordance with SC Res. 1988 (17 June 2011) and SC Res. 1989 (17 June 2011), she was reappointed as Ombudsperson for the Al-Qaida Sanctions Committee and she continues in that post currently.

2 SC Res. 1904 (17 December 2009).

3 The UNSC first adopted sanctions against the Taliban with SC Res. 1267 (15 October 1999), demanding that the Taliban turn over Usama bin Laden (para. 2), and imposing a flight restriction and financial measures (para. 4). The sanctions were expanded in SC Res. 1333 (19 December 2000) to include an embargo on arms and military training and assistance within territory controlled by the Taliban (para. 5), and imposing financial measures on 'Usama bin Laden and individuals and entities associated with him as designated by the [UNSC Sanctions] Committee, including those in the Al-Qaida organization' (para. 8). The sanctions targeting 'Usama bin Laden, members of the Al-Qaida organization and the Taliban and other individuals, groups, undertakings and entities associated with them' were expanded in SC Res. 1390 (28 January 2002) to include travel restrictions and an arms embargo (para. 2), and further strengthened in SC Res. 1455 (17 January 2003), SC Res. 1526 (30 January 2004), SC Res. 1617 (29 July 2005), SC Res. 1735 (22 December 2006), SC Res. 1822 (30 June 2008) and

SC Res. 1904 (17 December 2009). The Al-Qaida and Taliban Sanctions regimes were divided into two separate regimes with the adoption of SC Res. 1988 (17 June 2011) and SC Res. 1989 (17 June 2011), with the Ombudsperson mandate being limited to the latter – the Al-Qaida Sanctions regime.

4 SC Res. 1989 (17 June 2011), SC Res. 2083 (17 December 2012) and SC Res. 2161 (17 June 2014).

5 See, e.g. Florian Hoffmann and Frédéric Mégret, 'Fostering Human Rights Accountability: An Ombudsperson for the United Nations?' (2005) 1(1) *Global Governance* 43–63; Carolyn Stieber, '57 Varieties: Has the Ombudsman Concept Become Diluted?' (2000) 16(1) *Negotiation Journal* 49–57; Roy Gregory and Philip Giddings (eds), *Righting Wrongs: The Ombudsman in Six Continents* (Amsterdam, IOS Press, 2000); Linda C. Reif (ed.), *The International Ombudsman Anthology: Selected Writings from the International Ombudsman Institute* (The Hague, Kluwer Law International, 1999); Katja Heede, 'Enhancing the Accountability of Community Institutions and Bodies: The Role of the European Ombudsman' (1997) 3(4) *European Public Law* 587–605.

6 See, e.g. *Yassin Abdullah Kadi and Al Barakaat International Foundation* v. *Council of the European Union and Commission of the European Communities*, Joined Cases C-402/05 P and C-415/05 [2008] ECR I-6351 (3 September 2008); *European Commission & the Council of the European Union* v. *Yassin Abdullah Kadi*, Joined Cases C-584/10 P, C-593/10 P and C-595/10 P [2013] ECR not yet reported (18 July 2013); *Al-Jedda* v. *United Kingdom*, Appl. No. 27021/087, ECtHR, Judgment [Grand Chamber] (7 July 2011); *Nada* v. *Switzerland*, Appl. No. 10593/08, ECtHR, Judgment (Grand Chamber) (12 September 2012). For a discussion of these cases, see de Wet's chapter in this collection.

7 SC Res. 1904 (17 December 2009), paras 20–7; SC Res. 1989 (17 June 2011), paras 21–35; SC Res. 2083 (17 December 2012), paras 19–35.

8 See UN Doc. S/2014/73 (31 January 2014), *Seventh Report of the Ombudsperson to the Security Council*, para. 7.

9 SC Res. 2161 (17 June 2014), para. 3 of Annex II.

10 See UN Doc. S/AC.37/2013/Note/17/Add.3, *Guidelines of the Committee for the Conduct of its Work*, paras 7(gg) and (hh).

11 See discussion of appropriate procedural protections in *Suresh* v. *Canada* [2002] 1 SCR 3, paras 113–28 (Supreme Court of Canada). See also Article 6 of the European Convention on Human Rights, which sets out rights applicable in civil and criminal proceedings and those solely in criminal proceedings; discussion by the House of Lords of sufficiency of procedural protections under the Prevention of Terrorism Act 2005 in *Secretary of State for the Home Department (Respondent)* v. *MB (FC) (Appellant)* [2007] UKHL 46; and the decision of the European Court of Human Rights on the question of sufficiency of disclosure in the context of control orders in *A and others* v. *United Kingdom* (2009).

12 *European Commission & the Council of the European Union* v. *Yassin Abdullah Kadi*, joined Cases C-584/10 P, C-593/10 P and C-595/10 P [2013] ECR not yet reported (18 July 2013).

13 *Kadi* v. *Geithner*, 6 *US District Court*, DC, Case 1:09-cv-00108 (19 March 2012).

14 See comments by the United Nations Legal Counsel on behalf of the UNSC in UN Doc. S/PV.5474 (22 June 2006), *Security Council's 5474th Meeting*, p. 5 (reading from a letter and annexed non-paper from the Secretary-General to the UNSC, setting out his views concerning the listing and delisting of individuals and entities on sanctions lists).

15 The Analytical Support and Sanctions Monitoring Team was established by SC Res. 1526 (30 January 2004), paras 6–8, and subsequently extended, most recently by SC Res. 2083 (17 December 2012), paras 60–2. Operating 'under the direction of the Committee', the Monitoring Team's responsibilities are outlined in the Annex to SC Res. 1526 (30 January 2004), including 'to identify, gather information on, and keep

the Committee informed of instances and common patterns of non-compliance with the measures imposed in this resolution, as well as to facilitate, upon request by Member States, assistance on capacity-building'. See also UN Doc. S/2014/41 (23 January 2014), *Fifteenth Report of the Analytical Support and Sanctions Monitoring Team Submitted Pursuant to Resolution 2083 (2012) Concerning Al-Qaida and Associated Individuals and Entities.*

16 SC Res. 2083 (17 December 2012).

17 SC Res. 1989 (17 June 2011).

18 See SC Res. 1989 (17 June 2011), Annex II, para. 12.

19 See UN Doc. S/2011/29 (24 January 2011); UN Doc. S/2011/447 (22 July 2011); UN Doc. S/2012/49 (20 January 2012); UN Doc. S/2012/590 (30 July 2012); UN Doc. S/2013/71 (31 January 2013); UN Doc. S/2013/452 (31 July 2013); and UN Doc. S/2014/73 (31 January 2014).

20 Recall the Al-Qaida Sanctions measures target both designated individuals and entities.

21 The Al-Qaida Sanctions Committee Guidelines provide that '[i]n cases where the Ombudsperson recommends delisting in his/her Comprehensive Report, and after the Committee has completed its consideration of the Comprehensive Report, the Chairperson will circulate the delisting request with a no-objection period of 10 working days': www.un.org/sc/committees/1267/pdf/1267_guidelines.pdf., p. 10, para. 7(gg). If no objection is raised in this period, the listed name will be removed.

22 The only recourse for a state that disagrees with a recommendation to retain the listing is for that state to make a delisting request that will begin a separate process; no recourse is available through the original Ombudsperson process.

23 SC Res. 2161 (17 June 2014).

24 SC Res. 2083 (17 December 2012).

25 See, e.g. UN Doc. S/2014/73 (31 January 2014), *Seventh Report of the Ombudsperson to the Security Council.*

26 See UN Doc. S/2015/80 (2 February 2015), *Ninth Report of the Ombudsperson to the Security Council*, para. 43.

27 *European Commission and the Council of the European Union* v. *Yassin Abdullah Kadi*, Joined Cases C-584/10 P, C-593/10 P and C-595/10 P [2013] ECR (18 July 2013).

28 Australia, Austria, Belgium, Costa Rica, France, Germany, Liechtenstein, the Netherlands, New Zealand, Portugal, Switzerland and the United Kingdom.

29 US District Court, DC, Case 1:09-cv-00108 (19 March 2012).

30 *Kadi and al Barakaat International Foundation* v. *Council and Commission*, Joined Cases C-402/05 P and C-415/P (3 September 2008) ('Kadi I'); *Kadi* v. *European Commission*, Joined Appeal Cases C-584/10 P, C-593/10 P and C-595/10 P (18 July 2013) ('Kadi II'). For discussion of the European Kadi case, see de Wet's chapter in this collection.

31 UN Doc. A/67/396 (26 September 2012), *Report of the Special Rapporteur on the Promotion and Protection of Human Rights and Fundamental Freedoms while Countering Terrorism.*

32 State of Nationality or Residence of the Petitioner and the Designating State or States.

33 SC Res. 2161 (17 June 2014), Annex II, para. 13.

34 SC Res. 1904 (17 December 2009).

35 See, e.g. UN Doc. S/2015/80 (2 February 2015), paras 51–3; UN Doc. S/2014/553 (31 July 3014), paras 49–51.

14 Judicial challenges to the Security Council's use of sanctions

Erika de Wet[1]

Introduction

This chapter focuses on the role that courts, particularly in Europe, have played in the enforcement of United Nations (UN) Security Council (UNSC) sanctions-related resolutions that also affect the international human rights obligations of the state in question. At the outset, the chapter identifies the benchmarks for judicial protection, as developed by the courts of the European Union (EU), which are applicable within the EU legal order in relation to individuals and other entities that are subjected to targeted sanctions by the UNSC. The term judicial protection refers to the benchmarks of the right to a fair and public hearing (the term used in article 6(1) of the European Convention of Human Rights (ECHR)), as it has been developed and applied within the legal order of the EU. This identification of benchmarks is done against the backdrop of the so-called *Kadi* cases of 2005–2013, which served as a testing ground for the relationship between UNSC obligations and the law applied by the EU courts.

Thereafter Section 1.3 outlines the systemic challenges resulting from the benchmarks for judicial protection that developed within the EU. These challenges concern in particular the legal uncertainties that exist for those states that are members of both the EU and the UN. These states may face a situation where they cannot give effect to treaty obligations under the one regime without violating similar obligations under the other regime. The chapter further illustrates that the methodology applied by the EU courts has the potential to marginalise binding UNSC resolutions. On the positive side, however, the approach taken by the EU courts can result in bottom-up pressure on the UN sanctions system to introduce procedural fairness for those directly targeted by UN sanctions regimes. The EU courts have made clear that they will not enforce UNSC sanctions in the European legal order, if such enforcement implies a suspension of human rights standards. Therefore, unless some form of independent and even-handed judicial review is introduced within the UN sanctions system itself, UNSC sanctions measures that result in individual listing will continue to meet with resistance before the Court of Justice of the European Union (CJEU).

In Section 2, this chapter further illustrates how the European Court of Human Rights (ECtHR) attempts to overcome the systemic challenges outlined in Section 1, by applying a presumption of human rights friendliness. According to the ECtHR, there exists a very strong presumption that the UNSC would not expect UN member states to violate international human rights obligations, given that the development of human rights falls within the purposes and principles of the UN itself.

Section 2.2 subsequently illustrates that the technique of human rights-friendly interpretation indeed has the advantage of encouraging states to give effect to their human rights obligations while also implementing their obligations under the UN Charter. Stated differently, this technique appears to discourage states from outright rejecting UNSC obligations which could violate international human rights standards. However, Section 2.2 further illustrates that the technique of human rights-friendly interpretation is only effective if the text of the respective UNSC resolution is broad enough to accommodate the balancing of sanctions with human rights obligations. If the text of the UNSC resolution is (too) narrowly tailored, the presumption of human rights friendliness will not protect states against the dilemma of having to choose between giving effect to either their obligations under the UN Charter or to binding international human rights obligations. In essence, therefore, results produced by the technique of human rights-friendly interpretation can be similar to that produced by the dualist approach of the CJEU.

Finally, the conclusion suggests that the expansion and refinement of the procedure of the Ombudsperson within the UN sanctions system could go some way in providing procedural fairness for listed individuals and entities, while also reducing the onslaught of judicial rebellion of the regional courts in Europe against the UNSC in recent years. Without improved procedural fairness within the UN sanctions system, European courts will continue to rebel against UNSC sanctions that undermine human rights.

1 Benchmarks for judicial protection as developed by the EU courts

1.1 The context of the Kadi cases

Since 2006 the courts of the EU have developed a set of concrete benchmarks for the type of judicial protection that UNSC sanctions regimes must respect in order to be given effect within the EU legal order. The EU's General Court (GC) (formerly known as the Court of First Instance (CFI)) and its superior court, the CJEU, developed these benchmarks on the basis of EU law. Although the EU is not a state, it has a very sophisticated legal order with a centralised judiciary in the form of the GC and the CJEU. In the *Kadi* cases the CJEU treated the EU legal order as an autonomous legal order, i.e. a separate legal order that is comparable to that of a state. The seminal cases to date have been *Yassin Abdullah Kadi and Al Barakaat International Foundation* v. *Council and Commission* ('*Kadi* (CJEU I)'),[2] and *European Commission and the Council of the European Union* v. *Yassin Abdullah Kadi* ('*Kadi* (CJEU II)').[3]

The *Kadi* cases concerned targeted UN sanctions resulting from the UNSC Resolution 1267 (1999) sanctions regime.[4] This sanctions regime established the so-called Al-Qaida Sanctions Committee as a subsidiary organ of the UNSC. As with all UNSC sanctions committees, the membership of the committee mirrored the composition of the UNSC. Resolution 1267 (1999) and its follow-up resolutions, all of which were adopted under Chapter VII of the UN Charter, invested the Committee with the power to identify and place on the consolidated list individuals and entities that were suspected of involvement with the Taliban and Al-Qaida. Member states in which listed individuals or entities resided were required to freeze the listed parties' assets, impose travel bans and prevent the supply of arms.[5]

Within the UN sanctions system, these individuals and entities had no recourse to an independent and impartial judicial procedure to refute the allegations against them. The only body the UNSC resolutions in question authorised to consider delisting was the Al-Qaida Sanctions Committee. This procedure was intergovernmental in nature and listed individuals and entities had no direct access to the Committee. Moreover, the Committee took its decisions by consensus, as a result of which each member state could effectively veto a delisting request.[6]

On 19 December 2006 the UNSC adopted Resolution 1730 (2006), which introduced the so-called Focal Point for receiving delisting requests. This mechanism amounted to a human postbox whose competencies were limited to receiving and transmitting the requests for de-listing to the Al-Qaida sanctions committee. It did not have any power to amend or influence the decision-making procedure within the sanctions committee.[7] The most meaningful qualitative improvement from the perspective of listed individuals and entities has been the introduction of the Ombudsperson through Resolution 1904 (2009). The Ombudsperson is empowered to receive information from petitioners and states, assess the information and make suggestions ('observations') to the Sanctions Committee regarding delisting.[8] The first person appointed to the Office of the Ombudsperson was former Canadian judge Kimberly Prost.[9] By 31 July 2014 her efforts had resulted in the delisting of 34 individuals and 27 entities.[10] However, despite the relief that her conscientious efforts have brought to those delisted, the ultimate decision to delist remains a political one in the hands of the Sanctions Committee and the UNSC.[11]

By adopting Resolutions 1988 and 1989 on 17 June 2011, the UNSC created separate sanctions committees to deal with the threats posed by the Taliban and Al-Qaida, respectively. Resolution 1988 created a new Taliban Sanctions Committee with the authority to list individuals and entities who were deemed to pose a threat to peace, stability and security in Afghanistan. Those listed by the Taliban Committee still faced the freezing of their assets and travel bans, as was the case under the Al-Qaida Sanctions Committee.[12] However, they no longer had access to the Ombudsperson process.[13]

In accordance with Resolution 1989, the Ombudsperson procedure currently only applies to the Al-Qaida Sanctions Committee. This resolution also introduced a diluted sunset clause, i.e. a clause foreseeing the expiration of the sanctions under certain conditions. The resolution provides that once the Ombudsperson has recommended delisting or a state requested delisting, such delisting should occur unless all members of the Al-Qaida Sanctions Committee disagree with the recommendation or request within a 60-day period.[14] However, this reversal of the procedure from 'consensus required for delisting' to 'consensus required for continued listing' does not necessarily result in delisting where no consensus for continued listing can be achieved. If any state disagrees with the requested delisting within the 60-day period, the matter may be referred to the UNSC on that state's request and the UNSC then must take a decision concerning delisting within 60 days.[15] Given that in practice it usually is one of the UNSC permanent members opposing the delisting in the Sanctions Committee, delisting is likely to be blocked by the veto of a permanent member. Moreover, these amendments did not change the inter-governmental, essentially political nature of the delisting process.[16]

1.2 The legal reasoning of the Kadi cases: the right to be heard and the right to judicial review

The continued absence of an independent judicial procedure within the UN sanctions system, where listed individuals and entities can refute allegations made against them of terrorism, was bound to give rise to disputes in the European legal context about the legality of the measures implementing the Al-Qaida Sanctions regime. In the case of Mr Kadi – which has been extensively covered in academic debate[17] – such a dispute played out before the courts of the EU. The *Kadi* saga initially unfolded in 2005 before the CFI (as it then was) of the EU. That court considered Mr Kadi's listing to be immune from judicial scrutiny, as it originated from a binding UNSC sanctions regime that left no discretion for implementation.[18]

From there Mr Kadi launched a successful appeal to the CJEU (hereinafter referred to as *Kadi* (CJEU I)).[19] The CJEU formally separated the implementing measures within the EU legal order from the measures taken by the UNSC and the Al-Qaida Sanctions Committee. It applied a dualist approach, in so far as it reviewed the implementing measures without challenging the primacy of the UNSC measures at the global level.[20] The stated basis for this approach was the fact that within the EU legal order, fundamental rights such as the right to judicial protection formed an integral part of the general and constitutional order that could not be sacrificed.[21] The CJEU ordered the implementing measures to be annulled, so far as they concerned Mr Kadi, since the EU authorities had neither communicated any reasons to him regarding his listing, nor afforded him any opportunity to be heard.[22]

Subsequently the EU provided Mr Kadi with a summary of reasons made available by the Al-Qaida Sanctions Committee and allowed him a hearing, but only to dismiss his response and re-instate the sanctions within the EU legal order.[23] Mr Kadi once again turned to the GC (as the CFI had by then become) which – following the CJEU's line of reasoning – determined that the reasons forwarded to Mr Kadi were too vague to allow for meaningful review. The measures implementing the UNSC sanctions within the EU legal order were therefore once again struck down.[24] This decision gave rise to another appeal to the CJEU, this time by the European Commission (the Commission) and the Council of the European Union (the Council), which was decided on 18 July 2013.[25]

Supported by several EU member states, the appellants urged the CJEU to reconsider its position. According to the appellants, the EU was under a strict obligation to give effect to the Al-Qaida Sanctions regime and had been left with no discretion regarding the manner of implementation, as a result of which these measures should be immune from judicial review.[26] In the alternative, the appellants further argued for lowering the level of scrutiny applied during judicial review, due to the EU institutions' lack of any margin of discretion in relation to the manner of implementing the measures.[27] However, this argument failed to impress the court, which proceeded to apply a high level of scrutiny in reviewing and striking down the reasons submitted by the EU organs in relation to Mr Kadi's listing.

In coming to its decision the CJEU underscored that the right to be heard along with the right to judicial review constitute the two pillars of judicial protection in the EU. Both of these pillars apply to all decisions that can culminate in a measure adversely affecting the person in question. The right to be heard requires that once restrictive measures have been imposed, the relevant EU authority notify that person of the evidence against him or her, as well as provide the person with a statement of reasons for the decision and the opportunity to make his or her views known. Both the CJEU and GC/CFI, relying on jurisprudence of the ECtHR,[28] have accepted that not all relevant matters have to be conveyed to the affected persons in the notification of evidence or the statement of reasons,[29] and that a concise statement of reasons may sometimes suffice.[30] However, the decisive point with respect to UNSC sanctions regimes is that, under EU law, the listed individuals must be in a position to make their views known effectively in relation to the grounds advanced against them. They must be able to decide, with full knowledge of the relevant facts, whether there is any point in bringing an action before the EU courts.[31] Furthermore, according to the EU courts, the UNSC has to review the sanctions list at least once every six months to ensure that there are still grounds for sustaining it.[32] Where it decides to maintain a name on the list (a so-called subsequent decision), it must indicate the specific reasons why the sustained listing (and the restrictive measures resulting from such listing) remains justified.[33]

As far as the right to judicial review before the EU courts is concerned, the court must be placed in a position to determine whether the EU authority responsible for the listing has carefully considered all the relevant facts; whether the facts actually support the conclusions drawn by the EU authority; and whether the EU authority has given sufficient consideration to any exculpatory evidence. This implies that the provision of a statement of reasons for the listing is not only a crucial element of a fair hearing before the administrative organs, but also of judicial review by the EU courts. Just as the listed individual needs to know the gist of the allegations against him or her to be in a position to exercise review, the court itself must know to some extent the reasons for the listing.[34]

When exercising judicial review, the EU courts must strike a balance between deference to the UNSC's assessment of the evidence, on the one hand, and the level of scrutiny necessary, on the other hand, in order to guarantee a fair trade-off between the need to combat international terrorism and the protection of fundamental rights.[35] In striking this balance, the CJEU and the GC accept that certain evidence may be revealed only to the court, and that in some cases only part of the evidence may be revealed to the court and the affected individual. Even so, at least one of the reasons provided must be sufficiently detailed and specific, as well as substantiated with evidence directly linked to the listed person, to serve as the basis for the listing.[36]

In the case of Mr Kadi, none of the reasons put forward lived up to this requirement. Four of the five reasons elaborated in some detail upon Mr Kadi's acquaintance with and/or ties to individuals or entities that allegedly had close ties to Usama bin Ladin and allegedly supported terrorist activities. However, despite the specificity of these allegations, they all remained unsubstantiated so far as the actual link between those individuals or entities and terrorism. In addition, Mr Kadi was able to provide plausible alternative reasons for his contacts with the individuals and entities in question. The fifth reason for listing did not even meet the first hurdle of specificity: it amounted merely to a vague allegation of Mr Kadi's involvement with (unidentified) firms that were financing extremists.[37]

Since no evidence was produced in relation to Mr Kadi's listing, it remains unclear what type of evidence would suffice to convince the EU courts that the listing is justified. It also remains uncertain whether these courts would accept the appointment of special advocates or other procedures designed to defend the interests of the individual.[38] As far as the special advocate procedure is concerned, it is worth noting that the ECtHR has attached certain conditions to the acceptability of this procedure, which are likely to inform the position of the EU courts if they were at some point confronted with the issue. At the time the ECtHR was confronted with the issue, the special advocate procedure existed, *inter alia*, in the UK. It implied that while certain classified and unclassified materials were accessible to the court, it was not accessible to those individuals who were regarded as a national security threat and – as a result – were confronted with restrictive measures. Instead, the classified material was disclosed to one or more special advocates appointed by the Solicitor-General to act on behalf of the affected individuals. During closed sessions before the court, the special advocate could make submissions on behalf of these individuals regarding both procedural matters, such as the need for further disclosure, as well as the substance of the case. However, from the point that the special advocate first had sight of the closed material onwards, he was not permitted to have any further contact with the applicant and his representatives, save with the permission of the court.[39]

In the so-called *A* case, the ECtHR confirmed that the special advocate could perform an important role in counter-balancing both the lack of full disclosure, as well as the absence of a full, open adversarial hearing, by gauging the evidence and putting forward arguments on behalf of the detainee during closed hearings.[40] However, the special advocate could not perform this function in any useful way unless the detainee was provided with sufficient information about the allegations against him or her to enable him or her to instruct the special advocate effectively. This would be impossible if unclassified materials consisted purely of general assertions and the court's decision to uphold detention was based solely – or to a decisive degree – on closed material.[41]

1.3 Assessment of the approach of the EU courts

There is a high standard of judicial protection in the EU that needs to be upheld by EU administrative organs when implementing UNSC sanctions regimes. The benchmarks of the right to be heard and the right to judicial review are not directed at the UNSC sanctions committees; the EU courts do not have the judicial competence to order the UNSC or its sanctions committees to delist any particular individual or entity, nor to introduce effective judicial protection within the UN sanctions system. The practical outcome of this situation is that while the EU courts can order executive organs within the EU not to give (unqualified) effect to a particular UNSC listing, the individual or entity will formally remain listed by the UN sanctions committee in question. One can describe this as a 'limping situation', as those delisted still carry the chain of sanctions around their legs outside of the EU.[42]

On one hand, the bottom-up pressure the EU courts have generated in this manner on the UNSC to introduce judicial protection for listed individuals is positive, as it prompted the (albeit modest) reform at the UN in the form of the Ombudsperson procedure for those listed by the Al-Qaida Sanctions Committee. On the other hand, the technique the EU courts have applied carries with it the risk of devaluing and marginalising international human rights law. The EU courts based their findings exclusively on EU law and left unanswered the question of if and to what extent the UNSC has to or is presumed to act in accordance with international human rights standards, such as those contained in the ICCPR.[43]

This fuels the perception that an irreconcilable norm conflict exists between the legal regime the UNSC has created with its sanctions-related resolutions and domestic or regional regimes that value the protection of human rights – a conflict which could only be resolved by protecting either one of the regimes at the expense of the other. This in turn gives rise to legal uncertainty, as individuals and entities remain listed by the particular UN sanctions committee, while member states cannot give effect to the listings domestically, due to the requirements of the EU legal order. Moreover, such states are faced with the choice of triggering state responsibility either for not implementing UNSC decisions, or for not giving effect to EU standards of judicial protection.[44]

2 The alternative approach of the ECtHR

2.1 The context of the Nada case

This dilemma leads to the question of whether the systemic challenges resulting from the dualist technique applied by the CJEU can be overcome by human rights-friendly interpretation, otherwise known as harmonious interpretation or the systemic integration approach. Such an approach, which has been adopted by the ECtHR,[45] departs from the premise that any norm conflict stemming from different international obligations should be resolved through a balancing of the different obligations. More specifically, the ECtHR has adopted a strong presumption in favour of a human rights-friendly intention on the part of the UNSC.

In its 2011 judgment in the *Al-Jedda* case, the Grand Chamber of the ECtHR underscored that Article 24(2) of the UN Charter required the UNSC to act in accordance with the purposes and principles of the UN, one of which was the promotion of international human rights.[46] In the event of any ambiguity in the wording of a UNSC resolution, the Grand Chamber found, the court must choose that interpretation which was most in harmony with international human rights standards and which avoided any conflict of international obligations.[47] This reasoning implies that the ECHR sets out a legal regime that corresponds to the human rights standards underpinning the UN Charter itself. As a result, the UNSC must be presumed to have acted in accordance with the ECHR, as anything else would require member states to contravene standards which are not only embodied in the ECHR but also in the UN Charter. In line with this reasoning, the UNSC would have to use clear and explicit language in the relevant resolution if it intended states to take measures that would conflict with their international human rights obligations.

The implications of this approach became clear in the case of *Nada* v. *Switzerland*.[48] The Al-Qaida Sanctions Committee listed Mr Nada in November 2001 in accordance with the UNSC Resolution 1267 (1999) sanctions regime. As a result of this listing, he was subjected to a freezing of assets, as well as stringent travel restrictions, and had no recourse to judicial review. The travel restrictions, which effectively confined him to the Italian canton in Switzerland where he lived, *inter alia*, complicated his access to medical care outside the enclave. This was problematic in light of his health and his age. As the measures implementing the Resolution 1267 (1999) sanctions regime that resulted in these constraints were adopted by Switzerland – not an EU member state – the judicial review of their legality was initially undertaken by the Swiss Federal Tribunal.

This tribunal was of the opinion that Switzerland's obligation under Article 103 of the UN Charter, namely to give precedence to obligations under the UN Charter in instance of conflict with other treaty obligations, prevailed over the right to a fair hearing as provided for in Article 6(1) of the ECHR. More specifically, as the delisting procedure provided for by the sanctions regime left no room for discretion in interpretation, Mr Nada's right to a fair hearing in Article 6(1) of the ECHR was necessarily suspended.[49]

However, this conclusion was subsequently rejected by the Grand Chamber of the ECtHR in September 2012 and was found to be, *inter alia*, in violation of the right to a remedy in Article 13(1) of the ECHR. The ECtHR considered as its starting point whether Switzerland had done everything within its power to minimise the conflict between UNSC resolutions and the obligations resulting from the ECHR, and concluded that this had not been the case. According to the ECtHR, Switzerland should have provided Mr Nada with access to judicial review in Swiss courts, by which means he could have challenged the measures implementing the Resolution 1267 (1999) sanctions regime. In fact, Mr Nada had no effective means to obtain an exemption from the implementing measures within the domestic legal order, which amounted to a violation of Article 13(1) of the ECHR.[50]

Of particular interest is the ECtHR's assertion that there was nothing in the Resolution 1267 (1999) sanctions regime that prevented the Swiss authorities from providing effective domestic judicial review mechanisms.[51] This can be interpreted as implying that the Resolution 1267 (1999) sanctions regime necessarily and implicitly allowed states the discretion needed to enforce the respective sanctions regime in accordance with international human rights standards. Such an interpretation would amount to assuming the permissibility of judicial review in accordance with the standards of the ECHR (or other applicable international human rights instruments), unless this was explicitly excluded.[52]

2.2 Assessment of the ECtHR's approach

This conclusion that judicial review within the domestic legal order was permissible unless explicitly excluded by a UNSC resolution would in practice place implementing states and the affected individuals and entities in a similar 'limping situation' of legal uncertainty to that resulting from the *Kadi* (CJEU I and II) decisions. Whereas the individuals would regain access to their assets and freedom of movement within a particular jurisdiction, they would remain formally listed ('targeted') within the UN sanctions system until such time as the relevant sanctions committee delisted them. Furthermore, states that delist individuals within the domestic legal order subsequent to a court decision to this effect may incur state responsibility for acting in contravention with a UNSC obligation.[53]

In essence, the *Nada* case exposed both the strengths and weaknesses of the technique of systemic integration. On the positive side, this approach can have a defragmentary effect in that it attempts to find a resolution for international norm conflicts in a manner that upholds all the relevant international law obligations. In other words, this approach attempts to prevent the outright rejection of binding UNSC obligations. It also prevents states from hiding behind the excuse that such obligations require them to limit human rights in instances where such obligations in fact allow for discretion that can facilitate human rights-friendly interpretation.

The case of *The Netherlands* v. *A and Others*, which concerned domestic measures implementing UNSC Resolution 1737 of 23 December 2006, is one such instance.[54] This resolution, *inter alia*, called on

> all States to exercise vigilance and prevent specialised teaching or training of Iranian nationals, within their territories or by their nationals, of disciplines which would contribute to Iran's proliferation of sensitive nuclear activities and development of nuclear weapon delivery systems.[55]

The Supreme Court of the Netherlands rejected the Dutch Government's argument that this paragraph of the resolution necessitated the exclusion of Iranian nationals from certain specialised disciplines at Dutch universities. According to the Supreme Court, such an interpretation violated the principle of non-discrimination in Article 26 of the ICCPR (which was directly applicable in the Netherlands). The Dutch government had not provided convincing arguments why it could not follow less restrictive measures, similar to those practised in neighbouring countries.

On the negative side, however, the technique of human rights-friendly interpretation can lead to a distortion of the text of UNSC obligations, in instances where these obligations leave no margin for interpretation. This arguably occurred in the *Nada* decision. Moreover (and as already indicated above), the distortive interpretation ultimately leads to the same legally uncertain situation that resulted from the *Kadi* decisions. The technique of systemic integration is therefore only a workable solution where the text of the UNSC resolution does not clearly limit or even suspend certain human rights.[56]

As both Mr Kadi and Mr Nada have since been delisted by the Al-Qaida Sanctions Committee, issues regarding state responsibility for non-implementation of UNSC decisions are not likely to arise in relation to their specific situations. However, other EU and Swiss residents listed by the Al-Qaida Sanctions Committee may still avail themselves of the EU and/or Swiss courts, and eventually the ECtHR. The same applies to those individuals and entities listed by the Taliban Sanctions Committee and other country-specific sanctions committees with the competence to engage in direct listing.[57] As noted above, in terms of the UN sanctions system, these individuals and entities do not even have access to an Ombudsperson and are entirely dependent on the inter-governmental, political procedure for delisting as exercised by their respective sanctions committees.[58]

3 Conclusion

Elsewhere, this author has extensively argued that when the UNSC creates subsidiary organs that engage in direct listing for the purpose of assets freezing, this must be undertaken in accordance with basic standards of procedural justice as recognised in Article 14(1) of the ICCPR.[59] Of particular importance are principles of independence, even-handedness and impartiality. The special role and nature of the UNSC in the maintenance of international peace and security may require some leeway in the manner in which the UNSC gives effect to this obligation. It could not be expected that the UNSC follow, for example, exactly the same procedure as the CJEU.[60]

Even so, it remains essential that the listing and delisting procedures are subjected to a process that takes into account the principles of independence, even-handedness and impartiality. It is arguable that the procedure currently carried out by the Ombudsperson can live up to these criteria, if her proposals for delisting were made final and binding and not subjected to a veto by either the UNSC sanctions committee or the UNSC itself. Once such conditions existed within the UN sanctions system, it is very likely that European regional courts would exercise more judicial restraint when confronted with the legality of measures that implement sanctions resulting from the direct listing of individuals or entities by UN sanctions committees. These courts then may feel less compelled to engage in strict judicial review of the (lack of) evidence supporting the particular listing and instead defer to the opinion of the Ombudsperson in this regard.

However, until such a time as impartial and independent judicial review is introduced within the UN sanctions system for those individuals and entities directly listed by UNSC sanctions committees, the current judicial rebellion in Europe will continue. The next chapter in this rebellion is already looming around the corner, as the *Al-Dulimi* decision by the Second Chamber of the ECtHR has since been referred to the Grand Chamber, where it was pending at the time of writing.

Notes

1 Parts of this chapter are based on Erika de Wet, '(Implicit) Judicial Favoring of Human Rights over United Nations Security Council Sanctions: A Manifestation of International Constitutionalism?' in Federico Fabbrini and Vicki Jackson (eds), *Constitutionalism across Borders in the Struggle against Terrorism* (Cheltenham, Edward Elgar, 2015 forthcoming).

2 *Yassin Abdullah Kadi and Al Barakaat International Foundation* v. *Council of the European Union and Commission of the European Communities*, Joined Cases C-402/05 P and C-415/05 [2008] ECR I-6351 (3 September 2008) ('*Kadi* (CJEU I)').

3 *European Commission and the Council of the European Union* v. *Yassin Abdullah Kadi*, Joined Cases C-584/10 P, C-593/10 P and C-595/10 P [2013] ECR not yet reported (18 July 2013) ('*Kadi* (CJEU II)'). This case was preceded by *Yassin Adullah Kadi* v. *Council of the European Union and Commission of the European Communities*, Case T-315/01 [2005] ECR II-3649 (21 September 2005) ('*Kadi* (GC I)'); *Kadi* (CJEU I); and *Yassin Abdullah Kadi* v. *European Commission*, Case T-85/09 [2010] ECHR II-0000 (30 September 2010) ('*Kadi* (GC II)').

4 SC Res. 1267 (15 October 1999).

5 Ibid., paras 4 and 6; Dire Tladi and Gillian Taylor, 'On the Al Qaida/Taliban Sanctions Regime: Due Process and Sunsetting' (2011) 10(4) *Chinese Journal of International Law* 771–89; Erika de Wet, 'From *Kadi* to *Nada*: Judicial Techniques Favouring Human Rights over United Nations Security Council Sanctions' (2013) 12(4) *Chinese Journal of International Law* 787–808.

6 See Tladi and Taylor, 'Due Process and Sunsetting', 775ff.; de Wet 'From *Kadi* to *Nada*', 788.

7 Tladi and Taylor, 'Due Process and Sunsetting', 781; de Wet, 'From *Kadi* to *Nada*', 788–9.

8 SC Res. 1904 (17 December 2009), paras 20–1; see Tladi and Taylor, 'Due Process and Sunsetting', 782; de Wet, 'From *Kadi* to *Nada*', 789.

9 For a first-hand account of the Ombudsperson's efforts to improve the due process of listed individuals, see Prost's chapter in this collection.

10 UN Doc. S/2014/553 (31 July 2014), para. 6.

11 See also *Kadi* (GC II), para. 128; Tladi and Taylor, 'Due Process and Sunsetting', 782; de Wet, 'From *Kadi* to *Nada*', 789.

12 SC Res. 1988 (17 June 2011), paras 1, 6, 21.

13 Individuals who were moved from the Consolidated List of the Al-Qaida Sanctions Committee to the separate list of the Taliban Sanctions Committee through the adoption of SC Res. 1988 (17 June 2011) suddenly found themselves without any access to the Ombudsperson. For a critical analysis, see Tladi and Taylor, 'Due Process and Sunsetting', 786; de Wet, 'From *Kadi* to *Nada*', 789.

14 SC Res. 1989 (17 June 2011), paras 23 and 27; de Wet, 'From *Kadi* to *Nada*', 789.

15 Ibid.

16 Tladi and Taylor, 'Due Process and Sunsetting', 781, 787; de Wet, 'From *Kadi* to *Nada*', 789–90.

17 See, *inter alia*, Devika Hovell, 'A Dialogue Model: The Role of the Domestic Judge in Security Council Decision-Making' (2013) 26(3) *Leiden Journal of International Law* 579–97; Antonios Tzanakopoulos, 'Collective Security and Human Rights', in Erika de Wet and Jure Vidmar (eds), *Hierarchy in International Law: The Place of Human Rights* (Oxford, Oxford University Press, 2012), 42–70.

18 *Kadi* (GC I), paras 221ff.; see also Antonios Tzanakopoulos, 'Kadi Showdown: Substantive Review of (UN) Sanctions by the ECJ', sec. IV (26 July 2013): www.ejiltalk.org/kadi-showdown/#more-8613; Tladi and Taylor, 'Due Process and Sunsetting', 779; de Wet, 'From *Kadi* to *Nada*', 791.

19 *Kadi* (CJEU I).

20 See also *Kadi* (GC II), para. 119.

21 *Kadi* (CJEU I), para. 288; de Wet, 'From *Kadi* to *Nada*', 791.

22 *Kadi* (CJEU I), para. 334; see also Tzanakopoulos, 'Kadi Showdown', sec. II; de Wet, 'From *Kadi* to *Nada*', 791.

23 Tzanakopoulos, 'Kadi Showdown', sec. II–III; de Wet, 'From *Kadi* to *Nada*', 791.

24 *Kadi* (GC II), para. 157; Tzanakopoulos, 'Kadi Showdown', sec. II; Tladi and Taylor, 'Due Process and Sunsetting', 780; de Wet, 'From *Kadi* to *Nada*', 791.

25 *Kadi* (CJEU II); de Wet, 'From *Kadi* to *Nada*', 792.

26 See also Tzanakopoulos, 'Kadi Showdown', sec. II; de Wet, 'From *Kadi* to *Nada*', 792.

27 *Kadi* (CJEU II), paras 72–3; Tzanakopoulos, 'Kadi Showdown', sec. IV. Advocate-General Bot suggested a similar (ultimately unsuccessful) line of reasoning in his 'opinion to the CJEU regarding Joined Cases C-584/10 P, C-593/10 P and C-595/10 P, *European Commission, Council of the European Union, United Kingdom of Great Britain and Northern Ireland* v. *Yassin Abdullah Kadi*, paras 53ff. (19 March 2013): http://eurlex.europa.eu/LexUriServ/LexUriServ.do?uri=CELEX:62010CC0584:EN:NOT. See also de Wet, 'From *Kadi* to *Nada*', 792.

28 *Chahal* v. *United Kingdom*, ECtHR (1996-V), Series A No. 22 ('*Chahal* case'), para. 131; de Wet, 'From *Kadi* to *Nada*', 793.

29 *Kadi* (CJEU I), para. 344; *OMPI* (I), paras 135 and 146; Gattini, 'Joined Cases', 222.

30 *Melli Bank plc* v. *Council*, Joined Cases T-246/08 and T-332–08, Judgment (9 July 2009) ('*Melli Bank* case'); SC Res. 1737 (23 December 2006).

31 *Kadi* (CJEU II), paras 111–12; de Wet, 'From *Kadi* to *Nada*', 793.

32 *OMPI* (I), para. 116.

33 Ibid., paras 138, 143, 145.

34 *Kadi* (GC II) paras 89, 93, 143, 145; *Kadi* (CJEU II), paras 114–15, 119; de Wet, 'From *Kadi* to *Nada*', 793ff.

35 *OMPI* (I), para. 155.

36 Ibid., paras 155ff.

37 *Kadi* (CJEU II), paras 141ff.; see de Wet, 'From *Kadi* to *Nada*', 797–8.
38 *Kadi* (CJEU I), para. 344; *Kadi* (GC II), para. 134; *OMPI* (I), para. 135, 158; Gattini, 'Joined Cases', 222.
39 This was the procedure followed by the Special Immigration Appeals Commission (SIAC) in the UK and which gave rise to *A and Others* v. *United Kingdom*, Appl. No. 3455/05, ECtHR, Judgment (Grand Chamber) (19 February 2009) ('*A* case').
40 Ibid.
41 Ibid., paras 220, 215.
42 De Wet, 'From *Kadi* to *Nada*', 798–9.
43 Ibid., 799–800.
44 See also Tzanakopoulos, 'Kadi Showdown', sec. III.
45 *Al-Jedda* v. *United Kingdom*, Appl. No. 27021/087, ECtHR, Judgment (Grand Chamber) (7 July 2011) ('*Al-Jedda* case').
46 Ibid., para. 102. The case concerned the extent to which UNSC obligations authorising internment for security reasons in Iraq by British troops were compatible with art. 5(1) of the ECHR; de Wet, 'From *Kadi* to *Nada*', 801–2.
47 *Al-Jedda* case, para. 102; de Wet, 'From *Kadi* to *Nada*', 802.
48 *Nada* v. *Switzerland*, Appl. No. 10593/08, ECtHR, Judgment (Grand Chamber) (12 September 2012) ('*Nada* case').
49 *Nada* v. *State Secretariat for Economic Affairs and Federal Department of Economic Affairs*, Administrative Appeal Judgment, Case No. 1A 45/2007 (14 November 2007), ILDC 461 (CH 2007); de Wet, 'From *Kadi* to *Nada*', 803.
50 *Nada* case, paras 211–13; de Wet, 'From *Kadi* to *Nada*', 804.
51 *Nada* case, para. 212.
52 De Wet, 'From *Kadi* to *Nada*', 804–5.
53 Ibid., 805.
54 *The Netherlands* v. *A and Others*, Supreme Court of the Netherlands, Judgment (14 December 2012), LJN: BX8351.
55 SC Res. 1373 (23 December 2006), para. 17.
56 As arguably was the situation in the *Al-Jedda* case; de Wet, 'From *Kadi* to *Nada*', 805.
57 Such as the sanctions committee pursuant to SC Res. 1483 (22 May 2003); de Wet, 'From *Kadi* to *Nada*', 805.
58 See in this regard the case of *Al-Dulimi and Montana Management Inc.* v. *Switzerland*, Appl. No. 5809/08, ECtHR, Judgment (Second Chamber) (26 November 2013), currently pending before the Grand Chamber. The case concerned the sanctions regime against Iraq, imposed by SC Res. 1483 (23 May 2013), para. 23. It, *inter alia*, required the freezing of assets of the government of Saddam Hussein. See also Anne Peters, 'Targeted Sanctions after Affaire Al-Dulimi et Montana Management Inc c. Suisse: Is There a Way Out of the Catch-22 for UN Members?' (4 December 2013): www.ejiltalk.org/targeted-sanctions-after-affaire-al-dulimi-et-montana-management-inc-c-suisse-is-there-a-way-out-of-the-catch-22-for-un-members.
59 See, for example, Erika de Wet, 'Holding the United Nations Security Council Accountable for Human Rights Violations through Domestic and Regional Courts: A Case of "Be Careful What You Wish For?"', in Jeremy Farrall and Kim Rubenstein (eds), *Sanctions, Accountability and Governance in a Globalised World* (Cambridge, Cambridge University Press, 2009), 143–68.
60 See Hovell, '*Dialogue Model*', 585, who underscores the need to take account of the context of procedural fairness.

Part IV

The Security Council, use of force and the rule of law

15 Between flexibility and accountability

How can the Security Council strengthen oversight of use-of-force mandates?

Karine Bannelier and Théodore Christakis[1]

Introduction

Since 1990 the United Nations (UN) Security Council (UNSC) has authorised states or coalitions of states to use force on multiple occasions. It has done so in Iraq,[2] Bosnia-Herzegovina,[3] Somalia,[4] Rwanda,[5] Haiti,[6] Zaïre,[7] Albania,[8] the Central African Republic (CAR),[9] Guinea-Bissau,[10] Kosovo,[11] Timor-Leste,[12] Afghanistan,[13] Côte d'Ivoire,[14] the Democratic Republic of the Congo (DRC),[15] Chad,[16] Libya[17] and Mali.[18] Unlike use-of-force mandates given to 'robust' UN peacekeeping forces acting under UN flag and command,[19] these authorisations, given to individual states or 'coalitions of the willing', introduce into the collective security system a strong element of decentralisation. This system of delegating the power to use force under Article 42 of the UN Charter to individual states or coalitions raises various concerns, especially when the states that take action on the basis of these UNSC resolutions have a direct interest in the countries in which they are intervening. There is a clear danger that such states might use the UNSC's authorisation as a cover to pursue their own agenda and justify what would be otherwise an unlawful intervention.

While this risk of abuse and misuse of the collective security system is enough in itself to justify more effective oversight of a use-of-force mandate, things are not that simple. In practice there is always a tension between the need for such control, on the one hand, and the desire of states that carry out UNSC use-of-force mandates ('operating states') to benefit from maximum flexibility in order to perform costly and often dangerous missions, on the other hand.[20] Tying the hands of operating states by imposing rigorous oversight and control could prove counterproductive: the volunteers could vanish and the UN could revert to precisely the same kind of inaction that stigmatised the Cold War years and relegated the organisation to a helpless spectator role during the genocide in Rwanda. As Kolb has rightly observed, the choice in that instance was not between imperfect and perfect action, but rather between 'complete inaction and imperfect action'.[21]

When the Libyan crisis broke out in 2011, the UNSC was still struggling to balance the institutional requirement of centralisation and control, and the functional necessity of decentralisation and flexibility. The modalities of interpretation of the UNSC's Resolution 1973 (2011),[22] and its implementation by Operation Unified Protector, which was deployed by the North Atlantic Treaty Organization (NATO), raised critical issues concerning compliance by the coalition of operating states with the UNSC mandate. Several states within the UN considered that 'the Council's mandate for conducting the operation in Libya was disregarded',[23] or that there was an 'arbitrary interpretation of the Council's resolutions'.[24] Other states, such as South Africa, talked about a 'flagrant abuse of resolution 1973 [which] seriously undermined and damaged the reputation of [the doctrine of 'responsibility to protect' (R2P)]'.[25] Yet other states, like Cuba and Venezuela, even alleged that there lay behind Operation Unified Protector an 'imperialistic agenda' which should be avoided by all means in the future.[26] Even some states that participated in the coalition, like Norway, criticised the implementation of Resolution 1973 (2011), underlining that it was 'essential that such mandates [were] implemented strictly to protect civilians and [did] not go beyond that'.[27]

Motivated by these concerns, Brazil presented a concept note entitled 'responsibility while protecting' (RWP) at the UN in November 2011.[28] Although the note discussed all three pillars of R2P,[29] its primary purpose was to advance proposals designed to limit the risk of abuse of a UNSC use-of-force mandate.

The RWP concept has prompted much discussion within the UN.[30] While it was initially welcomed by several countries, it received a mixed, if not frosty, reception from several western countries who expressed the fear that the Brazilian proposals could lead to the institutionalisation of inaction.[31] In non-western countries, the concept of RWP originally received a fairly warm welcome but mistrust progressively took hold. The initial enthusiasm of South Africa and India gave way to scepticism, while China and Russia expressed strong reservations. The latter possibly feared that the concept of RWP, by proposing a series of checks and balances, might grant new legitimacy to R2P and thus weaken Russia's opposition to the use of force in cases like Syria.[32]

Important R2P theoreticians, such as Gareth Evans, have viewed RWP as an opportunity to restore the reputation of R2P.[33] Nonetheless, there was nothing particularly revolutionary in the Brazilian concept note. It merely elaborated on ideas already expressed by the UNSC in a presidential statement dated 30 November 1998 concerning the need for accountability and enhanced UNSC procedures to monitor and assess the manner in which use-of-force resolutions are interpreted and implemented.[34]

In this chapter we build upon the 1998 presidential statement and the Brazilian RWP proposals to propose and evaluate nine potential avenues of action to strengthen oversight and control of UNSC use-of-force mandates.

1 Better defining the scope of use-of-force mandates

The first idea that appears in all relevant discussions within the UN is that authorisations for the use of force must be clear and limited in scope with a statement of the specific objectives to be achieved.[35] Some scholars go so far as to identify an 'obligation' on the UNSC 'to ensure that it specifies in some detail the objectives for which Chapter VII powers are being delegated'.[36] Indeed, the UNSC has been accused of using open-ended expressions and thus failing to specify clear objectives for use-of-force missions. The best example is Resolution 678 (1990), authorising UN members 'to use all necessary means ... to restore international peace and security' after the invasion of Kuwait by Iraq.[37] As Kolb correctly points out, giving this kind of *carte blanche* to states is dangerous for the UN system: it is as if the UNSC is acting as a 'bailiff, who opens the door and disappears'.[38]

Following this initial criticism, the UNSC has tried in subsequent years to better define the scope of the use of force,[39] yet its mandates have often remained vague.[40] As the above discussion of Libya shows, even when the UNSC tries to define the mandate in a more precise way, major problems of interpretation can still arise.[41]

In some cases, the UNSC has not even bothered to define the scope of use-of-force mandates, instead using a technique of 'referrals'. In these instances, instead of specifying clearly and precisely in what situations and for what reasons multinational forces are authorised to use force, the resolution refers to another text. A problematic example of this was Resolution 1546 (2004) concerning Iraq, which decided that a multinational force would have 'the authority to take all necessary measures to contribute to the maintenance of security and stability in Iraq in accordance with the letters annexed to this resolution'.[42] One of the two annexed letters (and the only one relevant to the question of the scope of the mandate) was from US Secretary of State Colin Powell, who unsurprisingly framed the mandate in a very open way. In other words, instead of defining the objectives of the use of force, the UNSC spinelessly endorsed the will of the state that was to lead the multinational force that it was authorising to use force![43]

Respect for the rule of law, transparency and judicial security require a clear identification of the situations/objectives that permit the use of force. The practice of 'referrals' can make this identification difficult and create confusion as to the precise scope of the mandate. It is even more problematic to trust this mission to the intervening power, as in the case of Iraq. To limit the risks of abuse by intervening powers, it is necessary to define the scope and objectives of the use of force mandate in a *multilateral* way within the UNSC, and to include this directly within the relevant resolutions.

2 Avoiding the 'reverse veto' risk by fixing an expiration date

Once the UNSC authorises the use of force, it can in theory still clarify, amend or revoke that authorisation in case of conflicting interpretation, abuse or other problems.[44] However, in practice any such modifications must overcome the hurdle of the 'reverse veto', that is, a permanent member may use its veto power to block revising or ending an authorisation to use force.[45] As a result there is a risk of the UNSC entering into a kind of 'black hole' whenever it adopts a

Chapter VII resolution.[46] The refusal of a permanent member to authorise a modification of a Chapter VII resolution can make it impossible to end the authorised action and terminate the mandate.

One scholarly proposal to counter this risk of a reverse veto is the idea of a voluntary suspension of the right to veto.[47] This voluntary suspension would be exercised by permanent members in order to ensure the UNSC is always able to modify or terminate a Chapter VII action on a majority basis. However, this proposal seems impractical and hard to realise.

An easier way to mitigate the risk of a reverse veto would be to include a sunset clause in resolutions authorising the use of force, thus fixing a date on which the authorisation expires. This would avoid the 'black hole' effect of Chapter VII and strengthen the overall monitoring process, requiring the UNSC to assess the situation periodically in order to decide whether the mandate ought to be extended, modified or allowed to lapse.

Indeed, the UNSC faced heavy criticism in relation to Resolution 678 (1990) on Iraq because the resolution did not contain an expiration date. This led to major debates in 2003, when the US and the UK argued that the authorisation to use force given by Resolution 678 in 1990 still remained valid 13 years later.[48] Following this criticism, the UNSC initiated a systematic practice of introducing sunset clauses, beginning with Resolution 929 (1994) on the Rwandan crisis, and continuing steadily until Resolution 1973 (2011), which, in a striking departure, set no deadline for the expiration of the authorisation to use force against Libya. This constituted a major setback in UNSC practice. Avoiding such departures from established practice in the future will help establish mutual trust among UNSC members.

3 Ensuring operating states do not act *ultra vires*

A basic principle governing delegation of powers in general and authorisation to use force in particular is that the delegate cannot act *ultra vires*.[49] This means that the discretionary power of the states authorised to use force only exists as long as these states remain within the framework fixed by the act of delegation.[50]

This of course requires an interpretation of the limits of the mandate, which can be difficult if the mandate is open-ended and vague. The large margin of discretion enjoyed by operating states in implementing a UNSC mandate makes things even more complicated. Nonetheless, some scholars consider that this margin of discretion should be reconciled with the principle *exceptio est strictissimae interpretationis*, which, according to them, is applicable to use-of-force authorisations and the delegation of Chapter VII powers.[51] If this principle does prohibit a state from perverting or revising the objectives fixed by the UNSC, it would not become an impediment in relation to the *means* used to attain these objectives.

In the case of Libya, for example, the mandate was 'to take all necessary measures … to protect civilians and civilian populated areas under threat of attack'.[52] In that case, the principle *exceptio est* precluded the conclusion that the objective the UNSC fixed in Resolution 1973 (2011) was regime change. On the other hand, nobody seriously called into question whether the coalition had the discretion to read its mandate as authorising bombings not only against troops *directly* involved in the attacks against civilians, but also against other military targets and infrastructure of Gadhafi's army as a 'necessary measure' to reach the legitimate objectives stated in Resolution 1973 (2011).[53]

This also raises the question of *who* is entitled to interpret UNSC resolutions and decide whether a mandate has been exceeded.[54] There is little doubt that the UNSC itself has the capacity to proceed to such an assessment within its general power of review and control of the enforcement action. However, the UNSC is yet to call a state to task for exceeding one of its mandates.

In the case of Côte d'Ivoire, the Ivorian Government sent a letter to the UNSC in November 2004, arguing that French forces in command of Operation Licorne had violated their UNSC mandate.[55] The Ivorian Government thus sought 'prompt apologies from France and compensation for the damage which it caused'.[56] The UNSC rejected these claims and expressed 'its full support for the action undertaken by French forces'.[57] In 2011 France was again criticised by Ivorian President Laurent Gbagbo, as well as Russia, Angola and South Africa, for acting outside Resolution 1975 (2011) by attacking the Presidential compound in Abidjan, which ultimately led to the arrest of Laurent Gbagbo.[58] Once again the UNSC did not condemn or chastise France for its actions. Returning to the case of Libya, also in 2011, the UNSC again did nothing to address the criticism, directed by several states and international organisations, including the AU,[59] that the states participating in Operation Unified Protector were acting *ultra vires* in order to overthrow Colonel Gaddafi and achieve regime change in Libya.

Ultimately, even if one could imagine a hypothetical situation where a majority within the UNSC decide to criticise operating states for acting *ultra vires*, it is very hard to see how a draft resolution could avoid a veto, especially as permanent members are almost always involved in such use-of-force operations.

4 Imposing precise rules of engagement for operating states?

Another criticism of use-of-force mandates is that they are not accompanied by clear, transparent rules of engagement (ROE) to guide the parties responsible for implementation. Although clear and precise ROE would certainly be useful, especially where ground troops are deployed, such detailed and strict ROE could also act as a considerable constraint on military effectiveness and erode the necessary margin of discretion for operating states. This is especially so when ROE establish complicated 'dual-key' procedures. Dual-key procedures require the intervening state to get a 'green light' from the UN before using force, either by delegating the task to the UN Secretary-General (UNSG) or by entrusting it to the commander of a UN peacekeeping mission operating jointly with the operating states.

Past experience demonstrates that we should not underestimate the problems that might arise when the UNSC subordinates the use of force to a process of 'co-decision' or authorisation by the UNSG or the Chief of Staff of a UN peacekeeping operation also present on the ground. In the case of Bosnia-Herzegovina, Resolutions 816 (1993) and 836 (1993) authorised member states to take 'under the authority of the Security Council and subject to close coordination with the Secretary-General and UNPROFOR all necessary measures' in order to enforce the 'no-fly zone' over Bosnia and to protect the 'safe areas' in the Republic. The UNSG interpreted this mandate as requiring his consent for any military action by NATO forces.[60] Similarly, the commander of UNPROFOR, General Rose, stated that 'not a single NATO bomb will be launched without my order'.[61] Nonetheless, the very same day NATO launched not one but several missiles without consulting with General Rose or the UNSG.[62] More generally there were several operational difficulties in relation to this 'dual-key' mechanism, which led one NATO official to observe that 'in our cooperation with the UN we have violated the golden military rule to have one single command structure'.[63]

In subsequent resolutions the UNSC tried to deal with the issue of coexistence of UN peacekeeping forces and multilateral forces or states operating jointly on the ground either by asking them in general terms to 'cooperate' and coordinate their action,[64] or by asking them to 'reach an agreement' on the modalities of their cooperation.[65] In some cases, including Resolutions 2100 (2013) on Mali and 2149 (2014) on the CAR, the UNSC gave an authorisation to a specific state (France) to 'intervene in support' of elements of the peacekeeping operation 'upon request of the Secretary-General'.[66]

5 Regulating the requirement for necessity and proportionality

In its RWP concept note, Brazil emphasises that 'in the event that the use of force is contemplated, action must be judicious, proportionate' and 'must produce as little violence and instability as possible and under no circumstance can it generate more harm than it was authorized to prevent'.[67] The adjectives 'judicious' and 'proportionate' evoke the international law principles of necessity and proportionality.[68] These two principles apply to the implementation of UNSC use-of-force mandates.

The terminology used in the resolutions of the UNSC clearly invokes the principle of necessity: the UNSC authorises states to 'use all necessary means' or 'to take all necessary measures' in order to realise its objectives. This formula confers on operating states a large margin of discretion (they can use 'all necessary' force to accomplish their tasks), but also imposes a limit: states cannot do more than what is 'necessary' in order to implement a UNSC resolution.

Beyond the terminology used in UNSC resolutions, general international law also requires respect for the principles of necessity and proportionality in all cases of the use of force.[69] The International Court of Justice (ICJ), in its 1986 Judgment in the *Case Concerning the Military and Paramilitary Activities in and against Nicaragua*, found that while the UN Charter 'does not contain any specific rule whereby self-defence would warrant only measures which are proportional to the armed attack and necessary to respond to it', there was no doubt that this rule was 'well established in customary international law'.[70] It is therefore reasonable to conclude that any use of force under UNSC authorisation is subordinated to exactly the same 'customary' conditions that apply to the use of force in self-defence, namely respect for the principles of necessity and proportionality. Necessity requires force to be used only when there is no alternative, pacific solution. Proportionality, for its part, requires a balancing test between the military advantage anticipated by the use of force and the destruction created by the military action.

In practice, these two principles always give rise to difficult judgements concerning what is required in the circumstances. These difficulties are compounded when it comes to UNSC use-of-force mandates, raising several problems. First, there is the perennial problem of which organ possesses authority to make these judgements concerning prospective or actual UNSC action. It is hard to imagine how a judicial organ, such as the ICJ, could receive jurisdiction to conduct such an evaluation.[71] And as far as the UNSC is concerned, we have already seen its reluctance to criticise operating states for an *ultra vires* action; it is highly unlikely that the UNSC would call these same states to account for 'unnecessary' or 'disproportionate' actions.

Second, even if the UNSC were willing to engage in such an evaluation, its effect would be limited. The magical formula the UNSC uses to authorise the use of force (states can use '*all necessary means*') clearly indicates that states enjoy a large margin of discretion within the framework of the authorisation and objectives fixed by the UNSC. This leads to extensive freedom in relation to the planning, command and conduct of the military operations in order to achieve the UNSC's objectives. Thus in some cases those states authorised to use force have decided *not to use it* (because it was not necessary).[72] In other cases where states have found it necessary to resort to military action, they have insisted on being masters of the operation. Pushing the requirements of necessity and proportionality too far could therefore result in pushback from operating states, and lead to micro-management of the operations by the UNSC, which would in turn be counterproductive for the system of use-of-force mandates.

The UNSC should therefore only intervene to control how its authorisations to use force are interpreted and implemented when: (1) there is a manifest error of assessment on the part of the delegate/s (for example, if it becomes evident that the facts justifying a military operation do not actually exist); or (2) the military operation is manifestly disproportionate to the objectives that gave rise to the authorisation (for example, if there is a blatant and obvious mismatch between the military action undertaken, the facts on the ground and the objectives set by the UNSC).

6 Ensuring respect for international law

In the 1998 presidential statement noted above, the UNSC emphasised 'that missions and operations must ensure that their personnel respect and observe international law, including humanitarian, human rights and refugee law'.[73] Brazil similarly stressed in its RWP concept note that 'military action must ... be carried out in strict conformity with international law, in particular international humanitarian law and the international law of armed conflict'.[74]

States that conduct operations under a UNSC mandate are bound by the *jus in bello* (law of armed conflict (LOAC)) when the situation in which they are involved reaches the threshold of an armed conflict. However, applying the *jus in bello* rules is highly complex and problematic, with authorisations to use force being given in contexts of non-international armed conflict and even where there is no armed conflict at all. The question that arises, then, is to define the potential impact of such use-of-force mandates on the legal assessment of the situation. For example, under what conditions could the military intervention of a foreign state (authorised by the UNSC) trigger the application of the law of *international* armed conflict? Interestingly, in the 2013 Mali crisis, France considered its intervention to be subject to the law of non-international armed conflict, namely Common Article 3 to the four Geneva Conventions, and Additional Protocol II relating to the Protection of Victims of Non-International Armed Conflicts.[75]

Beyond international humanitarian law (IHL) and the LOAC, states should also respect other areas of international law, especially international human rights law (IHRL). It is now well recognised that IHRL is relevant during armed conflict and can, when applicable, supplement the protection given by IHL.[76] Since 1999 and the adoption of Resolution 1265,[77] the UNSC has consistently recalled the obligation of belligerents to respect IHRL during armed conflict in its resolutions concerning the protection of civilians.[78] But while in several of its resolutions the UNSC authorised a use-of-force mandate to protect human rights in a country,[79] it only recently began identifying respect for IHRL as a condition of an authorisation to use force.[80]

However, the requirement to respect IHRL when using force does not only extend to those forces acting on UNSC authorised use-of-force mandates. The UNSC should also ensure 'non-United Nations security forces' participating in the field of operations (especially local defence and security forces) also fully comply with IHRL, which connects with the idea of 'positive obligations' in the field of human rights.[81]

7 Resolving attribution problems

Affirming the principle of accountability is futile if it is not possible to attribute responsibility to individual states for violations of *jus in bello* or other rules of international law due to the usual nebula of actors undertaking military action.[82] Indeed, it is sometimes a multinational coalition that responds to the authorisation given by the UNSC.[83] In the case of Libya in 2011, for example, there was little or no transparency concerning which operating states undertook which actions in accordance with the UNSC's authorisation in Resolution 1973 (2011).

Factors that render attribution for violations of international law almost impossible in the case of actions of a multinational force include the extreme variety of rules binding each operating state (for example, due to uneven ratification of *jus in bello* and arms control treaties), the invocation of immunities rules, as well as problems of shared responsibility that have not been adequately addressed by the International Law Commission's Draft Articles on Responsibility of International Organizations.[84] The UNSC should reflect on this problem. Putting in place a process to ensure accurate determination of 'who did what' during an operation would serve the rule of law without constituting an impediment to action. In line with this, the UNSC could also deploy fact-finding missions or create commissions of inquiry in cases of serious allegations of violations of international law during military operations.

8 Enhancing reporting and monitoring

The UNSC generally requests operating states to report to it on a regular basis on the implementation of use-of-force mandates. This important measure seems to be required by the UN Charter itself.[85] But several things could be done to enhance the UNSC's reporting and monitoring systems.

First, the UNSC has never indicated what should be contained in these reports. Of course operating states should not be asked to divulge confidential military information, the disclosure of which could be detrimental to the accomplishment of the mission. On the other hand, it would be consistent with the principles of accountability and transparency to require states to include in their reports non-classified information that is relevant to the conduct of UNSC-authorised operations. The reporting requirement should not be a mere formality. Rather, it should enable the UNSC to have a clear idea about the situation on the ground and the respective roles of each participating state.

Second, the UNSC does not always fix a time frame for the submission of reports. In its early 1990s mandates, the UNSC only requested in general terms that states report 'on a regular basis', while sometimes fixing a deadline for the first report but not subsequently.[86] During the second half of the 1990s, the UNSC gave the impression of changing this practice by requesting states to report according to tight time frames (every two weeks).[87] Since then the UNSC's practice has been inconsistent. Sometimes the UNSC has asked operating states to present their report in a specific time frame,[88] while at other times it has used the expression 'regular basis' or 'periodic reports' without specifying a time frame.[89] There is no reason for the UNSC not to include in its authorising resolutions a provision requiring operating states to report to it according to a specific time frame. The UNSC should also issue stern 'reminders' in cases where operating states neglect their reporting requirements.[90]

The current system is essentially based on a process of self-reporting, with the implication that operating states may pick and choose what to mention and what to omit from their reports. One way to address this problem would be to establish a system of independent monitoring. For example, the UNSC could mandate the UNSG or another person to receive all relevant information (including from non-governmental organisations) and relay it in a report to the UNSC.[91]

9 Instituting a 'Use-of-Force Committee'?

There have been suggestions, inspired by the UNSC's sanctions committees, to create a new subsidiary organ of the UNSC entrusted with the task of monitoring implementation of use-of-force mandates. In a recent article two scholars suggested that a 'Use-of-Force Committee' should serve as 'an independent, quasi-judicial body',[92] the conclusions of which would be binding upon all states unless the UNSC acting in plenary decides otherwise. This would mean that the possible veto of a permanent member could only act in favour of the Committee's conclusions and interpretations, but never against them.[93]

Although we share the concerns that motivated these scholars to call for the establishment of such an independent oversight mechanism, we fear that the suggested committee is unrealistic and could also become counterproductive. It is unrealistic because it is hard to imagine a UN organ with the power to impose its findings and interpretations on the UNSC. It is also problematic from an institutional point of view: how could a subsidiary organ of the UNSC have primacy over its own creator? To recall the old 'omnipotence paradox', could the UNSC be so omnipotent as to create an organ even more powerful than itself? Moreover, it is highly unlikely that the UNSC's permanent members would accept such an evolution. Furthermore, the comparison between the UNSC's sanctions committees and the proposed Use-of-Force Committee is misleading because, whereas the sanctions committees adopt decisions concerning essentially private persons, the Use-of-Force Committee would judge the assessments and interpretations of sovereign states, including the permanent members of the UNSC, which often participate in authorised interventions.

In conclusion, although such a committee could have a useful monitoring and advisory function, it would be difficult to confer on it an adjudicative function or a capacity to impose its findings on the UNSC.

10 Conclusion

The UNSC's authorisation to use force is one of the two exceptions to the prohibition of the use of force in international relations recognised by positive international law – the other being the right to self-defence. These use-of-force mandates play an important role in the system of collective security. Since 1990 the UNSC has resorted widely to these mandates, sometimes in conjunction with the deployment of UN peacekeeping operations. It is thus particularly important to maintain and improve this essential tool in the 'Chapter VII toolbox'.

In this chapter we discussed and evaluated nine different avenues of action which could enable the UNSC to strengthen oversight and control of use-of-force mandates and introduce greater transparency and checks and balances in the system of collective security, without destroying the flexibility and discretion of operating states, which are essential parts of this 'decentralised' collective security system. Some of our proposals (better definition of the scope of use-of-force mandates; fixing a date of expiration of the mandate; criticising *ultra vires* actions; emphasising the principles of necessity, proportionality and accountability; enhancing reporting requirements and monitoring) are important, easy to realise and will strengthen the sustainability of the collective security system. Other proposals, such as imposing precise rules of engagement for operating states and instituting a Use-of-Force Committee, are more problematic. In any event, the widespread criticism that followed the broad interpretation of Resolution 1973 (2011) by operating states in Libya demonstrated the strong need for the UNSC to better frame use-of-force resolutions and to better monitor and assess the manner in which they are interpreted and implemented. As we have shown here, it is possible to fulfil this need. However, in doing so the UNSC must strike the right balance between the need for transparency and accountability, on the one hand, and the need for continuing flexibility, on the other.

Notes

1 The research base for this chapter is comprehensive up to May 2014.
2 SC Res. 678 (22 November 1990); SC Res. 1511 (16 October 2003); SC Res. 1546 (8 June 2004).
3 SC Res. 770 (13 August 1992).
4 SC Res. 794 (3 December 1992); SC Res. 1744 (21 February 2007); SC Res. 1816 (2 June 2008).
5 SC Res. 929 (22 June 1994).
6 SC Res. 940 (31 July 1994); SC Res. 1529 (29 February 2004).
7 SC Res. 1080 (15 November 1996).
8 SC Res. 1101 (28 March 1997).
9 SC Res. 1125 (6 August 1997); SC Res. 2121 (10 October 2013); SC Res. 2127 (5 December 2013); SC Res. 2134 (28 January 2014); SC Res. 2149 (10 April 2014); SC Res. 2162 (26 June 2014); SC Res. 2217 (28 April 2015).
10 SC Res. 1216 (21 December 1998).
11 SC Res. 1244 (10 June 1999).
12 SC Res. 1264 (15 September 1999).
13 SC Res. 1368 (20 December 2001).
14 SC Res. 1464 (4 February 2003); SC Res. 1528 (27 February 2004).
15 SC Res. 1484 (30 May 2003); SC Res. 1671 (25 April 2006).
16 SC Res. 1778 (25 September 2007).
17 SC Res. 1973 (17 March 2011).
18 SC Res. 2085 (20 December 2012); SC Res. 2100 (25 April 2013); SC Res. 2164 (25 June 2014).
19 The most 'robust' mandate of this kind was provided by SC Res. 2098 (2013) to the UN Intervention Brigade in the DRC. For discussion, see Oswald's chapter in this collection. We do not discuss here the problems related to oversight of use of force by UN forces acting under UN flag and command. For discussion of 'robust' peacekeeping, see Heathcote's chapter in this collection.
20 See Théodore Christakis and Karine Bannelier, 'Acteur Vigilant ou Spectateur

Impuissant? Le Contrôle Exercé par le Conseil de Sécurité sur les Etats Autorisés à Recourir à la Force' (2004) 37 *Revue Belge de Droit International* 498–528.

21 Robert Kolb, *An Introduction to the Law of the United Nations* (Oxford, Hart Publishing, 2010), p. 97.

22 SC Res. 1973 (27 March 2011).

23 Position of Russia in UN Doc. S/PV.6620 (16 September 2011), p. 3. See also UN Doc. S/PV.6528 (4 May 2011), p. 9; and UN Doc. S/PV.6531 (10 May 2011), p. 9.

24 Position of China in UN Doc. S/PV.6528 (4 May 2011), p. 10. See also UN Doc. S/PV.6531 (10 May 2011), p. 21.

25 Statement by Ambassador Baso Sangqu, Permanent Representative of South Africa to the UN, *Informal Meeting Hosted by the Minister of External Relations of Brazil*, 12 February 2012: http://cpdoc.fgv.br/relacoesinternacionais/rwpbrazil/informaldebate.

26 For Cuba's intervention in the 67th UN General Assembly debate, see Global Centre for the Responsibility to Protect, 'The Responsibility to Protect and the 67th Opening of the UN General Assembly', 4 October 2012, p. 50: www.globalr2p.org/media/files/compilation_of_r2p_related_unga_2012_quotes.pdf. For Venezuela's intervention, see p. 33.

27 UN Doc. S/PV.6531, Resumption 1 (10 May 2011), p. 13. See also Marcelo Kohen, 'The Principle of Non-Intervention 25 Years after the Nicaragua Judgment' (2012) 25(1) *Leiden Journal of International Law* 157–64, 162; Olivier Corten and Vaïos Koutroulis, 'The Illegality of the Military Support to the Rebels in the Libyan War: Aspects of *Jus contra Bellum* and *Jus in Bello*' (2013) 18(1) *Journal of Conflict and Security Law* 59–77; and Mehrdad Payandeh, 'The United Nations, Military Intervention, and Regime Change in Libya' (2012) 52(2) *Virginia Journal of International Law* 355–403.

28 UN Doc. A/66/551–S/2011/701 (11 November 2011). See also Harrington's chapter in this collection.

29 For a summary of the three pillars, see ICRtoP: www.responsibilitytoprotect.org/index.php/about-rtop. See also Harrington's chapter in this collection.

30 See the websites of the Global Centre for the Responsibility to Protect: www.globalr2p.org/about_r2p; and the ICRtoP: www.responsibilitytoprotect.org/index.php/component/content/article/35-r2pcs-topics/4002-informal-discussion-on-brazils-concept-of-responsibility-while-protecting.

31 See 'Statement by Ambassador Herman Schaper': www.responsibilitytoprotect.org/index.php/component/content/article/35-r2pcs-topics/4002-informal-discussion-on-brazils-concept-of-responsibility-while-protecting.

32 See Théodore Christakis, 'L'Encadrement Juridique des Autorisations et le Concept de Responsibility while Protecting', in Karine Bannelier and Cyrille Pison (eds), *Le Recours à la Force Autorisé par le Conseil de Sécurité: Droit et Responsabilité* (Paris, Pedone, 2014), pp. 143–5.

33 See Gareth Evans, 'The Responsibility to Protect after Libya and Syria', address to Annual Castan Centre for Human Rights Law Conference, Melbourne, 20 July 2012: www.gevans.org/speeches/speech476.html; and Gareth Evans, 'Responsibility while Protecting', *Project Syndicate*, 27 January 2012: www.project-syndicate.org/commentary/responsibility-while-protecting.

34 See UN Doc. S/PRST/1998/35 (30 November 1998).

35 See for example UN Doc. A/66/551–S/2011/701 (11 November 2011); and UN Doc. S/PRST/1998/35 (30 November 1998).

36 Danesh Sarooshi, *The United Nations and the Development of Collective Security: The Delegation by the UN Security Council of its Chapter VII Powers* (Oxford, Clarendon Press, 1999), p. 156.

37 SC Res. 678 (29 November 1990).

38 Robert Kolb, *Ius contra Bellum: Le Droit International Relatif au Maintien de la Paix* (Brussels, Bruylant, 2003), p. 98.

39 See, e.g. SC Res. 770 (13 August 1992), para. 2; SC Res. 794 (3 December 1992), para. 7; SC Res. 1101 (28 March 1997), para. 4; SC Res. 1125 (6 August 1997), para. 2; and SC Res. 1216 (21 December 1998), para. 4.
40 See, e.g. SC Res. 1264 (15 September 1999), para. 3, using the same terminology as in SC Res. 678 (29 November 1990).
41 See SC Res. 1973 (17 March 2011), paras 4, 8.
42 SC Res. 1546 (8 June 2004), para. 10.
43 For another example, see SC Res. 1031 (15 December 1995) and SC Res. 1088 (12 December 1996).
44 See Christakis and Bannelier, 'Acteur Vigilant ou Spectateur Impuissant?'.
45 See ibid., 519.
46 See Théodore Christakis, *L'ONU, le Chapitre VII et la Crise Yougoslave* (Paris, Monthchrestien, 1996), pp. 145–9. This idea was also used later in the Editorial, 'A Black Hole in the System of Collective Security' (2011) 16(3) *Journal of Conflict and Security Law* 415–16.
47 See David Caron, 'The Legitimacy of the Collective Authority of the Security Council' (1993) 87 *American Journal of International Law* 552–88, 584–6; Erica de Wet, *The Chapter VII Powers of the UN Security Council* (Oxford, Hart Publishing, 2004), p. 270.
48 See Olivier Corten, 'Opération *Iraqi Freedom*: Peut-on Admettre L'argument de L'"Autorisation Implicite" du Conseil de Sécurité?' (2003) 1 *Revue Belge du Droit International* 205–43.
49 See, e.g. Sarooshi, *Development of Collective Security*, p. 165; Philippe Lagrange, *La Sous-traitance de la Gestion Coercitive des Crises par le Conseil de Sécurité des Nations Unies* (doctoral thesis, Université de Poitiers, 1999), pp. 432ff.
50 See, e.g. UN Doc. A/66/551–S/2011/701 (11 November 2011), para. 11(d).
51 See Olivier Corten and Pierre Klein, 'L'Autorisation de Recourir à la Force à des Fins Humanitaires: Droit d'Ingérence ou Retour aux Sources? (1993) 4(4) *European Journal of International Law* 506–33, 525; Linos A. Sicilianos, 'Entre Multilatéralisme et Unilatéralisme: L'Autorisation par le Conseil de Sécurité de Recourir à la Force', *Collected Courses of the Hague Academy of International Law*, vol. 339 (Leiden, Brill, 2008), p. 75. For an analysis of the status of the principle *exceptio est strictissimae interpretationis*, see Robert Kolb, *Interprétation et Creation du Droit International* (Brussels, Bruylant, 2006), pp. 673–87.
52 SC Res. 1973 (17 March 2011), para. 4.
53 See, e.g. Corten and Koutroulis, 'Illegality of Military Support to Rebels'.
54 On the debate about the interpretation of UNSC resolutions, see Euthymios Papastavridis, 'Interpretation of Security Council Resolutions under Chapter VII in the Aftermath of the Iraqi Crisis' (2007) 56(1) *International and Comparative Law Quarterly* 83–118; Michael Wood, 'The Interpretation of Security Resolutions' (1998) 2 *Max Planck Yearbook of United Nations Law* 73–95; and Alexander Orakhelashvili, 'Unilateral Interpretation of Security Council Resolutions: UK Practice' (2010) 2(3) *Goettingen Journal of International Law* 823–42.
55 See UN Doc. S/2004/910 (16 November 2004).
56 Ibid., p. 2.
57 See UN Doc. S/PRST/2004/42 (6 November 2004) and SC Res. 1572 (15 November 2004).
58 See Olivier Corten, *Le Droit Contre la Guerre* (Paris, Pedone, 2014), p. 544 (and the sources he quotes). See also Antonios Tzanakopoulos, 'The UN/French Use of Force in Abidjan: Uncertainties Regarding the Scope of UN Authorizations', *EJIL Talk!*, 9 April 2011: www.ejiltalk.org/the-un-use-of-force-in-abidjan.
59 See, e.g. 'Communiqué of the African Union Peace and Security Council at its 275th Meeting Held on 26 April 2011, Held at Ministerial Level', PSC/MIN/COMM (CCLXXV), para. 11.

60 UN Doc. S/1994/50 (18 January 1994).

61 Interview published in the French journal *Libération* on 1 March 1994.

62 For an analysis of the coordination (or lack of it) between NATO and the UN in relation to the use of force during the conflict in Bosnia, see Christakis, *L'ONU*, pp. 165ff.

63 Quoted by Sarooshi, *Development of Collective Security*, p. 85.

64 See, e.g. SC Res. 1244 (10 June 1999) on the necessary cooperation between KFOR and UNMIK in Kosovo, and SC Res. 1401 (28 March 2002) on the necessary cooperation between ISAF and UNAM.

65 See, e.g. SC Res. 1528 (27 February 2004), para. 16; and SC Res. 1671 (25 April 2006), para. 8.

66 See SC Res. 2100 (25 April 2013), para. 18; and SC Res. 2149 (10 April 2014), para. 47. See also Karine Bannelier and Théodore Christakis, 'Under the UN Security Council's Watchful Eyes: Military Intervention by Invitation in the Malian Conflict' (2013) 26(4) *Leiden Journal of International Law* 855–74.

67 UN Doc. A/66/551–S/2011/701 (11 November 2011), paras 11(e)(f).

68 See Judith Gardam, *Necessity, Proportionality and the Use of Force by States* (Cambridge, Cambridge University Press, 2004); Théodore Christakis and Karine Bannelier (eds), *La Nécessité en Droit International* (Paris, Pedone, 2007), p. 384.

69 The same position has been defended by scholars like Michael Bothe, 'Les Limites des Pouvoirs du Conseil de Sécurité', in René Dupuy (ed.), *Le Développement du Rôle du Conseil de Sécurité: Colloque de l'Académie de Droit International de La Haye* (The Hague, Martinus Nijhoff, 1993), pp. 67–81, 76–9; Judith Gardam, 'Proportionality and Force in International Law' (1993) 87(3) *American Journal of International Law* 391–413; Judith Gardam, 'Legal Restraints on Security Council Military Enforcement Action' (1996) 17 *Michigan Journal of International Law* 285–321, 305ff.; Julian Lehmann, 'All Necessary Means to Protect Civilians: What the Intervention in Libya Says about the Relationship between the *Jus in Bello* and the *Jus ad Bellum*' (2012) 17(1) *Journal of Conflict and Security Law* 117–46, 132–3.

70 *Case Concerning the Military and Paramilitary Activities in and against Nicaragua*, Judgment, ICJ Rep. 1986, para. 176.

71 This is not completely excluded, however. We could imagine a contentious case brought to the ICJ under Article 36(2) of the Statute where a state 'victim' of a disproportionate use of force asks the Court to decide.

72 See, e.g. UN Doc. S/1996/1046 (16 December 1996).

73 See UN Doc. S/PRST/1998/35 (30 November 1998).

74 UN Doc. A/66/551–S/2011/701 (11 November 2011), para. 11(d).

75 See *Journal Officiel de la République Française*, 11 April 2013, p. 1126.

76 See Sicilianos, 'Entre Multilatéralisme et Unilatéralisme', 304–35.

77 SC Res. 1265 (17 September 1999).

78 See, e.g. SC Res. 1296 (19 April 2000); SC Res. 1738 (23 December 2006); and SC Res. 1674 (28 April 2006).

79 See, e.g. SC Res. 1528 (27 February 2004).

80 See, e.g. SC Res. 2100 (25 April 2013), para. 24; SC Res. 2134 (28 January 2014), para. 48; and SC Res. 2149 (10 April 2014), para. 42.

81 For developments in this field, see UN Doc. A/67/775–S/2013/110 (5 March 2013); SC Res. 2100 (25 April 2013), para. 26; and SC Res. 2149 (10 April 2014), para. 39.

82 Cf. UN Doc. A/66/551–S/2011/701 (11 November 2011), para. 11(i).

83 See, e.g. the 48-state coalition that made up Afghanistan's ISAF: www.isaf.nato.int/troop-numbers-and-contributions/index.php; and the United Nations Multidimensional Integrated Stabilization Mission in Mali, with force contributions from 36 states: www.un.org/fr/peacekeeping/missions/minusma/facts.shtml.

84 International Law Commission, 'Draft Articles on the Responsibility of International Organizations' (2011) 2(2) *Yearbook of the International Law Commission.*

85 See UN Charter, art. 54.
86 See, e.g. SC Res. 794 (3 December 1992), para. 18; SC Res. 929 (22 June 1994), para. 10; and SC Res. 940 (31 July 1994), para. 13.
87 See, e.g. SC Res. 1080 (15 November 1996), para. 11; SC Res. 1101 (28 March 1997), para. 9; and SC Res. 1125 (6 August 1997), para. 6.
88 See SC Res. 1511 (16 October 2003), para. 25. See also SC Res. 1546 (8 June 2004), para. 31.
89 See, e.g. SC Res. 1386 (20 December 2001), para. 9; SC Res. 1464 (4 February 2003); SC Res. 1528 (27 February 2004); SC Res. 1529 (29 February 2004); and SC Res. 2100 (25 April 2013), para. 18.
90 See preamble to SC Res. 2100 (25 April 2013).
91 See, e.g. SC Res. 929 (22 June 1994), para. 10; and SC Res. 794 (3 December 1992), para. 18.
92 Tamar Hostovsky-Brandes and Ariel Zemach, 'Controlling the Execution of a Security Council Mandate to Use Force: Does the Council Need a Lawyer?' (2013) 36 *Fordham International Law Journal* 657–705.
93 See ibid., 696–7.

16 Use of force, rule-of-law restraints and process

Unfinished business for the responsibility to protect concept

Joanna Harrington

Introduction

Despite the endorsement in 2005 of the principle that every state, as well the international community, has a 'responsibility to protect' (R2P) populations from genocide, war crimes, ethnic cleansing and crimes against humanity,[1] there remain concerns about the principle's implementation, especially when such implementation involves the use of force. With a view to building broader state support, United Nations (UN) Secretary-General (UNSG) Ban Ki-moon, with the assistance of a Special Adviser on the Responsibility to Protect, has published a series of annual reports offering guidance on how best to 'operationalise' the R2P concept. The first such report,[2] released in early 2009, was welcomed for its embrace of a 'three pillar' approach that tapped into state support for the concept's preventive and capacity-building roles, and the notion of the state as bearing the primary responsibility for the protection of its population. Drawing upon the language of the 2005 resolution, the UNSG's three-pillar approach identified the protection responsibilities of the state as pillar one, international assistance and capacity-building as pillar two, and the provision of a 'timely and decisive response' by the international community when a state is manifestly failing to provide protection as pillar three.[3] No set sequence between the three pillars was intended, and nor was one pillar identified as more important than the other – a point highlighted in the report's front-page summary. Caution was, however, expressed with respect to the international community's use of military force, with state concerns subsequently heightened by criticism that the UN-mandated intervention to protect civilians in Libya was misused, or abused, so as to achieve regime change.

Perceptions can influence international affairs, and the perception that the 2011 Libya intervention exceeded its 'responsibility to protect' mandate provoked a strong reaction from states, leading Brazil to call for the adoption of a set of 'principles, parameters and procedures' to govern any future exercise of the international community's responsibility to protect under the proposed banner of a 'responsibility while protecting' (RWP).[4] The RWP initiative, for its part, has also provoked controversy. For some, the proposal lacked clarity,[5] while others viewed it as a threat to a robust vision of R2P at a time when the consensus was under strain, most notably with regards to action to address atrocities in Syria.[6] But for many states, Brazil's strategic intertwining of the R2P concept with a concept of RWP provided a needed outlet for criticism, while also solidifying support for its starting point.

As a constructive step, the Brazilian proposal was based on an understanding shared by many states that any discussion of the R2P concept must respect that concept's boundaries as agreed in 2005. This understanding is also reflected in the support for a 'narrow but deep' approach (with a 'deeper' outlook for putting responsibility into practice relying on more than simply military intervention). As explained by the UNSG:

> From the outset, the importance of a narrow but deep approach has been highlighted – narrow, in terms of restricting its application to the crimes and violations cited in paragraph 138 of the *2005 World Summit Outcome* ... and deep, in terms of the variety of Charter-based tools that are available for this purpose.[7]

However, if the implementation of R2P is indeed at a crossroads, with reaction to its use in Libya contributing to inaction with regards to atrocities in Syria, then any future steps must address both perceptions, as well as criteria, with attention to matters of process, in addition to substance, being part of any governance structure that respects the rule of law (ROL).

The discussion in this chapter is organised into four sections. Section 1 provides an overview of the UN-approved military intervention in Libya and surveys the positions taken by the BRICS (Brazil, Russia, India, China, South Africa) states,[8] each being a member of the UN Security Council (UNSC) at the time. Section 2 reviews the proposal made by Brazil promoting criteria to guide the UNSC when authorising force and emphasising the need for a subsequent process of monitoring and review.[9] Section 3 examines the UNSG's 2012 report on R2P, given its express focus on the taking of 'timely and decisive' action by the international community and its engagement with the Brazilian initiative.[10] Of the six reports released to date, only the 2012 report has such an explicit focus, with the 2013 and 2014 reports returning to examine individual state responsibility and international assistance.[11] Section 4 then distils the guidance to be gleaned from these discussions, with state representatives and the UNSG indicating some degree of interest in the process aspects of the exercise of power to authorise the use of force, so as to ensure that decisions are made on the basis of timely access to information and assessment and not arbitrarily. While substantive principles clearly have a role in the making of any decision to use military force, how such decisions are made contribute to their reception and sense of legitimacy. It is also this focus on process, rather than substance, that may provide the more promising basis for taking any future steps towards resuscitating R2P in its fullest sense, with a fruitful link to be made to efforts to reform the working methods of the UNSC.

1 The UN-mandated military intervention in Libya

The concept of R2P gained serious operational teeth only two years after the UNSG's first report on implementation, and only six years after the concept's formulation had gained UN General Assembly (UNGA) endorsement. Here was responsibility in action, with R2P's most ardent supporters viewing the UNSC's invocation of the responsibility language as proof that the international community had the will to act in a decisive and timely manner to protect civilian populations from mass atrocities. But when the mandate to protect civilians came to be perceived as a UN-authorised mandate for regime change, the intervention in Libya came to be viewed, at least for some states, as the high point for operationalising the R2P concept when force is needed (and thus a low point if one supports the use of force to protect civilians).[12] It is also likely that the fallout from Libya contributed to the UNSC's far less robust response to the atrocities in Syria.[13]

The UNSC's involvement in Libya's 'Arab Spring' began in February 2011, soon after Colonel Muammar Gaddafi's forces brutally suppressed protests in the Libyan city of Benghazi. This in turn led to further rebellion across the country. Acting with uncharacteristic speed, the UNSC condemned the use of force against civilians in Libya,[14] and suspecting the commission of crimes against humanity quickly adopted a resolution to refer the situation to the Prosecutor of the International Criminal Court (ICC).[15] The text of Resolution 1970 (2011) included a preambular reference '[r]ecalling the Libyan authorities' responsibility to protect its population',[16] as well as operative paragraphs authorising an arms embargo, a travel ban against certain named individuals and an asset freeze.[17] The resolution received unanimous support from the 15-member UNSC, presumably so as to send a clear and unambiguous message to the Libyan authorities to halt the violence.

The Libyan authorities did not, however, take heed of the UNSC's demands, and on 17 March 2011, a second resolution was adopted. Using the preamble to '[r]eiterat[e] the responsibility of the Libyan authorities to protect the Libyan population and reaffirming that parties to armed conflicts bear the primary responsibility to take all feasible steps to ensure the protection of civilians',[18] the UNSC authorised the use of 'all necessary measures … to protect civilians and civilian populated areas under threat of attack in the Libyan Arab Jamahiriya, including Benghazi, while excluding a foreign occupation force of any form on any part of Libyan territory'.[19] Resolution 1973 (2011) also authorised the establishment of a no-fly zone over Libyan airspace to help protect civilians from aerial bombardment, and it contained several paragraphs aimed at enhancing the already imposed arms embargo and asset freeze. Two days later, on 19 March 2011, a coalition of states, including France, the United Kingdom and the United States, began to carry out air strikes against military targets in Libya.

The adoption of Resolution 1973 (2011) marks the first time that the responsibility to protect concept had been invoked, albeit implicitly,[20] to authorise the use of force by UN member states.[21] Ten states voted in favour (Bosnia-Herzegovina, Colombia, France, Gabon, Lebanon, Nigeria, Portugal, South Africa, the United

Kingdom and the United States), while five states abstained (Brazil, China, Germany, India and the Russian Federation). In their statements of explanation, the abstaining states emphasised the need to prioritise efforts at peaceful resolution, with China also stating that she had 'serious difficulty with parts of the resolution'.[22] But China refrained from exercising its veto power because she 'attached great importance' to the wishes of the Arab League and the African Union (AU),[23] with the Council of the Arab League having called upon the UNSC 'to bear its responsibilities towards the deteriorating situation in Libya' and requested the imposition of a no-fly zone.[24] The abstaining states also spoke against the use of force, both in general (India) and in international relations (China), and expressed concern about the potential risks and unintended consequences of military intervention. The exact scope of the authorisation being provided also attracted concern and uncertainty,[25] with Russia also critical of the process used for negotiating the text.[26]

Operative paragraphs 4 and 5 of Resolution 1973 (2011) provided a UN mandate for collective action, leading to a NATO-led military intervention in Libya that lasted several months, and resulted in the overthrow of the Gaddafi regime. Some critics believe more time should have been afforded for the exhaustion of all non-military options, while others who were initially supportive of certain elements of the mandate, such as the establishment of a no-fly zone and the destruction of Libya's air force, later complained that opportunities to secure a ceasefire were squandered by the desire for regime change. In turn, others have responded by noting that regime change must surely be inevitable when that government has been widely condemned for the commission of mass atrocities.[27] Moreover, the United Kingdom had made known its desire for a new government to replace the 'violent discredited regime' of Colonel Gaddafi at the time of the resolution's adoption, with the British representative declaring that '[t]he central purpose of the resolution is clear: to end the violence, to protect civilians and to allow the people of Libya to determine their own future, free from the tyranny of the Al-Qadhafi regime'.[28] Indeed, one scholar has described the Libya intervention as 'the first case of a Security Council-mandated operation conducted with the more or less openly admitted goal of overthrowing the government and changing the regime'.[29] Nevertheless, critics have voiced concern about the mission's evolution from the protection of civilians into a 'taking of sides', with the supply of arms to the rebels in defiance of the embargo also drawing ire.[30] In any event, whatever one's views as to who is correct, perceptions have an impact on international relations, including the building of cross-regional support, and clearly there are states now wary about the concept of the R2P as a result of the UN-sanctioned military intervention in Libya.

Leading the campaign of criticism have been the emerging powers of Brazil, Russia, India, China and South Africa (the BRICS group). Remarkably, all the BRICS states were members of the UNSC for the adoption of Resolution 1973 (2011), although their positions differed at that time. South Africa, being a member of the AU whose constitutive act embraces a right of collective intervention,[31] was one of ten states that voted for the resolution, although South Africa, along with the AU, was soon thereafter very critical of the resolution's implementation.[32] In addition to the criticisms noted above, the BRICS states also criticised the lack of information presented to the UNSC as the mission unfolded, leading others to respond that a military operation cannot be micro-managed from miles away.[33]

2 The Brazilian proposal for a 'responsibility while protecting'

As noted above, Brazil advanced the concept of 'responsibility while protecting' as a reaction to the perceived abuse of the mandate to protect civilians in Libya. The RWP concept emphasises prevention and the need to exhaust all peaceful means for conflict resolution before considering the use of military force to protect populations. It also encourages the development of criteria to guide the future exercise of the international community's responsibility to protect, with Brazil's RWP proposal also expressly calling for 'enhanced Security Council procedures' to monitor and assess the manner in which resolutions are interpreted and implemented,[34] to keep all UNSC members informed during the implementation of future 'use of force' mandates, and 'to ensure the accountability of those to whom authority is granted to resort to force'.[35]

The desire to instil a sense of responsibility while protecting was first articulated by Brazilian President Dilma Rousseff in her opening address to the UNGA on 21 September 2011,[36] a month before the official end of the Libya intervention mandate.[37] Taking note of the mass demonstrations that had taken place in Arab countries in 2010 and 2011, Rousseff urged states to 'find a legitimate and effective way to aid those societies that cry out for reform – without, however, depriving their citizens of a lead role in the process'.[38] She then made clear that while the people of Brazil 'strongly repudiate the brutal crack down episodes that victimize civilian populations[,] [w]e remain convinced that for the international community, resort to force must always be the last alternative'.[39] While not closing the door to military intervention, President Rousseff expressed a preference for efforts of conflict prevention through diplomacy and the promotion of development. She then delivered the first official expression of Brazil's position on RWP, stating:

> Much is said about the responsibility to protect; yet little is said about responsibility in protecting. These are concepts that we must develop and mature together. To that end, the role of the Security Council is critical, and the more legitimate its decisions are, the more appropriate that role will be.[40]

Two months later, at an open debate of the UNSC on the protection of civilians in armed conflict, a Brazilian representative again expressed the view that 'the international community, as it exercises its responsibility to protect, must demonstrate a high level of responsibility while protecting'. She also emphasised that '[b]oth concepts should evolve together, based on an agreed set of fundamental principles, parameters and procedures'.[41]

A concept note was also presented for wider distribution, consisting of 11 paragraphs intended to instigate further discussion, with the final paragraph repeating the call for 'an agreed set of fundamental principles, parameters and procedures' to govern the interweaving of the concepts of a responsibility to protect and a responsibility while protecting. The note also confirmed that '[t]here is a growing perception that the concept of the responsibility to protect might be misused for purposes others than protecting civilians, such as regime change'.[42]

Clearly one issue of concern to Brazil (and others) is the use of force and the perceived need post-Libya to impose greater restraint on its use. Brazil has placed much emphasis on prevention, suggesting that any listing of principles to guide the implementation of the responsibility to protect concept must stress the importance of preventive diplomacy and the exhaustion of all available peaceful means before there is resort to force.[43] Brazil also takes the view that

> the use of force, including in the exercise of the responsibility to protect, must always be authorized by the Security Council, in accordance with Chapter VII of the UN Charter, or, in exceptional circumstances, by the General Assembly, in line with its Resolution 377 (V),[44]

the latter opening the door to reviving interest in an old resolution[45] aimed at encouraging UNGA action when the UNSC is at an impasse.

Sequencing was also a notable feature of the Brazilian proposal, as first presented, with Brazil wanting further attention to be paid to the R2P concept's three-pillar structure, as embraced in 2005 and later confirmed by the UNSG in his 2009 implementation report.[46] Brazil took the position that the third pillar is only applicable 'in exceptional circumstances and when measures provided for in the first and second pillars have manifestly failed',[47] and 'upon the manifest failure of the individual State to exercise its responsibility to protect and upon the exhaustion of all peaceful means'.[48] In making this point, Brazil was pushing for the three pillars to 'follow a strict line of political subordination and chronological sequencing',[49] drawing a distinction between collective responsibility and collective security. In Brazil's view, the former can be fully exercised through non-coercive measures while the latter involves a case-by-case political assessment by the UNSC.

Another issue of clear concern to Brazil was the need for ensuring strict adherence to the specifics of any UN mandate to use force. In Brazil's view:

> The authorization for the use of force must be limited in its legal, operational and temporal elements and the scope of military action must abide by the letter and the spirit of the mandate conferred by the Security Council or the General Assembly, and be carried out in strict conformity with international law, in particular international humanitarian law and the international law of armed conflict.[50]

In the event that the use of force is contemplated, Brazil emphasised that 'action must be judicious, proportionate and limited to the objectives established by the

Security Council',[51] with any such mandate only to be issued after 'a comprehensive and judicious analysis of the possible consequences of military action on a case-by-case basis'.[52] Brazil's concept note also emphasised that 'under no circumstance' can the use of force 'generate more harm than it was authorized to prevent'.[53] While cognisant of the need to repudiate violence against civilian populations, Brazil also expressed a desire to draw attention to what it termed 'the painful consequences of interventions that have aggravated existing conflicts'.[54]

3 The Secretary-General's 2012 report on timely and decisive response

In August 2012, the UNSG released his fourth R2P report, and the first to be focused on the third component of the concept's three-pillar structure. Invoking the language of the 2005 resolution, the 2012 report examines the international community's responsibility to 'take collective action, in a timely and decisive manner, through the Security Council'.[55] Brazil's efforts in instigating further dialogue were also acknowledged,[56] with the UNSG mentioning the Brazilian proposal by name and noting 'that concerns have been raised by Member States about responsibility, the measures that might be used when a timely and decisive response is required, and about the management and oversight of those measures'.[57] The phrase 'responsibility while protecting' also served as one of the headings within the 2012 report.[58] (Use is also made of the phrase 'protecting responsibly'.)

But while the UNSG was willing to acknowledge Brazil's efforts, he had also identified a key weakness, with the report's second paragraph making clear that '[t]he three pillars are not sequential and are of equal importance; without all three, the concept would be incomplete'. It is later repeated in paragraph 13 that: 'Pillars are not sequenced'. One can assume that the UNSG chose to draw this bright line with some confidence that he had the backing of many states. The harshness of his message was softened somewhat by the express recognition that 'it may not always be possible to clearly determine whether an activity falls exclusively under one or another of the three pillars'.[59] It was also recognised that '[p]illar three is best understood in the context of the other two. It would make little sense standing alone'.[60]

As a result, the R2P concept continues to have three pillars, not two, notwithstanding a return to viewing 'responsibility as sovereignty',[61] with action taken under the first and second pillars working in tandem with respect for sovereignty and state consent.[62] As the report explains, '[r]esponsibility is an ally of sovereignty, in that collective action by the international community to protect populations is not called for where a State fully discharges its sovereign responsibility to protect'.[63] The UNSG's 2012 report does not foreclose the possibility of future military action by the UNSC under a 'responsibility to protect' banner, describing such action as 'part of the toolbox',[64] but emphasis is placed on prevention, drawing upon the very words of paragraph 138 of the *2005 World Summit Outcome* to remind us that states have declared that responsibility 'entails the prevention of such crimes, including their incitement, through appropriate and necessary means'.[65] While the 2012 report expressly recognised that 'prevention and response must be seen as closely connected', and stated that 'one should not draw too sharp a distinction between prevention and response',[66] it also accepted that '[e]ffective action under pillars one and two may make actions under pillar three unnecessary'.[67]

As for the tools available within pillar three, the 2012 report made clear that a wide range of non-coercive responses should be considered, including mediation and preventive diplomacy, public advocacy and media reporting, fact-finding missions and commissions of inquiry, monitoring and observer missions, and referrals to the ICC. Mention is also made of the 'critical role of partners', with the UNSG echoing his prior support for engaging with regional and sub-regional arrangements, while also drawing an express link between their 'critical role' and UNSC authorisation.[68]

With respect to the Brazilian proposal specifically, the 2012 report can be read as recognising the proposal's support for the responsibility to protect concept, while also suggesting ways to widen the focus of the Brazilian theme, noting that 'at every stage of the implementation process ... international actors need to act responsibly'.[69] According to the report, acting responsibly requires accurate and informed analysis, as well as early warning mechanisms and the provision of fair and timely assessments; thus sidestepping Brazil's call for a discussion of the criteria for future interventions by focusing on elements to improve the decision-making process. As the UNSG explained, '[t]imely and decisive action puts a premium on assessment, on understanding what is happening, why it is happening, and how the international community can keep a difficult situation from becoming worse'.[70] While recognising that concerns did exist with respect to the Libya intervention, the UNSG nevertheless eschewed the development of any template to guide future interventions and instead used his 2012 report to emphasise a message of flexibility and case-by-case assessment. He closed this section of the report with a hint that 'suggestions for improving decision-making in such circumstances and reviewing implementation' would be 'useful catalysts for further discussion'.[71]

4 Distilling the guidance for future authorisations of force

It has become standard practice for the UNSG's R2P report to serve as the prelude to, and focal point for, an annual 'informal interactive dialogue' within the UNGA on R2P. As to be expected, the chosen focus of the 2012 report stimulated a discussion of the R2P concept's third pillar, with many of the states participating in the debate held on 5 September 2012,[72] confirming their support for the focus on prevention, as well as the non-sequential nature of the three pillars. Prevention, however, is within the 'comfort zone' for most states, with at least one informed observer (who is now the Special Adviser on the Responsibility to Protect) having suggested earlier that 'there have been costs' (in the sense of political costs) associated with a strategy of preparing reports that have 'placed great emphasis on so-called root-cause prevention and state capacity building' at the expense of discussing collective action.[73] For some states, however, the annual dialogue held in 2012 was an opportunity to focus discussions on the role of the UNSC, with several expressing support for the Brazilian initiative, while still others reiterated their concerns about the misuse of the R2P concept to achieve regime change. Notably, Singapore, among others, used the dialogue to call for UNSC reform,[74] drawing a link to an earlier (unsuccessful) effort by the Small Five (S5) group of states to push for restrictions on the use of the veto power to block actions taken to address the four mass atrocity crimes that form the foundation of the R2P concept (specifically, genocide, war crimes, ethnic cleansing and crimes against humanity).[75]

As for the desire for a set of criteria to guide the UNSC when authorising force, any review of the Brazilian proposal inevitably leads back to a discussion of what may be termed the unfinished business of the R2P project. Clearly, the principles and parameters mentioned in the Brazilian concept note of November 2011 bear some resemblance to the six criteria for military intervention ICISS put forward in 2001,[76] and the five criteria the UNSG's High-level Panel on Threats, Challenges and Change set out in 2004.[77] It was, however, impossible to reach agreement on these criteria at the World Summit in 2005, and an agreement on the substantive principles or precise guidance for the use of force remains unlikely, notwithstanding post-2005 events.

Nevertheless, the discussions that Brazil's efforts instigated suggest a degree of coalescence around certain principles or guideposts that will likely arise within any future discussion on the use of force. These include the principles of last resort (including language on the exhaustion of all peaceful means and no practicable alternative) and proportionality (whereby the prospects of a reasonable chance of success to achieve a specified aim are weighted against the risk of unintended consequences), as well as the principle of right intention or proper purpose combined with defined objectives (reflecting a desire for clarity as to a mandate's aims, with the possibility of future mandates to be organised into phases so as to provide for periodic briefings).[78]

It is also clear that one must embrace 'the narrow', with the four atrocity crimes specified in the 2005 resolution continuing to serve as the threshold criteria for any future collective action. While states continue to differ as to the need to consider the position of the state concerned, many have articulated a desire for at least the representation of local views, perceptions and priorities, enhanced (or possibly balanced) by what appears to be a widely supported desire for an assessment of the situation from a relevant regional or sub-regional organisation. The UNSC has also confirmed, by way of a Presidential Statement, that it considers developing effective partnerships with regional and sub-regional organisations to be a useful means to enable early responses.[79]

In addition to the desire for substantive guidance, the discussion of 'principles, parameters and procedures' instigated by the Brazilian proposal has highlighted a number of process matters. The UNSG has suggested that 'acting responsibly' requires a process that ensures access to early and accurate threat identification and assessment.[80] His 2012 report also speaks of a need for the careful and timely assessment of situations, a review of the likely consequences and consideration of the most effective strategy – aspects on which action may be achieved through improvements to the working methods of the UNSC. The 2004 High-level Panel had similarly identified the seriousness of the threat as a criterion or guideline, leading to a need for access to timely, reliable and unbiased information, as well as its objective assessment, in relation to any of the four agreed atrocity crimes. In this way, Brazil's call for change, including changes in process, recognises that how one makes a decision may have an impact on the reception those decisions receive. It also complements the broader quest for overarching institutional reform for the UNSC.

The call for change to the UNSC's working methods dates back to 1993,[81] and attracted renewed attention in May 2012,[82] and again in May 2013 with the formation of a group of small- and medium-sized states pushing for 'Accountability, Coherence and Transparency' (ACT).[83] The interest suggests some desire (at least among some non-permanent members of the UNSC) to improve the transparency of UNSC decision-making, as a means of encouraging accountability for both UNSC action and inaction. It also suggests a desire for greater interactivity as between both UNSC states and non-UNSC members.[84] Securing change to the UNSC's working methods is also a means to facilitate greater interaction between the UNSC and the relevant regional organisations, as well as a means for continuing to facilitate improved interaction with troop-contributing countries.

Other possible reforms include the reinstatement (on a regular basis) of monthly 'horizon scanning' briefings by the UN's Department of Public Affairs (DPA) on emerging situations of concern,[85] the potential use of 'any other business' to place such situations on the UNSC's agenda, the holding of regular meetings with the UNSG to keep members apprised of regions at risk of armed conflict[86] and more flexible meeting formats, such as 'Arria-formula' meetings and informal interactive dialogues. Named after a Venezuelan Ambassador who arranged a meeting with a Croatian priest from Bosnia who was eager to provide UNSC members with an eyewitness account of the Balkan conflict, an 'Arria-formula' meeting is an informal, confidential gathering that enables UNSC members to have a frank and private exchange of views with persons from whom the inviting member or members of the UNSC believe it would be beneficial to hear or to whom they may wish to convey a message.[87] Changing the UNSC's working methods may also serve as an opportunity to unite unlikely allies if one includes the effort to establish 'an effective mechanism to monitor the implementation of the Council's mandates',[88] with China, among others, echoing earlier sentiments that having such a mechanism would serve 'to avoid acts that abuse or overstep' a UNSC mandate.[89]

5 Conclusion

There are never situations in which states do not have a responsibility to protect populations from mass atrocities. As the UNSG concludes in his 2012 report, '[i]t is clear that every State has an inherent responsibility to protect'.[90] The question is how best to operationalise that responsibility, with collective action, up to and including the use of military force, ideally to be guided by some sense of a shared agreement on the applicable criteria. Too often, however, one focuses on the substance of a legal framework as a means to achieve respect for the ROL, while discounting possible benefits to be gained from undertaking procedural reforms to enhance the legitimacy of the decision-making process. Process is also part of the ROL, with the recent ROL declaration endorsed by the UNGA in September 2012 acknowledging efforts to reform the UNSC and encouraging the UNSC to continue to ensure that 'fair and clear procedures are maintained and further developed'.[91] As the UNSG has stated,[92] disagreements about the past must not stand in the way of taking action in future to protect populations from mass atrocities. The Brazilian proposal for marrying the R2P concept with a concept of RWP provided the space that was needed for criticism and discussion, whether or not Brazil wishes to push further for its more concrete development or express adoption. Its content also relates to ongoing discussions concerning the UNSC's working methods, with procedural reforms equally important for ensuring a rule-of-law approach to future deliberations on using force.

Notes

1 GA Res. 60/1 (24 October 2005), *2005 World Summit Outcome*, paras 138–9.
2 UN Doc. A/63/677 (12 January 2009), *Implementing the Responsibility to Protect: Report of the Secretary-General.*
3 Ibid., para. 11.
4 'Responsibility While Protecting: Elements for the Development and Promotion of a Concept' in UN Doc. A/66/551–S/2011/701 (11 November 2011), *Letter Dated 9 November 2011 from the Permanent Representative of Brazil to the United Nations Addressed to the Secretary-General*, Annex.
5 Germany, for example, expressed concern that the Brazilian approach lacked 'a precisely defined concept of its own' – a point discussed in Thorsten Benner, *Brazil as a Norm Entrepreneur: The 'Responsibility while Protecting' Initiative* (Berlin, Global Public Policy Institute, 2013), pp. 4–5: www.gppi.net/fileadmin/media/pub/2013/Benner_2013_Working-Paper_Brazil-RWP.pdf.
6 The United States, for example, expressed concern that elements of Brazil's proposal might 'bind ourselves to inaction based on an unrealistic prerequisite of assured success': United States Mission to the United Nations, *Remarks by the United States at an Informal Discussion on 'Responsibility while Protecting'* (New York, 21 February 2012): http://usun.state.gov/briefing/statements/184487.htm.
7 See UN Doc. A/66/874–S/2012/578 (25 July 2012), *The Responsibility to Protect: Timely and Decisive Response – Report of the Secretary-General*, para. 9.
8 The leaders of Brazil, Russia, India and China have met annually since 2008 to discuss issues of global significance at high-level summits. South Africa joined the group in 2011, leading to the use of the term BRICS, instead of BRIC, to refer to the five-nation association. See further: University of Toronto, *BRICS Information Centre* (undated): www.brics.utoronto.ca.
9 See the statement of HE Ambassador Maria Luiza Ribeiro Viotti, Permanent Representative of Brazil to the United Nations, delivered during the UNGA's annual dialogue on R2P, 5 September 2012: http://responsibilitytoprotect.org/Brazil(1).pdf.

10 *Timely and Decisive Response Report*, para. 50.

11 UN Doc. A/67/929–S/2013/399 (9 July 2013), *Responsibility to Protect: State Responsibility and Prevention – Report of the Secretary-General*; UN Doc. A/68/947–S/2014/449 (11 July 2014), *Fulfilling Our Collective Responsibility: International Assistance and the Responsibility to Protect – Report of the Secretary-General.*

12 For discussion of the Libya intervention as a significant normative moment, see Catherine Powell, 'Libya: A Multilateral Constitutional Moment?' (2012) 106 *American Journal of International Law* 298–316. For the view that 'the legal significance of Libya is minimal', see Simon Chesterman, '"Leading from Behind": The Responsibility to Protect, the Obama Doctrine, and Humanitarian Intervention after Libya' (2011) 25(3) *Ethics and International Affairs* 279–85.

13 See further, Spencer Zifcak, 'The Responsibility to Protect after Libya and Syria' (2012) 13 *Melbourne Journal of International Law* 59–93.

14 UN Doc. SC/10180–AFR/2120 (22 February 2011), *Security Council Press Statement on Libya.*

15 SC Res. 1970 (26 February 2011), para. 4.

16 Ibid., preambular para. 9.

17 Ibid., paras 9–14, 15–16, 17–21, respectively.

18 SC Res. 1973 (17 March 2011), preambular para. 4.

19 Ibid., para. 4.

20 Some might describe the references as ambiguous, with Loiselle concluding that 'it is unclear whether the responsibility to protect principle even played such a central role in the decision to intervene'. See Marie-Eve Loiselle, 'The Normative Status of the Responsibility to Protect after Libya' (2013) 5(3) *Global Responsibility to Protect* 317–41, 319.

21 Powell notes that while the UNSC had not authorised *member states* to intervene or use force as done in the Libya resolution, the UNSC had previously authorised the UN Mission in Sudan (UNMIS) 'to use all necessary means … to protect civilians under threat of physical violence', referring to SC Res. 1706 (31 August 2006), para. 12(a). See Powell, 'Libya: A Multilateral Constitutional Moment?', 308.

22 UN Doc. S/PV.6498 (17 March 2011), p. 10 (Li Baodong).

23 Ibid.

24 See further, UN Doc. S/2011/137 (15 March 2011), *Letter Dated March 2011 from the Permanent Observer of the League of Arab States to the United Nations Addressed to the President of the Security Council.*

25 For a detailed analysis, see Mehrdad Payandeh, 'The United Nations, Military Intervention, and Regime Change in Libya' (2012) 52 *Virginia Journal of International Law* 355–404, 383–91.

26 UN Doc. S/PV.6498 (17 March 2011), p. 8 (Vitaly Churkin).

27 See, in particular, Barack Obama, David Cameron and Nicolas Sarkozy, 'Libya's Pathway to Peace', *New York Times* (New York), 14 April 2011: www.nytimes.com/2011/04/15/opinion/15iht-edlibya15.html?_r=0 ('Our duty and our mandate … is to protect civilians.… It is not to remove Qaddafi by force. But it is impossible to imagine a future for Libya with Qaddafi in power.')

28 UN Doc. S/PV.6498 (17 March 2011), p. 4 (Mark Lyall Grant).

29 Payandeh, 'Regime Change in Libya', 358.

30 See 'NATO Stretching UN Libya Mandate: Evans', *Sydney Morning Herald* (Sydney), 4 May 2011: news.smh.com.au/breaking-news-national/nato-stretching-un-libya-mandate-evans-20110504-1e7zj.html. See further, Olivier Corten and Vaios Koutroulis, 'The Illegality of Military Support to Rebels in the Libyan War: Aspects of *Jus Contra Bellum* and *Jus In Bello*' (2013) 18(1) *Journal of Conflict and Security Law* 59–93.

31 *Constitutive Act of the African Union*, opened for signature 11 July 2000, 2158 UNTS 33 (entered into force 26 May 2001), art. 4(h) (recognising 'the right of the

Union to intervene in a Member State pursuant to a decision of the Assembly in respect of grave circumstances, namely: war crimes, genocide and crimes against humanity').

32 See further, Theo Neethling, 'South Africa, the African Union and International Intervention in Libya: A Critical Appraisal' (2012) 33(2) *The Australasian Review of African Studies* 8–28.

33 See, for example, Gareth Evans, 'The Responsibility to Protect after Libya and Syria', an address to the Annual Castan Centre for Human Rights Law Conference, Melbourne, 20 July 2012: www.gevans.org/speeches/speech476.html.

34 'Responsibility while Protecting: Elements for the Development and Promotion of a Concept', para. 11(h).

35 Ibid., para. 11(i).

36 President Rousseff's statement is recorded in UN Doc. A/66/PV.11 (21 September 2011), pp. 6–9.

37 SC Res. 2016 (27 October 2011), para. 5.

38 UN Doc. A/66/PV.11 (21 September 2011), p. 8.

39 Ibid.

40 Ibid.

41 The remarks are recorded in UN Doc. S/PV.6650 (9 November 2011), pp. 15–17 (Maria Luiza Ribeiro Viotti).

42 'Responsibility While Protecting: Elements for the Development and Promotion of a Concept', para. 10.

43 Ibid., paras 11(a)(b).

44 Ibid., para. 11(c).

45 GA Res. 5/377 (3 November 1950), *Uniting for Peace*.

46 UN Doc. A/63/677 (12 January 2009), *Implementing the Responsibility to Protect: Report of the Secretary-General*.

47 'Responsibility While Protecting: Elements for the Development and Promotion of a Concept', para. 4.

48 Ibid., para. 5.

49 Ibid., para. 6.

50 Ibid., para. 11(d).

51 Ibid., para. 11(f).

52 Ibid., para. 9.

53 Ibid., para. 11(f).

54 Ibid., para. 8.

55 See *2005 World Summit Outcome*, para. 139.

56 *Timely and Decisive Response Report*, para. 50.

57 Ibid., para. 3.

58 Ibid., p. 13, section V.

59 Ibid., para. 12.

60 Ibid., para. 14.

61 For the origins of this concept, see Francis M. Deng, Sadikiel Kimaro and Terrence Lyons, *Sovereignty as Responsibility: Conflict Management in Africa* (Washington, DC, Brookings Institution, 1996). See also Francis M. Deng, 'From Sovereignty as Responsibility to the Responsibility to Protect' (2010) 2(4) *Global Responsibility to Protect* 353–70.

62 *Timely and Decisive Response Report*, para. 17.

63 Ibid., para. 18.

64 Ibid., para. 37.

65 Ibid., para. 7.

66 Ibid., paras 7–8.

67 Ibid., para. 15.

68 Ibid., paras 20 and 35. See also UN Doc A/65/877–S/2011/393 (28 June 2011), *The*

Role of Regional and Subregional Arrangements in Implementing the Responsibility to Protect: Report of the Secretary-General.

69 *Timely and Decisive Response Report*, para. 51.

70 Ibid., para. 53.

71 Ibid., para. 58.

72 A summary can be found in UN Doc. GA/11270 (5 September 2012), *World not Fulfilling 'Never Again' Vow, Secretary-General Tells General Assembly Meeting on Responsibility to Protect: Use of Force Must Be Last Resort, Says President before Panel Discussion.* For a scholarly account, see Alex J. Bellamy, 'Making R2P a Living Reality: Reflections on the 2012 General Assembly Dialogue on Timely and Decisive Response' (2013) 5(1) *Global Responsibility to Protect* 109–27.

73 Jennifer Welsh, 'Civilian Protection in Libya: Putting Coercion and Controversy Back into R2P' (2011) 25(3) *Ethics and International Affairs* 255–62, 255.

74 See Statement by HE Ambassador Albert Chua, Permanent Representative of Singapore to the UN, at the Informal Interactive Dialogue on the Responsibility to Protect, 5 September 2012: www.mfa.gov.sg/content/mfa/overseasmission/newyork/nyemb_statements/plenary/2012/201209/press_20120905.html.

75 UN Doc. A/66/L.42/Rev.1 (3 May 2012), *Costa Rica, Jordan, Liechtenstein, Singapore and Switzerland: Revised Draft Resolution – Enhancing the Accountability, Transparency and Effectiveness of the Security Council.*

76 See *The Responsibility to Protect: Report of the International Commission on Intervention and State Sovereignty* (Ottawa, International Development Research Centre, 2001), para. 4.16.

77 See UN Doc A/59/565 (2 December 2004), *A More Secure World: Our Shared Responsibility – Report of the Secretary-General's High-level Panel on Threats, Challenges and Change*, para. 207.

78 The UK invoked similar criteria in its position regarding the legality of military action in Syria: *Chemical Weapon Use by Syrian Regime: UK Government Legal Position* (London, Prime Minister's Office, 29 August 2013): www.gov.uk/government/publications/chemical-weapon-use-by-syrian-regime-uk-government-legal-position.

79 UN Doc. S/PRST/2013/12 (6 August 2013).

80 *Timely and Decisive Response Report*, paras 51–2.

81 As acknowledged in a concept note prepared for an open debate on UNSC working methods: UN Doc. S/2013/613 (17 October 2013), *Letter Dated 16 October 2013 from the Permanent Representatives of Azerbaijan to the United Nations Addressed to the Secretary-General.*

82 Included within the draft resolution concerning the non-exercise of the veto in relation to UNSC actions aimed at preventing genocide, war crimes and crimes against humanity are 19 other recommendations intended to 'institutionalize and/or improve current practices' within the UNSC: see *Costa Rica, Jordan, Liechtenstein, Singapore and Switzerland: Revised Draft Resolution*, Annex.

83 Volker Lehmann, *Reforming the Working Methods of the UN Security Council: The Next ACT* (New York, Friedrich-Ebert-Stiftung, 2013); William Pace, '21 Member States Launch New Initiative to Improve the Working Methods of the Security Council' (12 May 2013): www.centerforunreform.org/node/500.

84 See further, UN Doc. S/2010/507 (26 July 2010), *Note by the President of the Security Council.*

85 Similar to DPA briefings provided in the 1990s, the idea of 'horizon scanning' briefings was floated by the UK during the UNSC's July 2010 debate on preventive diplomacy. Regular briefings were discontinued in March 2012, amidst some concern about their format and content, but while a work-in-progress, the briefings are embraced by some as a step in the right direction. See further, Security Council Report, *In Hindsight: Horizon-scanning Briefings* (1 May 2013).

86 SC Res. 1625 (14 September 2005), paras 2(a) and 3(a), encourages the UNSG to

provide the UNSC with regular reports and analysis on developments in regions at risk of armed conflict and to keep the UNSC apprised of preventive-diplomacy initiatives.

87 See Security Council Report, *Security Council Transparency, Legitimacy and Effectiveness: Efforts to Reform Council Working Methods 1993–2007* (18 October 2007).

88 UN Doc. S/PV.6870 (26 November 2012), p. 10 (Li Baodong).

89 Ibid.

90 *Timely and Decisive Response Report*, para. 13. See also *Application of the Convention on the Prevention and Punishment of the Crime of Genocide (Bosnia and Herzegovina* v. *Serbia and Montenegro)*, Judgment [2007] ICJ Rep. 43, 115.

91 GA Res. 67/1 (24 September 2012), *Declaration of the High-level Meeting of the General Assembly on the Rule of Law at the National and International Levels*, paras 35 and 29, respectively.

92 *Timely and Decisive Response Report*, para. 58.

17 The Force Intervention Brigade and UN peace operations

Some legal issues

Bruce 'Ossie' Oswald[1]

Introduction

On 28 March 2013, the United Nations (UN) Security Council (UNSC) authorised a Force Intervention Brigade (FIB) – its 'first-ever "offensive" combat force' – for deployment in the Democratic Republic of the Congo (DRC).[2] The FIB was mandated to undertake 'targeted offensive operations'[3] to 'prevent the expansion of all armed groups, neutralize … and … disarm them'.[4] The FIB's first reported offensive operations occurred in August 2013, when it supported the Congolese armed forces against the 23 March Movement (M23) rebel group by providing 'ground troops, attack helicopters and artillery fire'.[5] The FIB also engaged in heavy combat with the M23 in October 2013, triggering its defeat.[6]

It is noteworthy that after almost 65 years of UN peacekeeping, the FIB represented the first time the UN had created a combat force under UN command and control. However, perhaps even more noteworthy are the various legal issues that arise from the FIB's creation and operation. Those issues include: (1) the UNSC's authority to establish a combat force to undertake 'targeted offensive operations' under the command and control of the UN; (2) whether UN peacekeeping forces engaged in armed conflict should be considered a party to the conflict for the purposes of international humanitarian law (IHL); and (3) the legal principles and rules that regulate the activities of peacekeepers engaged in armed conflict.

This chapter proceeds in three sections. Section 1 surveys the evolution of UN peacekeeping operations in the DRC. Section 2 examines UNSC Resolution 2098 (2013) pursuant to which the UNSC established the FIB. Section 3 explores the most important legal issues arising from the FIB's creation and deployment.

1 UN peacekeeping in the DRC (1960–2015)

The UN's involvement in peace operations in the DRC can be divided into three distinct periods. During the first period, 1960–1964, the UNSC established Operation des Nations Unies au Congo (ONUC).[7] During the second period, 1999–2010, the UNSC created the UN Organization Mission in the DRC (MONUC).[8] During the third period, the UNSC replaced MONUC with the UN Organization Stabilization Mission in the DRC (MONUSCO).[9]

1.1 ONUC (1960–1964)

ONUC undertook a variety of tasks, including restoring and maintaining law and order, supervising the withdrawal of Belgian forces and providing assistance to deal with the constitutional crisis that commenced in September 1960.[10] ONUC withdrew from the Congo on 30 June 1964, upon the completion of its mandate. ONUC's deployment was significant for a number of reasons. It was the first UN peacekeeping operation to contain a major civilian component. It was the first operation mandated to maintain law and order and to assist a government to establish its authority. Moreover, it was the first UN peace operation to undertake combat operations and to use force beyond the limits of self-defence.[11]

1.2 MONUC (1999–2010)

Thirty-five years later the UNSC deployed another peace operation to the Congo. MONUC's mandate included planning for the observation of a post-conflict ceasefire, providing information on security conditions in its areas of operation, and facilitating the delivery of humanitarian assistance.[12] MONUC's mandate expanded over the subsequent decade to include: assisting with voluntary disarmament, demobilisation, repatriation and resettlement of fighters; supporting confidence-building measures between the DRC, Rwanda and Uganda; assisting with protecting civilians; assisting with stabilising particular areas of operations, such as the Kivus; and assisting with elections. Interestingly, MONUC also deployed a 'neutral force' to provide security reassurance to those members of the Transitional Government who were assessed to require it.[13]

During MONUC's deployment the UNSC authorised two non-UN peace operations under national command and control to assist the UN peacekeepers to fulfil their mandate. In May 2003, the UNSC authorised the deployment of an Interim Emergency Multinational Force (IEMF) in Bunia, led by France with a mandate to work with MONUC to 'contribute to the stabilization of the security conditions … to ensure protection of the airport … and … to contribute to the safety of the civilian population, UN personnel and the humanitarian presence in the town'.[14] In April 2006 the UNSC authorised the deployment of an EU force to support MONUC by contributing to the protection of civilians under imminent threat, contributing to the protection of the Kinshasa airport and conducting operations in order to rescue individuals in danger.[15]

1.3 MONUSCO (2010–present)

MONUSCO's mandate initially included: protecting civilians, supporting efforts to bring perpetrators to justice, supporting the return of internally displaced persons (IDPs), supporting the Government of the DRC with ongoing operations against non-state armed actors such as the Lord's Resistance Army, supporting the reform of the police and assisting the Government of the DRC with demining.[16]

The strongest threat to civilians under MONUSCO's tenure arose in April 2012 when the M23 initiated attacks in the North Kivu region.[17] In a series of decisions in the second half of 2012, the UNSC condemned M23's actions and emphasised MONUSCO's role in supporting the DRC to take action against armed groups, including M23, and to 'restore order and bring the perpetrators to justice while ensuring the protection of the civilian population'.[18]

1.4 The evolution of peacekeeping use-of-force mandates in the DRC

From February 2000, UN peacekeepers acted in accordance with their Chapter VII mandate to protect civilians and use force in self-defence. In July 2003, the UNSC authorised MONUC to 'take all necessary means in the areas of deployment of its armed units, and as it deems it within its capabilities' to protect UN personnel, equipment and facilities, to ensure security and freedom of movement, to protect civilians and humanitarian workers and to improve security to facilitate the delivery of humanitarian assistance.[19] This mandate was expanded gradually to include ensuring the territorial security of the DRC, disarming and demobilising foreign and Congolese armed groups and protecting civilians.[20]

Both MONUC's and MONUSCO's mandates were framed in the context of supporting the DRC military forces, with the level of support escalating throughout both operations. MONUC started with military observer liaison responsibilities in 1999, and by 2004 it had shifted to supporting the Forces Armées de la République du Congo (FARDC).[21] In 2007 the UNSC authorised MONUC to engage in security sector reform (SSR) by providing to the FARDC short-term basic training in areas such as IHL and international human rights law (IHRL), among other responsibilities.[22] Later that year the UNSC went further by emphasising that joint MONUC–FARDC operations conducted with FARDC to disarm and demobilise should be planned jointly and undertaken in accordance with IHL, IHRL and refugee law, and with appropriate measures in place to protect civilians.[23]

Pursuant to their mandates, both MONUC and MONUSCO engaged in a range of military operations, often with the FARDC, against non-state actors. MONUC thus 'seized weapons in Bunia and detained a number of persons suspected of harbouring weapons',[24] conducted 'cordon and search operations',[25] established 'weapons free zones, and [...deterred and prevented] reprisal attacks',[26] and undertook reconnaissance missions.[27] MONUSCO, for its part, conducted several joint offensive combat actions with FARDC in 2012, targeting armed groups in a number of territories.[28]

1.5 Conclusions

Several conclusions can be drawn from the above overview of the three periods of UN peace operations in the DRC. First, in each period the Congolese military forces were unable to deal adequately with rebel forces or to provide appropriate levels of civilian protection. In fact, on various occasions the Congolese military forces were actually accused of committing serious criminal offences. Second, the Government of the DRC and the UN have both struggled to defeat the rebels and provide protection to the civilian population.[29] Third, despite all of the efforts by DRC authorities and the UN, the security situation in some areas of the DRC has not improved significantly. Fourth, in early 2012 the cross-border impact of the DRC conflict led the African Union (AU), the International Conference on the Great Lakes Region (ICGLR) and the South African Development Community (SADC) to float the idea of a Neutral International Force (NIF). Roux argues that this initiative by African states to create a force of their own to do what MONUSCO could not – i.e. protect civilians – 'galvanised' the UN 'into action, with the DPKO [UN Department of Peacekeeping Operations] proposing the deployment of a UN intervention brigade, utilising SADC troop components that would have deployed under the NIF'.[30] In February 2013 the UN Secretary-General (UNSG) thus recommended that the UNSC create such a brigade.[31]

2 Resolution 2098 (2013) and the deployment of the Force Intervention Brigade

In March 2013 the UNSC adopted Resolution 2098 (2013), establishing the FIB pursuant to its Chapter VII powers.[32] The FIB was created 'on an exceptional basis and without creating a precedent or any prejudice to the agreed principles of peacekeeping'.[33] The FIB was mandated 'to carry out targeted offensive operations … with the responsibility of neutralizing armed groups'.[34] The FIB was also to 'prevent the expansion of all armed groups … and to disarm them in order to contribute to the objective of reducing the threat posed by armed groups on state authority and civilian security in eastern DRC and to make space for stabilization activities'.[35] Based on the references to the armed groups made elsewhere in the resolution, it is reasonable to assume that the FIB was thus tasked with undertaking offensive operations against the M23, the Democratic Liberation Forces for the Liberation of Rwanda, the Lord's Resistance Army and various Mai Mai groups.[36]

The FIB falls under the direct command of the MONUSCO Force Commander.[37] Resolution 2098 (2013) provided that the UNSC would determine the ongoing presence of the FIB based on its performance and the progress made by the DRC in taking over 'responsibility for achieving the objective of the Intervention Brigade'.[38] The resolution also stipulated that the legal framework applicable to the FIB in carrying out its functions and tasks is international law, including IHL.[39]

Resolution 2098 (2013) further authorised MONUSCO to 'take all necessary measures' with the FIB to protect civilians, UN personnel, facilities, installations and equipment, and with the Government of the DRC, to identify threats to civilians.[40] The military component of MONUSCO was also authorised to support the implementation of tasks such as monitoring and reporting human rights violations, SSR, reform of the DRC army and action plans concerning the prevention of recruiting and using children.[41] Further, the UNSC established an accountability regime for MONUSCO and the FIB by noting the importance of UN peacekeepers being 'properly prepared' and 'effectively equipped' to carry out their tasks and requesting the UNSG to report to it every three months on the implementation of MONUSCO's mandate.[42]

In relation to risks, the UNSC required both MONUSCO and the FIB to 'mitigate the risk to civilians before, during and after any military operations',[43] and requested the UNSG to report to it on both these potential risks and steps taken to mitigate them.[44]

3 Key legal issues

The UNSC's innovation in establishing an offensive military peacekeeping force to 'neutralize' non-state actors raises important legal questions. First, does the UNSC have the authority to mandate a peacekeeping force to undertake offensive military operations? Second, should the FIB be considered a party to the conflict in the DRC? Third, if the FIB is a party to the conflict, what legal implications flow from this? Fourth, by using the term 'neutralize', what precisely did the UNSC authorise the FIB to do? Fifth, to what extent must UN forces comply with IHRL when conducting operations? Sixth, to what extent is the FIB liable to pay compensation or make reparations for deaths, injuries or damage of property caused by its offensive operations?

3.1 The UNSC's authority to mandate offensive military peacekeeping operations

It is universally accepted that the UNSC has the power to establish a peacekeeping force for any purpose associated with maintaining international peace and security, as a matter of both law and practice.[45] As a matter of law, when the UN 'takes action which warrants the assertion that it was appropriate for the fulfillment of one of the [UN's] stated purposes ... the presumption is that such action is not *ultra vires* the Organization'.[46] The UNSC is authorised to determine whether there is a threat to peace and may make recommendations or decide what peaceful or use-of-force measures it might take to maintain or restore international peace and security pursuant to Chapter VII, Article 39.

Moreover, the UN Secretariat has previously argued for the establishment of UN enforcement units, believing that such units could be created under the UNSC's Chapter VII powers.[47] In any case, it is clearly within the UNSC's powers to determine that the levels of violence, instability and breaches of fundamental principles of law in the DRC represent a threat to international peace and security. Furthermore, as the International Court of Justice (ICJ) has stated: '[i]t cannot be said that the Charter has left the Security Council impotent in the face of an emergency situation'.[48] Considering the levels of violence and the threat posed by armed groups such as the M23, particularly after the November 2012 attacks in the Goma area, it is difficult to argue that the Government of the DRC and MONUSCO were not facing an emergency situation when the FIB was created.

Some might argue that the FIB's creation goes against two of the basic principles of UN peacekeeping, namely impartiality and non-use of force except in self-defence or in defence of the mandate.[49] In Resolution 2098 (2013) the UNSC reaffirmed these principles but also recognised 'that the mandate of each peacekeeping mission is specific to the need and situation of the country concerned'.[50] As the principles are doctrinal and not legal, the UNSC does not act *ultra vires* if it overrides those principles where it is necessary and reasonable to do. As a matter of practice, it should also be noted that no member of the UNSC, and indeed no member of the UN more generally, has contended that the UNSC has acted *ultra vires* in establishing the FIB and giving the FIB its robust mandate.

3.2 Is the FIB a party to the conflict?

It is important to note that the UN has not publicly stated at any stage during its long engagement in the DRC that it has been a party to the conflict.[51] Patricia O'Brien, the former UN Under-Secretary-General for Legal Affairs and UN Legal Counsel, has stated that '[i]t is without doubt that MONUSCO must conduct any military operations in full compliance with IHL if and when it becomes a party to an armed conflict'.[52] Schindler has also argued that '[w]hen a UN peacekeeping force becomes involved in an armed conflict, the organization … will be the party to the conflict'.[53] Nevertheless, the UN is yet to admit that MONUSCO is a party to the conflict.

Is the mere fact that the UN is engaged in armed conflict sufficient to establish that it is party to armed conflict? Greenwood has argued that the test for establishing whether UN forces are parties to armed conflict is unlikely to be judged by the same standards as that used for other forces. In his view, UN forces should be considered parties to armed conflict 'only when they have engaged in hostilities on a scale comparable to those of a force established for the purpose of enforcement action'.[54] In Greenwood's view, the requisite scale of hostilities should be 'considerably higher than that which is used to define an armed conflict for other purposes'.[55]

The Special Court for Sierra Leone in *Prosecutor* v. *Sesay, Kallon and Gbao* ('RUF case') has taken another approach by concluding that peacekeepers only become combatants when they take a direct part in the hostilities.[56] The International Criminal Court (ICC) in the pre-trial hearings of cases against Nourain and Jamus,[57] and Garda,[58] reached similar conclusions concerning the combatant status of peacekeepers. The Rome Statute also provides that peacekeeping personnel 'are entitled to protection, unless and for such time as they take a direct part in hostilities, i.e. are engaged as combatants'.[59]

A narrow reading of the RUF case and both ICC pre-trial cases would lead to the conclusion that where there is a group of peacekeepers, for example on a military base, only those peacekeepers actually engaged in armed conflict (i.e. taking a direct part in hostilities)[60] would be parties to the conflict. The other peacekeepers in the base would retain their civilian status and would therefore not be directly targetable. This interpretation appears to be consistent with the view taken in the 1999 UNSG's Bulletin on the observance of IHL by the UN, which establishes a so-called 'double-key' test for the application of IHL principles and rules, set out in that Bulletin.[61] It stipulates that, first, there must be an armed conflict in the area at the time of the deployment and, second, there must be an engagement of members of the force in the conflict as combatants.[62]

Ferraro introduces a different test to determine whether UN forces are parties to armed conflict by arguing for a 'support-based approach'.[63] According to this test, four conditions apply cumulatively. First, there should be a 'pre-existing NIAC ongoing in the territory where multinational forces intervene'.[64] Second, any 'actions related to the conduct of hostilities' should be 'undertaken by multinational forces in the context of that pre-existing conflict'.[65] Third, those actions should be taken in support of a party to that conflict.[66] Fourth, the actions should flow from a decision by a troop-contributing country (TCC) or international organisation to support that party to the conflict.[67] Applying Ferraro's support-based approach to the FIB, the focus would be on whether the support provided by the FIB has a direct impact on the ability of, for example, the M23 to conduct hostilities.

Ultimately, whether the 'party to an armed conflict', the 'direct part in hostilities' or the 'support-based' approach is taken, it is clear that when the FIB engaged the M23 in North Kivu with troops, artillery, mortars and attack helicopters on 28 August 2013, those peacekeeping troops could themselves be targeted by the M23.[68]

3.3 The legal consequences of being a party to the conflict

One consequence of accepting that members of the FIB are lawful targets is that, as a matter of international law, M23 personnel would have combatant immunity: that is, immunity under international law from prosecution for attacking peacekeepers or their property.[69] The notion of combatant immunity for those that attack peacekeepers taking a direct part in hostilities is consistent with the interpretation given to the relevant provisions of the Rome Statute and the 1994 Convention on the Safety of UN and Associated Personnel.[70] This leads to the conclusion that it is not a crime to attack peacekeepers, their installations, material or vehicles for such time as the peacekeepers are undertaking combat.

Further, if it is accepted that the FIB personnel could be lawfully targeted, the question arises whether MONUSCO, as a whole, is also a party to the conflict. One could argue that, because the FIB is under the command and control of the MONUSCO Force Commander, the whole force is thus a party to the conflict – and therefore could be lawfully targeted by opposition forces. Alternatively, one could distinguish between members of MONUSCO on the basis that those taking an active part in hostilities could be targeted, and those who are not would retain their protected status. The second approach would appear to be supported by the RUF case: 'common sense dictates that peacekeepers are considered to be civilians only insofar as they fall within the definition of civilians laid down for non-combatants [...that is] they do not take part in hostilities'.[71]

A more nuanced approach might be to separate the FIB from MONUSCO by arguing that only those MONUSCO forces engaged in actual fighting in support of the FIB are parties to the conflict. Thus, those MONUSCO units carrying out humanitarian assistance or protecting vulnerable people would maintain their protected status and it would be unlawful to target them. In any event, it is also important to consider how the opposing parties to the conflict are expected to distinguish between members of the FIB and members of MONUSCO.

A political and practical difficulty that arises with declaring that UN peacekeepers may be lawfully targeted in some circumstances is that TCCs might be hesitant to contribute troops to peacekeeping operations where they might be targeted while carrying out a humanitarian mission. For this reason it might be argued that, regardless of whether peacekeepers are parties to an armed conflict, combatant immunity should never be granted to those who attack peacekeepers or their property.[72] Following this line of argument, the FIB and MONUSCO might be viewed as holding a privileged position that permits them to engage in armed hostilities without the opposing forces possessing combatant immunity.[73]

This approach is arguably taken by the UNSC in Resolution 2098 (2013), where it condemns all attacks against peacekeepers and emphasises that 'those responsible for such attacks must be held accountable'.[74] The UNSC thus attempts to make it unlawful to target UN forces in any circumstances. This approach is consistent with the view that UN peacekeepers have particular privileges and immunities when undertaking their official functions and consequently are not subject to the domestic criminal law of the state in which the peace operation is being conducted.[75] At the same time, however, this approach is problematic, as it undermines a key principle of both IHL and the rule of law more broadly, namely the importance of the equal application of the law.[76]

The question of whether the FIB is a party to armed conflict is also important in determining whether FIB peacekeepers must apply IHL during military operations. While the classification of a conflict involving international forces in a state engaged in an internal armed conflict is somewhat controversial, the better view is that 'such a conflict is ... non-international, regardless of the international components of the multi-national force'.[77] This is based on the reasoning that, given the FIB's operations are in support of the DRC and conducted with the DRC's consent, the conflict should be categorised as a non-international armed conflict for the purposes of applying either Common Article 3,[78] or Additional Protocol II to the Geneva Conventions.[79] The choice between Common Article 3 and Additional Protocol II will depend in large part on whether the armed groups that the FIB fights meet the threshold prescribed by Additional Protocol II – that they are 'under responsible command [and] exercise such control over a part of its territory as to enable them to carry out sustained and concerted military operations'.[80] Regardless of whether the FIB's adversaries meet this threshold, at a minimum, Common Article 3 will apply to the combat operations conducted by the FIB.[81] One also assumes that the FIB, having met the double-key test in the UNSG's Bulletin, will apply the provisions of the Bulletin when it takes a direct part in the hostilities. The view of the International

Committee of the Red Cross (ICRC) is that 'multinational forces are bound by IHL when conditions for its applicability have been met'.[82] Furthermore, troops engaged in combat operations must also apply their national IHL obligations.[83]

3.4 The legal significance of the term 'neutralize'

Why did the UNSC mandate the FIB to 'neutralize' armed groups when the FIB, as a subordinate component of MONUSCO, would have the ability to 'take all necessary measures' to complete its mandate?[84] Did the UNSC use that word as a term of art to mean that the FIB should 'render [the armed groups] ineffective or unusable'?[85] If so, did it intend to distinguish the FIB's mandate from other operational terms such as 'contain', 'defeat', 'destroy', 'disrupt', or 'exploit'? What ramifications does the term have for the FIB's functions and tasks? Should the FIB interpret 'all necessary measures' more narrowly because of the word 'neutralize'? Or should it employ 'all necessary measures' to carry out the mandate of 'neutralizing'?

Durch contends that the difference in mandates between MONUSCO and the FIB arises from the 'intent to force, as it were, the use of force – highlighting some Security Council members' growing impatience with peacekeeping mission leaders' failure to effectively use the tools, from political to military, that they were given to do their jobs'.[86]

If the term 'neutralize' is interpreted broadly, it is reasonable to assume that the FIB is mandated to target armed groups with lethal force. In line with the usual concept of offensive operations, the FIB could conduct ambushes and deliberate attacks, and hold ground against any armed group. Therefore if MONUSCO's rules of engagement do not authorise its forces to undertake offensive operations, then the FIB's rules of engagement would need to be amended to permit the FIB to take offensive action.[87] The rules of engagement would also have to deal with the question of whether the basis for targeting is that a rebel is a member of an organised armed group, or whether he or she is taking an active part in hostilities.[88]

It is also reasonable to assume that the FIB has the power to detain and capture members of the armed groups it is conducting operations against. Indeed, according to O'Brien, the UN has developed specific standard operating procedures to deal with the FIB capturing individuals during offensive operations.[89] It appears that there are four options for dealing with those captured: (1) put into a disarmament, demobilisation, and reintegration (DDR) programme or a disarmament, demobilisation, reintegration, resettlement and repatriation (DDRRR) programme; (2) hand over to the appropriate DRC authorities; (3) keep in detention by MONUSCO; or (4) release.[90]

3.5 The application of international human rights law

In paragraph 12(b) of Resolution 2098 (2013), the UNSC states that the FIB should act in strict compliance with international law, including IHL and the

Human Rights Due Diligence Policy on UN support to non-UN security forces (HRDDP).[91] The HRDDP, for its part, requires the UN to withdraw its support to an intended recipient where the UN has 'substantial grounds for believing that there is a real risk of the intended recipient committing grave violations of international humanitarian law, human rights or refugee law'.[92]

The UNSC's reference to the HRDDP does not equate to a broader requirement to apply IHRL to actions taken against armed groups. Indeed, DPKO doctrine provides that UN peacekeeping personnel '*should* act in accordance with international human rights law and understand how the implementation of their tasks intersects with human rights'.[93] Notwithstanding the reference to 'should' in the doctrine, a broad reading of the stipulation in Resolution 2098 (2013) that the FIB's operations are to be conducted in accordance with international law would require that IHRL also be complied with by FIB personnel.

Civil society, courts and tribunals are increasingly considering whether UN forces have unfettered powers when fulfilling their mandates. An important question is whether UN forces are able to interpret UNSC resolutions in a manner that adversely affects the fundamental rights of individuals. For example, one interpretation of the *Al-Jedda* v. *United Kingdom* case (even though that case does not address UN forces undertaking peace operations) is that the European Court of Human Rights will not look favourably on states asserting that they are exercising powers of indefinite detention based on a UNSC Resolution. In addressing the power of British forces to use internment in Iraq, the Court argued that the mandate provided by the UNSC to take measures to contribute to the maintenance of security and stability could not be interpreted as creating a 'binding obligation to use internment'.[94]

It is worth reflecting on whether the UNSC should be more nuanced when authorising peace operations to 'use all necessary measures', which can then lead peacekeepers, using the doctrine of implied powers, to undertake additional functions and tasks such as detention and targeting. Should the UNSC, for example, state explicitly that the FIB has the power to target and detain? If so, should it spell out the targeting and detention regimes it requires to be applied? One would assume that if the UNSC were to explicitly spell-out targeting and detention regimes, those regimes would comply with fundamental principles and rules that states have accepted in accordance with their international obligations.

3.6 Compensation and reparations

A final legal issue to discuss here is the extent to which the FIB is liable to pay compensation or make reparations for the deaths, injuries or damage of property caused by its offensive military actions.[95] If IHL applies, then the two provisions relevant would be the 1907 Hague Convention IV, Article 3,[96] and Additional Protocol I, Article 91.[97] Both provisions provide that where a party to a conflict violates IHL they shall be liable to pay compensation. In the ICRC's view both provisions apply as a matter of customary international law to non-international armed conflicts.[98] Victims wishing to claim compensation for violations of IHL by the FIB might also use treaty regimes such as the Rome Statute,[99] or the Convention Against Torture.[100]

Where the claim for compensation does not arise from a breach of IHL, the issue is dealt with primarily by Article II, section 2 of the Convention on Privileges and Immunities of the UN, which provides the UN with immunity from all legal process unless it expressly waives such immunity.[101] However, although the UN is immune from legal process and the jurisdiction of national courts, it is nevertheless obliged to settle disputes in respect of claims of a private law nature to which the UN is party, pursuant to section 29 of that Convention.[102] Furthermore, pursuant to the model status-of-forces agreement between the UN and host countries, the UN and the host country should settle such disputes through a standard claims commission.[103]

Since 1956 the UN has settled claims for compensation arising from its peace operations in this manner. However, in 1998 the UN General Assembly adopted Resolution 52/247, establishing specific guidelines for payment of compensation for damages to third parties arising from UN conduct.[104] The main limitation on victims accessing compensation relating to the FIB's operations is that compensation is not available for damage resulting from 'operational necessity'.[105] This means that victims of the FIB's operations are unlikely to be successful in establishing UN liability for compensation where the FIB's conduct is considered 'operationally necessary'. There does remain, however, the practice of making 'act of grace' payments for deaths, injuries or damage to property arising from military operations by the UN and relevant TCCs. Such act of grace payment schemes are sometimes criticised because of their ad-hoc nature.[106]

4 Conclusion

A sensational headline such as 'the UN creates a war fighting Brigade' might suggest to some that Resolution 2098 (2013) was a revolution in the means available to the UN to maintain international peace and security. However, viewed over the history of UN peace operations, the creation of the Intervention Brigade simply represents another step in the evolution of UN peacekeeping. The conduct of operations by ONUC, MONUC, MONUSCO and now the FIB has, at various times, crossed the line between the use of force in self-defence and the use of force in offensive operations. The innovative step taken by the UN in establishing the FIB is intended to send a clear message to rebel groups that offensive operations will be conducted against them and to provide a greater level of cohesion and efficiency by introducing a unified chain of command for all UN forces operating in the DRC.

UNSC members apparently shared the view that setting up a UN force under UN command and control to fight armed groups in the DRC was necessary for maintaining international peace and security, and to better protect the civilian population. However, this chapter has demonstrated that the FIB's operations raise two legal issues of particular concern. First, it is uncertain whether the

FIB's forays into offensive operations will render MONUSCO a party to the conflict for the purposes of applying IHL. Second, it is unclear what, if any, legal limits the term 'neutralize' places on the FIB when it is conducting operations. These important matters should be resolved definitively before the UNSC decides to establish another peace operation under UN command and control to undertake offensive operations.

Notes

1 Elements of this chapter are drawn from the substantially shorter online publication 'The Security Council and the Intervention Brigade: Some Legal Issues' (2013) 17(15) *Insights, American Society of International Law*. Ossie is grateful to Katarina Grenfell for her comments, Beth Wellington, Jane McCosker and Natasha Robbins for their editorial assistance, and Liz Saltnes for her support.
2 '"Intervention Brigade" Authorized as Security Council Grants Mandate Renewal', UN Press Release SC/10964 (28 March 2013): www.un.org/News/Press/docs/2013/sc10964.doc.htm.
3 SC Res. 2098 (28 March 2013), para. 12(b).
4 Ibid., paras 10, 12(b).
5 UN Doc. S/2013/581 (30 September 2013), *Report of the Secretary-General on the United Nations Organization Stabilization Mission in the Democratic Republic of the Congo*, paras 15, 37. For discussion of the 23 March Movement (M23), a rebel group formed in 2012, see UN Doc. S/2012/838 (14 November 2012), *Report of the Secretary-General: United Nations Organization Stabilization Mission in the Democratic Republic of the Congo*, paras 11–25.
6 SOLLIMS Lesson No. 1307, 'UN Force Intervention Brigade against the M23': http://nust.edu.pk/INSTITUTIONS/Schools/NIPCONS/nipcons-institutions/CIPS/Download%20Section/SOLLIMS_Lsn_1307_UN_Force_Intervention_Brigade_(20-Nov-2013).pdf; and UN Doc. S/PRST/2013/17 (14 November 2013).
7 For detailed discussion of ONUC, see Georges Abi-Saab, *The United Nations Operation in the Congo 1960–1964: Internal Crises and the Role of Law* (Oxford, Oxford University Press, 1978).
8 SC Res. 1279 (30 November 1999).
9 SC Res. 1925 (28 May 2010).
10 See UN Department of Public Information, *The Blue Helmets* (New York, United Nations, 1985), pp. 175–99.
11 See SC Res. 169 (24 November 1961), para. 4 (authorising the UNSG to take action, 'including the use of requisite measure of force, if necessary, for immediate apprehension, detention … of all foreign military and paramilitary personnel'. For discussion, see D.W. Bowett, *United Nations Forces: A Legal Study of United Nations Practice* (New York, Frederick A. Praeger, 1964), pp. 153–261.
12 SC Res. 1279 (30 November 1999).
13 UN Doc. S/2003/1098 (17 November 2003), *Fourteenth Report of the Secretary-General on MONUC*, para. 33.
14 SC Res. 1484 (30 May 2003), para. 1.
15 SC Res. 1671 (25 April 2006), para. 8.
16 SC Res. 1925 (28 May 2010), para. 12.
17 See UN Doc. S/2013/119 (27 February 2013), *Report of the Secretary-General: Democratic Republic of Congo and the Great Lakes Region*, para. 5.
18 SC Res. 2053 (27 June 2012), para. 20; SC Res. 2076 (20 November 2012), para. 1; SC Res. 2078 (28 November 2012), paras 6–7.
19 SC Res. 1493 (28 July 2003), para. 25; SC Res. 1565 (1 October 2004), para. 6; SC

Res. 1756 (15 May 2007), para. 4; SC Res. 1856 (22 December 2008), para. 5; and SC Res. 1906 (23 December 2009), para. 6.

20 SC Res. 1565 (1 October 2004), para. 6; SC Res. 1756 (15 May 2007), para. 4; SC Res. 1856 (22 December 2008), para. 5; SC Res. 1906 (23 December 2009), para. 6; SC Res. 1925 (28 May 2010), para. 11.

21 UN Doc. S/2004/650 (16 August 2004), *Third Special Report of the Secretary-General on MONUC.*

22 SC Res. 1756 (15 May 2007), para. 3(o).

23 SC Res. 1794 (21 December 2007), para. 7.

24 *Fourteenth Report of the Secretary-General*, para. 9.

25 UN Doc. S/2006/759 (21 September 2006), *Twenty-second Report of the Secretary-General on MONUC*, para. 42.

26 UN Doc. S/2008/433 (3 July 2008), *Twenty-sixth Report of the Secretary-General on MONUC*, para. 35.

27 *Twenty-first Report of the Secretary-General*, para. 35.

28 UN Doc. S/2012/355 (23 May 2012), *Report of the Secretary-General on MONUSCO*, para. 16; and UN Doc. S/2013/96 (15 February 2013), *Report of the Secretary-General on MONUSCO*, para. 37.

29 See UN Doc. S/2013/119 (27 February 2013), *Report of the Secretary-General on the Democratic Republic of Congo and the Great Lakes Region*, paras 2–5.

30 Andre Roux, 'South Africa and the UN Intervention Brigade in the DRC', *ISS Today* (online), 24 April 2013: www.issafrica.org/iss-today/south-africa-and-the-un-intervention-brigade-in-the-drc.

31 UN Doc. S/2013/119 (27 February 2013), *Special Report of the Secretary-General on the Democratic Republic of the Congo and the Great Lakes Region*, para. 60.

32 SC Res. 2098 (28 March 2013), paras 9–12.

33 Ibid., para. 9.

34 Ibid.

35 Ibid., para. 12(b).

36 Ibid., para. 8.

37 Ibid., para. 9.

38 Ibid., para. 10.

39 Ibid., para. 12(b).

40 Ibid., para. 12(a).

41 Ibid., para. 16.

42 Ibid., paras 29, 34(iii).

43 Ibid., para. 12(a)(i).

44 Ibid., para. 33(vi).

45 See *Certain Expenses of the United Nations (Article 17, Paragraph 2, of the Charter)*, Advisory Opinion [1962] ICJ Rep. 151, 168.

46 Ibid.

47 See UN Doc. A/47/277–S/24111 (17 June 1992), *An Agenda for Peace: Preventative Diplomacy, Peacemaking and Peace-keeping: Report of the Secretary-General Pursuant to the Statement Adopted by the Summit Meeting of the Security Council on 31 January 1992*, para. 44.

48 *Certain Expenses of the United Nations (Advisory Opinion)*, 167.

49 The third basic principle is the consent of the parties. For further discussion see DPKO, *UN Peacekeeping Operations: Principles and Guidelines* (2008), pp. 31–43.

50 SC Res. 2098 (28 March 2013), preambular para. 2.

51 For detailed discussion of the classification of conflicts in the Congo from 1993–2010, see Louise Arimatsu, 'The Democratic Republic of the Congo 1993–2010', in Elizabeth Wilmshurst (ed.), *International Law and the Classification of Conflicts* (Oxford, Oxford University Press, 2012), pp. 146–212.

52 Patricia O'Brien, statement at the 36th Round Table on Current Issues of International

Law, 'Respecting IHL: Challenges and Responses', Sanremo, Italy, 5 September 2013, p. 6.

53 Dietrich Schindler, 'United Nations Forces and International Law', in Christophe Swinarski (ed.), *Studies and Essays on International Humanitarian Law and Red Cross Principles in Honor of Jean Pictet* (The Hague, Martinus Nijhoff, 1984), pp. 521–30, 524.

54 Christopher Greenwood, 'International Humanitarian Law and United Nations Military Operations' (1998) 1 *Yearbook of International Humanitarian Law* 3–34, 25.

55 Ibid.

56 *Prosecutor* v. *Sesay, Kallon and Gbao* ('RUF case'), Special Court for Sierra Leone, Trial Chamber Judgment (2 March 2009), para. 233.

57 *Prosecutor* v. *Abdallah Banda Abakaer Nourain and Saleh Mohammed Jerbo Jamus*, ICC-02/05-03/09 (27 August 2009), paras 18–21.

58 *Prosecutor* v. *Bahar Idriss Abu Garda*, ICC-02/05-02/09 (8 February 2010), paras 83–4.

59 Knut Dormann, with contributions by Louise Doswald-Beck and Robert Kolb, *Elements of War Crimes under the Rome Statute of the International Criminal Court: Sources and Commentary* (Cambridge, Cambridge University Press, 2003), p. 455.

60 For further discussion, see Nils Melzer, *Interpretive Guidance on the Notion of Direct Participation in Hostilities under International Humanitarian Law* (Geneva, ICRC, 2009).

61 UN Doc. ST/SG/1999/13 (12 August 1999), *Secretary-General's Bulletin*: *Observance by United Nations Forces of International Humanitarian Law*, section 1.1.

62 Ibid.

63 Tristan Ferraro, 'The Applicability and Application of International Humanitarian Law to Multinational Forces' (2013) 95(891/892) *International Review of the Red Cross* 561–612, 584.

64 Ibid.

65 Ibid.

66 Ibid.

67 Ibid.

68 See UN Doc. S/2013/581 (30 September 2013), *Report of the Secretary-General on MONUSCO*, paras 15, 37.

69 Laurie R. Blank and Gregory P. Noone, *International Law and Armed Conflict: Fundamental Principles and Contemporary Challenges in the Law of War* (Aspen, Aspen Publishers, 2013), pp. 243–4.

70 See *Rome Statute of the International Criminal Court*, opened for signature 17 July 1998, 2187 UNTS 90 (entered into force 1 July 2002), arts 8(2)(b)(iii) and 8(2)(e)(iii); and *Convention on the Safety of the United Nations and Associated Personnel*, opened for signature 15 December 1994, 2051 UNTS 361 (entered into force 15 January 1999), art. 2(2). See also Dormann, *Elements of War Crimes under the Rome Statute*, pp. 159, 455.

71 *RUF* case, para. 233.

72 See Bowett, *United Nations Forces*, pp. 496–9.

73 I am grateful to Daniel Bethlehem for drawing this issue to my attention.

74 SC Res. 2098 (28 March 2013), preambular, para. 26. One way the UNSC has sought to pursue such accountability is by imposing financial and travel sanctions on all individuals or entities 'who plan, sponsor or participate in attacks against MONUSCO peacekeepers': see SC Res. 2078 (28 November 2012), para. 4(i).

75 Bruce Oswald, Helen Durham and Adrian Bates, *Documents on the Law of UN Peace Operations* (Oxford, Oxford University Press, 2010), pp. 34–66.

76 Marten Zwanenburg, *Accountability of Peace Support Operations* (Boston, MA, Martinus Nijhoff, 2005), pp. 159–60.

77 Wilmshurst, 'Conclusions', p. 487.

78 *Geneva Convention Relative to the Amelioration of the Condition of the Wounded and Sick in Armed Forces in the Field*, opened for signature 12 August 1949, 75 UNTS 31 (entered into force 21 October 1950), common art. 3; *Geneva Convention Relative to the Amelioration of the Condition of Wounded, Sick and Shipwrecked Members of Armed Forces at Sea*, opened for signature 12 August 1949, 75 UNTS 85 (entered into force 21 October 1950); *Geneva Convention Relative to the Treatment of Prisoners of War*, opened for signature 12 August 1949, 75 UNTS 135 (entered into force 21 October 1950); *Geneva Convention Relative to the Protection of Civilian Persons in Time of War*, opened for signature 12 August 1949, 75 UNTS 287 (entered into force 21 October 1950).

79 *Protocol Additional to the Geneva Conventions of 12 August 1949, and Relating to the Protection of Victims of Non-International Armed Conflicts*, opened for signature 12 December 1977, 1125 UNTS 609 (entered into force 7 December 1978) ('Additional Protocol II').

80 Additional Protocol II, art. 1(1).

81 Ola Engdahl, 'The Status of Peace Operation Forces Under International Humanitarian Law' (2008) 11 *Yearbook of International Humanitarian Law* 109–38.

82 ICRC, *International Humanitarian Law and the Challenges of Contemporary Armed Conflicts*, p. 33.

83 See UK Ministry of Defence, *The Manual of the Law of Armed Conflict* (Oxford, Oxford University Press, 2005), para. 14.3.

84 SC Res. 2098 (28 March 2013), para. 12.

85 US Department of Defense, *DOD Dictionary of Military Terms*: www.dtic.mil/doctrine/dod_dictionary.

86 William Durch, *Forceful Peacekeeping: Shared Risk, Sustainable Engagement* (5 December 2013): www.stimson.org/spotlight/forceful-peacekeeping-shared-risk-sustainable-engagement.

87 The UN rules of engagement for MONUSCO and the FIB are not in the public domain. However, Patricia O'Brien has stated that 'the rules of engagement of MONUSCO have … been adapted to the new mandate of MONUSCO, and […her] Office has ensured that they are in full compliance with the IHL rules relating to the conduct of hostilities'. See O'Brien, Statement at the 36th Round Table, p. 6.

88 Melzer, *Interpretive Guidance on the Notion of Direct Participation in Hostilities*. See also the questions raised in the context of targeting by Ashley Deeks, 'How Does the UN Define "Direct Participation in Hostilities?"' (21 October 2013): www.lawfareblog.com/2013/10/how-does-the-un-define-direct-participation-in-hostilities.

89 O'Brien, Statement at the 36th Round Table, p. 7.

90 Ibid., pp. 7–8.

91 The HRDDP was endorsed by the UNSG in July 2011. For details of the policy, see UN Doc. A/67/775–S/2013/110 (5 March 2013), *Human Rights Due Diligence Policy on United Nations Support to Non-United Nations Security Force* ('HRDDP').

92 HRDDP, para. 16. However, the Policy recognises that in some circumstances withdrawing support because of human rights abuses might make it difficult for a UN mission to fulfil its mandate. In such circumstances the UNSG 'should advise the Council … and seek the Council's advice regarding the way forward': see para. 28.

93 DPKO, *United Nations Peacekeeping Operations: Principles and Guidelines* (New York, United Nations, 2008), pp. 14–15 (emphasis added).

94 *Al-Jedda* v. *United Kingdom*, Application. No. 27021/08, Council of Europe: European Court of Human Rights, 7 July 2011, p. 109.

95 On violations of IHL by FIB members, see Keiichiro Okimoto, 'Violations of International Humanitarian Law by United Nations Forces and their Legal Consequences' (2003) 6 *Yearbook of International Humanitarian Law* 199–236.

96 *Convention (IV) Respecting the Laws and Customs of War on Land*, 18 October 1907, UKTS 9 (1910), Cd. 5030 (adopted 18 October 1907, entered into force 26 January 1910).

97 *Protocol Additional to the Geneva Conventions of 12 August 1949, and Relating to the Protection of Victims of International Armed Conflict* ('Protocol I'), opened for signature 12 December 1977, UKTS 29 (1999), Cm. 4338 (entered into force 7 December 1978).

98 Jean-Marie Henckaerts and Louise Doswald-Beck, *Customary International Humanitarian Law, Volume I: Rules* (Cambridge, ICRC and Cambridge University Press, 2005), rule 150, pp. 547–8.

99 See Rome Statute, art. 75.

100 See *Convention Against Torture and Other Cruel, Inhuman or Degrading Treatment or Punishment*, opened for signature 10 December 1984, 1465 UNTS 85 (entered into force 26 June 1987) ('CAT'), art. 14; and Committee against Torture, General Comment No. 3, CAT/C/GC/3 (19 November 2012), interpreting art. 14.

101 *Convention on the Privileges and Immunities of the United Nations*, opened for signature 13 February 1946, 1 UNTS 15 (entered into force 17 September 1946).

102 The UN Office of Legal Affairs has reaffirmed that the UN is capable of incurring obligations and liabilities of a private law nature. See United Nations, *United Nations Juridical Yearbook* (New York, United Nations, 2001), pp. 381.

103 UN Doc. A/45/594 (9 October 1990), *Report of the Secretary-General: Model Status-of-Forces Agreement for Peace-keeping Operations*, para. 51. Such a claims commission has never been established.

104 GA Res. 52/247 (26 June 1998), *Third-party Liability: Temporal and Financial Limitations*. See also Daphna Shraga, 'UN Peacekeeping Operations: Applicability of International Humanitarian Law and Responsibility for Operations-Related Damage' (2000) 94 *American Journal of International Law* 406–12.

105 GA Res. 52/247 (26 June 1998), *Third-party Liability: Temporal and Financial Limitations*, para. 6.

106 See Bruce Oswald and Bethany Wellington, 'Reparations for Violations in Armed Conflict and the Emerging Practice of Making Amends', in Rain Liivoja and Timothy McCormack (eds), *Routledge Handbook of the Law of Armed Conflict* (Abingdon, Routledge, 2015).

18 Peace through law and the Security Council

Modelling law compliance

Mary Ellen O'Connell[1]

Introduction

The United Nations (UN) was founded in 1945 to 'save succeeding generations from the scourge of war'.[2] This phrase from the first line of the UN Charter makes clear, together with the Charter as a whole, that the purpose of the organisation is to prevent and end major armed conflict. Law dominates the UN approach to preserving the peace, beginning with the fact that the UN Charter is a multilateral treaty with binding obligations for all member states. Those obligations include, most importantly, the interconnected set of substantive rules prohibiting resort to force except in limited circumstances.[3] The substantive rules further mandate the peaceful settlement of disputes and empower the UN Security Council (UNSC) to respond to threats to the peace, breaches of the peace and acts of aggression. The UNSC has the power to authorise the use of force if alternative measures short of force prove 'inadequate'.[4] The Charter also responds to the problem of war indirectly through promoting human rights and economic development.[5] The third component of the Charter is the UN itself, which provides opportunities for states to consult long before any dispute reaches a crisis stage. The UN has various agencies able to assist in conflict prevention and peaceful settlement of disputes, such as the International Court of Justice (ICJ) and the office of the UN Secretary-General (UNSG).[6]

Since 1945, the world has experienced over 300 armed conflicts.[7] We cannot know, of course, how many armed conflicts might have occurred were it not for the UN. We can conclude, however, that the UN's capacity to prevent and end armed conflict must be improved. Over the years, UN members and officials have sought to enhance the UN's effectiveness in preventing armed conflict. In the 1960s, the concept of peacekeeping was developed based on a creative reading of the Charter.[8] More recently the UN has promoted the rule of law (ROL) within nations as a means of promoting peace.[9] The focus of this chapter is on a new proposal, a strategy the UNSC could adopt in support of the intra-state ROL. The UNSC, both as a body and in the individual capacity of members, can model law compliance with respect to the use of force. To 'model law compliance' refers to the rules, norms and principles governing the UNSC and its members. The UNSC is an entity established under international law, and subject to treaty rules, customary international law rules, general principles, *jus cogens* norms and its own procedural rules.[10]

The UNSC has a good deal of discretion in fulfilling its mandate under the Charter, but does have limitations in law outside the Charter. For example, with respect to authorising the use of force, in addition to limits within the Charter, the UNSC has a duty to respect the general principles of necessity and proportionality.[11] These principles apply to all lawful coercive action in international relations.[12] Other law-imposed restrictions found outside the Charter include human rights and international humanitarian law and the structural rules of international law, such as the rules on sources, jurisdiction, interpretation and responsibility.[13] The most important structural rule for states may be the general principle of non-intervention.[14]

The value of complying with this law should be self-evident. Even beyond the more intangible benefits of law compliance, failing to adhere to the law governing resort to armed force has been linked to failure in accomplishing the very purpose of using force. The principle of necessity, for example, restricts resort to the use of force to situations where it can be expected to accomplish the military objective. Sending under-resourced, poorly trained peace enforcement missions into armed conflict hostilities will predictably fail to accomplish the purpose. Thus authorising such a mission conflicts with the principle of necessity. Since the end of the Cold War, the UNSC has authorised numerous peace enforcement missions without taking the principle of necessity into consideration. In some cases, such as Srebrenica and Rwanda, the mission not only failed to accomplish the purpose, but also became more violent and unstable than before peacekeepers arrived.[15]

Modelling law compliance also means that, in addition to the UNSC as a whole, individual members of the UNSC, especially the five permanent members, should support the international law that governs UNSC action. When members defy the law, it not only weakens the prohibition on the use of force, it may retard attempts to build respect for law in other contexts. By contrast, following the law on the use of force has multiple benefits, from effectuating that law's purpose to setting an example of respect. Compliance with international law on the use of force is more closely associated with positive social outcomes over time than violations of the law. Using unlawful military force even to stop a tyrant's use of excessive force against peaceful demonstrators has had counterproductive results. Diplomacy, targeted sanctions, positive incentives supporting good governance and the ROL, have all produced superior results at far lower costs, certainly in the long run.

Much of the scholarship on the use of force being produced in western states with advanced military forces focuses on re-interpreting UN Charter rules to relax the prohibition on resort to force. These arguments for the right to use force for arms control, regime change and human rights protection are often based on the false assumption that force is effective for achieving these and other desiderata.[16] By contrast, my argument is that, rather than relax the law against violence, strengthening and extending it will support the use of alternative solutions.

Rather than 'paralysing' states or the UNSC, the limits on force channel action into non-violent and more successful avenues.

The chapter begins with a brief look at how promoting the ROL promotes peace. It continues by considering how the UNSC as a body can better adhere to international law and model law compliance, and how, in addition to the UNSC as a whole, individual UNSC members can support the ROL by demonstrating greater respect for legal obligations. The chapter's final section reviews practical and politically attainable ways to improve UNSC and UNSC member compliance with law in the interest of promoting the ROL more generally.

1 The peace–law interconnection

Law is the principal alternative to violence for settling disputes and ordering societies.[17] When the ROL prevails, violence does not. Definitions of the ROL are premised on these understandings. A handbook on the ROL prepared for US military lawyers describes the ROL as existing when seven criteria are met: the state monopolises the use of force in the resolution of disputes; individuals are secure in their persons and property; the state is itself bound by law and does not act arbitrarily; the law can be readily determined and is stable enough to allow individuals to plan their affairs; individuals have meaningful access to an effective and impartial legal system; the state protects basic human rights; and individuals rely on the existence of legal institutions and the content of law in the conduct of their daily lives.[18]

The UNSG provides a similar description of what 'rule of law' means:

> The 'rule of law' … refers to a principle of governance in which all persons, institutions and entities, public and private, including the State itself, are accountable to laws that are publicly promulgated, equally enforced, and independently adjudicated, and which are consistent with international human rights norms and standards. It requires, as well, measures to ensure adherence to the principles of supremacy of law, equality before the law, accountability to the law, fairness in the application of the law, separation of powers, participation in decision-making, legal certainty, avoidance of arbitrariness and procedural and legal transparency.[19]

Thus, if a robust ROL is established, the use of violence will by definition be the exceptional and not the normal means of establishing social order.

In some cases, it will be necessary to first end high levels of violence or actual armed conflict before the ROL can take hold to supplant violence. Once sufficient order is established, however, preserving the peace generally requires rule-of-law institutions. The argument here is that order – particularly the absence of armed conflict – is essential to the existence of the ROL, but also that the ROL is a key tool in the prevention of armed conflict. Attempting to impose order or governance institutions through external military intervention is unlikely to succeed.[20] Empirical research indicates that military intervention and targeted assassination can undermine the conditions required for peace.[21] Evidence also shows that, like the promotion of good governance and human rights, terrorism suppression and arms control is more likely to be successful by using means other than the use of force.[22]

Such uses of military force and violence are also prominent acts of law violation; they can incite revenge, disrupt institutions, destroy infrastructure and the natural environment, and cause deaths and injury – including long-lasting mental health injury.[23] The use of military force by permanent members of the UNSC in defiance of the law sends a message that disrespect of the law is acceptable conduct even on the part of states that benefit most from the current legal order.

Military intervention since the end of the Cold War has often been justified as supporting democracy, human rights and arms control. As will be discussed in the next section, however, international law does not generally permit the use of force in pursuit of these goals. Nevertheless, the US, Britain and Australia claimed to be enforcing international law – specifically, UNSC resolutions – when they invaded Iraq in 2003. Other permanent members and a majority of rotating members rejected the claim that the invasion was lawful. The rhetoric around a possible attack on Syria in 2013 was even more counter-intuitive. In order to enforce the Chemical Weapons Convention,[24] France, the US and several other states announced their intention to use force in violation of the UN Charter.

Not only does such conduct defy common sense, the results of such interventions demonstrate how inappropriate the use of military force is for advancing complex social goals such as promoting the ROL, enforcing treaty obligations, protecting human rights and establishing effective government institutions. In addition, as explained above, social science research indicates that this sort of external intervention is ineffective in realising the stated aims of the interveners. Such intervention is also associated with moral hazard. Invading to assist rebels in overthrowing a government invites rebels in other states to do what it takes to create enough sympathy for the North Atlantic Treaty Organization (NATO) or the west to come to the rescue.[25] This can be seen in the case of Syria. After NATO intervened to assist rebels fighting to overthrow the government of Libya in 2011, government opponents in Syria abandoned non-violence and began fighting to try to oust the government – something they were unlikely to accomplish without outside assistance.

2 Security Council legal obligations

2.1 The law governing Security Council authorisations of force[26]

For some decades international law scholars have debated whether or not the UNSC had a duty to comply with general international law when acting within its area of authority over peace and security. The argument for interpreting the Charter as leaving the UNSC unfettered in peace and security matters is based principally on the lack of any express provision listing restrictions. The argument gained support from the ICJ's advisory opinion on Namibia in the *South West Africa* case.[27] The ICJ cited a statement of the UNSG that 'the Members of the [UN] have conferred upon the Security Council powers commensurate with its responsibility for the maintenance of peace and security. The only limitations are the fundamental principles and purposes found in Chapter I of the Charter.'[28]

The weight of authority is today on the side of seeing the UNSC as having considerable discretion with respect to peace and security matters, but not complete discretion. Important principles do circumscribe UNSC action.[29] Article 24(2) of the Charter states that 'in discharging [its] duties the Security Council shall act in accordance with the Purposes and Principles of the United Nations'. Chapter I of the Charter sets out the purposes and principles, including in Article 1(1): to bring 'about by peaceful means, and in conformity with the principles of justice and international law, adjustment or settlement of international disputes'. Article 1(1) could be seen as linking 'conformity' with international law as a requirement for the settlements reached to end international disputes rather than general action by the UNSC. On the other hand, Article 1(1) plus Article 24 could be read together as requiring that the UNSC comply generally with relevant international law.

A more persuasive argument respecting the UNSC's binding obligations under international law beyond the Charter was made by Elihu Lauterpacht, sitting as judge ad hoc in the *Bosnia* v. *Serbia* case: 'one only has to state the proposition thus – that a Security Council Resolution may even require participation in genocide – for its unacceptability to be apparent'.[30] Judge Weeramantry has also expressed the view that the history of the UN Charter provides evidence that UNSC powers 'must be exercised in accordance with well-established principles of international law'.[31]

The International Criminal Tribunal for Yugoslavia (ICTY), which the UNSC established as an exercise of its authority to take measures to respond to armed conflict, determined that the UNSC did have the authority under the Charter to establish courts. The ICTY went on to say:

> It is clear ... that the Security Council plays a pivotal role and exercises a very wide discretion under this article. But this does not mean that its powers are unlimited.... In any case, neither the text nor the spirit of the Charter conceives of the Security Council as *legibus solutus* (unbound by law).[32]

UNSC decisions to authorise the use of force in international relations are limited by the Charter's terms in Articles 39 and 42. These reference the UNSC's right to act to 'restore international peace and security'. At the 2005 World Summit in New York, UN members agreed that the UNSC may also act in situations of severe humanitarian crisis.[33] Beyond the Charter, the UNSC is limited by the principles of necessity and proportionality – not only in how force is used, but in the decision to resort to force in the first place.[34] Thus the ICJ held in a 2003 decision: 'whether the response to the [armed] attack is lawful depends on observance of the criteria of the necessity and the proportionality of the measures taken'.[35]

The principle of necessity has two components: resort to force must be a last resort and it must offer a reasonable prospect of success in accomplishing the military objective.[36] If alternatives to military force have yet to be exhausted or if the military predicts the resort to force will have little or no chance of succeeding, resort to military force is unlawful. Even if resort to force meets these conditions, the principle of proportionality requires that the cost in lives lost and property destroyed not be disproportionate to the value of the military objective.[37]

These legal principles are reflected in a 2004 UN High-level Panel report, which set down guidelines for the UNSC drawing on the Just War Doctrine.[38] According to these guidelines, before authorising the use of force the UNSC must take into consideration: the seriousness of the purpose in using force; whether the purpose will be proper for resort to force; whether force is a last resort; whether the means used will be proportional to the purpose; and whether the negative consequences are balanced compared with the purpose.[39]

Peters explains the policy involved in finding the UNSC subject to law:

> Interrelated considerations of legitimacy and effectiveness suggest acknowledging legal limits for the Security Council. The Council's behavior is morally consistent and thus credible only if the Council itself satisfies the standards it imposes on its members.... Members are likely to comply with what they perceive as lawful decisions. If one does not concede to the members the authority to contest a flagrantly illegal act of the Council with legal arguments, they will try to sneak out secretly, and simply obstruct Security Council resolutions.[40]

2.2 Security Council corporate failures[41]

Soon after the UNSC began meeting in the 1940s, it deployed truce observers and then peacekeeping missions despite the lack of express provision for such initiatives in the Charter.[42] Nevertheless, these missions had consent from all the parties to the conflict, remained neutral in the conflict, deployed only after a ceasefire was in effect and used force only for personal defence.[43] These four criteria came to characterise 'traditional peacekeeping', which drew its legality from general international law, especially consent, as opposed to the UN Charter.[44] At the end of the Cold War, however, the UNSC began to authorise missions that departed significantly from traditional peacekeeping. The new missions have often been deficient in meeting the requirements of international law on the use of force. The poor results of these deficient missions may be compared with the success of traditional peacekeeping. Curiously, the UNSC, rather than revising peacekeeping policy to recapture past success, has authorised ever more aggressive and legally questionable missions, as well as the intervention in the Libyan civil war.

Peace enforcement

The UNSC's aggressive new missions have been authorised under Chapter VII of the UN Charter, permitting 'all necessary means' to achieve the UNSC's goals. These goals, however, as in the cases of Haiti, Bosnia, Rwanda, Congo and so many other places, are about establishing better governance through the use of offensive force. As Russell Buchan observes, '[s]pecifically, peacekeeping missions are now being deployed by the UN in order to promote respect for democracy, human rights and the rule of law'.[45] The rationale for this new style of mission, he argues, is 'the normative commitment of the UN to promoting respect for liberal values and a correlative weakening of its concern for protecting state sovereignty and, in particular, respecting the right to non-intervention in domestic political affairs'.[46]

This rationale is highly problematic for promoting the good order associated with the ROL. First, the UNSC gives little indication that it applies the principle of necessity in terms of assessing alternatives to force and the likelihood of success. Peace enforcement missions rarely have the resources UN planners say they need. Even if they did, outside intervention of this type has little chance of re-organising societies for the purposes of establishing democracy, respect for human rights or the ROL.

Perhaps of even greater concern is the evidential finding set out in the *Human Security Report 2012* that when outside militaries intervene, civil wars tend to be twice as deadly as without external intervention.[47] Another researcher has found that intervention on the side of rebels increases the lethality of a civil war by 192 per cent.[48] Yet, there is no indication that the UNSC considers such information in authorising peace enforcement missions.

Force Intervention Brigade

The poor record of peace enforcement supports an argument for a return to traditional peacekeeping. Instead, in the midst of one of the most unsuccessful UN efforts of all – the peace enforcement mission to the long-running armed conflict in the Democratic Republic of the Congo (DRC) – the UNSC authorised a new type of operation, called a 'Force Intervention Brigade' (FIB). The brigade has authority to use offensive force to 'neutralize and disarm' fighters in the DRC.[49] The authorising resolution, however devotes more space to emphasising that troop-contributing countries (TCCs) must fulfil their promises than to the details respecting what the FIB will do. The troop-contribution agreements are actually appended to the resolution. The UNSC apparently expects the challenge of finding sufficient troops and resources to be even more serious in the case of the FIB than peace enforcement.

In the short run, the FIB did push some of the DRC's most brutal rebel fighters, the M23, out of the eastern town of Goma.[50] On the other hand, no sooner had the FIB provided a military advantage to government forces than the government walked out of peace talks.[51] Three months later, no further attempts were underway at achieving a political solution, despite the fact that all experts agree peace will only come to the DRC through a political settlement, not an intervention force of a few thousand foreign troops. Nicholas Kulish and Somini Sengupta have pointed out that '[a]nalysts warn that the defeat of a single group like the M23, which was plagued by internal dissent and weakened even before the latest offensive, is no reason for triumphalism'.[52] Intense pressure was also put on Rwanda, together with a 'handsome' financial package from the World Bank,[53] as part of the strategy for getting the M23 to relinquish Goma. The prospects for peace in the DRC seem slim, despite the FIB and the additional 17,000 troops in the DRC at a cost of US$1.5 billion dollars per year.

Six months after the deployment of the FIB to the DRC, Fiona Blyth reached two critical conclusions that are worth repeating here:

> The UN is authorized to take proactive military action under Chapter VII, but the articles are interpreted differently by troop contributors, some of whom are reluctant to acknowledge that Chapter VII supports the use of force beyond self defense. Peacekeepers can already take action to disrupt rebel activity through preemptive operations … but it requires political will.
>
> […]
>
> The deployment of an intervention brigade should not be used as a substitute for a longer-term strategy of security sector reform and a review of the force requirements of the mission.[54]

Force authorisation in Libya

In March 2011, the UNSC authorised the imposition of a no-fly zone to protect civilians from the Libyan government. About 172 peaceful demonstrators had been killed in the capital, Tripoli, in February 2011. As soon as the resolution passed, NATO forces began a campaign far in excess of a no-fly zone. NATO forces came to the aid of government opposition forces driving Colonel Gaddafi from Tripoli and to his death at the hands of a mob. Despite the clear violation of international humanitarian law (IHL) in the killing of Gaddafi while a detainee, no attempt has been made by the Government of Libya or NATO governments to bring any of the perpetrators to justice. The killing was filmed by many, providing much better evidence of who the suspects are than has often been the case in mass war crimes trials, such as those organised for Rwanda and the former Yugoslavia.

When challenged that the UNSC resolution did not authorise regime change, only a no-fly zone to protect civilians, the answer has been that the only effective way to protect civilians was to remove Gaddafi from power.[55] This is, at best, an unsupported extrapolation from the text of the resolution and an unsupported assumption about how to protect civilians. As a matter of law, a waiver of the otherwise prevailing rule should be narrowly construed.

Beyond the debate on whether NATO exceeded its authority under Resolution 1973 (2011), there is the question of whether the UNSC should have even authorised a no-fly zone. The debate on the Libya crisis omitted discussion of the necessity of using force.[56] According to Hugh Roberts, writing at the time of the Libya intervention, the claim that the international community had no alternative to military intervention was false. Roberts noted that an 'active, practical, non-violent alternative' had been floated but rejected, on the grounds that only a no-fly zone and military intervention employing 'all necessary measures' could end the regime's repression and protect civilians.[57] However, in his words, 'many argued that the way to protect civilians was not to intensify the conflict by intervention on one side or the other, but to end it by securing a ceasefire followed by political negotiations'.[58]

The International Crisis Group advocated the formation of a contact group to negotiate among the Libyan factions. The African Union (AU) offered high-level mediation, which Colonel Gaddafi accepted, but the rebels and their western sponsors rejected.

NATO's intervention was anything but a last resort. Nor was success a predictable outcome. US President Obama spoke of Gaddafi going, but did not say how removing him would assist civilians. Richard Falk predicted that the Libyan intervention would follow the disastrous fate of so many interventions in the region.[59] He was correct. The fighting resulted in an estimated 30,000 lives lost. Libya has been the scene of lawlessness, militant activity and vicious human rights violations, especially aimed at minorities and immigrants from sub-Saharan Africa. Some parts of the country are attempting to secede.[60] By 2014, the country was clearly again in a civil war. The results follow closely the data reviewed above on how interventions have fared.

2.3 Security Council member failures

The failures of the UNSC just reviewed have serious implications for the ROL. Permanent members of the UNSC have committed even more egregious violations. While UNSC members acting without UNSC authorisation are independent from the UNSC, as prominent and privileged UNSC members their actions in violation of the law are highly visible. Attempts to reform the veto and other aspects of UNSC practice have failed, but it is within the realm of the possible to demand compliance with international law on the use of force as the price for permanent member status. Looking just at the period since the end of the Cold War, the most significant violations of the *jus ad bellum* include NATO's 78-day bombing campaign of Serbia during the 1999 Kosovo crisis;[61] the 2003 invasion of Iraq by the US, UK, Australia and Poland;[62] the ongoing US campaign of targeted killing with military force, often drones, beyond armed conflict zones;[63] and the 2014 Russian intervention in Crimea to support secession from Ukraine.[64] Human rights organisations have also criticised China's and Russia's excessive use of force in internal conflict situations. Russia used excessive force in responding to Georgia's unlawful attack on Russian troops in South Ossetia in 2008.

In addition to actual violations of the prohibition on the use of force, the US has taken public positions in conflict with the UN Charter. Two recent dramatic examples involve threats to use force in Syria and in Iran.[65] US Ambassador to the UN, Samantha Power, was asked in an interview in September 2013 whether a US attack on Syria would be 'legal'.[66] She answered that it would be a 'legitimate, necessary, and proportionate response'.[67] She did not say it would be lawful but nevertheless lobbied the US Congress to authorise the President to attack.

3 Improving law compliance at the Security Council

As discussed above, the UNSC is already obligated to follow relevant, general international law in addition to specific UN Charter rules in fulfilling its mandate to preserve peace and security in the world. Unlike amending the veto power or other politically difficult change, improving UNSC compliance with the law is achievable through informal measures. The permanent members of the UNSC are unlikely to initiate such steps. The rotating members, by contrast, have every interest in leaving the UNSC more securely anchored in the world's law at the end of their terms. Rotating members can continue to work for reform after their terms end, but while members of the UNSC they have greater opportunity to set agendas, make proposals and negotiate. It is difficult to think of a more important legacy to leave than reform of the UNSC through promoting adherence to law as a path to peace.

A tangible step towards law compliance could take the form of a UNSC resolution or presidential statement acknowledging the obligation to comply with the general principles of necessity and proportionality, as well as the rules of the Charter. The UNSC's rules of procedure could be amended to include consideration of necessity and proportionality. When deciding to authorise force or to assess an unauthorised resort to force, the UNSC could require as an additional procedural matter a public statement of the authority in the Charter for any decision taken, as well as how the decision meets the requirements of necessity and proportionality.[68]

A number of other measures are available if needed to move the UNSC to publicly acknowledge its obligations and to reveal how they have been complied with in particular cases. The UNSC may request advisory opinions from the ICJ respecting aspects of general international law relevant to its conduct.[69] The UNSC has only been involved in one advisory opinion, concerning Namibia.[70] If the UNSC were hesitant, the UN General Assembly (UNGA) could also request such an opinion, as it did in the *Certain Expenses* case, which specifically dealt with UNSC authority.[71]

The UN also has extensive education and training capacity. The *jus ad bellum* might be an unusual area of instruction for the UN University or other programmes, but the rules on resort to force are just as critical as arms control, IHL and human rights law, which are regularly taught. Rotating members of the UNSC could initiate a required programme for all UNSC member staff to receive an immersion in objective, solid courses on the Charter, rules of customary international law and general principles.

International law has also always relied on its 'publicists' to inform government ministers, courts and the public about the content of international law.[72] A good deal of writing in the area of *jus ad bellum* seems more supportive of government policy than objective analysis of international law. This problem seems especially prevalent among international law scholars based in the US and Britain. UNSC members, particularly rotating members, could make greater demands on international law scholars, insisting that they ground their work in international legal authority. Preferring scholarship that is independent of government policy could help create a virtuous cycle of better scholarship in support of better outcomes at the UNSC.

Notes

1 With thanks for research assistance to Sean Parish and Sarah Bosha.
2 *Charter of the United Nations*, opened for signature 26 June 1945, 1 UNTS 16 (entered into force 24 October 1945), preamble.
3 Ibid., art. 2(4).
4 Ibid., arts 39–42.
5 Ibid., art. 55.
6 Ibid., art. 99.
7 M. Cherif Bassiouni, *The Pursuit of International Criminal Justice: A World Study on Conflicts, Victimization, and Post-conflict Justice* (Antwerp, Intersentia, 2010), p. 79. See also Peter Wallensteen, 'What's in a War? Insights from a Conflict Data Program', in Mary Ellen O'Connell (ed.), *What is War? An Investigation in the Wake of 9/11* (Leiden, Brill, 2012), pp. 261–72.
8 Nigel D. White, 'Peacekeeping or War-fighting?' in Nigel D. White and Christian Henderson (eds), *Research Handbook on Conflict and Security Law: Jus Ad Bellum, Jus In Bello, Jus Post Bellum* (Cheltenham, Edward Elgar, 2013), pp. 572–97, 572.
9 United Nations Development Programme, *Strengthening the Rule of Law in Crisis-affected and Fragile Situations 2012–2015* (New York, United Nations, 2011): www.undp.org/content/dam/rbas/doc/Crisis%20prevention/Global%20Programme%20Phase%20II%20-%20FINAL.pdf.
10 *Reparations for Injuries Suffered in the Service of the United Nations*, Advisory Opinion [1949] ICJ Rep. 174, 182. See also UN Doc. S/96/Rev. 7 (1983), *Provisional Rules of Procedure of the Security Council*. However, when the UN acts within the territory of member states, some national law will be relevant to UN personnel in addition to the international law under which they operate.
11 For a detailed discussion of the principles of necessity and proportionality in the law on resort to force, see Judith Gardam, *Necessity, Proportionality and the Use of Force by States* (Cambridge, Cambridge University Press, 2004). See also UN Doc. A/59/565 (2 December 2004), *A More Secure World: Our Shared Responsibility, Report of the High-level Panel on Threats, Challenges and Change*, para. 207.
12 *Legality of the Threat or Use of Nuclear Weapons*, Advisory Opinion [1996] ICJ Rep. 226 ('Nuclear Advisory Opinion'), in which the ICJ referred to necessity and proportionality as rules of customary international law. See also Mary Ellen O'Connell, 'Jus Cogens, International Law's Higher Ethical Norms', in Donald Earl Childress III (ed.), *The Role of Ethics in International Law* (New York, Cambridge University Press, 2012), pp. 78–98, 84.
13 Anne Peters, 'Article 25', in Bruno Simma, et al. (eds), *The United Nations Charter: A Commentary* (Oxford, Oxford University Press, 2012), pp. 787, 821, 826–7. See also Louise Doswald-Beck, *Human Rights in Times of Conflict and Terrorism* (Oxford, Oxford Publishing, 2011).

14 See GA Res. 25/2625 (24 October 1970), *Declaration on Principles of International Law Concerning Friendly Relations and Co-operation Among States in Accordance with the Charter of the United Nations*, para. (c). See also Brad R. Roth, *Sovereign Equality and Moral Disagreement, Premises of a Pluralist International Legal Order* (Oxford and New York, Oxford University Press, 2011), pp. 7–8; and UN Charter, art. 2(7), which restricts interference by the UN in a state's internal affairs.

15 See UN Doc. A/54/549 (15 November 1999), *Report of the Secretary-General Pursuant to General Assembly Resolution 53/55* (concerning the Srebrenica massacre); and UN Doc. S/1999/1257 (16 December 1999), *Report of the Independent Inquiry into the Actions of the United Nations During the 1994 Genocide in Rwanda.*

16 See, e.g. Daniel Bethlehem, 'Self-defense against an Imminent or Actual Armed Attack by Non-state Actors' (2012) 106 *American Journal of International Law* 770–7 (advocating a significant expansion of the right to resort to major military force in the counter-terrorism context). See also Lee Feinstein and Anne-Marie Slaughter, 'A Duty to Prevent' (January/February 2004) *Foreign Affairs* 136–50 (advocating that organisations other than the UNSC have the power to authorise military intervention for such purposes as arms control).

17 Elizabeth Zoller, *Peacetime Unilateral Remedies: An Analysis of Countermeasures* (New York, Transnational Publishers, 1984), p. 4.

18 Center for Law and Military Operations and Joint Force Judge Advocate, *Rule of Law Handbook: A Practitioner's Guide for Judge Advocates* (Charlottesville, Center for Law and Military Operations and Joint Force Judge Advocate, 2007), p. 6.

19 UN Doc. S/2004/616 (23 August 2004), *Report of the Secretary-General: The Rule of Law and Transitional Justice in Conflict and Post-conflict Societies*, para. 6.

20 See, e.g. Goran Peic and Dan Reiter, 'Foreign-Imposed Regime Change, State Power and Civil War Onset, 1920–2004' (2011) 41(3) *British Journal of Political Science* 453–75; Andrew J. Enterline and J. Michael Greig, 'Beacons of Hope? The Impact of Imposed Democracy on Regional Peace, Democracy, and Prosperity' (2005) 67(4) *Journal of Politics* 1075–98; Andrew J. Enterline and J. Michael Greig, 'Perfect Storms? Political Instability in Imposed Polities and the Futures of Iraq and Afghanistan' (2008) 52(6) *Journal of Conflict Resolution* 880–915; Alexander B. Downes and Jonathan Monten, 'Forced to Be Free? Why Foreign-Imposed Regime Change Rarely Leads to Democratization' (2013) 37(4) *International Security* 90–131; and Bruce Bueno de Mesquita and George W. Downs, 'Intervention and Democracy' (2006) 60(3) *International Organization* 627–49.

21 Ibid.

22 With respect to terrorism, see Seth G. Jones and Martin C. Libicki, *How Terrorist Groups End: Lessons for Countering Al Qa'ida* (2008): www.rand.org/pubs/monographs/2008/RAND_MG741-1.pdf; and Louise Richardson, *What Terrorists Want: Understanding the Enemy, Containing the Threat* (New York, Random House, 2006). As for arms control, the example of nuclear weapons is telling. Since the adoption of the Nuclear Non-Proliferation Treaty in 1970 (*Treaty on the Non-Proliferation of Nuclear Weapons*, opened for signature 1 July 1968, 729 UNTS 161 (entered into force 5 March 1970)), a number of states, including Brazil, Libya, South Africa and Ukraine, have ended nuclear weapons programmes as a result of diplomacy. We have no examples of states ending programmes because of the use of force, such as Israel's attack on Iraq in 1981.

23 Mary Ellen O'Connell, 'Review of Thomas Weiss, Humanitarian Intervention: Ideas in Action' (2009) 7 *Perspectives in Politics* 712–13, 712.

24 *Convention on the Prohibition of the Development, Production, Stockpiling and Use of Chemical Weapons and on their Destruction*, opened for signature 13 January 1993, 1974 UNTS 45 (entered into force 29 April 1997).

25 Alan J. Kuperman, 'The Moral Hazard of Humanitarian Intervention: Lessons from the Balkans' (2008) 52 *International Studies Quarterly* 49–80. See also Timothy W.

Crawford and Alan J. Kuperman, *Gambling on Humanitarian Intervention: Moral Hazard, Rebellion, and Civil War* (Abingdon, Routledge, 2006).

26 This section draws on ideas presented in Mary Ellen O'Connell, 'The United Nations Security Council and the Authorization of Force: Renewing the Council through Law Reform', in Niels Blokker and Nico Schrijver (eds), *The Security Council and the Use of Force: Theory and Reality, A Need for Change?* (Leiden, Martinus Nijhoff Publishers, 2005), pp. 47–63.

27 *Legal Consequences for States of the Continued Presence of South Africa in Namibia (South West Africa) Notwithstanding Security Council Resolution 276 (1970)*, Advisory Opinion [1971] ICJ Rep. 16, 52 ('*South West Africa* case').

28 Ibid.

29 Peters, 'Article 25', pp. 828–33.

30 *Application of the Convention on the Prevention and Punishment of the Crime of Genocide (Bosnia and Herzegovina* v. *Yugoslavia (Serbia and Montenegro))*, Provisional Measures [1993] ICJ Rep. 325, 444 ('*Bosnian Genocide* case') (Separate Opinion of Judge Lauterpacht).

31 *Questions of Interpretation and Application of the 1971 Montreal Convention Arising from the Aerial Incident at Lockerbie (Libya* v. *UK; Libya* v. *US)*, Provisional Measures [1992] ICJ Rep. 114, 175 (Dissenting Opinion of Judge Weeramantry).

32 See *Prosecutor* v. *Dusko Tadic*, Appeals Chamber of the ICTY, IT-94-1 (2 October 1995), para. 28.

33 GA Res. 60/1 (24 October 2005), *2005 World Summit Outcome*, p. 30.

34 In addition to the UN Charter, the rules on the use of force have been construed in a series of ICJ decisions: *Corfu Channel (United Kingdom of Great Britain and Northern Ireland* v. *Albania)*, Judgment [1949] ICJ Rep. 244; *Military and Paramilitary Activities in and against Nicaragua (Nicaragua* v. *United States of America)*, Judgment [1986] ICJ Rep. 14; Nuclear Advisory Opinion; *Oil Platforms (Islamic Republic of Iran* v. *United States of America)*, Judgment [2003] ICJ Rep. 161, paras 61–4 ('*The Oil Platforms* case'); *Legal Consequences of the Construction of a Wall in the Occupied Palestinian Territory*, Advisory Opinion [2004] ICJ Rep. 136, paras 33–4 (Separate Opinion of Judge Higgins); *Armed Activities on the Territory of the Congo (Democratic Republic of Congo* v. *Uganda)*, Judgment [2005] ICJ Rep. 168, paras 146 and 301; *Bosnian Genocide Case*, Judgment [2007] ICJ Rep. 43, para. 391.

35 *The Oil Platforms* case, para. 74. The case concerned self-defence, but necessity and proportionality apply to all coercive action taken on the basis of a permissive legal rule.

36 O'Connell, 'The Prohibition of Force', p. 89.

37 Peters, 'Article 25', p. 820. The author confirms that the UNSC is bound to respect the principle of proportionality in authorising resort to force. She does not discuss necessity *per se*, but does say of proportionality, '[a] decision is proportionate if it is an appropriate and necessary means to serve the stated end'.

38 UN Doc. A/59/565 (2 December 2004), *A More Secure World: Our Shared Responsibility – Report of the High-level Panel on Threats, Challenges and Change*. It is important to point out, however, that unlike the Just War Doctrine, international law binds the UNSC, and does not just guide it. Arguably, therefore, the High-level Panel report should have included reference to the UNSC's binding legal obligations.

39 Ibid., para. 207.

40 Peters, 'Article 25', p. 810.

41 For discussion of several issues addressed in this section, see Heathcote's chapter in this collection.

42 Traditional peacekeeping was famously argued to be on the basis of 'Chapter VI ½' because it fell between the strictly peaceful measures of Chapter VI and the use of troops provided for in Chapter VII.

43 White, 'Peacekeeping', pp. 572–83.

44 Ibid., p. 574. Cf. Heathcote's chapter in this collection.

45 Russell Buchan, *International Law and the Construction of the Liberal Peace* (Portland, OR, Hart Publishing, 2013), pp. 1–2.
46 Ibid., quoting Outi Korhonen, Jutta Gras and Katja Creutz, *International Post-conflict Situations: New Challenges for Co-operative Governance* (Helsinki, Erik Castrén Institute Research Reports 18/2006), p. 3. Cf. Roth, *Sovereign Equality*, who argues that a central purpose of international law is to provide for the diversity of states through its principle of non-intervention.
47 Human Security Project, *Human Security Report 2012* (London, Oxford University Press, 2012), pp. 157–61.
48 Kristine Eck, 'From Armed Conflict to War: Ethnic Mobilization and Conflict Intensification' (2009) 53 *International Studies Quarterly* 369–88.
49 SC Res. 2098 (28 March 2013). For discussion of the Force Intervention Brigade, see Oswald's chapter in this collection.
50 Nicholas Kulish and Somini Sengupta, 'New UN Brigade's Aggressive Stance in Africa Brings Success, and Risks', *New York Times* (New York), 12 November 2013, A10.
51 Ibid.
52 Ibid.
53 Ibid.
54 Fiona Blyth, 'Too Risk-Averse, UN Peacekeepers in the DRC Get New Mandate and More Challenges', *Global Observatory (International Peace Institute)*, 10 April 2013: www.theglobalobservatory.org/analysis/475-too-risk-averse-un-peacekeepers-in-the-drc-get-new-mandate-and-more-challenges.html.
55 Hugh Roberts, 'Who Said Ghaddafi Had to Go?' (2011) 33(22) *London Review of Books*: www.lrb.co.uk/v33/n22/hugh-roberts/who-said-gaddafi-had-to-go.
56 Mary Ellen O'Connell, 'Remarks, Revolution and Intervention in the Middle East ASIL Proceedings' (2011) 105 *American Society of International Law Proceedings* 555–76, 563–4.
57 Roberts, 'Who Said Ghaddafi had to go?'
58 Ibid.
59 See Richard Falk, *Can Humanitarian Intervention ever be Humanitarian?* (4 August 2011): mwcnews.net/focus/editorial/12577-humanitarian-intervention.html?tmpl=component.
60 'Libya Threatens to Bomb North Korean Flagged Tanker', *BBC* (online), 8 March 2014: www.bbc.com/news/world-africa-26495625.
61 Bruno Simma, 'NATO, the UN and the Use of Force: Legal Aspects' (1999) 10 *European Journal of International Law* 1–22.
62 Sean Murphy, 'Assessing the Legality of Invading Iraq' (2004) 92 *Georgetown Law Journal* 173–257.
63 Christine Gray, 'Targeted Killings: Recent US Attempts to Create a Legal Framework' (2013) 66(1) *Current Legal Problems* 1–32.
64 See Bill Neely and M. Alex Johnson, 'Russian Troops Flood Crimea: Ukraine Warns of War', *NBC News* (online), 1 March 2014: www.nbcnews.com/storyline/ukraine-crisis/russian-forces-flood-crimea-ukraine-warns-war-n42066.
65 Ewen MacAskill, 'Obama not Bluffing Over Iran Military Threat, Biden Tells Aipac', *Guardian* (online), 5 March 2013: www.theguardian.com/world/2013/mar/04/biden-aipac-speech-iran-threat/print.
66 'US Ambassador Samantha Power Presses for Strike On Syria', *National Public Radio*, 9 September 2013: www.npr.org/2013/09/09/220586231/u-s-ambassador-susan-rice-makes-case-for-strikes-on-syria.
67 Ibid.
68 Anna Spain, 'The UN Security Council's Duty to Decide' (2013) 4 *Harvard National Security Journal* 320–84, 352. The author provides an analysis of why the UNSC is already obligated under international law to provide reasons for its decisions.

69 Peters, 'Article 25', pp. 834–6.
70 *The South West Africa* case.
71 *Certain Expenses of the United Nations (Article 17, Paragraph 2 of the Charter)*, Advisory Opinion [1962] ICJ Rep. 151.
72 *Statute of the International Court of Justice*, 1 UNTS 993 (entered into force 18 April 1946), art. 38(1) lists the three primary and two secondary sources of international law: treaties, customary international law, general principles of law, judicial decisions and the 'teachings of the most highly qualified publicists'.

19 Protecting responsibly

The Security Council and the use of force for human protection purposes

Alex J. Bellamy

Introduction

Since the turn of the century, the United Nations (UN) Security Council (UNSC) has become gradually more proactive in relation to the protection of civilians in armed conflict. This coincides with the adoption of the concept of the 'responsibility to protect' (R2P) by the 2005 World Summit, the largest-ever gathering of heads of state and government, and its reaffirmation by the UNSC in Resolution 1674 (2006),[1] Resolution 1894 (2009),[2] Resolution 2150 (2014)[3] and a Rwandan Presidential Statement in 2013,[4] as well as its application in relation to situations in Darfur (Sudan), African Great Lakes, Libya, Cote d'Ivoire, South Sudan, Somalia, Yemen, Mali, Central African Republic (CAR) and Syria. From hesitant beginnings in Sierra Leone and the Democratic Republic of the Congo (DRC), the UNSC has gradually moved human protection to the centre of UN peacekeeping, with a majority of its ongoing missions having protection mandates.[5] These mandates were established under Chapter VII of the UN Charter and permit the use of 'all necessary measures' to protect civilians.

This trend towards human protection as a core purpose of the UNSC and a more robust approach to protection accelerated markedly in early 2011. Since that time, the UNSC has authorised the use of force to protect populations in Libya and Cote d'Ivoire, which in both cases resulted in a change of government; mandated a UN mission (MINUSMA)[6] to assist the government of Mali to protect the population from Tuareg/Islamist militia alongside a French deployment that has applied extensive coercive force; established an international intervention brigade in the DRC mandated to use force to protect civilians against M23 and other militia, but also ostensibly intended as an armed deterrent to Rwandan interference in the country's east;[7] and authorised a UN mission (MINUSCA)[8] to use all means necessary (i.e. force if needed) to protect civilians in the CAR.[9] The UNSC also responded quickly to the deterioration of the situation in South Sudan in late 2013 by authorising an unprecedented redeployment of peacekeeping forces to reinforce the beleaguered UNMISS[10] mission there.

These mandates and missions have not been without controversy. Critics complained that UN forces in Cote d'Ivoire and the North Atlantic Treaty Organization (NATO)-led mission over Libya exceeded their mandates to protect civilians and that the UNSC did not hold properly accountable the UN officials and states that assumed responsibility for discharging the UNSC's mandates. Among UN officials and peacekeeping experts, concerns are re-emerging about the UNSC's growing willingness to mandate UN peacekeepers to conduct robust missions involving the use of force to protect populations in semi-hostile environments – a task for which the UN is ill-prepared. At the same time, the capacity of two permanent members of the UNSC to block decisive collective action on Syria – in the face of a clear majority of UNSC members who support such action and sharp criticism from the UN General Assembly (UNGA), where large majorities have voiced concern about the UNSC's inability to take meaningful steps – has prompted a resurgence of interest in the idea of voluntary restraint in the use of the veto.

Two trends seem to be at play here. First, the deepening international consensus on R2P and the protection of civilians in armed conflict is creating new expectations about the UNSC's role in responding to genocide and mass atrocity crimes. Sentiments expressed in the UNGA demonstrate a very clear – if still emerging – expectation that the UNSC has a responsibility to take reasonable measures to protect populations from atrocity crimes. Second, as the UNSC becomes more proactive, and especially as it turns to more robust measures to protect civilians from genocide and atrocity crimes, demands for accountability – in particular the accountability of states acting on UNSC mandates to the UNSC itself – are becoming more significant. These two, seemingly divergent, trends are connected inasmuch as that further deepening of consensus on the use of force or other coercive means for protection purposes – a seemingly necessary response to underlying normative shifts in international society – will require steps to address the question of accountability. With that in mind, this chapter examines the evolution of these two trends in the context of the Syrian crisis and recent discussion about the concept of 'responsibility while protecting' (RWP),[11] proposed by Brazil to remedy problems it saw with the implementation of Resolution 1973 on Libya.[12]

1 Divided counsels: differences between the Security Council and the General Assembly on Syria

It is commonly argued that concerns arising from the implementation of Resolution 1973 on Libya prevented international society from adopting a robust response to the crisis in Syria.[13] The UNSC's inability to find consensus on Syria reflects a combination of concerns specific to that case and issues relating to the use of force for protection purposes more broadly. It resulted in the vetoing of three draft UNSC resolutions by China and Russia. The wider crisis in Syria has been well documented elsewhere and so need not detain us here. This section briefly examines the background to the three vetoed draft resolutions concerning Syria and their content.

The first draft resolution on Syria came to a vote on 4 October 2011.[14] It recalled the Syrian government's 'primary responsibility to protect' its population from war crimes and crimes against humanity,[15] and condemned the systematic violation of human rights and targeting of civilians by the regime. It demanded that the Syrian government take steps to remedy the problem, including by immediately ceasing violations of human rights, ending the use of force against civilians, alleviating the humanitarian situation and allowing safe return for the displaced. It also called for an inclusive 'Syrian-led' political process.[16] The most controversial elements of the draft resolution were paragraphs 9 and 11 which, respectively, called for member states to exercise vigilance and restraint in relation to the types of assistance they provided to the Syrian government and expressed the UNSC's intention to review compliance with the measures within 30 days and adopt further measures under Article 41 of the UN Charter (i.e. sanctions) if necessary. Nine states voted in favour (including African Union (AU) members Gabon and Nigeria), four abstained (Brazil, India, Lebanon and South Africa) and two permanent members voted against (China and Russia).[17] Having achieved the required nine votes, it was the two permanent member vetoes that blocked the draft's adoption.

The second draft resolution was presented for a vote on 4 February 2012,[18] in the context of the suspension of the League of Arab States (Arab League) Monitoring Mission due to the deteriorating situation in Syria and mounting violence there. Its principal purpose was to support the Arab League Plan of Action to which Damascus had agreed on 2 November 2011. Under the Plan, armed and military personnel were to be withdrawn from the streets, Arab League monitors deployed and both foreign reporters and Arab monitors granted unfettered access. The parties to the conflict also agreed to begin a political process. However, the monitoring mission was suspended when it became clear that none of these terms were being honoured.

There were clear signs that this second draft resolution sought to accommodate some of the concerns expressed by more cautious UNSC members. Most notably, the draft condemned 'all violence' regardless of its source, in addition to condemning human rights violations by the Syrian regime.[19] It demanded compliance with the Arab League action plan, called for an inclusive Syrian-led political process, and called upon the Syrian government to cooperate with the Arab League. In a further sign that the new draft was trying to accommodate concerns about the earlier text, it contained no explicit reference to potential Article 41 measures, though it did stipulate that the UNSC would review compliance within 21 days and consider 'further measures' if necessary.[20] This draft secured 13 positive votes, including those of two of the most strident critics of the NATO-led intervention in Libya: India and South Africa. Other notable supporters of the resolution were Pakistan, Togo and Azerbaijan. However, two permanent members, China and Russia, again cast negative votes, blocking its adoption.[21]

The UNSC's failure to reach consensus prompted renewed diplomatic efforts. On 23 February 2012, Kofi Annan was appointed as the first joint UN–Arab League Envoy charged with assisting the Syrian parties to reach a negotiated settlement. The result was a six-point plan, which the Syrian government agreed on

27 March to implement. The six points were: (1) work with the Envoy in an inclusive Syrian-led political process; (2) stop the fighting and achieve urgently an effective UN-supervised cessation of armed violence in all its forms by all; (3) ensure timely provision of humanitarian assistance to all areas affected by the fighting; (4) intensify the pace and scale of release of arbitrarily detained persons; (5) ensure freedom of movement throughout the country for journalists and a non-discriminatory visa policy for them; and (6) respect freedom of association and the right to demonstrate peacefully as legally guaranteed.[22]

The UNSC then adopted two resolutions by consensus, Resolution 2042 (2012) and Resolution 2043 (2012),[23] which voiced support for the plan and mandated the deployment of an observer mission, the UN Supervision Mission in Syria (UNSMIS) to report on compliance. When the Syrian government dragged its feet, a ceasefire meant to come into effect on 10 April in fact commenced on 14 April.

It was immediately apparent, however, that neither side was complying with the agreement. Syrian government forces refused to cease firing and withdraw unless the rebels did so first, and the Syrian armed opposition made precisely the same argument and even launched offensives at some points along the front line. On 1 May, the UN's Under-Secretary-General for Peacekeeping, Herve Ladsous, reported that both sides had violated the ceasefire.[24] Attempts to persuade the parties to implement the agreement limped on, but on 25 May regime-backed militia killed over 100 civilians in Houla, prompting an outpouring of international condemnation.[25] The UNSC issued a press statement condemning the attack and assigning responsibility to the Syrian government. The Free Syrian Army reacted by stepping up its offensive and the regime responded in early June by vowing to crush 'anti-regime elements', effectively terminating the ceasefire and with it the Annan plan.

Within this context of a rapidly deteriorating situation and generalised non-compliance with the Annan plan, a third draft resolution was tabled in July to indicate the UNSC's resolve and introduce the possibility of enforcement measures against the government in the event of its continued disregard of the UNSC's past demands.[26] The key elements of this draft were a general demand that the parties immediately implement all aspects of the six-point plan, a demand that all parties – including the opposition – cease all armed violence, and the extension of UNSMIS's mandate by 45 days. Most controversially, draft paragraph 4 'decided' that the Syrian government should verifiably implement its commitments to cease troop movements towards population centres, cease use of heavy weapons in such centres and pull back military concentrations in and around such centres. The draft resolution gave the government ten days to comply and requested that the UN Secretary-General (UNSG) report to the UNSC on compliance. It also warned that in the event of non-compliance, the UNSC would adopt measures under Article 41 of the Charter. The draft text secured 11 affirmative votes, including those of India, Morocco and Togo. Pakistan and South Africa abstained, while China and Russia again voted against.[27]

In summary, the story of the UNSC's failure to respond effectively to the crisis in Syria revolves around these vetoed resolutions. However, this is not simply a story of the UNSC refusing to take up its protection responsibilities or a more general backtracking on the part of international society. This is clear for two reasons. First, interwoven into the story told above were moments of consensus: two adopted resolutions supporting a peace plan self-consciously aimed at addressing the 'legitimate grievances' of the Syrian people,[28] and a press statement condemning a massacre of civilians in Houla.

Second, and perhaps more interestingly, there is another story to tell – one about the UNGA's response to the crisis in Syria and, in particular, its response to the UNSC's actions. An additional sign that the UNSC's inability to reach a consensus on timely and decisive action in Syria is not a product of a wider political backlash against human protection and the use of robust measures to achieve its goals is that the UNGA resoundingly endorsed many of the measures proposed for Syria that were blocked in the UNSC. On 16 February 2012, two weeks after the second vetoed draft resolution, the UNGA voted by 137 to 12 (with 17 abstentions) to adopt a resolution that contained much of the text from the rejected UNSC draft. The UNGA resolution 'strongly condemned' the 'widespread and systematic violations of human rights and fundamental freedoms by the Syrian authorities', called on all armed groups to put an immediate end to violence and reprisals, supported the Arab League's peace initiative, and called on the UNSG to lend his support.[29] Among the states voting against the resolution were Russia, China, North Korea, Iran, Syria itself, Zimbabwe and Venezuela. Interestingly, for our purposes, among those states that supported the resolution were some of the most strident critics of the NATO-led intervention in Libya, including Brazil, India, South Africa and Pakistan.

A few months later, on 3 August 2012 – a day after Kofi Annan announced his decision to resign as the joint envoy for Syria, citing the parties' unwillingness to abide by their commitments and the UNSC's inability to impose consequences on the parties for non-compliance – the UNGA adopted a second resolution on the situation in Syria, again by a huge majority of 132 votes to 12.[30] This resolution, principally drafted by Qatar and Saudi Arabia, proved somewhat more controversial than the first because it heaped all its criticism on the Syrian authorities and did not condemn atrocities committed by opposition groups, a problem identified especially by India. Significantly, for our purposes, the resolution 'deplored' the failure of the UNSC to adopt measures on Syria,[31] sending a clear signal that the UNSC's position did not reflect that of the wider UN membership. The controversy over the lack of even-handedness created more abstentions (31), including those of India and Pakistan, than in the first vote, but no more negative votes. Despite these concerns, however, Brazil and South Africa voted in favour of the resolution.

For our purposes, there are two key points that stem from this discussion. First, there are indeed heightened sensitivities about the use of coercion against member states as a tool of human protection, but these do not necessarily represent a backtracking on commitments to human protection or wholesale rejection of coercion as a potential instrument of protection in some cases. Second, UNSC members want to ensure the proper calibration and accountability of measures adopted by the UNSC and are concerned that some might interpret loosely worded mandates in an expansive fashion to justify policies of regime change sometimes only tangentially linked to human protection. There are therefore good grounds for thinking, as Gareth Evans does,[32] that without efforts to address these accountability concerns, it will be difficult to move towards a deeper consensus on timely and decisive responses to atrocity crimes – especially when the principal perpetrator is the state itself.

2 Responsibility while protecting

One useful way of thinking about the lessons that need to be learnt about the design and oversight of mandates to use force in order to protect populations in the wake of the controversy over Libya can be found in some aspects of the concept of RWP championed by Brazil. The concept was proposed first by Brazilian President Dilma Rousseff at the September 2011 plenary of the UNGA. The Brazilian Permanent Mission to the UN circulated a note outlining the concept in more detail towards the end of 2011,[33] and co-hosted an informal dialogue in February 2012. Although there was some initial scepticism among some western states, who saw the concept as an attempt to derail implementation of R2P, the initiative was widely welcomed, including by the UNSG, for providing fresh ideas to stimulate discussion about how to implement those most controversial aspects of R2P that relate to coercion and the use of force.

In relation to the issues of accountability mentioned earlier, there are three particularly important elements of this concept: decision-making criteria for the use of force; the provision of judicious analysis to guide decision-making; and the establishment of an accountability mechanism to oversee the UNSC's work.

2.1 Decision-making criteria

The concept of RWP revived longstanding proposals for the development of criteria to guide UNSC decision-making about the use of force. A proposal for such criteria was a centrepiece of the 2001 report of the International Commission on Intervention and State Sovereignty (ICISS), which coined the phrase 'responsibility to protect',[34] but the idea – and some of the criteria – had been aired two years earlier by British Prime Minister Tony Blair as part of his 'doctrine of the international community'.[35] These two sets of advocates articulated the need for criteria on very different bases.

First, from the perspective of the Brazilian government, Gareth Evans',[36] and others', criteria guard against the abuse, misuse or over-extension of UNSC mandates by ensuring that the UNSC adopts resolutions for the correct reasons and that there is a shared understanding among UNSC members of what has been agreed to. Second, from the perspective of Blair,[37] and to some extent ICISS,[38] criteria help establish a legitimate basis – founded on agreed principles

– upon which to advance the case for armed intervention for human protection purposes. By this logic, once there is agreement on the principle of the need for action in the face of mass killing and on the relevant prudential checks, it becomes more difficult to justify the blocking of collective action when those conditions are met.

Although decision-making criteria have been widely taken as the centrepiece of RWP, including by Brazil itself in 2012,[39] the concept note which set out the concept in 2011 did not in fact spell-out a list of criteria. Rather, it limited itself to proposing some common principles, some of which – such as 'prevention is always the best policy'[40] – were clearly not intended as decision-making criteria. Nonetheless, it is possible to discern some such criteria in the Brazilian concept note. Table 19.1 compares these with the criteria proposed by Blair and ICISS.

Despite suggestions that RWP is an echo of the ICISS notion of R2P, direct overlap is limited to the 'last resort' and 'proportionality' criteria, arguably two of the most problematic when applied in a *jus ad bellum* context. On the question of 'right authority', both were notably more permissive than what the UNGA agreed in 2005 and the UNSG advanced thereafter, but they differed in the important respect that the ICISS countenanced the possibility that armed intervention might be legitimate even if not authorised by the UNSC or UNGA. What is more, Brazil's President, Dilma Rousseff, sharply contradicted her own government's concept note when, at the opening of the 67th UNGA in September 2012, she insisted that 'the use of force without authorization by the UNSC is illegal, yet it is beginning to be regarded in some quarters as an acceptable option. This is by no means the case.'[41] This was a remarkable statement given that only 11 months earlier Brazil had written to the UNSG that the UNGA, too, could, 'in exceptional circumstances', authorise the use of force. But it further distinguished RWP from ICISS.

Before assessing the capacity of decision-making criteria to improve accountability, it is important to stress that they enjoy relatively little political support and that what support they do have evaporates very quickly when discussion turns to what specific criteria should be used and what baselines for assessment should be employed. Key opponents of criteria have included three of the five permanent members (P5) of the UNSC (US, China and Russia), India, several other Asian states, and even some progressive Europeans, though their reasons for scepticism were quite different.[42]

Whatever their intuitive appeal, there are few grounds for thinking that criteria would help to address concerns about accountability. First, in terms of crystallising understanding of the circumstances in which force might be needed – and legitimate (the ostensible purpose of the ICISS's 'just cause' thresholds) – it seems reasonable to suggest that the R2P principle already achieves this goal by defining the atrocity crimes that give rise to the special responsibilities it enumerates. This perhaps explains why Brazil did not include 'just cause' thresholds among its criteria. The 2005 World Summit Outcome Document identified the crimes from which governments had a responsibility to protect populations and the circumstances in which that responsibility ought to be taken

Table 19.1 Proposed criteria for armed interventions for humanitarian protection

Blair 1999	*ICISS 2001*	*Brazil 2011*
Just cause (are we sure of our case?)	Just cause (large-scale loss of life/ethnic cleansing)	–
Last resort (have we exhausted peaceful means?)	Last resort (non-military measures must have been explored)	Last resort (exhaust all peaceful means)
Prudence (are there sensible military options?)	Reasonable prospects (good chance of success)	–
Long-term commitment (are we committed for the long term?)	–	–
National interests	–	–
–	Right intention (purpose must be humanitarian)	–
–	Proportional means (scale of military action should be minimum needed)	Use of force must produce as little violence as possible/must be proportionate/judicious
–	Right authority (UNSC, UNGA, regional organisation)	Right authority (UNSC or in exceptional circumstances UNGA)
–	Operational principles (clear objectives, coordination, proportionate rules of engagement, etc.)	–
–	–	Use of force strictly limited to that which is authorised

up by the international community, acting through the UNSC. In the Outcome Document, member states agreed that they have a responsibility to protect their populations from genocide, war crimes, ethnic cleansing and crimes against humanity, and that the UNSC should stand ready to take up this responsibility, on a case-by-case basis, in situations where a government is 'manifestly failing' to protect its own population.[43] There is broad agreement that the UNSC should be engaged in such circumstances. For example, the Chinese government's 2005 position paper on UN reform agreed that 'massive humanitarian' crises were 'the legitimate concern of the international community'.[44]

Of course, agreement on the relevant crimes does not guarantee agreement on whether the thresholds have been breached and the most appropriate response in actual cases. This problem was raised throughout the ICISS consultation process and has been aired many times since.[45] It has also been evident in practice: in relation to Darfur, governments more or less agreed on the gravity of the threat but disagreed about the most appropriate course of action and the responsibility of the Sudanese Government;[46] on Syria, the P5 disagreed about whether one side (the government) was primarily responsible or whether blame – and hence punitive action – should be shared more evenly among the armed actors.

What is more, even if voluntary recognition of criteria – and shared understandings of them – could be negotiated, there is little reason for confidence that criteria would serve the goals of accountability. In the hands of skilled diplomats, criteria would likely merely become the language used to justify pre-determined positions. Indeed, in classroom exercises undergraduate students have proven capable of plausibly arguing the case for and against intervention in Kosovo and Syria by reference to criteria. Thus, in a case such as Syria, it is hard to the point of fanciful to suppose that the protagonists in the UNSC would employ the criteria for any other purpose than to justify their own positions. The problem is exacerbated by the fact that some criteria – precisely those on which ICISS and Brazil agreed – such as 'last resort' are vague in the extreme and open to subjective interpretation, and others, especially 'proportionality', are impossible to calculate with any degree of precision prior to the use of force (and difficult and subjective even afterwards when all the data are in). This has long been understood in the tradition of thought from which they arose: the Christian Just War tradition.

Therefore, neither criterion provides meaningful external benchmarks except, perhaps, in the most extreme of cases, such as Rwanda, and even then actual lived history shows that there remain grounds for arguing that there are viable alternatives to the use of force. Given this, it is difficult to see how criteria would have helped avoid the controversies stemming from the implementation of Resolution 1973. The only obvious way in which criteria might have had this effect would have been by providing additional arguments and legitimacy to those governments that were uncomfortable with the resolution. Perhaps Russia and China could have used criteria to argue that the 'last resort' had not been found or that NATO's proposed action was disproportionate. In such a scenario, criteria would not have produced 'responsible protection', it would have led to the people of Benghazi and elsewhere receiving no protection at all.

There is a counter argument here, that by setting clear thresholds for action, criteria may actually make it more difficult for states to oppose decisive action in clear cases of genocide and mass atrocities. There is not much evidence, however, to suggest that the thresholds could limit the use of the veto. In relation to the crisis in Darfur, it was suggested that Russia and China might have been 'compelled' into abstaining on a resolution authorising intervention were such a resolution tabled, backed by arguments grounded in shared criteria.[47] Actual voting behaviour regarding Darfur, as well as the more recent performance of Russia and China in relation to Syria, suggests that this may be based more on wishful thinking than political practice. China's performance in the UNSC regarding the situation in Darfur suggests that it would have been more than willing to use its veto: China threatened to veto measures far less intrusive than non-consensual military intervention, such as comprehensive targeted sanctions and no-fly zones. Likewise, in relation to the situation in Syria, both Russia and China have defied large majorities in the UNSC and UNGA and even voted against measures to encourage compliance with their own earlier demands (when they vetoed a resolution threatening sanctions for non-compliance with the Annan plan). Criteria could hardly be expected to alter geopolitical calculations in these cases. It is much more likely that they would simply add an extra layer of argument in defence of pre-determined positions.

Moreover, when considered more systematically, the whole issue of criteria seems disconnected from the main point of concern that many member states have: the question of accountability. On that score, criteria would only rule out the blatantly obvious abuses – of which I can think of no clear examples in the UNSC's history; after all, the UNSC refused US entreaties regarding Iraq without the need for criteria – and rule in the most obvious of genocides. Again, Rwanda stands out as an example, but at the time even this was disputed; debate raged about whether the killing was part of the civil war or whether it was genocidal. Although we are all wise with hindsight, at the time even several NGOs on the ground in Rwanda were reluctant to categorise what they were seeing as genocide until several weeks into the killing. Given the immense amount of political capital that would be required to secure agreement on criteria and the limited potential gains in terms of accountability, this element of responsible protection seems less than propitious.

2.2 Judicious analysis

A second key element of Brazil's concept note on RWP was its call for judicious analysis in advance of decisions to use force. The note argued that the 'use of force must … be preceded by a comprehensive and judicious analysis of the possible consequences of military action on a case-by-case basis'.[48] This is entirely sensible. Decision-making is clearly improved if it is based on a solid understanding of the situation at hand and likely consequences of different potential courses of action. Moreover, anything that can help the UNSC reach a shared understanding of the situation can assist in building a united approach to the problem. However, the UNSG's first Special Adviser on R2P, Edward Luck, detected in RWP the potential for further delaying action in response to atrocity crimes, with this demand for 'judicious' analysis chief among the factors that could be used to promote delay.[49] While information and assessment is a necessary component of decision-making, building a 'judicious' assessment can take months, if not years. Further delay would be caused by the proliferation of competing assessments from different member states and other interested parties. The time required to conduct 'judicious' analysis and pit it against alternative assessments gives those states that would be opposed to decisive action a route by which to delay action indefinitely while claiming to be acting in a manner consistent with R2P. An additional problem is that states may simply refer to their own analysis, thereby entrenching and formalising existing divisions.

There are three ways around these potential pitfalls. First, and most obviously, the requirement for analysis to be 'judicious' should be rethought. International events, especially those characterised by armed conflict and mass atrocities, are simply too fast-paced and fluid to permit truly 'judicious' analysis. The response of any government to a pressing international crisis is seldom properly described as 'judicious' and so it makes little sense to impose on the UNSC a standard of analysis that no government would expect of itself.

Second, to ensure that the burden of analysis is not entirely directed at forestalling international action, analysis should also include assessment of the possible consequences of *not* taking military action and the likely consequences of a range of other potential measures.

Third, to avoid the proliferation of analyses each claiming to be authoritative, the UNSC should look to the UN Secretariat to provide it with the assessments it needs. As the UN system's repository of expertise on the prevention of genocide and mass atrocities, the UN's Office on Genocide Prevention and R2P would be the most promising candidate to provide this sort of advice to the UNSC on request and through the Special Advisers. The Office would be able to draw upon its regional experts to provide analysis of the consequences of various courses of action, but its analytical capacity would need to be augmented. With greater expertise regarding their own regions, relevant regional arrangements could also feed their analysis of a situation and likely consequences of different courses of action into this process.

2.3 Accountability mechanism

The Brazilian concept note calls for 'enhanced Security Council procedures' to 'monitor and assess the manner in which resolutions are interpreted and implemented to ensure responsibility while protecting',[50] and for the UNSC to ensure 'the accountability of those to whom authority is granted to resort to force'.[51] These are important considerations if the UNSC is to continue to play an active role in the protection of populations from atrocity crimes. UNSC resolutions generally do contain reporting requirements, as indeed Resolution 1973 did, but there is concern that these requirements are not sufficiently complied with. For example, there was little transparency in the way in which NATO reported its activities in Libya to the UNSG during its Libyan campaign. Moreover, when the Libyan regime made entreaties about a negotiated ceasefire, NATO rejected those entreaties out of hand, without first discussing the issue with the UNSC.[52] This raised concerns among some UNSC members that, in effect, NATO had assumed control over the intervention, denying the UNSC the primacy on the issue that it is entitled to by virtue of the Charter.[53]

Brazil's calls for strengthened procedures to allow the UNSC to hold to account states that act on its mandate flow directly from the Libya experience. However, although there is clear merit in the argument for stronger accountability, there are problems with Brazil's initial proposal for special mechanisms to govern R2P enforcement operations. First, the UN Charter gives to the UNSC wide flexibility in terms of the actions it can take in pursuit of its primary responsibility for international peace and security and deliberately makes the UNSC self-regulating. This has allowed the UNSC to be innovative when it has needed to be and has helped the UNSC find consensus when that has proven difficult. New permanent mechanisms to regulate the UNSC would require a change to the Charter, which could have unintended negative consequences. Second, the UNSC's responsibility covers international peace and security and not just R2P cases. It would make no practical sense to have one set of rules for some Chapter VII resolutions on the use of force and another set for others – not least because 'R2P' cases could be easily re-labelled. Third, the UN has had bad experience in the past with excessive political interference in military matters. The experience of the UN Protection Force (UNPROFOR) in Bosnia is testament to what can happen when the UNSC tries to micro-manage military operations. Fourth, excessive political requirements might inhibit states from implementing UNSC mandates by pushing them to the view that they cannot translate a resolution into a viable military strategy that they can sell to their publics. This would reduce implementation of UNSC mandates, weakening the UNSC's credibility and legitimacy, and inhibiting protection.

These problems should not mean that nothing is done to improve accountability. Clearly, the UNSC itself needs to engage in dialogue – informally at first – about how to improve this accountability loop. Instead of a new layer of procedural rules, the UNSC should make use of the powers it already has by writing specific accountability measures into its resolutions. The UNSC has already developed a strong repertoire of accountability measures that might be appropriate. One way forward may be to foster informal dialogue on the various accountability measures that the UNSC already has at its disposal and to inform non-permanent members in particular about what these measures are and when they might be employed.

Five such measures might be included. The first is to include *sunset clauses* in UNSC resolutions. This would make authorisations to use force time-limited, forcing states acting on mandates to return to the UNSC for a renewal. This is standard practice for UN peacekeeping operations and helps build an accountability loop. The second suggestion is to include *specific and frequent reporting requirements*. The UNSC can, and does, require reports from those acting on its mandates. In the case of Libya, Resolution 1973 required that implementing states report their activities to the UNSG.[54] In future, the UNSC might also require that the UNSG brief it on these reports or demand that implementing states report directly to the UNSC. The third suggestion is for the UNSC to include *specific limitations* to rule out certain courses of action. For example, Resolution 1973 forbade the deployment of ground troops as an occupying force in Libya. The fourth suggestion is *direct action*: the UNSC might directly mandate or require diplomatic activity, the dispatch of envoys or acceptance of negotiated agreements. And the fifth suggestion is to mandate *information gathering*: to supplement or replace reporting from implementing states, the UNSC might mandate its own fact-finding mission to gather information about the implementation of its mandates.

Pursuing this route to greater accountability would reduce the likelihood of unintended negative consequences, would allow the tailoring of accountability measures to individual circumstances, and would make use of the UNSC's existing authority under the UN Charter.

3 Conclusion

The UNSC's response to the crisis in Syria ought to be viewed in the wider context of its evolving practice on human protection and its general history and politics. As Edward Luck explained, the UNSC's efforts are constrained and shaped by two conditions: there are some problems that do not have feasible near-term solutions and the UNSC is 'not above the vagaries of international politics. Indeed it is all about politics: local, national, regional and global.'[55] As a result, from case to case the UNSC is inconsistent and unpredictable and it is not always possible to draw clear connections between its handling of different situations. Such inconsistencies – inevitable given the nature of the UNSC and of international order – should not blind us, however, to the deeper, longer-term transformations in the UNSC's practice, chief among which is the rise to prominence of human protection, in part facilitated by R2P. As the UNSC has become more assertive in the field of human protection – an assertiveness increasingly demanded by the international community more broadly, as evidenced by the UNGA's position on the UNSC's response to the crisis in Syria – so too have demands arisen for greater accountability. This is to be expected, as the more active the UNSC gets, the more UN member states will want to ensure that it acts for the common good.

In that regard, the concept of RWP marks a useful contribution to thinking about how best to balance the UNSC's protection responsibilities with increasing demands for accountability. Drawing on this concept, I argue that the best approaches to strengthening the UNSC's accountability in relation to use of force for protection purposes would be to strengthen the flow of information and analysis from the UN Secretariat to the UNSC and to improve the UNSC's own working practices to enhance oversight of its mandates and accountability.

Notes

1 SC Res. 1674 (28 April 2006).
2 SC Res. 1894 (11 November 2009).
3 SC Res. 2150 (16 April 2014).
4 UN Doc. S/PRST/2013/4 (15 April 2013).
5 Siobhan Wills, *Protection of Civilians* (Oxford, Oxford University Press, 2011).
6 UN Multidimensional Integrated Stabilization Mission in Mali.
7 For discussion of the intervention brigade, see Oswald's chapter in this collection.
8 UN Multidimensional Integrated Stabilization Mission in the Central African Republic.
9 SC Res. 2149 (10 April 2014).
10 UN Mission in the Republic of South Sudan.
11 'Responsibility While Protecting: Elements for the Development and Promotion of a Concept' in UN Doc. A/66/551–S/2011/701 (11 November 2011), *Letter Dated 9 November 2011 from the Permanent Representative of Brazil to the United Nations Addressed to the Secretary-General*, Annex. For discussion of R2P and RWP, see Harrington's chapter in this collection.
12 SC Res. 1973 (17 March 2011).
13 See, e.g. Ramesh Thakur, 'R2P after Libya and Syria: Engaging Emerging Powers' (2013) 36(2) *The Washington Quarterly* 61–76, 62.
14 UN Doc. S/2011/612 (4 October 2011).
15 Ibid., p. 1 (preamble).
16 Ibid., para. 5.
17 UN Doc. S/PV.6627 (4 October 2011), p. 2.
18 UN Doc. S/2012/77 (4 February 2012).
19 Ibid., para. 3.
20 Ibid., para. 15.
21 UN Doc. S/PV.6711 (4 February 2012), p. 2.
22 See SC Res. 2042 (2012), *Annex: Six-Point Proposal of the Joint Special Envoy of the United Nations and the League of Arab States*.
23 SC Res. 2042 (14 April 2012) and SC Res. 2043 (21 April 2012).
24 United Nations Public Affairs Section, 'Herve Ladsous, Under-Secretary-General for Peacekeeping Operations, Press Conference, 1 May 2012: Near-Verbatim Transcript' (1 May 2012): www.un.org/en/peacekeeping/articles/usg_ladsous_press_conf01052012.pdf.
25 See, e.g. 'Annan Condemns "Appalling Crime" on Syria Visit as Damascus Denies Houla Killings', *Al Arabiya News* (28 May 2012): http://english.alarabiya.net/articles/2012/05/28/217134.html.
26 UN Doc. S/2012/538 (19 July 2012).
27 UN Doc. S/PV.6810 (19 July 2012), p. 2.
28 See point 1 of Annan's Six-Point plan: SC Res. 2042 (2012), Annex.
29 GA Res. 66/253 (21 February 2012).
30 GA Res. 66/253 B (7 August 2012).
31 Ibid., para. 11.
32 Gareth Evans, 'Responding to Atrocities: The New Geopolitics of Intervention', *SIPRI Yearbook 2012: Armaments, Disarmament and International Security* (Oxford, Oxford University Press for the Stockholm International Peace Research Institute, 2012), pp. 15–38.
33 'Responsibility While Protecting: Elements for the Development and Promotion of a Concept' in UN Doc. A/66/551-S/2011/701 (11 November 2011), *Letter Dated 9 November 2011 from the Permanent Representative of Brazil to the United Nations Addressed to the Secretary-General*, Annex.
34 International Commission on Intervention and State Sovereignty (ICISS), *The*

Responsibility to Protect: Report of the International Commission on Intervention and State Sovereignty (Ottawa, International Development Research Centre, 2001).

35 Tony Blair, 'Doctrine of the International Community' (Chicago, 24 April 1999): www.britishpoliticalspeech.org/speech-archive.htm?speech=279.

36 Thakur, 'R2P after Libya and Syria'.

37 Tony Blair, 'Doctrine of the International Community'.

38 ICISS, *The Responsibility to Protect.*

39 See the statement of HE Ambassador Maria Luiza Ribeiro Viotti, Permanent Representative of Brazil to the UN, delivered during the UNGA's annual dialogue on R2P, 5 September 2012: http://responsibilitytoprotect.org/Brazil(1).pdf.

40 'Responsibility While Protecting' in UN Doc. A/66/551–S/2011/701 (11 November 2011).

41 Statement by HE Dilma Rousseff, President of the Federative Republic of Brazil, at the Opening of the General Debate at the 67th Session of the UNGA, 25 September 2012: http://gadebate.un.org/sites/default/files/gastatements/67/BR_en.pdf.

42 Jennifer M. Welsh, 'Conclusion: Humanitarian Intervention after 11 September', in Jennifer M. Welsh (ed.), *Humanitarian Intervention and International Relations* (Oxford, Oxford University Press, 2004), p. 180.

43 GA Res. 60/1 (24 October 2005), para. 139.

44 *Position Paper of the People's Republic of China on the United Nations Reforms* (8 June 2005): www.china.org.cn/english/government/131308.htm.

45 See Thomas G. Weiss and Don Hubert, *The Responsibility to Protect: Supplementary Volume to the Report of the International Commission on Intervention and State Sovereignty* (Ottawa, IDRC, 2001), pp. 351–2.

46 Alex J. Bellamy, 'Responsibility to Protect or Trojan Horse? The Crisis in Darfur and Humanitarian Intervention after Iraq' (2005) 19(2) *Ethics and International Affairs* 31–54.

47 Nicholas J. Wheeler and Justin Morris, 'Justifying the Iraq War as a Humanitarian Intervention: The Cure is Worse than the Disease', in Ramesh Thakur and Waheguru Pal Singh Sidhu (eds), *The Iraq Crisis and World Order* (Tokyo, UN University Press, 2006), pp. 444–63, 460.

48 'Responsibility While Protecting' in UN Doc. A/66/551–S/2011/701 (11 November 2011), para. 7.

49 Opening statement by Edward C. Luck, Special Adviser to the UNSG on the Responsibility to Protect at the 'Informal Discussion on the Responsibility While Protecting Initiative', organised by the Permanent Mission of Brazil, New York, 21 February 2012: www.globalr2p.org/media/files/edluckrwp.pdf.

50 Ibid., para. 11(h).

51 Ibid., para. 11(i).

52 'Libya: Rebels and NATO Dismiss Gaddafi Ceasefire Offer', *BBC News* (30 April 2011): www.bbc.co.uk/news/world-africa-13249923.

53 Discussed in Alex J. Bellamy and Paul D. Williams, 'The New Politics of Protection: Cote d'Ivoire, Libya and the Responsibility to Protect' (2011) 87(4) *International Affairs* 825–50, 847.

54 SC Res. 1973 (17 March 2011), paras 4 (relating to protection of civilians) and 8 (relating to no-fly zone).

55 Edward C. Luck, *The Security Council* (London, Routledge, 2006), pp. 7–8.

Part V

Strengthening the rule of law through the Security Council

20 The UN Security Council as regulator and subject of the rule of law

Conflict or confluence of interest?

Jeremy Farrall and Marie-Eve Loiselle

A central theme to emerge from this volume is how the UN Security Council's decision-making process shapes, and in turn is shaped by, the idea of the rule of law (ROL). As all chapters demonstrate in one way or another, the Council's engagements with the ROL tend to unfold on two separate but connected fronts. First, there is the external front, where the UNSC acts as promoter, enforcer or protector of the ROL. As Terence Halliday insightfully observed at one of the workshops from which this book evolved, when engaging with the ROL in this way the UNSC strengthens the ROL 'on the offence', thus playing the role of *regulator* of the ROL. The key question on the external front is how UNSC-authorised activities in the areas of peacekeeping, sanctions and force might better promote the ROL. Second, there is the internal front, where the UNSC acts as subject of the ROL. When engaging with the ROL in this way, the UNSC strengthens the ROL 'on the defence', thus playing the role of *subject* or *regulatee* of the ROL. The key question on the internal front is how the ROL as an important principle of governance might be better respected in the UNSC's decision-making processes that lead to the authorisation of peacekeeping, sanctions and force.

This chapter draws on the contributions to this collection to explore how the UNSC's actions on the external and internal fronts enhance (or indeed impede) the Council's capacity to regulate international peace and security. The chapter argues that the Council's capacity to strengthen the rule of law on the external front will be stronger when it respects the rule of law on the internal front. Put another way, the more responsive the Council is as both regulator and subject of the ROL, the greater its capacity will be to strengthen the ROL. The chapter proceeds in three sections. Section 1 examines how the UNSC can strengthen the ROL when playing the role of regulator of the ROL. Section 2 then explores how the Council can strengthen the ROL when playing the role of subject or regulatee of the ROL. Section 3 turns to the future, drawing on the analysis in both this chapter and the collection as a whole to advance proposals designed to increase the capacity of the UNSC to strengthen the ROL through its future practice on both the external and internal fronts, whether as regulator or subject of the ROL.

1 The Security Council as a regulator of the rule of law

The UN Charter identifies the UNSC as the primary regulator of threats to international peace and security.[1] Yet regulating such threats requires substantial capacity and resources.[2] While the Charter gives the UNSC considerable power to authorise coercive action to maintain or restore international peace and security,[3] the Council does not take this action itself. Rather, it must rely on other actors, in particular UN member states, to take the direct action necessary to implement or enforce its decisions. In order to access and activate the economic, human and informational resources required to implement its mandate, the UNSC must therefore set in motion an effective division of labour between UN member states, UN agencies and transnational institutional actors. Thus the UNSC itself is just one player, albeit a very important one, in the regulatory space for the maintenance of international peace and security.[4]

At first glance the concept of the ROL offers both guidance and legitimation for the UNSC's external efforts to regulate international peace and security. However, as the chapters in this collection demonstrate, the ROL's utility as a regulatory instrument is complicated by its contested meaning and influence at the international level (see the chapters by Natarajan, Sampford, Simpson and Grenfell), by the proliferation of actors at the international, regional, national and local levels who claim a stake in the 'rule-of-law industry' (see the chapters by Taylor, Whalan and Thomson), and by the concept's inherent promise not just to *facilitate* but also to *constrain* regulatory activities (see the chapters by Prost, O'Connell, and Bannelier and Christakis).

Rule-of-law challenges and the interventions they prompt tend to take shape in diverse ways in different contexts, involving a wide range of actors. The 2004 definition of the ROL advanced by Kofi Annan sought to provide conceptual clarity and articulate marching orders for UN rule-of-law promotion activities.[5] The definition provides helpful guidance on elements that typically feature in democratic societies that adhere to the ROL. It emphasises the need for functional procedural checks and balances to moderate the exercise of political power. Yet it also connects the ROL with international human rights standards, thus framing the ROL as a concept with both procedural and substantive roots.

A number of the authors in this collection engage with the question of whether the ROL should be understood in procedural ('thin') or substantive ('thick') terms. Sampford advocates a thin version of the ROL on the pragmatic ground that it is more amenable to promotion in diverse contexts. Natarajan also employs a 'thinner' understanding of the ROL, describing its primary benefits as creating order and predictability and ensuring equal treatment. At the same time, however, she cautions against the assumption that the ROL can be swiftly introduced in contexts where there is not a sufficiently enabling environment to support the emergence of a genuine rule-of-law culture. Devereux, for her part, argues that efforts to promote the ROL must place human rights front and centre, thus demanding a substantive understanding of the ROL.

Taylor and Simpson provide sobering reminders of the potential unintended consequences of unreflective rule-of-law promotion. Taylor describes how the ROL can be commoditised as a label in the pursuit of corporate profit, while Simpson explains how the concept of the ROL has been used and abused for destructive ends. For this reason, Krygier emphasises the need to focus on the essence, rather than the means, of the ROL, arguing that this essence lies in preventing the abuse of power. This focus on the essence of the ROL as preventing the abuse of power holds potential to facilitate regulatory refinement and innovation specific to each context, increasing the ROL's potential to travel across and adapt to different situations. This resonates with the idea of responsive regulation, which seeks to promote attention to regulatory context and support for regulatory innovation.[6]

A constructive way for the UNSC to approach the problem of the proliferation of actors in the 'rule-of-law industry' is to harness rather than compete with other efforts to regulate the ROL. Indeed, in each of the three areas of UNSC practice highlighted in this collection, namely peacekeeping, sanctions and force, effective UNSC interventions not only benefit from, but also rely on, effective cooperation with a variety of actors. The field of peacekeeping is characterised by a division between those who possess the legitimate authority to intervene and those who possess the resources to implement the measures envisaged. As the chapters by Sannerholm and Wall, Devereux and Grenfell illustrate, the UNSC's peacekeeping operations are only possible with the participation of states and/or regional organisations, which provide the necessary human and material resources to carry out the mandate. Moreover, the Council's efforts to regulate activities on specific important issues within areas of peacekeeping deployment necessitate the development of sophisticated strategies of regulatory engagement with and responsiveness to these different actors. Sannerholm and Wall identify the complexities involved in promoting an understanding of the ROL that is faithful to the Annan definition and thus moves beyond a narrow focus on police, courts and prisons. Heathcote and Whalan demonstrate some of these challenges in relation to UN efforts to regulate sexual exploitation and abuse. Thomson, for his part, advocates the need to build on synergies between the webs of actors involved in the promotion of the ROL and the protection of civilians.

The need to harness and manage the activities of different actors is equally strong for mandates that authorise states or groups of states to use force to achieve the objectives identified in a UNSC resolution (see Bannelier and Christakis). The chapters by Oswald, Bellamy and Harrington each examine different dimensions of the considerable challenge of regulating downstream the activities of those actors who are authorised to employ force in the UNSC's name. Equally, in the area of sanctions, the chapters by de Wet and Prost make it clear that the UNSC must rely on the support and good faith engagement of member states and private institutions to implement its sanctions regimes. In other words, the UNSC is not a leviathan that can impose its will downward upon its subjects. Instead, the Council must participate in a negotiated relationship of interdependence that is subject to constant flux and evolution.[7] In this environment, one of the key challenges for the UNSC, and indeed for the UN more broadly, is to enlist actors who possess the resources required to achieve the objectives of its peacekeeping, sanctions and use-of-force initiatives, within the boundaries of the Council's overarching responsibility for the maintenance of international peace and security.

The idea of a responsive approach to governance (or responsive regulatory theory) was articulated by Ayres and Braithwaite in the early 1990s.[8] This model is premised on features of responsiveness that include plurality, dynamism and deliberation, all of which are often encountered in UNSC activities.[9] Responsive governance aims to exploit and reinforce the strengths of the network of actors involved in a specific endeavour by drawing on their capacity to regulate themselves. It is usually illustrated through a metaphorical model of dual pyramids of support and sanctions.[10] The presumption underpinning this theory is that it is easier to secure compliance through dialogue than through coercion. This resonates with O'Connell's argument that the use of force is often based on the false assumption that force is effective in achieving desirable ends such as human rights protection and arms control, while in practice more peaceful channels of action offer greater prospects of success.

At the same time, however, enlisted actors such as states, regional organisations and civil society,[11] which deploy their respective resources in the form of legal and political authority, wealth, information and organisational capacities, also have the potential to encroach on the UNSC's interpretative authority of the ROL as it applies to their activities (see, for example, the chapters by Krygier, Taylor and Grenfell). While their behaviour may reinforce the UNSC's authority, it may also challenge the Council's legitimacy if the power it delegates is not exercised legitimately. As noted by Sampford, the ROL can only emerge in a host country if the mission participants are themselves subject to the ROL. Heathcote also makes this point in relation to sexual exploitation and abuse committed by troop-contributing countries (TCCs).

The primary regulatory challenge for the UNSC in strengthening the rule of law is therefore to retain the clout necessary to enlist the actors it needs to implement its mandates, while at the same time maintaining the capacity to hold them accountable for unauthorised, illegitimate activity. In order to do this the UNSC must be creative in its engagement with other rule-of-law actors, and as Bannelier and Christakis put it, the Council must navigate a path between flexibility and accountability. One way to do this is to employ a responsive model of governance, which favours a flexible approach to regulation contingent on the specific context of each case, rather than a command-and-control-driven approach that relies principally on predetermined sanctions to influence the actors that implement the Council's mandates.

A responsive regulation paradigm supports a dialogue between stakeholders with a view to achieving agreement on the desired outcomes.[12] It aims to cultivate a collaborative relationship between the 'regulator' and the 'regulated' where the former appeals to the values and motivations of the latter to generate the preferred behaviour. One advantage of this process is that it permits, and indeed facilitates, a reflective contest of ideas on the meaning of the ROL itself in the UNSC's practice. Such an approach, in turn, helps imbue the regulatory process with legitimacy and fairness.

In this context, legitimacy becomes an extremely important feature of the UNSC's bargaining power. If the UNSC wishes to enlist the cooperation of states and non-state actors in the area of peacekeeping, sanctions and the use of force, it must demonstrate that its decisions and actions are legitimate (O'Connell). As Braithwaite has put it, responsive regulators should demonstrate that they are 'listening, fair, and therefore legitimate'.[13] This underlines the importance of the UNSC employing and promoting models of governance that embody rule-of-law principles.[14]

This said, the risk remains that the network of actors engaged in ROL interventions might undermine the legitimacy of the UNSC itself. The UNSC's decision-making process and the implementation of its mandates take place at a juncture where diverse actors with various interests and goals, only one of which is the maintenance of international peace and security, gather to influence and secure an outcome that best suits their own national or organisational interests. This contest of influences on both the national and international planes increases the risk that the ROL will be superseded by principles that are characteristic of these global bargaining processes, such as national sovereignty and reciprocity.[15] It would be naive to assume that persuasion will always suffice to reach agreement on how to best promote ROL in a given context. This is why it is important to flag the potential for escalation to more coercive forms of control by the UNSC in the event that persuasive efforts fail. This can take diverse forms, from education about a problem to naming and shaming and sanctions. But coercion should only be used when more collaborative methods have failed.[16]

2 The Security Council as regulated by the rule of law

While networks of ROL actors can be harnessed by the UNSC to regulate the ROL, these same networks can also be used to challenge the UNSC's legitimacy as ROL regulator. As a number of contributors to this collection note, the ROL struggles to exert the same influence at the global level that it does within many nation-states. Many contributors voice particular concern about the lack of effective checks and balances to guarantee the accountability of the UNSC.

Nevertheless, the UNSC does not enjoy unconstrained powers. From a legal standpoint, Article 25 of the UN Charter precludes the UNSC from acting *ultra vires* of the powers given to it by the Charter. In practical terms, checks and balances are deployed through various regulatory influences; between the states that together compose the UNSC and between the Council itself and other states and non-state actors and regional and domestic institutions. Hence, while the UNSC can use its influence to shape the behaviour of others, so too can other actors employ their resources to steer the Council towards a more inclusive and engaged relationship with the ROL. Concrete examples include the rulings of domestic and regional courts in relation to the listing of individuals on sanctions blacklists (see Prost, de Wet) and in relation to the criminal liability of UN peacekeepers (Oswald).

The advantage of a responsive approach to regulating the ROL is that it allows the Council to maintain a workable balance between collaborative engagement and coercive enforcement, which in turn reinforces its most salient resource: legitimacy. A loss of legitimacy, however, could prove costly for the UNSC, as stakeholders might decide to engage in other forums that appear more legitimate and responsive to their concerns and interests.

The chapters in this collection articulate various concerns pertaining to the Council's working methods. These revolve around the UNSC's inability to adequately promote and respect key rule-of-law principles, such as transparency, consistency, accountability and due process. The failure to accord sufficient respect to these rule-of-law principles is most evident in the area of sanctions, where national and regional courts have overtly criticised UN sanctions regimes. As the chapters by Prost and de Wet discuss, national and regional courts have expressed concerns about the extent to which targeted sanctions against individuals clash with due process requirements.

Prost's chapter describes how the actions she has taken herself in the capacity as UN Ombudsperson for the 1267/1989 Al-Qaida sanctions regime have substantially increased the fair process extended to individuals on the Al-Qaida individual sanctions blacklist. The creation and empowerment of the Al-Qaida Ombudsperson could be described as the UNSC at its most responsive, providing an effective response to the chorus of criticisms about its due process failures. Yet as de Wet's chapter describes, these responsive innovations have not been interpreted by the European Court as sufficiently responsive. For the European Court, nothing short of full judicial protection would appear likely to satisfy its due process concerns. The manner in which the UNSC manages this continuing debate about its responsibilities as a subject of the ROL will in turn affect its ability to act as an effective regulator of the ROL.

In the area of peacekeeping, civil society's outrage following scandals of sexual exploitation and abuse committed by troops and UN personnel triggered concerted attempts to regulate peacekeepers' behaviour (see chapters by Heathcote and Whalan). This was reflected in the UN Secretary-General's zero-tolerance policy with respect to sexual exploitation and abuse, which sought to regulate the behaviour of peacekeeping personnel and restore the public's confidence in UN peacekeeping.[17] In an effort to govern the conduct of troops contributed by member states, there is now compulsory training on UN standards of conduct related to sexual exploitation and abuse for peacekeeping personnel. The 2007 Amendments to the Model Memorandum of Understanding also sought to increase the criminal accountability of military personnel.[18] Yet, as Whalan illustrates, sometimes a simple, pragmatic, local response to accountability problems, such as the creation of a community relations office in Cambodia, might be more responsive and effective in terms of achieving genuine accountability and legitimacy outcomes than more ambitious, sophisticated or legalistic global responses.

With regard to the use of force, the indignation of states and non-state actors following the failure to intervene in Rwanda and the former Yugoslavia prompted an extensive effort to re-interpret the UNSC's Chapter VII powers. This effort culminated in the adoption of the 2005 World Summit Outcome Document, which endorsed the view that states possessed a responsibility to protect their civilian populations from genocide, war crimes, ethnic cleansing and crimes against humanity (R2P).[19] This responsibility also extended beyond the domestic context where other states were unwilling or unable to take action to protect their own populations at risk of these atrocity crimes. Yet, Bannelier and Christakis argue that, while the rationale underpinning the development of R2P was to embolden the UNSC to use force when necessary,[20] the most prominent example of the UNSC doing so, in Libya in 2011, was considered so unsatisfactory that it triggered concerted efforts on the part of certain states to promote effective regulation of such action. These efforts culminated in the Brazilian government's release of a 'responsibility *while* protecting' (RWP) proposal to safeguard the international community against an unconstrained application of R2P.[21] Yet the RWP approach itself is not unproblematic, as Harrington and Bellamy both describe. Harrington thus advocates reform of the UNSC's working methods as one way to increase the legitimacy of its decision-making process surrounding the use of force. Bellamy, for his part, argues for the inclusion of direct accountability mechanisms in the text of resolutions that authorise force. We return to this theme in the following section.

These examples demonstrate that actors who use their influence and resources wisely can mitigate governance and accountability deficits within the UNSC.[22] This leverage is not only available to powerful actors such as the five permanent UNSC members. Weaker actors can also mobilise and pool their resources to increase their 'bargaining power', in and over the UNSC, to promote a governance model that is more responsive to and respectful of the rule-of-law principles of accountability, transparency and due process.

3 Policy proposals for strengthening the rule of law through the Security Council

How might the insights presented in this collection in relation to the UNSC's engagements with the ROL, whether as ROL regulator or subject, be harnessed to improve the UNSC's future engagements with the ROL? This question prompted the development of a series of policy proposals designed to strengthen the UNSC's capacity to strengthen the ROL.[23] These policy proposals advance concrete steps that can be taken by the UNSC to strengthen the ROL both externally, as ROL regulator, and internally, as ROL subject. They employ a pragmatic, responsive model of the ROL that balances an openness to robust deliberation on contextual approaches to strengthening the ROL with an uncompromising commitment to counter the misuse and abuse of power. While the model is flexible and open to context, it holds firm to four basic rule-of-law decision-making principles, namely transparency, consistency, accountability and due process.

In accordance with a responsive framework, the policy proposals seek to foster a deeper agreement about the role and responsibility of the UNSC as both regulator and subject of the ROL in the areas of peacekeeping, sanctions and the use of force. The proposals advocate an approach by the UNSC as regulator that prioritises support and persuasion while nevertheless retaining the background potential for more coercive measures in cases of non-compliance. With regard to the position of the UNSC as a subject of the ROL, the recommendations are premised on the assumption that the best way for the UNSC to maintain and enhance its legitimacy, and therefore to retain the support and engagement of the international community, is to regulate itself in response to increasing demands from a range of stakeholders for increased transparency, consistency, accountability and due process.

3.1 Responsive peacekeeping operations

When promoting the ROL through peace operations, the UNSC should be mindful that the UN's capacity to implement reforms within the host country depends on the buy-in of national actors. These actors include government authorities, civil society and the population itself. To increase the legitimacy of UN-supported reforms and secure the engagement of local actors, UN missions should aim to balance the human rights principles they seek to promote with appropriate local justice principles and mechanisms. As noted by Grenfell in relation to constitutional reform, the challenge is to ensure that international law principles incorporated into the domestic legal order intersect with local understandings of law and justice. In keeping with this position, civilian and military members of UN peace operations should ensure that their acts do not violate informal justice norms and practices. At the same time, however, UN peacekeepers must be careful not to promote any informal justice norms and practices that violate fundamental human rights.

The following policy proposals flow from these insights:

> **Recommendation:** UN peace operations should engage national and local actors in ongoing consultations about how to reconcile the tensions between their commitment to and obligations under international law, on the one hand, and local laws, customs and traditions, on the other.

> **Recommendation:** The Security Council should ensure that UN peace operations respect local laws, customs and practices where these are consistent with international human rights standards.

As a subject of the ROL, it is important for the UNSC to ensure that UN personnel working under its authority do not appear to be above the law. The chapters by Heathcote and Whalan demonstrate how the reputation of UN peace operations has been severely tarnished by the criminal behaviour of its personnel, including sexual exploitation and abuse. Little progress has been made to strengthen the accountability of peacekeeping missions despite negotiations between UN member states towards a convention on the criminal accountability of UN officials and experts on mission. Even if such a convention were adopted it would not cover military personnel from TCCs.

While a responsive regulation model favours a conciliatory approach to governance, it also recognises that coercive measures may be required if more lenient mechanisms fail. However, in the case of the pursuit of criminal accountability of peacekeeping personnel, including military personnel, there appears to be a lack of will from member states to regulate criminal conduct effectively either through a UN mechanism or through national prosecution. In this case, where escalating regulatory intervention is not currently possible, it becomes even more important to explore creative alternative regulatory options. These options might include the creation of a community engagement office of the kind employed by UNTAC and referred to by Whalan, or the creation of a local ombudsperson process to investigate allegations of misconduct brought by the local population against UN personnel.

The following policy proposals flow from these insights:

> **Recommendation:** The Security Council should provide for the creation of a well-resourced ombudsperson in all UN peace operation mandates, based on the principles of answerability, independence, accessibility and responsiveness.

> **Recommendation**: The Security Council should affirm the importance of the principles relevant to troop discipline and investigation procedures contained in the Model Memorandum of Understanding between the UN and TCCs, and the UN standards of conduct set out in Annex H of the same document. The Council should also affirm the applicability of the Human Rights Due Diligence Policy on UN support to non-UN security forces.

> **Recommendation:** The Security Council should engage in ongoing dialogue with TCCs concerning the need for accountability for the investigation and prosecution of allegations of all serious crimes committed by their troops.

3.2 Responsive sanctions regimes

Criticisms levelled against the UNSC in the area of sanctions relate mostly to the Council's role as a subject of the ROL. UN sanctions regimes have thus been criticised for their lack of compliance with rule-of-law principles, especially transparency and due process. A number of states and non-state actors have, for example, voiced their concerns that UN sanctions regimes do not afford individuals subjected to targeted UN sanctions an appropriate level of due process during the listing and delisting phases of the process. Litigation in the European courts has reinforced the need for the UNSC to improve its due process procedures.

In its current form, the UNSC's practice suggests a presumption of guilt rather than innocence concerning the individual to be listed. In order to promote rule-of-law principles, the UNSC should thus provide an opportunity for individuals targeted by UN sanctions measures, such as an asset freeze or a travel ban, to hear and contest the basis for their targeting, as a matter of due process. The creation of the Office of the Ombudsperson is a positive development that was possible largely due to the sustained criticisms of actors outside the UNSC, including national and regional courts (see Prost and de Wet). The Office provides an independent mechanism for individuals to challenge their listing on the Al-Qaida sanctions list. However, this mechanism is not available to individuals who are inscribed on the lists pertaining to other sanctions regimes. This creates inconsistencies between sanctions regimes with respect to due process rights, thus undermining the legitimacy of the whole UN sanctions system.

The following policy proposals flow from these insights:

> **Recommendation:** The Security Council should employ a conditional initial listing strategy for individuals inscribed on consolidated lists. Under this process, individuals would be placed on a temporary consolidated list for a period of three months. If the relevant sanctions committee is satisfied within this period, based on evidence including the opinion of the Ombudsperson, that the statement of cases and reasons for listing is based on solid evidence, then the individual would be moved to the consolidated list.

> **Recommendation:** The Security Council should make the current Al-Qaida Ombudsperson process available to all individuals and entities inscribed on UN sanctions lists. The most efficient way to do this would be to create a new general Office of the Ombudsperson covering all UN sanctions regimes.

3.3 Responsive use-of-force mandates

In the area of the use of force, contributors to this collection identify weaknesses in the UNSC's engagements with the ROL both as regulator and subject. As noted by O'Connell, the discretion of the UNSC to decide which actions to take for the maintenance of international peace and security is not without limit. When authorising the recourse to force under Chapter VII of the UN Charter, the UNSC should respect international law and its general principles. Here, as Bannelier and Christakis also point out, respect for the recognised general principles of necessity and proportionality would substantially increase the transparency, consistency and legitimacy of the UNSC's decisions. This would also go a long way in demonstrating that the UNSC does not consider itself to be above the law, thus providing a powerful example to those required to embody rule-of-law principles in their conduct.

In line with these two principles, the UNSC's decision to authorise the use of force should be contingent on an assessment of the contemplated intervention based on its necessity for the maintenance of peace and security and its proportionality with the objective it seeks to achieve. Necessity and proportionality should also guide the UNSC when exercising regulatory control over those whom it authorises to use force.

In certain situations, what is considered necessary and proportional may be contested. Despite strong criticisms about how the 2011 intervention in Libya was carried out by NATO forces, there was no strategic dialogue to address concerns of misinterpretation or excess in NATO's implementation of its mandate. When faced with disagreement of this nature, a responsive approach would pursue dialogue among stakeholders with the aim of reaching an agreement on what action is permitted and what is not permitted when acting in accordance with a UNSC authorisation to use force. This could lead to the clarification or amendment of authorisations to use force in specific situations. However, where these less coercive measures fail to influence positively the behaviour of actors implementing use-of-force mandates, it would be legitimate for the UNSC to use stronger measures to promote regulatory control over its delegates.

The following policy proposals flow from these insights:

> **Recommendation:** Security Council resolutions should clearly express the objectives of use-of-force missions, to serve as an interpretative guide for the implementation of the mandate.

> **Recommendation:** The Security Council should establish a reporting schedule and specify the information to be included in reports by states and groups of states implementing use-of-force mandates.

> **Recommendation:** The Security Council should specify a sunset clause (expiration date) for all use-of-force authorisations.

4 Conclusion

In this chapter we have examined how the UNSC's dual roles of regulator and subject of the ROL relate to each other. These two different modes of interaction with the ROL potentially represent a conflict of interest and there will always be a temptation for the members of the UNSC to invest more energy in how to increase the Council's regulatory capacity than in how to meet its rule-of-law obligations. Yet as we have argued here, there is in fact a confluence of interest in the manner in which the Council carries itself both as a regulator and a subject of the ROL. Ultimately the UNSC's capacity to act as an effective regulator of the ROL is inextricably tied to its willingness to serve as a respectful subject of the ROL. Returning to Halliday's neat characterisation of the UNSC's rule-of-law dilemma, the Council cannot expect to make advances in its promotion of ROL on the offence without diligently modifying its adherence to ROL on the defence. The best way for the UNSC to strengthen its capacity to strengthen the

ROL is thus for it to respect and promote the key rule-of-law principles of transparency, consistency, accountability and due process, whether acting externally as regulator of the ROL or internally as subject of the ROL.

Notes

1 UN Charter, art. 24.
2 Jennifer Wood and Clifford Shearing, *Imagining Security* (Cullompton, William Publishing, 2007), p. 4.
3 UN Charter, Chapter VII in general (arts 39–51).
4 Stephen Humphreys, *Theatre of the ROL: Transnational Legal Intervention in Theory and Practice* (Cambridge, Cambridge University Press, 2010), p. 161.
5 For discussion of UNSG Annan's definition, see the chapters in this collection by, *inter alia*, Charlesworth and Farrall, Sampford, Krygier and Grenfell.
6 John Braithwaite, 'The Essence of Responsive Regulation' (2011) 44(3) *UBC Law Review* 475–520, 476.
7 Colin Scott, 'Analysing Regulatory Space: Fragmented Resources and Institutional Design' (2001), Summer, *Public Law* 329–53, 330.
8 See Ian Ayres and John Braithwaite, *Responsive Regulation: Transcending the Deregulation Debate* (Oxford: Oxford University Press, 1992).
9 Braithwaite, 'The Essence of Responsive Regulation', 480.
10 Ibid., 482.
11 John Braithwaite and Peter Drahos, *Global Business Regulation* (Cambridge, Cambridge University Press, 2000), p. 25.
12 Ayres and Braithwaite, *Responsive Regulation*, 496
13 Ibid., 488.
14 Scott, 'Analysing Regulatory Space', 330.
15 Braithwaite and Drahos, *Global Business Regulation*, pp. 21, 30.
16 Braithwaite, 'The Essence of Responsive Regulation', 482.
17 UN Doc. ST/SGB/2003/13 (9 October 2003) *Special Measures for Protection from Sexual Exploitation and Sexual Abuse*.
18 See Zsuzsanna Deen-Racsmàny, 'The Amended UN Model Memorandum of Understanding: A New Incentive for States to Discipline and Prosecute Military Members of National Peacekeeping Contingents?' (2011) 18(3) *Journal of Conflict and Security Law* 1–35, 14.
19 UN Doc. A/RES/60/1 (24 October 2005) *2005 World Summit Outcome*, para. 139.
20 For a contrasting view arguing that the decision to intervene in Libya was a classic application of Chapter VII of the UN Charter, see generally: Marie-Eve Loiselle, 'The Normative Status of the Responsibility to Protect after Libya' (2013) 5(3) *Global Responsibility to Protect Journal* 317–41.
21 See UN Doc. A/66/551–S/2011/701 (11 November 2011).
22 Wood and Shearing, *Imagining Security*, p. 99.
23 Jeremy Farrall, Hilary Charlesworth, Shane Chalmers and Marie-Eve Loiselle, *Policy Proposals for Strengthening the Rule of Law through the UN Security Council* (Queanbeyan, Australian Civil-Military Centre, 2015).

Index

www.ingramcontent.com/pod-product-compliance
Ingram Content Group UK Ltd.
Pitfield, Milton Keynes, MK11 3LW, UK
UKHW020018200926
475702UK00014B/1959
* 9 7 8 1 1 3 8 4 8 8 1 9 9 *